EXCELSIOR

Assemblers and BAL

PRENTICE-HALL INTERNATIONAL, INC., *London*
PRENTICE-HALL OF AUSTRALIA, PTY. LTD., *Sydney*
PRENTICE-HALL OF CANADA, LTD., *Toronto*
PRENTICE-HALL OF INDIA PRIVATE LIMITED, *New Delhi*
PRENTICE-HALL OF JAPAN, INC., *Tokyo*

Assemblers and BAL

Ivan Flores

Computer Consultant

Professor of Statistics, Baruch College

The City University of New York

PRENTICE-HALL, INC., ENGLEWOOD CLIFFS, N. J.

Current printing (last digit):

10 9 8 7 6 5 4 3 2 1

13-049569-7

Library of Congress Catalog Card Number 79-125289

Printed in the United States of America

PREFACE

Everybody today seems to be writing Elementary programming books. This one is Intermediate to Advanced. That means that some programming background is presupposed. I am not going to discuss the important program components, loops, and subroutines, since I have gone that route at least once.† Although a knowledge of a higher language (FORTRAN, COBOL, etc.) is helpful, assembly language, even if seemingly unrelated (Autocoder, for example), is much more helpful.

This text has at least five aims, in the following order:

1. To describe assembly languages in a more or less general way (Chapter 1);
2. To examine BAL in particular and the programming for it;
3. To describe macro and conditional assembly facilities, how they are used, and how they work;
4. To describe system macros and their implementation;
5. To explain how assemblers work.

Since you are reading this preface, you obviously are aware of the importance of assembly language (AL) to computer science—most operating systems, utilities, and translations are written in AL. The only *real* programmers in my opinion are AL programmers.

How general can I make this book? The generality and motivation come in Chapter 1 where the various machine and assembly command types are given as much attention as needed to get a grasp of the potential of AL for most computer systems.

Chapter 2 is the point of no return; sadly I make a full commitment to BAL—sadly, because the byte oriented computer is not the end-all.

I make the commitment to BAL because:

* I have seen the light; commitment to a synthetic language can really turn people off.
* If you're going to learn an AL, you want to learn a *real* one.
* Why not learn the one most universally available (60%?)?
* OS will operate on a growing percentage of systems.

†Ivan Flores, *Computer Programming* (Englewood Cliffs, N.J.: Prentice-Hall, Inc., 1966).

* The BAL features are the same for DOS and BOS, Spectra 70 TOS, POS, and TDOS, except with regard to SET variables, which are explained when encountered. UNIVAC 9000 AL is pretty close, too.

Chapter 2 is devoted to BAL mnemonics and extended mnemonics. Most higher level language programmers who work with S360 or the like will have a little understanding here but should intensively review or study this material.

Chapter 3 concentrates on data and space pseudos, for with them the BAL programmer incorporates data he will reference and defines working space he will use in his program. The nature of S360, whether through versatility or complexity, poses so many kinds of data that knowledge of their nature is essential. Enough JCL is introduced in this chapter, along with specific macros, so that the reader can assemble simple programs if he can get near an S360. After finishing this chapter, the reader should be able to write an AL program which runs. So, why not find out how the assembler works by reading Chapter 4?

A disclaimer: The description of how the assembler works, although in many regards approximating the OS360 assembler F, is *not supposed to be an exact* description of it.

I am not going to stop to teach AL programming per se. And I do hope you already know what a *macro* is. Nevertheless, you should be sure to study Chapter 5 to be absolutely clear about this. The great power of AL resides in the macro; two-thirds of the book is spent on the *how* and *why* of macros. The introduction to macros, Chapter 5, deserves attention, if just to get *my* terms straight.

Chapters 6 through 10 are the meat:—how to use macro facilities—and the drink—how the assembler makes the macros work. Only a full repast can suffice: knowing *how* helps the programmer figure out *what to do*. The examples of Chapter 11 should top off the meal!

Chapters 12 and 13 may seem to come late. No BAL program can work without USING and all that jazz. But these details are unique to BAL. The savvy programmer is already advanced in BAL by now. The *how* and *why* of the pseudos should be rather easy.

Chapter 14 discusses system macros used by both OS and OS Access Methods. Hence, some time is spent looking at OS principles. System macro principles are similar regardless of the system.

Chapter 15 looks at the many alternatives for closed SR's and external code calls. Chapter 16 winds up the "big picture" of how a typical assembler might work.

Chapter 17 conveys how the assembler talks to the programmer. He will make mistakes! Whatever errors are detected are conveyed to him by diagnostics discussed here. Finally, the macros designed to help the novice produce running programs are analyzed and dissected. They are complicated. Hence, this is good review of how complex conditional macros are designed.

Note the many appendices; they may be useful as you plow through the text.

I wish to express my appreciation to those who have helped me in this effort. Paul Levin did a fine job in creating three macros SETUP, ENDUP, and REG which have enabled two classes, so far, to get their programs on the 360 after only four or five hours of instruction. Vennessa Pace produced a beautiful and lucid manuscript.

I.F.

CONTENTS

1

INTRODUCTION

1.0 CONVENTIONS

Here are the conventions I shall use:

1. Mnemonics appear in Gothic type. This includes normal commands such as AP, pseudos such as DC or MACRO, macros such as CALL, and quasis such as ENTRY.
2. Subsystems and hardware are in small caps such as CONTROL, MEMORY, and IO.
3. Classes of symbols are in lowercase italics in the text, such as *opcode* or *location,* whereas they are in Roman type in displays and equations such as

   name ADD location (1.0.1)

4. Software components are in script, such as McGen and Symb.
5. Tables are in Gothic italics, such as *HASHTAB.*
6. When definitions are made, the word defined is in boldface type; viz., **bit** is a binary digit.
7. English language command description adjectives are usually italicized; thus I speak of an *add* command or a *load* command.

1.1 MACHINE LANGUAGE

The assembler The assembler reduces the job of the programmer by making it easier for him to write programs. He writes in

assembly language (**AL**) wherein each command expresses one (or more) machine language command to be done by the computer. Of course, he has other choices of what languages he might use:

- At the very lowest level is the **binary machine language, BML,** which consists entirely of 0's and 1's.
- At the next level, for some machines, we find the **character machine language, CML.** For instance, in the IBM 1401, the programmer can write his program with characters. These are punched into punchcards and the punchcards can be run directly on the machine since translation from character to binary is done with the CARD READER/computer combination.
- Either of these is **machine language, ML.**
- **Assembly language, AL,** actually has three different grades of difficulty which we discuss later.
- The **procedure-oriented language, POL,** such as FORTRAN and COBOL, allows the programmer to write a single program regardless of the machine on which it will be run. This has a definite advantage but removes the programmer from the machine and requires much less in the way of programming technique—both an advantage and disadvantage.
- At the highest level, we have the **problem-oriented language,** such as RPG, and the special higher procedure-oriented language, such as LISP and GPSS. I call both these **HLL**s. The programmer talks in these languages because they resemble the way he might state his *problem* in ordinary English. They remove the programmer *even further* from the machine.

At the bottom of all higher level languages is the assembler language because it is used by the people, the system programmers, who design translators from converting POL or HLL to ML. Further, all software programs (which supervise the machine) are written in assembly language. Hence, it behooves the system programmer to learn assembly language, to know its potentialities, and even further, to understand the translator, the **assembler** (affectionately called $\mathcal{A}\mathfrak{SLR}$), for this will give him a deeper knowledge of how he can use assembly language.

Whatever language the programmer writes is called the **source language.** The translator sees this as data. The result it produces, the translation, is the object code in **object language.** Generally most translators, regardless of source language, produce ML as the object code but there are many notable exceptions, e.g.,

- SIMSCRIPT (HLL) translates into FORTRAN (POL).
- FORTRAN for the 709 translates into FAP or MAP (AL).

An assembly language is modeled after the machine on which it will run and its command structure. Therefore, we have to find out something about machine language to understand the structure of an assembly language.

The commands The **machine command** is a set of bits in MEMORY which tells the computer what to do next. At least some of these commands reference MEMORY. When the command is brought from MEMORY, CONTROL uses it to direct the other subsystems and interprets the address. Therefore, the command contains two main parts:

- ***opcode*** describes the task to be performed by the computer.
- ***location*** indicates one or more places where data are found.

A command is an element of all computer language. Hence, its use is only clear through context:

- It is a set of bits at the ML level.
- It is a formatted multicharacter string in AL.
- It is a sentence-like statement in HLL.

Class notation At least, in some sense, the command is one unit of language. At the lowest level, it consists simply of zeros and ones. At assembly level, it consists of letters and characters. At the highest levels, it consists of words arranged in "sentences" and has grammar or syntax associated with them.

We are concerned only with assembly language. When characters appear in AL, I use Gothic type to distinguish them from English which describes them and appears elsewhere in the book. An example is ADD, an AL instruction to *add*.

Sometimes a command requires specific combinations of letters in one of its parts. When this information is displayed (in a numbered equation), the display uses the required assembly language characters where needed. Other places in the command may permit a variety of combinations of characters and numerals for which rules (which are described in the text) prevail. The rules distinguish a class of letter combinations. In a display, this class is written with normal text letters and in lowercase. In the text, when speaking of these classes, again, lowercase text letters are used but they appear in italics.

Here is an example of what I mean:

name ADD location (1.1.1)

This describes the format of an assembly language command called ADD (written in Gothic typeface). *Name* is a combination of characters which is known as a name and has rules for its formation. For instance, it must start with a letter, etc. Similarly, *location* is a symbolic name used for an address in MEMORY, and it is also a set of characters which has rules governing what letters and numbers can be used. Of course, the rules will be discussed later; it is just the notation which I describe now.

1.2 MACHINE COMMANDS

It is obvious that the machine command and its format depend upon the machine. Soon we direct our attention to S360 which has a rather complicated command structure. At this point let's restrict the discussion to fixed word-type machines.

Fixed word machines All machines procure a fixed amount of data from MEMORY during each MEMORY cycle. This amount, called the **word size**, varies from eight bits (S360 Model 20) to sixty or more (CDC 6600). For a given machine and model it remains fixed.

The size of the data manipulated—the operand—is fixed in the **fixed word machine** at one word (generally). In this respect it is different from the other types of machines discussed later where variable amounts of data can be associated with a single command.

Since the fixed word machine always handles a single word of data, it is often convenient to make the command size identical to the word size. Thus, the IBM 7090 has exactly one command in each word (thirty-six bits). Where word size is larger, two commands may be packed in a word such as for the Philco 2000 (which has a forty-eight bit word).

The command of a fixed word machine refers to a fixed number of operands. The most popular is the **one address structure** where each command contains *one* operand address as in the IBM 7090. The Honeywell 800/1800 requires three operand addresses in each command; hence it is a **three address machine.** Here the *add* command contains the locations of the two numbers to be added and a place to put the sum. Old, first generation computers, such as the IBM 650, has a **one-plus-one address structure:** the command contains the address of an operand *and* of the next command. This permitted the program to skip around in MEMORY from one location to another which was a better policy because a DRUM *was* the MAIN MEMORY.

Modern computers sequence through MEMORY from one command to the next at successive MEMORY locations.

Field-oriented machines Commands for this class of machines are not limited to acquiring and processing a single MEMORY word. The command can request the processing of a field of information—several words from MEMORY. There are several alternatives on how a field is specified.

PUNCTUATION

In punctuation machines, such as the IBM 1401 or the H200, a field is delimited by a special bit in each character, a **word mark,** used only to signal the end of a field. A word corresponds generally to a character so that a command can request the processing of a number of characters. The command names the first character in the field. The punctuation distinguishes the last character.

QUANTITY

Quantity machines permit the command to specify the number of characters upon which the command is operating. Hence, each command includes an address *and* a length. Examples are the RCA 301 and 3301 and NCR 325. The IBM 7070 does the same job by specifying the start and finish locations of the field.

Combination machines Some machines permit both field- and word-type commands. The Control Data 3300 is primarily a word-oriented machine but has a repertoire of field-oriented commands. Third generation machines use combination commands: fixed word commands are word oriented; character commands are field oriented.

Command size It is convenient in a fixed word machine to have the command of fixed size as found with the IBM 7090 series and the CDC 3300. For field machines using quantity specification it is preferable to have commands of fixed size; otherwise it is difficult to know where a command begins and ends. Hence, we find that the RCA 3301 and NCR 325 both have fixed command size.

Where punctuation is used for data acquisition, it can also come in handy for commands. Now commands are of a **variable size.** CONTROL obtains characters of a command until it encounters one with punctuation indicating that *this* character is part of the *next* command and not this one. Hence, punctuation machines such as the IBM 1401, IBM 1620, and the Honeywell 200 use variable size commands.

The **multiple size command** found in third generation computers such as the S360 and the Spectra 70 has several (three) alternative sizes: two bytes, four bytes, and six bytes. The size depends on the function requested by the command and therefore upon the opcode. Hence, it is the opcode itself which indicates command size to CONTROL.

Assembly language To simplify our explanation of assembly language in this chapter, we examine the fixed word computer with fixed size commands. This enables us to have a fairly standard machine language form to the command. Chapter 2 is a thorough discussion of IBM System 360 (S360) explaining the commands, their mnemonics, and their actions, to enable us to explore assembler functions oriented to S360. Chapter 3 describes how directions are given to the assembler itself and Chapter 4 describes the simple symbolic assembler.

1.3 ABSOLUTE ASSEMBLY LANGUAGE

Discussion No programmer likes to write in 0's and 1's, so the very first and simplest assembly languages permitted the programmer to use mnemonics and decimal addresses which the assembler replaced by the proper configuration of bits. The machine command—fixed word computer, fixed command size—often has this format:

opcode,tags location (1.3.1)

Here *opcode* is a set of bits which tells CONTROL the operation to be performed; *location* is a set of bits representing a MEMORY address; *tags* are bits which tell CONTROL the kind of addressing to do and which INDEX REGISTERS (if any) to involve if requested.

The absolute assembly language command corresponding to (1.3.1) might have the format

step opcode,tags location (1.3.2)

Here *opcode* is a mnemonic, one of a set of multiletter combinations, a unique one for each machine language opcode. *Tags* are letters or digits which tell the assembler which bits to set for the kind of addressing requested by the programmer. *Location* is a decimal (or alphanumeric as in the IBM 1401) combination which conveys an address converted into binary by the assembler. Notice a fourth field, *step*, the MEMORY location at which this command will be stored at run time. This is converted by the assembler into a number, probably binary, used by the loader, telling it where to place the command.

Here is an example of an absolute assembly language command:

```
22      ADD      325
```
(1.3.3)

It requests addition of the operand located at 325 to the A REGISTER, AR, returning the sum to the AR. The command will be loaded into word 22. Here is another example:

```
29      STA,3    401
```
(1.3.4)

Here indexing is called for because *tag* is three. What this command does might be described as

$$(\text{AR}) \longrightarrow 401 + (\text{NR}3) \tag{1.3.5}$$

where NR3 is INDEX REGISTER 3. The contents of AR are placed at the effective address, the sum of *loc* and (NR3).

Usefulness Usefulness of absolute assembly language is apparent, for now the programmer writes only letters and numbers instead of bits. The limitation is that the assembler only goes so far and does not provide the features discussed in the next section. Each feature costs time and assembler complexity but the results more than compensate for the cost.

1.4 SYMBOLIC ASSEMBLY LANGUAGE

Description For absolute assembly language the programmer should be cognizant of all MEMORY locations, know what is in each, and make all correlations as he writes the program. The main purpose of the $\mathcal{ASLR}$ is to relieve the programmer of this "MEMORY mapping." The universal means is symbolic addressing which also provides a mnemonic (memory aid) to the programmer about the assignments. So symbolic assembly language permits him to use symbols instead of absolute addresses.

The programmer makes up the names of symbols he uses. They should have a mnemonic quality to tell the programmer what they represent. (TAX represents tax.) The programmer labels both commands and data so that each can be referenced symbolically. Thus, he can branch to symbolic locations or move a command around within his program.

Command The format of a fixed word, fixed size command in symbolic assembly language takes the form

name   opcode,tags   location   (1.4.1)

Here *name* is a symbolic name which the programmer assigns to the command he is writing. Not all commands are named, in which case *blanks* appear in this field. *Opcode* is a mnemonic as before. *Tags* distinguish the kind of addressing used. *Location* contains symbols by which the programmer refers to *all* MEMORY addresses required in the command.

Symbols As the programmer needs a new place to put information, he creates a name for it, a set of characters called a **symbol.** It is possible to design the assembler so that a cell is set aside and an address allocated whenever the assembler encounters a *new* symbol. It is simple to do this with a fixed word computer since data are all the same size. Any new datum the programmer needs is expected to be contained in a word and the assembler can allocate this address on its own.

For field-oriented computers, data size varies tremendously as well as the type of information to load in a data cell. Hence, simply naming a datum does not provide enough information for the assembler. The programmer uses **pseudocommands** (or simply **pseudos**) to tell the assembler the name, size, and other characteristics of his datum. He also may place a datum in the program where he wants it. However, he does not need to know its relative or absolute address; this is managed by the assembler.

When an array is defined in the fixed word computer, the size of the array cannot be guessed by the assembler; the programmer not only names but reserves the required amount of space for his array by giving a pseudocommand to the assembler.

Expressions It would be wasteful to require all locations which contain meaningful expressions for this program to be labeled by the programmer. Hence we permit him to reference any unlabeled word relative to a nearby label. For instance, suppose he labels a command CALC. He refers to the command which follows this one as CALC+1; he refers to a word which is three words previous to CALC by CALC−3. Hence only key commands in the program need be labeled. 𝒜𝒮ℒℛ "replaces a symbol by an address"; it replaces an expression by doing a simple calculation. Having found the address which applies to the symbol. It performs the arithmetic requested in the expression to provide the value to be inserted as the required address in the machine language output.

The same technique is applied to naming an array of data. If the program requires a set of twenty words, the programmer can call the entire array AR. To get to the ninth word in his array, he calls for AR+8. It makes no sense to talk about AR−3 since this word does not lie in his array.

SELF-RELATIVE

Sometimes the programmer wants to reference locations in terms of the command which is doing the referencing. If that command is labeled, his referencing is done as described above. For an unlabeled command, he can talk about its position in the program by using *. For instance, to jump ahead three commands, the command which makes the request refers to $*+3$; to jump backward five steps, the command refers to $*-5$.

𝒜𝒮ℒℛ knows the address of *this* command and can easily form the address of the object command.

Arithmetic To evaluate an expression, 𝒜𝒮ℒℛ itself does addition and subtraction. Will it ever have to do multiplication and division? Need sometimes arises for more complicated arithmetic. For instance, consider that the programmer has set aside a file area which begins at F. He has records of size R for this file. For him to address the sixth record in the file, he uses the expression F+5*R. Notice that R is not an address but a number. The result of adding the product of two numbers to an address is a valid address.

In doing arithmetic and setting up an expression, the programmer must be careful about which symbols represent *addresses* and which represent *numbers*. Usually he has a different way to set up the two (in OS360AL, it is explained later that DC and DS are for addresses and EQU for numbers.

1.5 MACRO ASSEMBLY LANGUAGE

Macro facility Programmers have found that sets of code occur repeatedly in their program. The programmer should not have to rewrite the code each time it is required. It is simple for him to give the code a name and then require that this set of code is inserted wherever the name appears (replacing that name). The **macrocommand, macrocall,** or simply **macro**, then, is the name which appears at *opcode* and which 𝒜𝒮ℒℛ replaces by the set of commands.

This makes it incumbent upon the assembler to recognize macrocalls and distinguish them from mnemonic opcodes. Macrocall names and the code they represent could be made known to the 𝒜𝒮ℒℛ before the program is ever presented for assembly or the program can transmit this information to the assembler at assembly time.

The macro facility has even further general application, for it permits the programmer to make macrocalls without even knowing the code to be produced and inserted by them. Instead he may simply know the function they perform in the program at run time. These are then called **system macros** or **library macros**.

Definitions There are three main sources of macro-definitions—the set of code to be replaced when the macrocall appears.

These are

- system macros,
- installation macros,
- programmer macros.

SYSTEM MACROS

The manufacturer has found it increasingly effective to write system macros, name them, and place these names at the disposal of the programmer. There is no need for the assembly language programmer to distinguish a normal opcode from a macrocall as long as he knows the function of each. He can then use this macrocall as any other mnemonic in the machine language repertoire. During assembly, the assembler, of course, replaces the call by the code which it represents and then translates this into machine language wherein the computer executes the machine steps required to implement the more complicated process represented by the call.

PROGRAMMER MACROS

The macro capability has extreme power which the programmer can use effectively. The manufacturer provides macros for functions which he feels most programmers need. The programmer uses the same tool to create functions unique to his problem or class of problems. He can both name and define his own macros as he sees fit. Then, *as a separate activity*, he calls the macro which the assembler replaces by the assembly language code that he defined and thereafter it translates.

INSTALLATION MACROS

The programmer's macros help him to write his program by obviating repetitious code patterns. The macros he creates solve portions of his problems. If other programmers find similar aspects to their programs, they might need the same macros. They could make similar definitions and calls in their own programs.

There is an easier way to do things. After a programmer writes a macro which seems useful to his associates or which he may need in several of his programs, he can call in a computer utility to place this macrodefinition in a macro library. Then, whenever the macrocall appears, the calling program need not contain the definition. The assembler goes to the macro library, looks up the call, finds the definition, and enters the corresponding code to the problem program and, thereafter, translates it into machine language.

Parameters The macrocall produces a copy of a set of code. If this copy were identical for every occurrence of the macrocall, its usefulness would be diminished. To permit variation from one call to the next, a **parameter list** is provided. This allows certain parts of the code to vary from one call to the next. The assembler also manages references to parameters as discussed in Chapter 5.

Importance Macros bear the same importance to assembly language as procedures do to problem-oriented languages. It is the macro facility which so enhances assembly language as to bring it almost to the level of the problem-oriented language. Certainly it will never replace the POL which resembles English, at least as far as the expression of procedures and problems is concerned. However, the POL is limited in relating the hardware to the software. Hence it is not strange that we find that most operating systems from the very smallest to the largest ones, typified by OS360, are written entirely in their macro assembly language. Not only is the assembler itself written in assembly language but the compilers which translate from a POL into machine language are also usually written in MAL.

Hence you will not find it inappropriate that about two-thirds of the book is devoted to features associated with the macro assembly language.

Choice We have examined three kinds of AL languages. How does the programmer choose one? Generally he doesn't! He is presented with a computer, operating system, and a hardware configuration. Usually the assembler which goes with this is fixed also: small computers have no macros; large computers have full macro facility. He gets a total system; how much of it can he use?

1.6 ASSEMBLY LANGUAGE COMMANDS

Format The programmer talks to the assembler with commands. The form of each assembly language command is fixed for several reasons:

1. The information conveyed in each command is quite simple.
2. Not much variation is required among the commands.
3. The assembler is a program to do the translating and its structure can be simplified if it receives information in a uniform format.

The result of this standardization improves the assembler in several ways:

1. The fixed format permits the assembler input component to find and manipulate command fields quickly and easily.

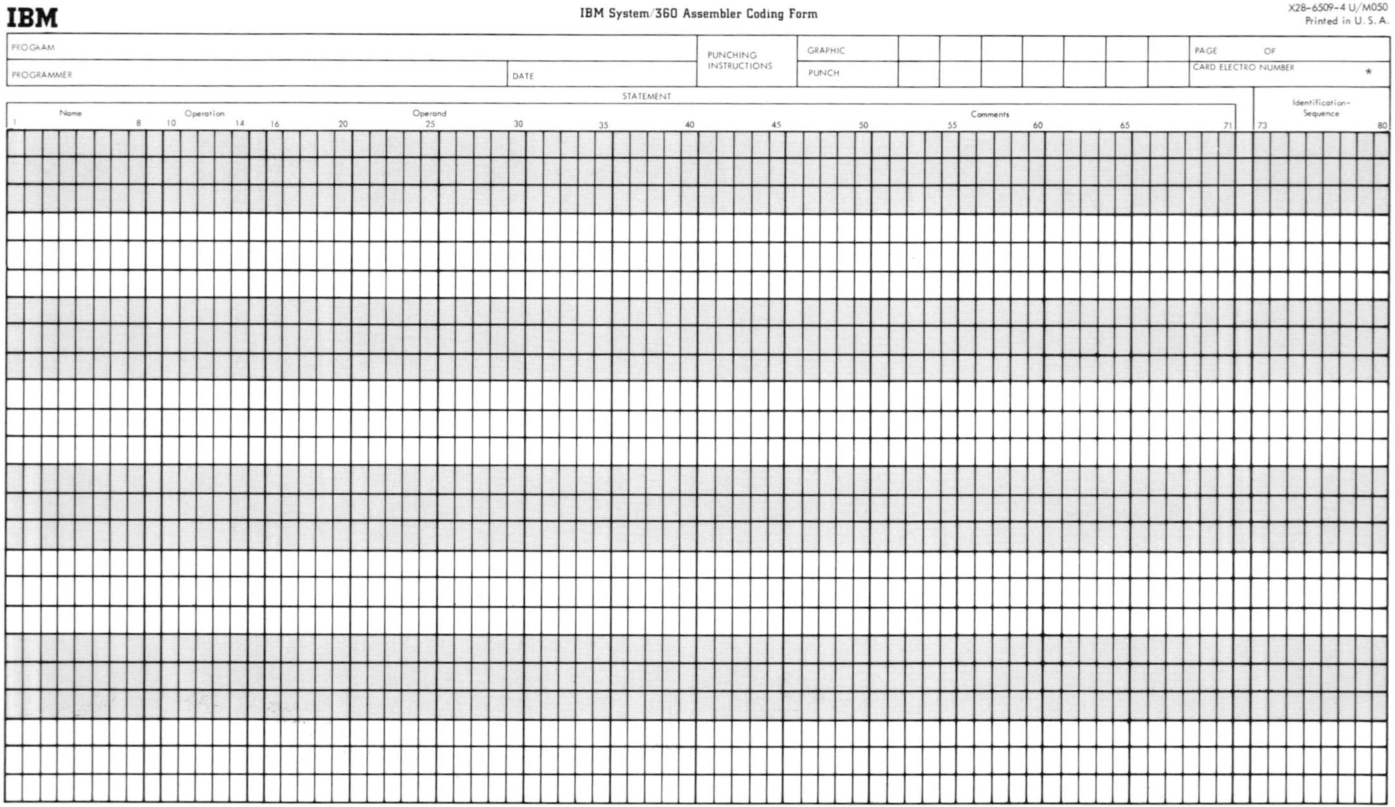

IBM

IBM System/360 Assembler Coding Form

X28-6509-4 U/M050
Printed in U.S.A.

PROGRAM		PUNCHING INSTRUCTIONS	GRAPHIC	PAGE OF
PROGRAMMER	DATE		PUNCH	CARD ELECTRO NUMBER *

STATEMENT

Name 1 8 | Operation 10 14 | 16 20 Operand 25 30 35 40 45 50 55 Comments 60 65 71 | Identification-Sequence 73 80

* A standard card form, IBM electro 6509, is available for punching source statements from this form.
Instructions for using this form are in any IBM System/360 Assembler Reference Manual.
Address comments concerning this form to IBM Corporation, Programming Publications, Department 232, San Jose, California 95114.

Fig. 1.6.1 IBM System/360 Assembler long coding form.

2. The assembler is consequently smaller.
3. It takes less time to operate.

Fields One format for an assembly language command is

name opcode,tag location comments sequence (1.6.1)

- *name* is the name which the programmer assigns to *this* command, if any.
- *opcode* is a mnemonic or other alternative which we explore later in the book.
- *tag* distinguishes different forms of addresses but is neither necessary nor present in BAL.
- *location* contains operands or addresses. Both IBM and RCA call this the operand field. However, I refer to it as *location* because I don't like to consider the address associated with the *branch* instruction as an operand.
- *comments* permits the programmer to document his program by writing statements in English about what the command does. This information is not translated by the assembler but only duplicated in the assembly printout to help the programmer debug his program.
- *sequence* permits the programmer to order his cards and then keep them in order. This is not reproduced in the machine language output but may be replaced by a sequence number used to keep machine language statements in order when they appear on punchcards.

Position The programmer writes assembly language code which is transcribed somehow before it gets to the computer. He usually writes this code on a format supplied by the manufacturer so as to make programming more uniform. The coding form, a sample of which appears in Fig. 1.6.1, has a single column for each of the letters or characters which the programmer might write. Further, the fields are set off by heavy lines to aid the programmer in keeping his fields in the proper position.

For BAL, blanks must exist between fields; other ALs may not require this. The form is set up so that a blank is automatically created between fields.

The exception is the *comments* field. Since *location* varies in size from one command to another, it is impossible to predict where it ends. It is up to the programmer to insert a blank before he writes his *comment*.

Punchcard Generally the way the assembly language programmer gets his program to the assembler is with punchcards. That is why the form of Fig. 1.6.1 has eighty columns to it. The punchcard has eighty columns which are formatted just the same as this form. An example of it appears in Fig. 1.6.2.

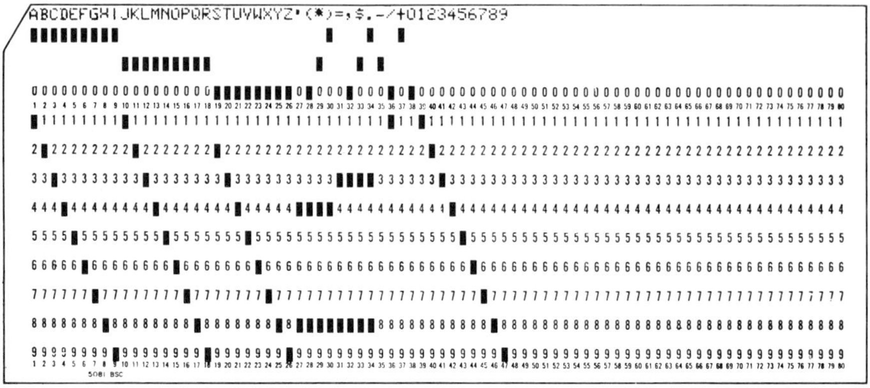

Fig. 1.6.2 An 80-column punched card.

Opcode I have noted the occurrence of a mnemonic which is translated into a machine language opcode. Also I have discussed the use of a macrocall in place of an opcode; this will be elaborated on extensively.

EXTENDED MNEMONICS

Occasionally, we find a situation where we would like to have a mnemonic for a nonexistent command which has a correspondent in machine language where one or more *location* fields are fixed. This is called an **extended mnemonic** and is treated in the next chapter. The symbol at *opcode* is then translated by the assembler into a machine language command with particular characteristics.

PSEUDOS

A command appearing at *opcode* for which we expect no translation but with which we talk to the assembler is called a **pseudocommand** or simply **pseudo**. One or two of these are examined early in the game but most of them are postponed until Chapter 12.

QUASI

I have coined the term **"quasicommand"** or simply **"quasi"** for a command which creates no code, talks to the assembler, but *does* create information in the machine language output which will be used by some other piece of software, such as the linkage editor or loader. These are discussed in Chapter 13.

Location *Location* generally contains addresses which may designate REGISTERS or MEMORY locations. Often they are the addresses of operands. Because S360 has a multiple size command structure computer, we postpone this topic until we examine the S360 mnemonics, Chapter 2.

PROBLEMS

1.1 Discuss for BML, CML, AL, POL, and HLL the following:
  (a) the *raison d'être;*
  (b) the programmer's "need to know,"
  (c) the name of the translator for it and the usual object language.

1.2 Discuss the need, usefulness, and occurrence of commands of:
  (a) fixed size;
  (b) variable size;
  (c) multiple size.

1.3 Distinguish AAL, SAL, and MAL.

1.4 What are *pseudos, expressions, macros, quasis?*

2

S360

2.1 THE STRUCTURE

Programmer's view We all know that what the programmer sees depends on "where he stands." Most often he stands at an application and looks at a language. These languages are mostly machine independent—mostly but not entirely—S360 COBOL is different from another COBOL.

We, too, are standing "near" applications and looking at assembly language S360AL. We expect it to be machine dependent since all ALs are. The peculiar thing is that *it is machine dependent and hardware independent!* Regardless of the model we choose, S360AL looks the same. From a $50K machine to a 5 megabuck machine, BAL looks the same. Obviously the programmer doesn't see the entire edifice; IBM says he sees "architecture."

What I see appears as Fig. 2.1.1. We examine the system for Models 25 and up, omitting Model 20. The components we find are

- MEMORY,
- GENERAL PURPOSE REGISTERS—GPR,
- FLOATING POINT REGISTERS—FPR,
- the PROCESSOR,
- an operating system—OS360,
- DEVICES attached to the system.

From our vantage point we not only look but we can also talk, and through talk, control. We talk with three languages:

- commands (both ML and AL),
- systems macros to talk to 𝒪𝒮360, DEVICES and files,
- job control language, JCL, to talk to 𝒪𝒮360 during loading cursorily examined in Sections 3.6 and 3.7.

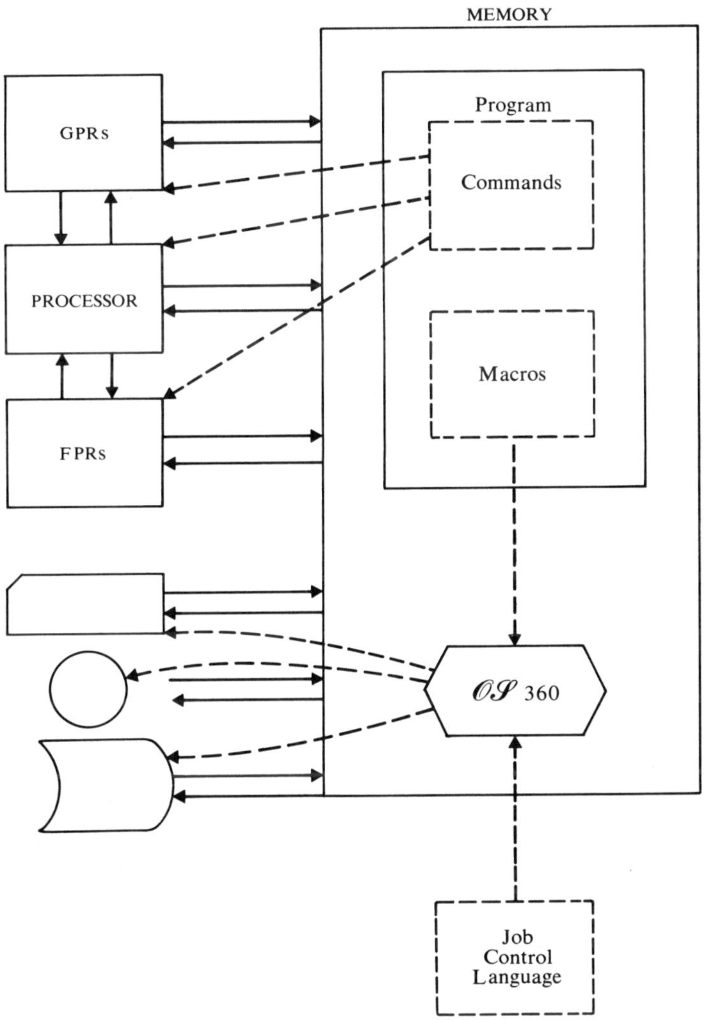

Fig. 2.1.1 View of System/360 as seen by the programmer.

Memory MEMORY is **byte addressable**—some commands select one or more bytes from MEMORY regardless of the word size of the user's model. It is convenient to have several other units of information:

- The **byte** contains eight bits.

- The **nibble** is a right or left half byte and hence contains four bits.
- The **Word** is four bytes.
- The Word contains a right and left **half Word**.
- The **doubleWord** contains a right and left Word and so is sixty-four bits.

The capacity of MEMORY is measured in bytes. 32K is rather small but will accommodate the disk operating system, DOS. 131K is about the minimum one could use for the main operating system, OS360. We can extract a reasonable profit out of OS360 only with multiprogramming which requires a minimum of 265K, or better, 531K. Provisions are made to address up to 16,000K, sixteen megabytes—twenty-four bits are allowed for addresses.

BOUNDARIES

The bottom byte of MEMORY is at address 0. It is the beginning of a doubleWord. Byte 8 starts the next doubleWord; addresses divisible by 8 are hence called doubleWord boundaries. We have these boundaries then:

- doubleWord with address divisible by 8,
- Word with address divisible by 4,
- halfWord with address divisible by 2.

These are important because some commands expect data to be aligned on specific boundaries; e.g., binary commands operate on Words which must start on Word boundaries. If a binary command uses an address which is not a Word boundary—pow—the computer stops working on the program and calls in OS360!

Commands themselves must be aligned on halfWord boundaries.

GPRS There are sixteen GPRS bearing labels 0 thru 15. Each holds one Word. A nibble suffices to identify a GPR, which has many uses:

- *arithmetic:* Binary numbers, Words, can be put in GPRS where they may have arithmetic done on them.
- *index:* The Word in a GPR may be used as an INDEX to be added to an address in a command; the left byte is then discarded.
- The Word in a GPR may also modify an address to obtain a relative address.

FPRS There are four doubleWord FPRS labeled 0, 2, 4, and 6. They are *only* used for floating point arithmetic. If a model does not have an FP option, FP commands won't work and the FPRS are not accessible.

PROCESSOR Here we find the functional units which do the work requested by each command. How data are moved about among MEMORY, the PROCESSOR, and the GPRS is not important to the programmer;† he need only know the result of the command.

OS360 The operating system is a hexagon in Fig. 2.1.1. It gets control from the program in one of the two ways:

- The hardware causes an interrupt.
- The program issues an interrupt thru an SVC.

We examine operations only in terms of OS360, although other systems such as DOS, BOS, etc., work similarly.

When OS360 gets control, an interrupt intervenes and provides the required services without "the program knowing about it." That is, the programmer never knows where in his program an interrupt takes over; but he need not know, since whatever is done does not generally interfere with the program. The exception to this is when OS360 detects trouble with which it cannot cope and hence must discontinue the performance of the program—a catastrophic error for the program.

If OS360 gets control by an SVC which originated as a macro in the program, the program needs a service which is either performed or initiated before the program regains control. OS360 gets instructions about new jobs, etc., via JCL. Only when OS360 has terminated a program or job step when successfully completed or because unsurmountable trouble has arisen, does it examine the job stream. Here it finds requests for new jobs.

Then JCL is the way OS360 goes from one job to another and finds out about the disposition of both hardware (DEVICES) and software (Access Methods) resources.

OS360 has total responsibility for hardware IO:

- The programmer
  - * deals with files mainly;
  - * can also choose and allocate DEVICES;
  - * can request operations with respect to the file.
- OS360 delegates requests to DEVICES:
  - * it gives commands to start IO;
  - * it receives an interrupt when the DEVICE action is completed for whatever reason;
  - * it chooses the next IO activity.

† Details about how the processing is done may be found in Ivan Flores, *Computer Organization*. Englewood Cliffs, N.J.: Prentice-Hall, Inc., 1969, Chapter 9. At least how System 360, Model 50 does things is described there.

2.2 DATA

We now talk about the AL for S360 which is called BAL for Basic Assembly Language.

Bytes When speaking of the *value* of a byte, it is inconvenient to use straight binary notation consisting of only 0's and 1's. We might use octal notation but manufacturers did not favor this because

1. Three octal digits are required for each byte.
2. Octal does not contain decimal numbers as a subset, so that packed numbers (see later) are not easily represented.
3. Octal is not as amenable to shift operations and their descriptions as applied to binary numbers.
4. Three punched columns per byte are needed for octal (versus two for hexadecimal) for binary numbers. A similar saving results for other media.

A *base 16* system is called **hexadecimal.**

HEXADECIMAL

Base 16 needs zero and fifteen other digits; the decimal system only provides ten usable digit symbols. Hence use the first six capital letters of the alphabet as auxiliary symbols. Each symbol has a four-bit combination (**combo**) corresponding to it. Combos are changed in natural succession in the same way as binary numbers. Thus the four-bit combo for six in binary, 0110_2, is assigned to six in hexadecimal and is represented as 6_H. The later combos are assigned to the letters in order of appearance: 1010 to A, etc. This code should be called **Natural Binary Coded Hexadecimal** or **NBCH.** Sometimes manufacturers erroneously call it **NBCD.** The NBCH code appears in Table 2.2.1.

Table 2.2.1 NBCH COMBOS

Hexadecimal	0	1	2	3	4	5	6	7	8	9	A	B	C†	D†	E	F
Decimal	0	1	2	3	4	5	6	7	8	9	+	−	+	−	+	+
Combo	0000	0001	0010	0011	0100	0101	0110	0111	1000	1001	1010	1011	1100	1101	1110	111

† Preferred sign combos.

EXAMPLES

To illustrate how NBCH is used, two examples follow:

$$11001000\ 11110101 \equiv \text{C8F5} \tag{2.2.1}$$

$$00111010 \equiv \text{3A} \tag{2.2.2}$$

Packed A byte can hold two decimal digits in NBCD form. The digits may be placed into designated bytes by PACK, described later. Decimal arithmetic commands expect to find two decimal digits per byte. This format is called **packed decimal**. Each digit is coded in NBCD, using the first ten combos in Table 2.2.1. Thus for packed decimal each byte is considered as two nibbles, each a four-bit combo. Only ten combos are admissible NBCD symbols. The other six are admissible as plus or minus signs, as noted from the table, only when they appear in the rightmost nibble of a decimal field (group of bytes): in any other position a sign is recognized by the hardware as invalid.

To reiterate, in a valid packed field, the rightmost nibble must be a sign; the other nibbles must *not* be signs—they must be NBCD combos. The hardware checks *all* bytes but *only* when a packed command is given. Invalid data cause an interrupt—intervention by OS—with possible job termination.

Unpacked When a byte carries **alphanumeric** or **unpacked information,** all eight bits participate. This provides 2^8 or 256 combos per byte. Two standard eight-bit codes are available. They are called USASCII–8 (USA—Standard Code for Information Interchange and EBCDIC (Extended Binary Coded Decimal Interchange Code). The codes themselves are found in S360 manuals.

With so many combos available, we find many unassigned combos in each code. Even so, there are combos for the following:

1. digits,
2. uppercase alphabetic,
3. lowercase alphabetic,
4. special characters such as asterisk, question mark, etc.,
5. special symbols such as carriage return, line advances, etc.

Packing Original data are always entered or transmitted to the computer from a KEYBOARD or CARDREADER input unpacked —one digit, character, or symbol per byte. Numerals are a subset of the eight-bit input code. There is no reasonable way to have the INPUT DEVICE handle numerical and alphabetic information differently.

Thus, information from PUNCHCARD READERS, PAPER TAPE READERS, CONSOLES, and so forth is unpacked (in alphanumeric form) even if it is numeric. Numerals which will not be processed arithmetically can be left *unpacked* and transferred directly as any other *alpha* byte to an output area without intermediate conversion.

Numeric data which are to be treated arithmetically must be *packed.* PACK takes numerals coded in an eight-bit code and changes them to four-bit NBCD by stripping the left four bits. PACK then *packs* them two digits per byte. This is possible because for both codes the numerals have their NBCD equivalent in the right nibble and 0101 (for USA–CII) or 1111 (for EBCDIC) as the left nibble. But *packing* takes time and also requires MEMORY for storing the number and the PACK and UNPK commands.

Hereafter I consider only *unpacked* EBCDIC decimal bytes which contain 1111, F_H, in the left nibble and the NBCD equivalent of the digit in the right nibble. The exception is the least significant digit which may have another combination in the left nibble to convey the sign. *Packed* data should always contain a sign in the rightmost nibble. *Packing* preserves the sign nibble, positioned as in Fig. 2.2.1.

Other decimal nibbles are prepared by *stripping* the left nibble from the *alpha* byte. These are assembled to produce the proper NBCD image as shown in Fig. 2.2.1.

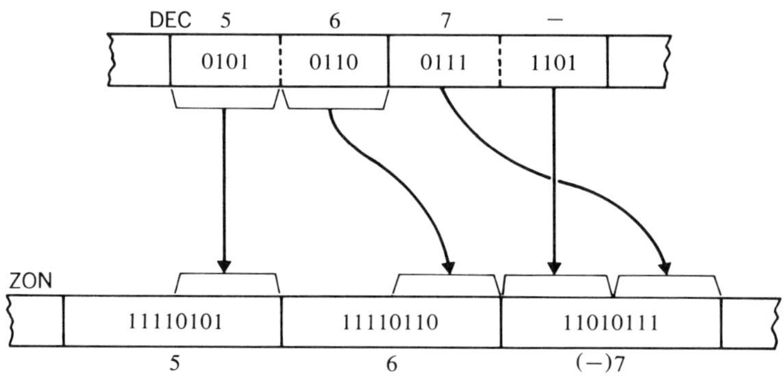

Fig. 2.2.1 Unpacking from DEC to ZON using: UNPK ZON,DEC.

Consider that if alpha rather than *numeric* data are used for packing inadvertently, *stripping* is performed automatically. The hardwave does not (cannot) check data presented for PACK or UNPK. If arithmetic is later performed on *packed* data, an error may be detected if invalid combos appear: only nonsign combos (NBCD) in nonsign positions may appear; a sign combo must appear in the sign position.

Unpack a numeric datum, N, using unpack, UNPK. The reverse operations to those in Fig. 2.2.1 are done to produce an *unpacked* datum, U.

1. The N rightmost (sign) nibble is placed in the left nibble of the U rightmost byte.

2. The next (going leftward) N nibble is placed in the right U nibble.
3. Succeeding N nibbles (going leftward) are placed in right nibbles of succeeding (going leftward) U bytes.
4. Hex F's (1111) are placed in the left nibbles of all U bytes.

Conversion For fixed point binary arithmetic, packed (decimal) information is next converted into binary using *ConVert to Binary*, CVB. S360 does binary arithmetic with fixed length thirty-two-bit Words or sometimes with sixteen-bit halfWords. Binary commands expect binary format but do not check for it.

Binary information for output must go through both *reconversion* and *unpacking* procedures:

- The *ConVert to Decimal* command, CVD, goes from binary to packed decimal.
- Packed decimal is converted to alphanumeric using UNPK.

When information is for later computer consumption and not to be used by the humans, we can really take advantage of packed decimal or fixed word binary format. In this case, a core image can be placed on magnetic tape, disk, or drum without conversion and later returned to MEMORY in its original state.

2.3 COMMANDS

Multiple length The advantage of multiple length commands becomes apparent at the inception of the IBM 1401. This philosophy has been carried over to System 360 which provides three command lengths:

- two bytes when MEMORY is *not* referenced,
- four bytes for a single MEMORY reference,
- six bytes when two separate MEMORY areas need reference.

For all commands the first byte conveys the opcode. Further, the first two bits of the opcode describe the command length so that CONTROL knows how many bytes must be *fetched.*

General format To introduce S360 commands, we consider only three of the five available formats. Assume first that two operands are required and that these are found in either a GPR or MEMORY. Table 2.3.1 shows the alternatives.

Addresses In describing the action of a command, it is the **effective address, M,** which interests us. We define M as the designation of the GPR, FPR, or the MEMORY address of the first byte of the operand.

Table 2.3.1 THREE S360 COMMAND FORMATS, LENGTHS IN NIBBLES

Name	*Opcode length*	*First operand Residence*	*First operand Length*	*Second operand Residence*	*Second operand Length*	*Other*	*Total*
RR	2	GPR	1	GPR	1	0	4
RX	2	GPR	1	MEMORY	5	0	8
SS	2	MEMORY	4	MEMORY	4	2	12

Then M1 is the effective address of the first operand, named first in the command; M2 is the effective address of the second operand.

Most operations work on two operands to create a result which is placed at M1 thereafter. We indicate this symbolically as

$$(\text{M1})\theta(\text{M2}) \longrightarrow \text{M1} \tag{2.3.1}$$

where θ is some operation requested by the opcode.

Register commands

RR commands require no MEMORY references. They have the format

$$\text{RR:}\quad \text{OP R1 R2} \tag{2.3.2}$$

where M1 = R1 and M2 = R2. Hence this requests

$$(\text{R1})\theta(\text{R2}) \longrightarrow \text{R1} \tag{2.3.3}$$

An example is *add register* with mnemonic AR:

$$\text{AR: } (\text{GPRR1}) + (\text{GPRR2}) \longrightarrow \text{GPRR1} \tag{2.3.4}$$

The opcode for AR is 1A in hexadecimal, so the machine language command 1A57 does

$$\text{1A57: } (\text{GPR5}) + (\text{GPR7}) \longrightarrow \text{GPR5} \tag{2.3.5}$$

It should be clear that this command is found in MEMORY in binary terms:

$$\text{1A57} \equiv 0001101001010111 \tag{2.3.6}$$

The AL equivalent, more important to us, is

```
AR      5,7                                  (2.3.7)
```

All RR mnemonics end in R.

RX commands

These have the ML format

$$\text{RX:}\quad \text{OP R1 X2 B2 D2} \tag{2.3.8}$$

where OP is a byte describing the command;

X2 is a nibble naming an INDEX REGISTER;

B2 is a nibble naming a BASE REGISTER;

D2 consists of three nibbles comprising a displacement of twelve bits.

The effective address, M2, is formed thus:

$$M2 = (\text{GPR}X2)_M + (\text{GPR}B2)_M + D2 \qquad (2.3.9)$$

where the subscript M indicates that only the rightmost 24 bits of the GPR are considered. Several observations are now essential:

- All GPRS contain thirty-two bits.
- Only twenty-four-bit addresses are valid.
- The subscript M above conveys that the left-hand eight bits of a GPR are discarded and only the right-hand twenty-four bits participate.
- The resulting address, M2, is hence twenty-four bits.

The processing requested is stated symbolically as

$$(R1)\theta(M2) \longrightarrow R1 \qquad (2.3.10)$$

An example of *add* with mnemonic A is given in AL as

$$\text{A:}\quad R1, D2\,(X2, B2) \qquad (2.3.11)$$

$$\text{A:}\ (\text{GPR}R1) + (M2) \longrightarrow \text{GPR}R1 \qquad (2.3.12)$$

or

$$\text{A:}\ (\text{GPR}R1) + ((\text{GPR}X2) + (\text{GPR}B2) + D2) \longrightarrow \text{GPR}R1 \qquad (2.3.13)$$

The opcode for A is 5A. Here is an example using both AL and hexadecimal ML:

$$\text{A} \qquad 3{,}1A0(4,\ 5) \qquad (2.3.14)$$

$$5A3451A0\text{:}\ (\text{GPR}3) + ((\text{GPR}4) + (\text{GPR}5) + 1A0) \longrightarrow \text{GPR}3 \qquad (2.3.15)$$

Notice the order for M2 in AL: displacement, then in parentheses, index and base. Suppose that (GPR4) = 00000028 and (GPR5) = 00020B00; then M2 is given as

$$M2 = 28 + 20B00 + 1A0 = 020CC8 \qquad (2.3.16)$$

Note how the left-hand "00" is dropped from (GPRS) since only twenty-four bits are used and (2.3.15) becomes

$$5A3451A0\text{:}\ (\text{GPR}3) + (20CC8) \longrightarrow \text{GPR}3 \qquad (2.3.17)$$

This adds the binary Word in GPR3 and the Word in MEMORY starting at address 20CC8 (last byte at 20CCB), placing the sum in GPR3.

Index or base suppression There are times when the calculation of M2 should exclude the use of a BASE REGISTER or INDEX REGISTER or both. It would be wasteful to require a GPR which always contained 0. The alternative adopted is to suppress reference to a GPR when either X2 or B2, or both, is 0. Hence it is impossible to index or relocate using GPR0, a minor penalty. We have

$$\text{A} \quad 3,1\text{A}0(0,5) \tag{2.3.18}$$

or

$$\text{A} \quad 3,1\text{A}0(5) \tag{2.3.19}$$

or

$$5\text{A}3051\text{A}0\text{: } (\text{GPR}3) + ((\text{GPR}5) + 1\text{A}0) \longrightarrow \text{GPR}3 \tag{2.3.20}$$

or

$$5\text{A}3051\text{A}0\text{: } (\text{GPR}3) + (20\text{CA}0) \longrightarrow \text{GPR}3 \tag{2.3.21}$$

where (GPR5) = 00020B00 but

$$\text{A} \quad 0,1\text{A}0(4,5) \tag{2.3.22}$$

or

$$5\text{A}0451\text{A}0\text{: } (\text{GPR}0) + [(\text{GPR}4) + (\text{GPR}5) + 1\text{A}0] \longrightarrow \text{GPR}3 \tag{2.3.23}$$

or

$$5\text{A}0451\text{A}0\text{: } (\text{GPR}0) + (20\text{CC}8) \longrightarrow \text{GPR}0 \tag{2.3.24}$$

where (GPR4) = 00000028 and (GPR5) = 00020B00. Again the AL order—displacement, index, base—is different than for the ML command.

Field commands For these commands, both operands are in MEMORY and the result is also returned there. The format depends upon whether the size of these two operands must be the same. If so, we have

$$\text{SS: } \quad \text{OP L B1 D1 B2 D2} \tag{2.3.25}$$

Here L is one byte which specifies the length of either operand where 00 denotes one byte and FF_H denotes 256 bytes. Also

$$\text{M1} = (\text{GPRB1}) + \text{D1} \qquad \text{M2} = (\text{GPRB2}) + \text{D2} \tag{2.3.26}$$

As an example, take the move character command MVC:

$$\text{MVC: } (\text{M2}) \xrightarrow{\text{L}} \text{M1} \tag{2.3.27}$$

Let (GPR5) = 000F1200. Then we have for MVC = D2

$$\text{MVC} \quad 15(5,12),21(5) \tag{2.3.28}$$

or

$$\text{D20D50015021: } (\text{F1221}) \xrightarrow{14} \text{F1201} \tag{2.3.29}$$

Here the fourth nibble, D, is $13_{\#}$ which requests $14_{\#}$ bytes moved. Again displacement is mentioned first; then base and actual length, if any. S360 provides decimal commands which operate on fields of packed numerics (hence the suffix P in the mnemonic). Fields may be of *different* size. Thus when posting weekly pay onto year-to-date pay, we would expect the receiving field to be larger than the source field. Such commands have the format

$$\text{SS:} \quad \text{OP L1 L2 B1 D1 B2 D2} \tag{2.3.30}$$

where M1 and M2 are calculated with (2.3.26) and L1 and L2 are each nibbles which convey the number of *bytes* in each field: L1 $= F_H$ means (M1) is sixteen bytes long; L2 $= 0$ means (M2) is one byte long. Take as an example *subtract packed*, SP:

$$\text{SP: } (\text{M1})_{L1} - (\text{M2})_{L2} \longrightarrow \text{M1} \tag{2.3.31}$$

Since SP $= \text{FA}_H$, an example of this is

$$\text{SP} \quad 10(3,7),20(3,5) \tag{2.3.32}$$

or

$$\text{FA6430103020: } (\text{AB10})_6 - (\text{AB20})_4 \longrightarrow \text{AB10} \tag{2.3.33}$$

where (GPR3) $=$ 0000AB00 and AL operand form: displacement (base, actual length).

Base suppression No base suppression is provided for SS commands. Hence GPR0 is used in (2.3.26) if specified.

2.4 FIXED BINARY COMMANDS

Assumptions Fixed binary commands have these similarities:

- At least one GPR is involved.
- The operands are generally treated as signed binary numbers.
- For arithmetic to produce correct results, the operands must have been packed (with PACK) and converted (with CVB) beforehand.

Data can be one of two lengths:

- fullWord—thirty-two bits—sign and thirty-one bits,
- halfWord—sixteen bits—sign and fifteen bits at the right of the GPR.

Three kinds of commands are applicable:

- fullWord register commands, RR, with suffix R,
- fullWord MEMORY commands, RX with no suffix,
- halfWord MEMORY commands, RX, with suffix H,
- There are *no* halfWord register commands.

Operands For these commands we have

$$\text{M1} = \text{R1} \tag{2.4.1}$$

For the RR commands we have

$$\text{RR: M2} = \text{R2} \tag{2.4.2}$$

For the RX command we have

$$\text{RX: M2} = (\text{X2}) + (\text{B2}) + \text{D2} \tag{2.4.3}$$

Descriptions of commands which follow apply equally regardless of how the operand is specified or its type. The commands are contrasted in Table 2.4.1.

Table 2.4.1 FIXED BINARY COMMANDS

Operation	*Register* *AL*	*ML*	*Word* *AL*	*ML*	*HalfWord* *AL*	*ML*	*Operator*
Store	—	—	ST	50	STH	40	none
and	NR	14	N	54	—	—	&
Logical compare	CLR	15	CL	55	—	—	:
or	OR	16	O	56	—	—	∨
exclusive or	XR	17	X	57	—	—	⊕
Load	LR	18	L	58	LH	48	none
Compare	CR	19	C	59	CH	49	:
Add	AR	1A	A	5A	AH	4A	+
Subtract	SR	1B	S	5B	SH	4B	—
Multiply	MR	1C	M	5C	MH	4C	*
Divide	DR	1D	D	5D	—	—	/

Arithmetic The operation of those commands is to perform algebraic addition or subtraction thus:

$$\text{A,AH,AR,S,SH,SR: (M1)} \pm \text{(M2)} \longrightarrow \text{M1} \tag{2.4.4}$$

As an example, we have

$$\text{AR} \quad \text{7,8: (GPR7)} + \text{(GPR8)} \longrightarrow \text{GPR7} \tag{2.4.5}$$

MULTIPLY

The product of two Words is a doubleWord requiring two GPRS. This is always a pair of successively numbered registers, the first of which *must be even*. Since GPRR1 always gets the result, R1 must be even. Then we have

$$\text{M or MR: (M2)}*(\text{GPRR1}) \longrightarrow \text{GPRR1} \smile \text{GPR(R1}+1) \tag{2.4.6}$$

For example

$$\text{M} \quad 8,\text{MPR: (MPR)}*(\text{GPR8}) \longrightarrow \text{GPR8} \smile \text{GPR9} \tag{2.4.7}$$

where the symbol $\smile$ indicates the combination of two GPRS.

For halfWords, the result is one Word and hence GPRR1 can hold it. The multiplicand is a Word and the product is truncated at the left before returning it.

$$\text{MH: (M2)}*(\text{GPRR1}) \longrightarrow \text{GPRR1} \tag{2.4.8}$$

For example,

$$\text{MH} \quad 10,\text{SHORT: (SHORT)}*(\text{GPR10}) \longrightarrow \text{GPR10} \tag{2.4.9}$$

DIVIDE

Stated symbolically, we have

$$\text{D or DR: } \frac{(\text{GPRR1} \smile \text{GPR(R1 + 1))}}{(\text{M2})} \longrightarrow \text{GPR(R1 + 1)} \tag{2.4.10}$$

$$\text{Remainder} \longrightarrow \text{GPRR1}$$

where R1 *must be even*. So we might give

$$\text{DR} \quad 6,8\text{: } \frac{(\text{GPR6}) \smile (\text{GPR7})}{(\text{GPR8})} \longrightarrow \text{GPR7} \tag{2.4.11}$$

Logical θ may be one of three logical operations. The operation works on corresponding bits in (GPRR1) and (M2) to create the bit for that position in GPRR1. The rules for the bit manipulation are found in Table 2.4.2.

Table 2.4.2 LOGICAL OPERATIONS

and = &(N)	*or* = ∨(O)	*exclusive or* = ⊕(X)
0 & 0 = 0	0 ∨ 0 = 0	0 ⊕ 0 = 0
0 & 1 = 0	0 ∨ 1 = 1	0 ⊕ 1 = 1
1 & 0 = 0	1 ∨ 0 = 1	1 ⊕ 0 = 1
1 & 1 = 1	1 ∨ 1 = 1	1 ⊕ 1 = 0

Transfers *Load* fills a GPR or copies one GPR into another: LOAD

$$\text{L,LR,LH: (M2)} \longrightarrow \text{GPRR1} \tag{2.4.12}$$

$$\text{L} \quad 3,\text{ Q: (Q)} \longrightarrow \text{GPR3} \tag{2.4.13}$$

Store copies a GPR into MEMORY; hence there is no R store. STORE

$$\text{ST,STH: (GPRR1)} \longrightarrow \text{M2} \tag{2.4.14}$$

$$\text{ST} \quad 4,\text{AWAY: (GPR4)} \longrightarrow \text{AWAY} \tag{2.4.15}$$

Compare All *compares* do this:

$$\text{C,CR,CH,CL,CLR:} \begin{cases} (\text{M1}) < (\text{M2}):\ 01 \longrightarrow \text{CCR} \\ (\text{M1}) = (\text{M2}):\ 00 \longrightarrow \text{CCR} \\ (\text{M1}) > (\text{M2}):\ 10 \longrightarrow \text{CCR} \end{cases} \tag{2.4.16}$$

where CCR is the **CONDITION CODE REGISTER**, a two-bit INDICATOR which can be tested as described in Section 2.5.

Table 2.4.3 OTHER BINARY COMMANDS

Operation	*AL*	*ML*	*Description*	*Note*
Load positive	LPR	10	$\|(\text{GPRR2})\| \rightarrow \text{R1}$	Set CCR + = 2, − = 1, 0 = 0
Load negative	LNR	11	$-\|(\text{GPRR2})\| \rightarrow \text{R1}$	
Load and test	LTR	12	$(\text{GPRR2}) \rightarrow \text{R1}$	
Load complement	LCR	13	$-(\text{GPRR2}) \rightarrow \text{R1}$	
Add logical	AL	5E	$(\text{M1}) \pm (\text{M2}) \rightarrow \text{M1}$	Add as unsigned integers and record carry from sign
	ALR	1E		
Subtract logical	SL	5F		
	SLR	1F		
Load address	LA	41	$\text{M2} \rightarrow \text{GPRR1}$	
Store character	STC	42	$(\text{GPRR1}) \rightarrow \text{M2}$	Rightmost byte only
Insert character	IC	43	$(\text{M2}) \rightarrow \text{GPRR1}$	Rightmost byte only
Convert to decimal	CVD	4E	$(\text{GPRR1}) \xrightarrow{2/\#} \text{M2}$	
Convert to binary	CVB	4F	$(\text{M2}) \xrightarrow{\#/2} \text{GPRR1}$	

Table 2.4.1 reveals *two* kinds of *compare*. The *arithmetic compare* views the Word or halfWord as a signed binary number. The left bit is 0 for positive and 1 for negative and, naturally, the former is always larger than the latter. *Logical compare* views the Word (halfWord) as a pure collection of bits; with this command the negative binary numbers turn out to be larger than positive ones. It is useful in comparing sets of letters.

EXAMPLE

Suppose (GPR6) = $00000400_H = 1024_\#$ and (GPR7) = $\text{FFFFFFFB}_H = -5_\#$, then we have

$$\text{CR} \quad 6,7:\ 10 \longrightarrow \text{CCR} \tag{2.4.17}$$

$$\text{CLR} \quad 6,7:\ 01 \longrightarrow \text{CCR} \tag{2.4.18}$$

Others Other commands are only of specialized interest. These are listed in Table 2.4.3 and described there symbolically.

2.5 BRANCHES

Reflexive commands When a command is executed, CONTROL goes to the byte after the last one used and gets the first byte of the next command there. Thus if AR at 370 has just been done, the next command starts at 372. If it is CVD, the next command is at 376, etc. Reflexive commands cause CONTROL to take a command from a different byte. This is usually a ***branch***, meaning that normal sequencing takes up from a new designated address. A *branch* is **conditional** if it is taken only when a specified condition prevails. Below, the double arrow, ⇒, indicates the address from which the *next* command is fetched.

Branch on condition The RX form of this command is

$$\text{BC(47)}: (\text{CCR}) \leftrightarrow \text{R1} \Rightarrow \text{M2} \tag{2.5.1}$$

and the RR form is

$$\text{BCR(07)}: (\text{CCR}) \leftrightarrow \text{R1} \Rightarrow (\text{GPRR2}) \tag{2.5.2}$$

where we have

- R1 is the set of four bits in the command.
- CCR is the condition code register.
- ↔ means the two are matched up as described below.
- ⇒ means the next instruction comes from M2 or (GPRR2) if the match is found, but in normal sequence otherwise.

MASK

The CCR has two bits to record one of four combinations. These combinations correspond to conditions which can arise during execution of only certain commands. For instance, LTR (see Table 2.4.3) sets CCR according to the sign of the number loaded; C sets CCR according to which operand, if either, is larger.

There is one bit in the mask, R1, corresponding to each condition which might be recorded in the CCR. The CCR is set by the *most recent* command which announces a condition (such as C or LTR). Table 2.5.1

Table 2.5.1 MASK BIT SETTINGS FOR BC AND BCR

R1				*CC*	
B8	*B9*	*B10*	*B11*	*Hexadecimal*	*Binary*
1	X	X	X	0	00
X	1	X	X	1	01
X	X	1	X	2	10
X	X	X	1	3	11

shows which CC (condition circle) will cause a branch when a corresponding bit of R1 is set to 1. Contrariwise, if a bit (say B9) is 0, then that CC (01) is ignored and cannot cause a *branch*. Then for BC or BCR, *for the* branch *to be made, the bit in* R1 *for the* CC *now in the* CCR *must be 1.*

Note these two special cases:

- If all bits of R1 are 0, then no CC causes a *branch* and BC acts like NOP.
- If all bits of R1 are 1, then *any* CC causes a branch and BC acts like an unconditional branch (B).

Examples Table 2.5.2 shows some arrangements for R1, their meaning, and their equivalent symbol.

Table 2.5.2 MEANING OF SOME VALUES OF R1 FOR BC, BCR AFTER C

R1 Hex	*Binary*	*CCs which cause a branch*				*Equivalent symbol*
2	0010	—	—	10	—	$>$
6	0110	—	01	10	—	$\neq$
C	1100	00	01	—	—	$\leq$
8	1000	00	—	—	—	$=$
0	0000	—	—	—	—	NOP
F	1111	00	01	10	11	B

In AL we have

BC 0,NEXT1: $\Rightarrow$ (IAR) (2.5.3)

BC 15,NEXT2: $\Rightarrow$ NEXT2 (2.5.4)

BC 2,NEXT3: (CCR) $=$ 10 $\Rightarrow$ NEXT3 (2.5.5)

BC 12,NEXT4: (CCR) $=$ 00 or 01 $\Rightarrow$ NEXT4 (2.5.6)

Extended mnemonics BAL provides extended mnemonics. These combine the BC or BCR with the condition required to make a new mnemonic. This is translated by the assembler into the proper opcode *and* setting of R1. BR is *branch, register,* for example, and is unconditional. Since BCR $=$ 07 and R1 should be set to F_H, we have

BR 2 (07F2): $\Rightarrow$ (GPR2) (2.5.7)

which says "branch to the address contained in GPRR2."

The *unconditional branch* and *noop* are independent of preceding commands. Other extended mnemonics provided are listed against the command type which precedes it in Table 2.5.3.

Table 2.5.3 EXTENDED MNEMONICS

AL	*Anytime* *Means*	*ML†*	*AL*	*After TM* *Means*	*ML†*
B	Branch	47F/M2	BO	Branch if ones	471/M2
BR	Branch register	07F/R2	BM	Branch mixed	474/M2
NOP	Noop	470/M2	BZ	Branch if zeros	478/M2
NOPR	Noop register	470/R2	BNO	Branch not ones	407E/M2
	Compare			*Arithmetic*	
BH	Branch high	472/M2	BO	Branch on overflow	471/M2
BZ	Branch low	474/M2	BP	Branch plus	472/M2
BE	Branch equal	478/M2	BM	Branch minus	474/M2
BNH	Branch not high	47D/M2	BZ	Branch zero	478/M2
BNL	Branch not low	47B/M2	BNP	Branch not plus	47D/M2
BNE	Branch not equal	477/M2	BNM	Branch not minus	47B/M2
			BNZ	Branch not zero	477/M2

† Where R2 is a register nibble and M2 a five nibble address in MEMORY.

Alignment We have seen that alignment is an important consideration. The AL programmer often needs to make sure that the next command given is on a particular boundary. He uses CNOP to do this; it has the following format:

CNOP byte,word (2.5.8)

where both *byte* and *word* are even numbers. *Word* is 4 for Word alignment and 8 for doubleWord alignment. *Byte* is 0, 2, 4, or 6 to request initial, second, third, or fourth halfWord alignment. Although IBM calls CNOP a pseudo, I insist it is an extended mnemonic since it usually *produces* ML code and it never "talks" to the assembler.

The assembler produces the number of NOPRs required to get the desired alignment specifying R2 = 0, which is unimportant since a branch is never taken. Hence CNOP produces in machine language a number of halfWords of the form 4700 where 47 stands for BCR, 0 says never *branch*, 0 says GPR0 *would* be used if a branch were ever taken.

Why are off-boundary alignments needed? The programmer may need a specific alignment later, which he provides for now. For instance, suppose he needs a doubleWord at 310 (command number) and a *compare*, C, at 309. He can place CNOP at 308 to ensure this, thus:

308	CNOP	2,8	
309	C	3,TEST	
310	doubleWord		(2.5.9)

If 308 is at the last halfWord of a doubleWord, the assembler produces two NOPRs to take us to the second halfWord of a doubleWord.

2.6 REFLEXIVE COMMANDS

Branches give control to a new sequence of commands. We may wish to return to the old sequence. CONTROL keeps track of the next command address in the INSTRUCTION ADDRESS REGISTER, IAR. This is part of the PROGRAM STATUS WORD REGISTER, PSWR, which also contains the CCR and a mask for suppressing interruptions arising from various program sources.

Linkage Getting back and forth to subroutines is done with *branch and link*, BAL, which stores the exit in a named GPR. However, a GPR holds thirty-two bits; an address is twenty-four bits; why not use the extra space for (CCR) and the mask? This is done: the right Word of the PSW doubleWord is stored during linkage; call this (PSWRR). Then we have

$$\text{BAL(45): (PSWRR)} \longrightarrow \text{GPRR1}; \Rightarrow \text{M2} \qquad (2.6.1)$$

There is an RR equivalent, BALR, described thus:

$$\text{BALR(05): (PSWRR)} \longrightarrow \text{GPRR1}; \Rightarrow \text{(GPRR2)} \qquad (2.6.2)$$

Both of these provide for access to the call sequence and return to the main program or highest level subroutine.

Execute *Execute*, EX, permits *one* command to be executed out of sequence and then control returns to the main program. The out-of-sequence command is at M2. Then we have

$$\text{EX(44): } \Rightarrow \text{M2}; \Rightarrow \text{(IAR)} \qquad (2.6.3)$$

What about R1? If it is 0, nothing changes; for R1 anything else, the rightmost byte of that GPR is *or*'ed with the second byte of the object instruction (at M2). This permits register specification by EX, etc., for the object instruction.

If the object instruction is a successful *branch*, the new sequence is pursued and return is *not* ordinarily made to the command after EX. It is not permissible to have EX as an object command for EX.

Count The *branch on count*, BCT, is for looping:

$$\text{BCT(46)}: (\text{GPR}R1) - 1 \longrightarrow \text{GPR}R1: (\text{GPR}R1) \neq 0 \Rightarrow M2 \qquad (2.6.4)$$

The GPR is decremented and checked and the *branch* taken only if the new contents of GPRR1 are nonzero. Similarly we have

$$\text{BCTR(06)}: (\text{GPR}R1) - 1 \longrightarrow \text{GPR}R1: (\text{GPR}R1) \neq 0 \Rightarrow (\text{GPR}R2) \qquad (2.6.5)$$

These commands are useful for loops performed a number of times, that is, determined by a count stored in GPRR1. Remember that sequencing through a list cannot be done with this command *alone*. When an INDEX REGISTER is used to monitor a list, the length of each datum must be kept in mind. For fixed data size, the INDEX REGISTER must be incremented or decremented by the *number of bytes* required for each datum. For instance, sequencing through a list of items each of Word size, the increment or decrement is 4.

Branch on index Instead of a count, an INDEX REGISTER may be checked directly. For these commands, four separate quantities are incorporated into the command:

1. The branch address is M2.
2. The index quantity is in GPRR1.
3. The increment to be added to the index is in GPRR3.
4. The test quantity is in GPR(R3 + 1) (for R3 even or GPRR3, also, for R3 odd).

The format of the two *branch on index* commands, BXH and BXLE, is

$$\text{BXH,BXLE}: \quad OP \ R1 \ R3 \ B2 \ D2 \qquad (2.6.6)$$

The commands are

$$\begin{aligned} \text{BXH(86)}: \quad & (\text{GPR}R1) + (\text{GPR}R3) \longrightarrow \text{GPR}R1; \\ & (\text{GPR}R1) > (\text{GPR}(R3+1)): \Rightarrow M2 \qquad (R3 \text{ even}) \end{aligned} \qquad (2.6.7)$$

$$\begin{aligned} \text{BXLE(87)}: \quad & (\text{GPR}R1) + (\text{GPR}R3) \longrightarrow \text{GPR}R1; \\ & (\text{GPR}R1) \leq (\text{GPR}(R3+1)): \Rightarrow M2 \qquad (R3 \text{ even}) \end{aligned} \qquad (2.6.8)$$

In both cases the increment and index are added together and the sum replaces the index; then the test is made. Generally (R3 even) a new GPR is used to test against the new index content and the *branch* taken if the test "succeeds."

Examples We're going to see how a simple problem can be programmed in 360AL using BCT, BXLE, and BXH.

BCT PROBLEMS

There are seven binary Words. The first is at NUM; the second is at NUM+4; . . . ; the last is at NUM+24. Add them. Place the sum at SUM.

This method, shown in Fig. 2.6.1, uses GPR4 for the number of Words, GPR3 for the sum, and GPR5 for the address of the next number to be

```
                (GPR3) = sum
                (GPR4) = count
                (GPR5) = address of next number

1       SR      3,3       Clear GPR3
2       LA      4,7       Put 7 in GPR4
3       LA      5,NUM     Put address of NUM in GPR5
4   ┌──►A       3,0(5)    Add next number
5   │   LA      5,4(5)    Increment address
6   └──►BCT     4,*-8     Decrement count and test
7       ST      3,SUM     Store sum
```

Fig. 2.6.1 Adding seven numbers using BCT.

added. GPR3 is cleared (1) when it is subtracted from itself with SR. GPR4 is filled with 7 by LA. Since the displacement is a number, $\mathcal{ASLR}$ sets X2 and B2 to 0 to suppress indexing and relocation.

The address of the first number, NUM, is placed in GPR5 with LA also (3).

After addition (step 4), the address is advanced by 4 (we're adding Words) to yield the address of the next Word(s). The count is decremented and tested (6). Looping is done as long as numbers remain. Note no indexing was done; self-relative addressing, *–8 counts the *branch* length from the *beginning* of *this* command to the *beginning* of the *object* command.

BXLE

Fig. 2.6.2 uses BXLE. After initialization (1–4) each number is added in turn to GPR5. The index is incremented and tested and if it is now 28 (why?), processing stops.

(GPR2) = sum (GPR3) = index
(GPR4) = increment (GPR5) = criterion

```
1      SR       2,2          Clear GPR2
2      SR       3,3          Clear GPR3
3      LA       4,4          Put 4 into GPR4
4      LA       5,28         Put 28 into GPR5
5   ┌─►A        2,NUM(3)     Add next number
6   └─►BXLE     3,4,*-4      Increment index and test
7      ST       2,SUM        Store sum
```

Fig. 2.6.2 Adding seven numbers using BXLE.

In Fig. 2.6.3 the numbers are added in reverse order, starting with the last at NUM+24 by setting the index to 24 (step 2). The increment is

BXH

GPR2 = sum GPR3 = index
GPR4 = increment GPR5 = criterion

```
1      SR       2,2          Clear GPR2
2      L        3,=F'24'     Put 24 into GPR3
3      L        4,=F'-4'     Put -4 into GPR4
4      L        5,=F'-1'     Put -1 into GPR5
5   ┌─►A        2,NUM(3)     Add next number
6   └─►BXH      3,4,*-4      Increment index and test
7      ST       2,SUM        Store sum
```

Fig. 2.6.3 Adding seven numbers with BXH.

negative, −4 (step 3). Since we wish to add the first number (when the index holds 0), we set the criterion to −1 (step 4).

2.7 VARIABLE FIELD LENGTH COMMANDS

Format Variable field length (hereafter, VFL) commands have an opcode D*H* where *H* is a hexadecimal digit. Each contains a length specifier tag, L, and two addresses, M1 and M2. Each effective address is formed by adding the displacement contained in the command (D1 and D2) to the contents of the GPR, designated in the command (B1 and B2). GPR0 is a valid base register.

M2 is the address of the first (leftmost) byte of the source datum of length, given by L. *L is one less than the desired length in bytes.* M1 is the address of the leftmost byte of the destination field whose length also is given by L. The opcode names an operation to be performed on the operands, the result being placed in the destination field starting at M1.

Each VFL field can begin at any byte in MEMORY—there are no boundary limitations. Table 2.7.1 presents a description of each command.

Table 2.7.1 VFL COMMANDS

Operation	*AL*	*ML*	*Description*	*Note*
Move numeric	MVN	D1	$(M2)_N \longrightarrow M1_N$	Only right nibbles moved
Move	MVC	D2	$(M2) \longrightarrow M1$	
Move zone	MVZ	D3	$(M2)_z \longrightarrow M1_z$	Only left nibbles moved
and	NC	D4	$(M2)\ \&\ (M1) \longrightarrow M1$	
Compare logical	CLC	D5	$(M2)\!:\ (M1) \longrightarrow$ CCR	
or	OC	D6	$(M2) \vee (M1) \longrightarrow M1$	
exclusive or	XC	D7	$(M2) \oplus (M1) \longrightarrow M1$	
Translate	TR	DC	$[M2 + (M1)] \neq 0$:	Byte for byte replacement
Translate and test	TRT	DD	$[M2 + (M1)] \neq 0$: $[M2 + (M1)] \longrightarrow$ GPRR2; $M1 \longrightarrow$ GPRR1; $\Rightarrow$ (IAR)	No bytes replaced, only examined
Edit	ED	DE	$(M2)\ E\ (M1) \longrightarrow M1$	
Edit and mark	EDMK	DF	$(M2)\ E\ (M1) \longrightarrow M1$	

Move There are three commands which *move* (unary) VFL operands. M2 is the starting address of the source and M1 is the starting address of the destination.

- MVC (opcode D2) moves characters without alteration.
- MVN (opcode D1) moves the right (numeric) nibble of each source (M2) byte into the right nibble of the corresponding destination (M1) byte. The destination field is altered only in the right nibble positions.
- MVZ (opcode D3) moves only the *zone* or *left nibble* from source to destination as for MVN described above.

In BAL, length of defined fields may be implied or it is parenthesized after the first mentioned symbolic address. The latter case *overrides* an implied length. An example is

$$\text{MVC} \quad \text{THERE(8),HERE: (HERE)} \xrightarrow{8} \text{THERE} \qquad (2.7.1)$$

Logical The three commands, NC, OC, and XC, with opcodes, respectively, D4, D6, and D7, perform, respectively, the logical functions *and*, *or*, and *exclusive or* with corresponding source and destination bytes on a bit basis as presented earlier in Fig. 2.4.2.

Compare CLC, with opcode D5, compares the two fields logically on a bit for a bit basis, viewing the fields as collections of bits of length 8(L + 1) and determining the larger of the two numbers. The result of the comparison is recorded in the CONDITION CODE REGISTER:

$$\begin{aligned}&0 \text{ for } (M1) = (M2)\\&1 \text{ for } (M1) < (M2)\\&2 \text{ for } (M1) > (M2)\\&3 \text{ not used}\end{aligned} \tag{2.7.2}$$

For example, we have

$$\text{CLC A,B: } 10 \longrightarrow \text{CCR} \quad \text{for} \quad (A) > (B) \tag{2.7.3}$$

Translate The translate command is useful in translation from one code to another. M2 is the address of a table, generally 256 bytes of the combos for the designation code. Each source byte acts as an address to enter the table. That is why 256 bytes of table are needed, even for an incomplete code. Examine the command below:

$$\text{TR(DC): } \quad (M2 + (M1)) \longrightarrow M1 \tag{2.7.4}$$

M1 is the address of a field of length L + 1 which is to be translated. Starting at the left, a byte is obtained from M1. This byte *is* the displacement for entering the table at M2. Hence M2 + (M1) is the address in MEMORY where the translated byte is found. When it is acquired, it replaces the original byte at M1. Lookup continues for L + 1 cycles.

Translate and test This command should be called *lookup and test* since, as opposed to TR, no translation is done. Again the table is entered but different action is taken:

$$\begin{aligned}\text{TRT(DD)} \quad [M2 + (M1)] \neq 0\text{: } [M2 + (M1)] &\longrightarrow \text{GPRR2}\\ M1 &\longrightarrow \text{GPRR1}\\ &\Rightarrow (\text{IAR})\end{aligned} \tag{2.7.5}$$

Each destination byte is obtained and a table address found, M2 + (M1). The table is entered and the "translate" byte examined. If it is 00_H, a new M1 byte is obtained until L + 1 bytes starting at M1 are used up. If the byte is nonzero, it is placed in GPRR2 and the address of the M1 byte just looked up is placed in GPRR1.

This command is useful in two special applications:

1. For data formatting where special characters are used for field separators. Only these characters have nonzero "translate" bytes.

TRT then determines the position of the delimiters and can have the program create commands for processing.

2. For compiling. A sum of the import field can distinguish operators (+, −, *, etc.) from data names providing easy parsing.

Edit Both *edit* (ED) and *edit and mark* (EDMK) are very complicated. In both cases M1 is the address of a pattern field and M2 that of a data field, each of length L + 1. Characters of M2 are manipulated as specified by the pattern bytes in M1, whereafter the resulting character replaces that of M1.

The purpose of *edit* is to do insertion, deletion, and alteration functions such as

- insert decimal points,
- replace signs by credit symbols,
- remove leading nonsignificant zeros, etc.

2.8 DECIMAL COMMANDS

All decimal commands are SS format, have opcode F*H*, and are described in Table 2.8.1.

Table 2.8.1

Operation	*AL*	*ML*	*Description*	*Note*
Move with offset	MVO	F1	$(M2) \longrightarrow M1$	Operand offset, one nibble left, preserving "sign" position of M1
Pack	PACK	F2	$(M2) \xrightarrow{C/P} M1$	
Unpack	UNPK	F3	$(M2) \xrightarrow{P/C} M1$	
Zero add positive	ZAP	F8	$(M2) \longrightarrow M1$	Zeros to M1 first to most significant positions
Compare packed	CP	F9	$(M1) = (M2)$: $00 \longrightarrow$ CCR $(M1) < (M2)$: $01 \longrightarrow$ CCR $(M1) > (M2)$: $10 \longrightarrow$ CCR	
Add packed	AP	FA	$(M1) + (M2) \longrightarrow M1$	(CCR) = 11 for overflow
Subtract packed	SP	FB	$(M1) - (M2) \longrightarrow M1$	(CCR) = 11 for overflow
Multiply packed	MP	FC	$(M2)*(M1) \longrightarrow M1$	CC not set
Divide packed	DP	FD	$(M1)/(M2) \longrightarrow M$	CC not set

Each decimal field is specified by the address of its left-hand byte (M1 and M2) and the number of bytes it contains (L1 + 1 and L2 + 1). Notwithstanding, decimal commands handle information from right to left since for arithmetic the sign (at the right) is needed first. Further, as the digits of each number are operated upon, carries may be propagated leftward.

Arithmetic commands require two operands but there are three single operand commands.

As noted earlier, PACK converts from *unpacked* or character format to packed format thus:

$$\text{PACK(F2)}:\ (\text{M2}) \xrightarrow{\text{C/P}} \text{M1} \qquad (2.8.1)$$

where C/P indicates the conversion. In AL, L1 and L2 are parenthesized after the symbolic name of the field where each represents the *actual* length in bytes.

As an example, we have the command

$$\text{PACK: DEC(2),CHAR(3)} \qquad (2.8.2)$$

which produces this result in Fig. 2.8.1.

	Before	*After*
CHAR	F3F4F5	F3F4F5
DEC	ABCDEF	345FEF

Fig. 2.8.1 The action of (2.8.2).

The destination may be padded on the left with 0's as would be needed by

$$\text{PACK: DEC(4),CHAR(3)} \qquad (2.8.3)$$

which from Fig. 2.8.1 would produce

$$\text{DEC: 0000345F} \qquad (2.8.4)$$

The fields can overlap as long as it is remembered that the action takes place from right to left and duplication might occur if the programmer is not wary. This request is OK:

$$\text{PACK: FIELD+2(3),FIELD(5)} \qquad (2.8.5)$$

and produces

$$\text{FIELD before: F1F2F3F4F5} \qquad \text{FIELD after: F1F212345F} \qquad (2.8.6)$$

The format of this command is UNPK

$$\text{UNPK(F3)}:\ (\text{M2}) \xrightarrow{\text{P/C}} \text{M1} \qquad (2.8.7)$$

and has the reverse effect of PACK. Thus unpacking of DEC is done into CHAR as in Fig. 2.8.1 by

UNPK CHAR(3),DEC(2) (2.8.8)

When this command is given

UNPK F(5),F(3) (2.8.9)

this result obtains:

F before: 12345FABCD F after: F1F2F3F4F5 (2.8.10)

Notice that the results of (2.8.5), namely (2.8.6), are not directly reversible. If we give

UNPK FIELD(5),FIELD+2(3) (2.8.11)

then look what happens:

FIELD before: F1F212345F FIELD after: FFFFFFF4F5 (2.8.12)

But this command may be used:

UNPK FIELD+2(5),FIELD+2(3) (2.8.13)

to yield an offset but correct result:

FIELD before: F1F212345F9876
FIELD after: F1F2F1F2F3F4F5 (2.8.14)

MVO *Move with offset*, MVO, moves (M2) to M1, except that the sign nibble in M1 is not stepped on. One purpose of MVO is to provide shifts in decimal fields without disturbing the sign. For example, we apply

MVO NUM(4),NUM(2) (2.8.15)

and find the result

NUM before: 7654321F NUM after: 0007654F (2.8.16)

Here NUM(2) is 7654. It is placed at NUM(4) starting at the right after skipping over the sign, F. When we run out of nibbles, 0's are filled in.

Using the same philosophy to shift *left*, MVO does not help. Instead, MVC is sometimes better:

MVC NUM(2),NUM+2 (2.8.17)

but yields

NUM before: 7654321F NUM after: 321F321F (2.8.18)

This is remedied by *and*ing the proper constant

NC NUM+1(3),=X'F0000F' (2.8.19)

to obtain

NUM before: 321F321F NUM after: 3210000F (2.8.20)

Thus MVC is good for an even shift left. An odd shift left is achieved with MVC thus:

MVO NUM(3),NUM+1 (2.8.21)

NUM before: 7654321F NUM after: 4321F21F (2.8.22)

NC NUM+2(2), = X'000F' (2.8.23)

NUM before: 4321F21F NUM after: 4321000F (2.8.24)

Arithmetic Packed commands expect a sign in the right nibble and NBCD digits elsewhere in both numbers addressed as defined in Table 2.2.1. If this is not so, the hardware detects invalid numbers and gives control to OS360. The sign in the right nibble of the result is always in preferred form, C for +, D for −. ADD/SUBTRACT

The commands for *add* and *subtract* are simple to visualize:

$$\begin{matrix}\text{AP(FA)}\\ \text{SP(FB)}\end{matrix}: \text{(M1)} \pm \text{(M2)} \longrightarrow \text{M1} \qquad (2.8.25)$$

where L1 and L2 are associated with M1 and M2 and the CCR records; thus

$$0 = 00 \qquad + = 10 \qquad - = 01 \qquad \text{Overflow} = 11 \qquad (2.8.26)$$

MP does MULTIPLY

$$\text{MP(DC): (M2)}*\text{(M1)} \longrightarrow \text{M1} \qquad (2.8.27)$$

with these restrictions

1. $L2 \leq 7$
2. $L2 < L1$
3. As many high order 0's in M1 as there are significant digits in M2.

An example appears in Fig. 2.8.2.

Command:	MP	PRICE, QUANT
	Before	*After*
PRICE	0000500F	0012500C
QUANT	025F	025F

Fig. 2.8.2 MP example.

DP does DIVIDE

$$\text{DP(FD)}: \frac{\text{(M1)}}{\text{(M2)}} \longrightarrow \text{M1} \qquad (2.8.28)$$

where the quotient is at the left of M1 and the remainder occupies the right part of M1 and is of size L2 + 1 where L2 $\leq$ 7.

ZERO, ADD

ZAP moves a small numeric field into a large one, clearing the latter first, thus:

$$\text{ZAP(F8): (M2)} \longrightarrow \text{M1} \tag{2.8.29}$$

It may be applied to truncate a larger number; ZAP will indicate an overflow by setting CCR to 0.

COMPARE

This command compares two fields arithmetically setting CC accordingly:

$$\begin{aligned} \text{CP(F9): } &\text{(M1)} = \text{(M2): } 00 \longrightarrow \text{CC} \\ &\text{(M1)} < \text{(M2): } 01 \longrightarrow \text{CC} \\ &\text{(M1)} > \text{(M2): } 10 \longrightarrow \text{CC} \end{aligned} \tag{2.8.30}$$

2.9 THE SYSTEM

It is the operating system, OS360 (or DOS360 or BOS360, neither of which we examine), which performs all the complicated service required by the installation. There are two ways in which the OS360 takes over:

- The programmer gives it CONTROL by using an SVC.
- The hardware gives it CONTROL by initiating an interrupt.

Residence There are actually three parts of the system which are clearly distinguishable.

- The nucleus of resident portion of OS360 which is *always* immediately available in MEMORY.
- The transient supervisor called in from disk when needed.
- The Access Method (AMethod) used by the program:
  * brought into the program only when needed,
  * maintained there while used,
  * eliminated when no longer needed.

Figure 2.9.1 shows the areas of MEMORY described above. Three aspects are important about each.

- Control inward:
  * OS360 gets control *only* by an interrupt.
  * AMethods and program requests normally set control by linkage (BAL, etc).
- Loading:
  * The OS360 nucleus is created only by system generation (not discussed). It is loaded by IPL (Initial Program Load).

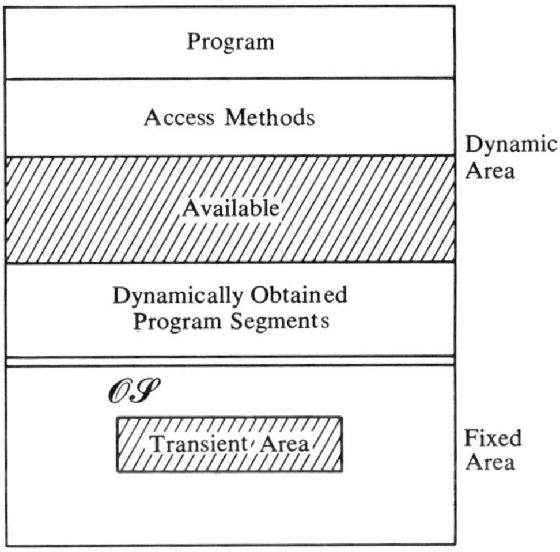

Fig. 2.9.1 Memory map, OS360.

  * OS360 segments are placed in the transient areas by OS360.
  * A program is loaded by OS360 as directed by the job steam.
  * AMethods are loaded by OS360 when OPEN (macro) appears in the program.
  * Dynamic segments are loaded by OS360 when macros such as LOAD, etc. (see Chapter 15) appear in the program.
- Return of control:
  * OS360 turns over control to the program with a special command, LPSW.
  * AMethods and segments return control with sample branches.

Interrupt The only way to get to OS360 is via an interrupt. Interrupts generally occur when various error or exception conditions are detected by the hardware. But there are times when OS360 should be given control *without* an error or exception. The trick is to *simulate* an interrupt. The SVC command does this. It has the form

$$\text{SVC(OA)}:\ \text{R1R2} \longrightarrow \text{PSW};\ \Rightarrow \text{OS360} \qquad (2.9.1)$$

The second byte of the command is placed in the program status word (PSW) and control is passed to OS360. It is R1R2 which conveys the program request to OS360 upon which it may then act.

Mode There are a number of commands which could prove extremely harmful if the normal program had them available to it.

This is prevented by establishing two modes:

- *All* commands are available in **supervisor mode.**
- Some commands, called **privileged**, are unavailable and illegal in **problem mode** and cause an interrupt when deleted.

The present PSW in the PSWR establishes the mode by the setting of its **mode bit.** When an interrupt occurs, a new PSW is placed in the PSWR, turning over control to 𝒪S360 and setting 𝒪S360 into the supervisor mode. Thereafter the full repertoire is available to 𝒪S360.

𝒪S360 returns control to the program with *load PSW*, LPSW, which sets the old PSW into the PSWR, reestablishing the program (and the limited repertoire) where it was interrupted. Thus

$$\text{LPSW(82): (M1)} \longrightarrow \text{PSWR} \qquad (2.9.2)$$

Since the PSW contains (IAR) for the interrupt program, this is reinstated causing the program to take up where it was left off.

Privileged commands A number of commands listed in Table 2.9.1, of which we have already noted LPSW, can only be executed in supervisor mode.

Table 2.9.1 PRIVILEGED COMMANDS

SPM	04	Reset the program mask and condition check
SSK	08	Set storage lock
ISK	09	Read storage lock
SSM	80	Reset the system mask
LPSW	82	Load PSW into PSWR
SIO	9C	Start IO
TIO	9D	Test IO
HIO	9E	Halt IO
TCH	9F	Test CHANNEL

PROTECT

For each set of 2K bytes of MEMORY, a hardware **lock** of five bits may be set (IBM calls it a key, not a lock). The lock means this 2K is available to be written into only if the key in the current PSW is identical to it (proper problem program) or is 00000 (the system key in the system PSW). The MEMORY lock is set with SSK. The lock setting can be checked by reading it into a GPR with ISK.

INTERRUPTS

The system mask in the PSW governs which classes of interrupts are permissible. It may be reset by SSM. The program mask in the PSW controls which conditions within the program and arising during execution can cause a program interrupt. It is reset with SPM.

Since all IO commands are privileged, none can be given by the program or even the AMethod. IO

Macros All system macros given in AL are converted by the assembler into either

- SVC and parameters or
- a linkage and a call sequence.

In the first case, an interrupt results at run time calling in OS360. The interrupt is analyzed and if a nonresident service is required, the desired routine is brought into the transient area of the nucleus. There it is given control to run in supervisor mode. When done, it returns to OS360 which, in turn, goes to the problem program with LPSW.

An AMethod or dynamically acquired segment is given control through a linkage. It operates in problem mode in the program area.

2.10 FLOATING POINT

Format Floating point numbers are much more convenient to use than fixed point binary or decimal numbers because they don't present the problems of overflow scaling and variable length which the latter have. However, they do involve a lot of trouble in conversion, which we shall mention later. They are very similar in use to commands in fixed Word computers.

Floating point numbers are explained at length elsewhere.† System 360 uses a base of 16. A number is represented as two factors. The first is a **fraction,** a number, in absolute value less than unity and of a magnitude representative of the original number. The second factor is a power to raise the base 16, the **exponent,** so that the product of these two is the original number.

For very large numbers, the exponent is a large positive number; for very small numbers, the exponent is a large negative number. We should be content with two signs in our representation:

- the sign of the exponent telling if the magnitude of the number is greater or less than unity;
- the sign of the fraction expressing the sign of the number.

System 360 obviates the first sign using a seven-bit exponent to which sixty-four has been added. This is equivalent to multiplying the second factor, as described above, by 16^{64}.

† Ivan Flores, *The Logic of Computer Arithmetic*. Englewood Cliffs, N.J.: Prentice-Hall, Inc., 1963.

The format of the short floating point number (E type) is

$$\begin{array}{ccc} \text{fraction sign/} & \text{exponent/} & \text{fraction} \\ \text{1 bit} & \text{7 bits} & \text{24 bits} \end{array} \tag{2.10.1}$$

This enables the size of two numbers to be compared by examining them, bit by bit, from left to right.

Sometimes this format does not provide a precise enough fraction. To get more significance, a doubleWord format is used. The sign of the fraction again occupies the leftmost bit and the exponent of the base 16 is again seven bits long. However, the fraction portion, which spreads over two words, is fifty-six bits. System 360 also supplies an extended format of fourWord length which we shall not discuss.

Examples Let's see how a few numbers are represented in floating point. *Fraction* is always a fraction. Let's convert a fraction first, namely $\frac{1}{2}$. Use # as a subscript to show a decimal number; we have

$$0.5_{\#} = 0.1_2 \tag{2.10.2}$$

Now the exponent: it should be 0 regardless of the base since we wish the other factor to be 1 and $x^0 = 1$. The seven-bit exponent is reset midway by addition of 1000000. Since this is a positive number, the first or sign bit is 0. The first two nibbles, i.e., sign and exponent, are 01000000 $= 40_H$ and we have

$$0.5_{\#} = 40800000;\ \text{sign} = 0;\ \text{exponent} = 1000000;\quad \text{fraction} = 100000000\ldots0 \tag{2.10.3}$$

It is easy to see that

$$0.25_{\#} = 40400000;\ 0.0625_{\#} = 40100000 \tag{2.10.4}$$

To represent 1, we need two factors which multiply to 1. From (2.10.4) we have $\frac{1}{16}$; this will produce 1 when multiplied by $16_{\#} = 16^1_{\#}$; hence,

$$1.0_{\#} = 41100000 \tag{2.10.5}$$

Notice also that

$$1.0_{\#} = 42010000 = 43001000 = 44000100,\ \text{etc.} \tag{2.10.6}$$

A representation is **normalized** when the third hexadecimal digit is nonzero. Thus (2.10.5) is the only normalized form for 1 and we have, as the normalized form for $10_{\#}$,

$$10_{\#} = 41B00000 \tag{2.10.7}$$

Negatives A negative number is represented in the same way as a positive one except that the initial bit is 1. Thus we have

$$-0.5_{\#} \equiv \text{C0800000} \qquad -1 \equiv \text{C1100000} \qquad -10_{\#} \equiv \text{C1B00000} \tag{2.10.8}$$

Zero As long as the fraction is 0, any exponent would produce 0. Contrary to what we might expect,

$$0 \not\equiv 40000000 \tag{2.10.9}$$

That would use up addition significance, as shown later. Hence we have

$$0 \equiv 00000000 \tag{2.10.10}$$

which is convenient from many points of view.

Conversion The floating point representation we have examined uses a binary fraction and a hexadecimal exponent. The human uses decimal information, primarily straight decimal or fixed point notation. In both cases, data he supplies must be converted into properly scaled fixed point if fixed point commands are to be used.

When numbers are defined by the programmer and appear as constants *in his program*, it is the *assembler* which converts these constants and assigns locations for them, making sure these constants are available in the referenced symbolic locations at *run* time.

Data supplied at program run time may be entered in the proper System 360 floating binary format, but this is unlikely. It will probably enter in a decimal floating point format such as would be used in the FORTRAN language. The program will either contain or link to a subroutine which converts the decimal floating point numbers into System 360 format binary floating point numbers while the program is running. The extensiveness of such a routine should not be underestimated. IBM does not supply such as a utility. It may be "stolen" from FORTRAN if the programmer knows how to get back and forth to it.

Reconversion—going from floating binary to decimal—is no less a problem.

Options Floating point commands refer to one or two of four evenly numbered FPRS, namely 0, 2, 4, and 6. Both short and long words are manipulated in these REGISTERS. Short words use only half of a doubleWord REGISTER, the even half; but the odd numbered SEMIREGISTERS are not accessible to the programmer. Therefore, FPRS which can only be the source or destination of floating point numbers are designated by 0, 2, 4, or 6 in the floating point command.

Table 2.10.1 FLOATING POINT COMMANDS

Operation	Description	Short RR AL	Short RR ML	Short RX AL	Short RX ML	Long RR AL	Long RR ML	Long RX AL	Long RX ML	Notes
Load	$(M2) \longrightarrow M1$	LER	38	LE	78	LDR	28	LD	68	
Compare	$(M1) = (M2)\ 00 \longrightarrow$ CCR $(M1) < (M2)\ 10 \longrightarrow$ CCR $(M1) > (M2)\ 01 \longrightarrow$ CCR	CER	39	CE	79	CDR	29	CD	69	
Store	$(M1) \longrightarrow M2$			STE	70			STD	60	
Add, normalized	$(M1) + (M2) \xrightarrow{N} M1$	AER	3A	AE	7A	ADR	2A	AD	6A	
Add, unnormalized	$(M1) + (M2) \xrightarrow{U} M1$	AUR	3E	AU	7E	AWR	2E	AW	6E	Postnormalized
Subtract, normalized	$(M1) - (M2) \xrightarrow{N} M1$	SER	3B	SE	7B	SDR	2B	SD	6B	
Subtract, unnormalized	$(M1) - (M2) \xrightarrow{U} M1$	SUR	3F	SU	&F	SWR	2F	SW	6F	Postnormalized
Multiply	$(M2) \overset{N}{*} (M1) \longrightarrow \underline{M1}$	MER	3C	ME	7C	MDR	2C	MD	6C	Prenormalized
Divide	$(M1)^N/(M2) \longrightarrow M1$	DER	3D	DE	7D	DOR	2D	DD	6D	Prenormalized
Halve	$(M2)/2 \xrightarrow{N} M1$	HER	34			HDR	24			Postnormalized
Load positive	$\lvert(M2)\rvert \longrightarrow M1$	LPER	30			LPDR	20			
Load negative	$-\lvert(M2)\rvert \longrightarrow M1$	LNER	31			LNDR	21			
Load and test	$(M2) \longrightarrow M1$	LTER	32			LTDR	22			Set CC
Load complement	$-(M2) \longrightarrow M1$	LCER	33			LCDR	23			

Notice that the FPRS differ from the GPRS used for other purposes such as indexing and relativizing. Hence, for instance, while GPR2 is referred to as a base or INDEX REGISTER in one portion of a floating point command, FPR2 may be used as an operand location (by making for R1 = 2) for instance.

There are three variations to floating point commands:

- The command may apply to a short or a long number.
  - * A short number is indicated by a suffix E.
  - * A long number is indicated by the suffix D (for Double).
- Floating point commands may take RR or RX format.
  - * A REGISTER to REGISTER command has a final suffix R.
  - * A MEMORY to REGISTER transfer has no final suffix.
- The result of add/subtract may or may not be normalized.
  - * Suffix U is for unnormalized short numbers.
  - * Suffix W is for unnormalized long numbers.
  - * No suffix is required for normalized numbers.

We shall generally use only short number floating point commands. However, to illustrate some variations, we have

- AE is the *short*, MEMORY *to* REGISTER, *floating point*, *add* command.
  - * Suffix W is for unnormalized long numbers.
  - * No suffix is required for normalized numbers.

Commands Table 2.10.1 presents floating commands. Their explanation is pretty clear except for the concept of normalization. Recall that a number is normalized when its third nibble is nonzero.

MULTIPLY

Both *multiply* and *divide* produce normalized numbers by hardware postnormalization. It is impossible for the programmer to suppress this, a complaint of the numerical analyst. When two unnormalized numbers in floating point (subscript F) are multiplied, the product is unnormalized; i.e.,

$$\tfrac{1}{2} \times \tfrac{1}{2} = \tfrac{1}{4}\colon\ 410B0000_F * 410B0000_F = 40400000_F \qquad (2.10.11)$$

ADD

For both *add* and *subtract*, one of the numbers must be unaligned—**unnormalized**—before arithmetic can be done.

$$35 + 0.5 = 35.5\colon\ 42230000_F + 40100000_F$$
$$= 42230000_F + 42001000_F = 42231000_F = 35.5 \qquad (2.10.12)$$

Although the sum above is normalized, this is not always the case:

$$138.25 + (-138.125) = 0.125\colon\ 4310B400_F + C310B200_F$$
$$-43000200_F = 40200000_F = 0.125_{\#} \qquad (2.10.13)$$

The result of this *addition* is a small unnormalized number. For AE or AER, the result is left that way; for AU or AUR, it is postnormalized as at the right of (2.10.13).

2.11 OTHERS

Some few commands yet remain to be explained to be complete. They are found in Table 2.11.1.

Multiple It is useful to be able either to fill or to store a number of GPRS at once. A continuous set of GPRS can be specified by naming the first with R1 and the last with R3. The MEMORY address is then composed of a BASE REGISTER contents named by B2 plus the displacement but no INDEX REGISTER. If B2 is 0, no base is used. The format is then

$$\begin{matrix}\text{STM(50)}\\ \text{LM(58)}\end{matrix} : \quad \text{OP R1 R3 B2 D2} \qquad (2.11.1)$$

Wrap around is the name applied to fact that, when R3 < R1, all the GPRS from GPRR1 through GPR15 are referenced, then GPR0 through GPRR3; thus

$$\begin{aligned} \text{LM} \quad 14, 2, \text{AREA} \equiv \text{58D20AA0: } & (\text{AA0}) \longrightarrow \text{GPR14} \\ & (\text{AA4}) \longrightarrow \text{GPR15} \\ & (\text{AA8}) \longrightarrow \text{GPR0} \qquad (2.11.2) \\ & (\text{AAC}) \longrightarrow \text{GPR1} \\ & (\text{AB0}) \longrightarrow \text{GPR2} \end{aligned}$$

Immediate For **immediate commands,** the second byte *is* the operand and **we label it I**. M2 then is formed only with (GPRB2) since there is no room to mention an INDEX REGISTER, the format being

$$\text{Immediate: } \quad \text{OP I B2 D2} \qquad (2.11.3)$$

The operation of MVI, NI, OI, and XI is obvious from Table 2.11.1. CLI tests the byte, I, against (M2) bit for bit to determine the *logically* larger byte. The CCR is then set accordingly.

TM provides a mask at I; where there are 1's in I, those bits of (M2) are tested. The CCR is set *for these* masked bits only and set thus:

- 00—masked bits are all 0
- 01—some masked bits are 0 and some are 1
- 11—masked bits are all 1

Table 2.11.1 OTHER COMMANDS

Operation	*AL*	*ML*	*Symbolic*	*Note*
Store multiple	STM	90	(GPRR1) $\longrightarrow$ M2	Wrap around
			(GPRR + 1) $\longrightarrow$ M2 + 4	
			⋮	
			(GPRR3) $\longrightarrow$ M2 + 4(R3 − R1)	
Test under mask	TM	91	I: (M2)	Set condition code according to bit settings
Move immediate	MVI	92	I $\longrightarrow$ M2	
Test and set	TS	93	$O(M2)_0 \longrightarrow$ CC	For multiprocessor
			FF $\longrightarrow$ M2	
And immediate	NI	94	I & (M2) $\longrightarrow$ M2	
Compare immediate	CLI	95	I: (M2)	Set CCR
Or immediate	OI	96	I ∨ (M2) $\longrightarrow$ M2	
Exclusive or immediate	XI	97	I ⊕ (M2) $\longrightarrow$ M2	
Load multiple	LM	98	(M2) $\longrightarrow$ GPRR1	Wrap around
			(M2 + 4) $\longrightarrow$ GPR(R1 + 1)	
			⋮	
			(M2 + 4(R3 − R1)) $\longrightarrow$ GPRR3	
Shift right logical	SRL	88	GPRR1 $\xrightarrow{M2}$ GPRR1	
Shift right arithmetical	SRA	8A		
Shift left logical	SLL	89	GPRR1 $\xleftarrow{M2}$ GPRR1	
Shift left arithmetical	SLA	8B		
Shift right double logical	SRDL	8C	R $\xrightarrow{M2}$ R	R = GPRR1 ⌣ GPR(R1 + 1)
Shift right double arithmetic	SRDA	8E		
Shift left double logical	SLDL	8D	R $\xleftarrow{M2}$ R	
Shift left double arithmetic	SRDA	8F		

EXAMPLES

TM 9,(9),X'C3' ≡ 91C39009: if ((GPR9) + 009) = FB, 11 ⟶ CC (2.11.4)

TM 9(9),X'C3' ≡ 91C39009: if ((GPR9) + 009) = B9, 01 ⟶ CC (2.11.5)

TM 9(9),X'C3' ≡ 91C39009: if ((GPR9) + 009) = 00, 00 ⟶ CC (2.11.6)

Shifts For all shifts the number of bit places shifted is given by M2; indexing is not provided; B2 = 0 suppresses the use of a base. Further I is ignored. Only the less significant bits of M2 are examined: six bits of M2 for single shifts; seven bits of M2 for double shifts. The characters in the mnemonic tell all about the shift:

- S—for shift,
- R or L—for right or left,
- D or none—for double or single,
- A or L—for arithmetic or logical.

The **direction** of the shift is the movement of the data with respect to the GPR.

A **double shift** applies when R1 is even: GPRR1 and GPR(R1 + 1) are considered to be a single REGISTER and the contents moved with respect to the composite.

A **logical shift** enters 0's at the left (right) for a right (left) shift. For the **arithmetic shift,** the sign is duplicated as the datum is shifted right; 0's are entered at the right for a shift left.

Test and set TS is used for multiprocessing. FF is entered at M2. First, though, the left bit is tested and CCR is set to 01 if it is 1 and 00 if it is 0.

PROBLEMS

2.1 (a) What is the difference between a GPR and an FPR?
(b) A command reference register 2; what determines if there is a GPR or an FPR?

2.2 Distinguish *Word* from *word.*

2.3 Describe NBCH, accurately explaining the derivation.

2.4 Assume that 3456 is at ZONA.
(a) Pack it into the doubleWord DW;
(b) What, in hex, is then at DW?
(c) Convert DW into binary in GPR4;
(d) What is in GPR4?

2.5 Repeat Prob. 2.4 for -3456 at ZONB.

2.6 Write BAL to find $Y = AX^2 + BX + C$ where $A =$ (A), $B =$ (B), etc., and Y is put into Y.

2.7 Similarly, write BAL to find $R = (DF - DI)/KT$.

2.8 Use BCT, C, and a *conditional branch* to find the largest of seventeen fullWord numbers stored in a list which starts at LIST, and put it at MAX.

2.9 Use BXLE to find the sum of the squares of numbers in LIST (see Prob. 2.8), placing it at SUMSQ.

2.10 Use BXH to find the least of the numbers in LIST (see Prob. 2.8), placing it in MIN and its location at LOCMIN.

2.11 Find the number in LIST (see Prob. 2.8) with the largest *absolute* value and put it at ABSMAX.

2.12 Given constants A, B, C, and the list X, find the value for Y given by

$$\mathrm{Y = AX^2 + BX + C}$$

and Y is the position in the Y list corresponding to the position of X in the X list. There are twenty-three values of X and Y.

2.13 A list of twenty-seven three-byte packed numbers (five digits and sign) is stored starting at PLIST. Add them and place the result at TOT.

2.14 As for Prob. 2.13, find the largest and put it at PMAX.

2.15 As for Prob. 2.13, find the sum of squares and put it at PSUMSQ using a word area of the proper size.

2.16 Repeat Prob. 2.12 when all numbers are three bytes except those in the Y list, which are nine bytes. Use work areas of sufficient size.

2.17 A macro called CREAD reads a card image into an eighty-byte area called CARD. Write BAL to read forty-five cards, extracting the *first eight* bytes of each, converting these bytes into a binary Word, and placing these into successive Words in CLIST.

2.18 Repeat Prob. 2.17 where now the eight-byte number in *first* card *is* the number of data cards which follow, the length of CLIST.

2.19 As for Prob. 2.18, the first card indicates how many data cards follow. Now, however, do not count after packing. Instead, *square* the packed number and print *each* square when calculated (unpacking first?) with the macro PRINT.

3

DATA AND SPACE

3.1 DEFINITION

Define pseudo Data are inserted in the program by the programmer using the pseudo, DC (for define constant). The format of this pseudo is

name DC numberletterlength'datum' (3.1.1)

The constant is placed in the machine language output in a position corresponding to where it appears in the assembly language program. It is converted into binary because, after all, binary *is* machine language—all information eventually ends up as 0's and 1's.

We now examine the fields which comprise the DC pseudo (3.1.1):

- *Name* can be any legal symbol, as discussed in Section 3.3.
- *Number* indicates the number of times the constant should be repeated. When *number* is blank or missing, the constant is inserted only once.
- *Letter* tells the assembler the type of constant being defined. These are itemized in Table 3.1.1 and discussed shortly.
- *Length*: when the programmer wishes to state the length of the constant categorically, he places an L at *length* followed by the number of bytes which comprise the constant.
- *Datum* is the field to be converted into binary using the proper rules and *lengthening* or *shortening* the result according to *length*. Note carefully that the datum is always enclosed in apostrophes.

Table 3.1.1 TYPE OF CONSTANTS, LITERALS, AND STORAGE RESERVATIONS

Code	*Type*	*Produced*	*Example*	*Converted to (Hex)*
C	Character	8-Bit code for character	C'A3X'	C1F3E7
X	Hexadecimal	4-Bit code for digit	X'C4D4'	C4D4
B	Binary	Bit for bit	B'0110'	06
F	FullWord	32-Bit binary fullWord equivalent of decimal number,	F'23'	00000017
		2's equivalent for negative number	F'—23'	FFFFFFE9
H	HalfWord	16-Bit binary fullWord, 2's complement representation of decimal number	H'29' H'—29'	001D FFE3
E	FullWord floating	Binary equivalent in floating point format of decimal number	E'37E—2'	
D	DoubleWord floating	As for E	D'3.7E+4'	
P	Packed decimal	4-Bit NBCD with sign	P'38'	038C
Z	Zoned decimal	8-Bit coded digit	'38'	F3C8
A	Full address	Word with binary address corresponding to symbol	A(HARRY)	
Y	Half address	HalfWord with binary address corresponding to symbol halfWord	Y(HARRY)	
S	B/D address	Base/displacement for symbol	S(HARRY)	
V	External address	Space for symbol defined externally	V(HARRY)	

Hexadecimal A simple way to define information is using hexadecimal format. This defines a nibble, indicating it with a decimal digit or a letter A through F. In the rest of the section we give examples of unlabeled DC pseudos showing the content of *location* followed by the colon and then by the hexadecimal datum produced in the machine language output stream. The simplest DC defines a hexadecimal constant. *Letter* then contains X. An example is

DC X'C4D4': C4D4 (3.1.2)

Information is entered only in multiples of bytes. If less than a byte is presented, 0's are entered at the left to fill up to a full byte. Thus, for instance, we have

DC X'3F1F2': 03F1F2 (3.1.3)

Since only five nibbles were defined, the nibble 0 was added by $\mathcal{ASLR}$ at the left to make a total of three bytes.

MULTIPLE

To define several sets of identical bytes, a number is placed at *number* in front of the type letter, X, thus:

DC 3X'F1': F1F1F1 (3.1.4)

Here the byte F1 is repeated three times because of the prefix 3 in *location.*

The field is repeated only after it has been filled to an integral number of bytes. Thus for

DC 2X'345': 03450345 (3.1.5)

an extra nibble of 0 is added to the field before it is repeated.

LENGTH

When *data* are longer than the amount specified in *length*, nibbles are removed from the left to produce the proper field thus:

DC XL2'A6F4E': 6F4E (3.1.6)

When *data* are too short, 0's are added at the left to fill up the field thus:

DC XL3'ABCD': 00ABCD (3.1.7)

Obviously, if *length* and *data* agree, the field is neither lengthened nor shortened.

Characters Characters are defined when the letter is C. The result produced is always in Extended Binary Coded Decimal Interchange Code or EBCDIC. Below, in describing the output field produced, we use hexadecimal representation. For instance, the three character field for *datum* is translated into six nibbles thus:

DC C'A3X': C1F3E7 (3.1.8)

It should be clear that the code for A is 11000001 or C1 in hex; similarly, 3 is 11110011 or F3 in hex. To define a field which is a repeated set of characters, the number of representations are given by *number*, thus:

DC 3C'AX': C1E7C1E7C1E7 (3.1.9)

LENGTH

The length attribute is overriding. When *datum* is too short, we enter *blanks*, hexadecimal 40, at the right; if too long, we remove characters from the right. This is shown in these two examples:

DC CL3'AX': C1E740 (3.1.10)

and

DC CL3'B5Y6': C2F5E8 (3.1.11)

BLANKS

It is permissible to have a blank within *datum*; for example,

DC C'S ABC': F540C1C2C3 (3.1.12)

There are additional rules regarding the use of apostrophes, ampersands, and other special characters, but these are not necessary to the exposition.

Fixed point numbers There are two kinds of fixed point numbers:

- FullWord numbers are type F.
- HalfWord numbers are type H.

The user furnishes a decimal number at *datum* and this is converted into its binary equivalent by 𝒜𝒮ℒℛ and placed on the proper boundary—halfWord for H, fullWord for F, etc. It is then filled with 0's in order to make a full- or halfWord accordingly.

An unsigned or a positive number is converted into a positive binary number (with 0 in the sign position). A negative number is converted into two's complement notation which necessarily has a one in the left-hand bit position.

Let us examine a few simple numbers defined

DC F'5': 00000005=0 . . . 0101 (3.1.13)

DC F'29': 0000001D=0 . . . 00011101 (3.1.14)

DC F'−5': FFFFFFFC=1 . . . 1011 (3.1.15)

DC H'97': 0061=0 . . . 01100001 (3.1.16)

The programmer may scale numbers. This is a tricky option. It simply moves the nonzero portion of the number left, the number of places indicated by the program. If he scales numbers before arithmetic, he must be careful to unscale them before printing or outputting the result and according to the arithmetic performed on the numbers.

Floating point Floating point numbers are represented as fullWords or doubleWords. These bear the type letters, respectively, E and D. Numbers can be presented for conversion with or without an exponent part. All numbers are presented in decimal form. When an exponent is present, it applies to a multiplier using base 10.

To define a floating point fullWord, we could simply use this pseudo (I make no attempt this time to translate):

DC E'4.5678' (3.1.17)

To put this into exponent form, a number is followed by the letter E which in turn is followed by an exponent applicable to the base 10. For instance, to get the same result as (3.1.17), we use

DC E'45678E−4' (3.1.18)

or we could use

```
        DC    E'.456781'E+1                                    (3.1.19)
```

Of course the number itself can be signed, in which case still another alternative of the number 4.5678 is

```
        DC    E'+456.78E-2'                                    (3.1.20)
```

To define the sum number as a doubleWord, we use D instead of E, thus:

```
        DC    D'4.5678'                                        (3.1.21)
```

To understand better what $\mathcal{ASLR}$ does to convert a decimal number into floating point representation, we now examine the steps:

1. When the number is first encountered by the assembler, it is in alpha. It is changed into packed decimal. The fraction and exponent are kept separate.
2. The number is converted from fraction and exponent form to a straight numerical form. This requires finding the power of the base 10 and then multiplying that by the fraction.
3. This number is converted into binary. There are different rules for converting the integer and a fractional part of the number. Hence, this may be done separately and the results added.
4. We want a binary fraction which is less than one. To get it, we divide the binary number we now have by 16 until it becomes a number which is smaller than one. If we started with a fraction, we have to multiply by 16 repeatedly until this condition prevails.
5. We keep track of the number of divisions or multiplications we have made. This becomes the hexadecimal exponent. However, floating point form requires that 64 is added to this exponent.
6. The fraction should now be in proper binary form. We check to see if there is an overflow or underflow in the exponent before packing the number into its word.

Decimal There are two kinds of decimal numbers which the programmer might create: packed and zoned are indicated, respectively, by the type letters P and Z. The programmer is permitted to indicate a decimal point for his own convenience but it is disregarded in fabricating the constant. As usual, if the sign is absent or positive, the constant acquires a positive sign; a negative number acquires a negative sign. Since the standard form is created by the assembler, a negative sign is represented by hexadecimal D and the positive sign hexadecimal C.

PACKED

A packed decimal number uses one nibble per digit. A sign is always included in the result. A nibble of 0's is filled in on the left if required. For example, we have

```
DC     P'38': 038C                                    (3.1.22)
DC     P'+127': 127C                                  (3.1.23)
```

As noted above, the decimal point is dropped and the negative sign is represented by D, thus:

```
DC     P'−7.6': 076D                                  (3.1.24)
```

For repeating definitions we have

```
DC     2P'12.34': 01234C01234C                        (3.1.25)
```

ZONED NUMBERS

For the zoned number a sign is placed in the left nibble of the last significant byte. Digit nibbles are placed in the right nibble of their respective bytes. For all but the right byte the zoned nibble is a hexadecimal F. Hence, the zoned number produced has as many bytes as there are in the original constant. For example, we have

```
DC     Z'38': F3C8                                    (3.1.26)
DC     Z' + 127': F1F2C7                              (3.1.27)
DC     Z' − 1.6': F1D6                                (3.1.28)
```

A repeated zone number can be designated by prefixing *location* with *number*, thus:

```
DC     2Z'12.34': F1F2F3C4F1F2F3C4                    (3.1.29)
```

Binary Binary constants are specified by the programmer who writes in *datum* the bit configuration he desires. For instance, we have

```
DC     B'11011011': DB                                (3.1.30)
```

When less than a full byte is specified, 0's are added at the left, thus:

```
DC     B'101': 05                                     (3.1.31)
```

If a larger datum is shown than is specified by *length*, we eliminate bits from the left thus:

```
DC     BL1'101010101': 55                             (3.1.32)
```

Multiple definitions A single DC pseudo can define several dissimilar constants where these constants appear at *datum* separated by commas. For example,

```
CONS     DC     F'9,16,66,24': 00000009000000100000004200000018
                                                      (3.1.33)
```

3.2 SPACE

Definition To define space, use the pseudo DS (define space). The salient difference between DS and DC is that DS does not enter anything into the space defined. The space is not cleared. Anything left over from the previous program will remain in the space set up by this DS pseudo. DS has the format

label DS numberletterlength'datum' (3.2.1)

The use of the fields of this pseudo are identical with those for the DC pseudo and are listed at the beginning of Section 3.1.

The field *datum* is generally omitted (as are the apostrophes surrounding it). When *datum* is present, it is ignored except for making a measurement. For instance, the pseudo,

NOW DS C'HARRY' (3.2.2)

defines a field of five bytes at a position for which the label is NOW. The only purpose of HARRY is to tell us that five characters are to be stored.

Quantities The amount of storage reserved by DS is the product of *number* and *length*. A question remains about *name*—which bytes does it apply to. Some examples should clear this up.

First we set aside an area of 100 bytes thus:

AREA1 DS CL100: 100 bytes (3.2.3)

then

L'AREA1=100 (3.2.4)

This tells us that AREA1 has a length of 100 bytes. A statement with the format

L'label=number (3.2.5)

means that the length of the field *label* is *number*.

We could define another area thus:

AREA2 DS 100C: 100 bytes (3.2.6)

This area is also 100 bytes, but *label* only applies to the *first* byte so that we have

L'AREA2=1 (3.2.7)

We can set aside an area of twenty bytes starting on a fullWord boundary thus:

AREA3 DS 5F (3.2.8)

However, again the label applies only to the first unit. In this case, we deal with Words so that we have

$$L'AREA3=4 \tag{3.2.9}$$

Multiples of fullWords and doubleWords are defined and aligned on the proper boundaries with these two pseudos:

```
R       DS    2D: 16 bytes          (3.2.10)
S       DS    3E: 12 bytes          (3.2.11)
```

Forcing factor Sometimes we wish to allocate space starting at a boundary which is not implied in the definition (as it would be for F). We might need a halfWord, fullWord, or doubleWord boundary. We can force the next DS to begin at a boundary by defining storage for which *number* is 0 and a boundary designator follows; thus we have

```
        DS    0D
AREA4   DS    CL32                  (3.2.12)
```

Here AREA4 begins on a doubleWord boundary and consists of thirty-two bytes.

Subdivision Often, it is advantageous to divide an area more finely into subdivisions. The main area is set up using the DS pseudo where *number* is 0. Thus, an area called REC is set up with

```
REC     DS    0CL80                 (3.2.13)
```

Suppose the first five bytes of this area are used for the employee number. This is set off from the next field by four unused bytes with

```
EMP     DS    CL5
        DS    CL4                   (3.2.14)
```

Several more fields are recorded with

```
NAME    DS    CL24
DATE    DS    0CL6
MO      DS    CL2                   (3.2.15)
DA      DS    CL2
YR      DS    CL2
```

Notice that the field DATE has been set up and contains three subdivisions.

We finish the eighty-byte field thus:

```
IN      DS   CL4
OUT     DS   CL4
DEPT    DS   CL5          (3.2.16)
JOB     DS   CL6
        DS   CL22
```

The unnamed field is not used.

Subdividing with DS Consider a large area called SP. Suppose we wish to divide it after it has been established. We can partition it using DSs where *loc* is an expression. We rename the beginning P1 thus:

```
P1      DS   SP           (3.2.17)
```

Another part, P2, is defined thus:

```
P2      DS   SP+100       (3.2.18)
```

and a third, P3, thus:

```
P3      DS   SP+200       (3.2.19)
```

etc.

3.3 SYMBOLS

Definition The symbolic assembler permits the programmer to use a symbol to represent a location. The assembler assigns and keeps track of all symbols, and this simplifies the programmer's job.

BAL requires that symbols *must* be defined in one of three ways:

- by a DC pseudo,
- by a DS pseudo,
- as the name for a command.

Since both DC and DS place the symbol being defined at *name*, we could simplify the statement above by saying, simply, all symbols must appear sometime or other at *name* in either a command or a pseudo. This is necessary but not sufficient; that is, what is found at *name* could be a section name (Chapter 13) or a sequence symbol (Chapter 10).

The definition of a symbol need not be made before the symbol is used. As long as the definition occurs somewhere in the program, this is sufficient. Of course, if data appear in the midst of commands, the programmer should precede the data with B, a *branch* around the data.

Assemblers work with several passes—several reviews of the source program. Suppose all symbols can be resolved on one pass; location substitution is made on a subsequent pass.

Why is it necessary that all symbols are defined? System 360 is a variable field length machine. This means that a command can reference a datum which ranges in size from one byte to hundreds of bytes. For ASLR to do its allocation properly, it must be told the length of the datum by one of the options above. When the symbol is a command name, the opcode distinguishes different command lengths: two, four, or six bytes. It is easy for ASLR to determine the length attribute of a symbol which labels a command.

Restrictions There are three restrictions on symbols which we now examine. They are

- length of the symbol,
- the characters used in the symbol,
- the first character in the symbol.

LENGTH

There is a limitation on the size of the symbol. In BAL, symbols are limited to eight characters. Each symbol winds up in a symbol table. If there were no restrictions on the length of symbols, the length of this table would become extremely difficult to manipulate. Since symbols are limited to eight characters, each symbol space in the table can be the maximum length and a uniform table format results.

CHARACTER SET

In BAL, only letters and numerals are valid characters in the symbol. This eliminates problems with special characters. For instance, if + were allowed, it would be difficult for ASLR to distinguish a simple symbol from an expression.

The assembler uses *blank* to set off the end of a symbol. If *blank* were permitted within the symbol, this too would complicate matters.

The symbol must start with a character. This simplifies evaluating expressions. Now when a numeric starts a term in an expression, it must be part of a complete number; when a letter is encountered, a symbol is being designated.

Location It is easy for ASLR to determine the location to which the symbol applies:

- A **location counter** within ASLR keeps track of each command.
- A symbol at *name* for a command is assigned a location in the program which *is* the value in the location counter.
- For DC or DS, again the value of the location counter is assigned to the symbol at *name*.

- The amount by which the location counter is incremented is determined
  - * by the command (from its opcode),
  - * by the length attribute of the symbol (from *location* in DC or DS).

Length Since *opcode* determines the length of the command, the length attribute of the symbol which represents the command is similarly determined. The length for DC and DS is determined as mentioned earlier by *number * length.*

Modifiers Definition of an area or constant generally carries with it a length and type. In a command it may be desirable to state explicitly a length for one of several reasons such as

- to override defined length,
- when two fields are involved and they have different lengths.

This is done in this format:

symbol(length) (3.3.1)

For instance

MVC A(3),B (3.3.2)

moves three bytes from B, B+1, and B+2 into A, A+1 and A+2.

Base registers Since relocating is the rule rather than the exception, it is customary for the assembler to accept BASE REGISTER assignment from the programmer with USING discussed in Chapter 12 and thereafter $\mathcal{ASLR}$ automatically uses this assignment, relieving the programmer of this chore. Table 3.3.1 shows how the assembler inserts the BASE REGISTER indicator and also supplies index indicators if it can.

Table 3.3.1 EXPLICIT VERSUS IMPLICIT BASE REGISTER DESIGNATION

Type	*Explicit*	*Implicit*	*Default* (*no parenthesized numbers*)
RX	Disp(index,base)	Symbol(index)	*Index*=0
	Disp(,base)	Symbol	
RS	Disp(base)	Symbol	
SI	Disp(base)	Symbol	
SS	Disp(length,base)	Disp(length)	Length as defined

where *disp* is a three nibble displacement
base is a one nibble GPR indicator
index is a one nibble GPR indicator
length is a nibble or byte length indicator

As an example we have

$$\text{M} \quad 4,\text{X}(2) \tag{3.3.3}$$

requesting that X is indexed by (GPR2) when we multiply.

Also we have

$$\text{AP} \quad \text{R}(4),\text{A}+2(3) \tag{3.3.4}$$

requesting that the three-byte field at A+2 is added to the four-byte field at R.

Alternatives In some computers it would not be necessary to require definition of all symbols. For instance, commands and operands have a fixed size; in a fixed word length computer, it is easy to assign a length attribute of 1 to all symbols. As symbols are encountered at *location* in commands, they can be automatically allocated within a fixed area of MEMORY.

Then, as a programmer needs a new field such as EMPNO, he just uses it in a command and it is automatically allocated. The trouble is in catching the programmer's errors. Suppose he forgets how he has spelled the symbol and refers to it later as EMPNUM. $\mathcal{ASLR}$ does not know this is a mistake, sees it as a new symbol, and assigns a new location for it.

Errors As far as symbols are concerned, several kinds of errors can occur which the assembler should point out to the programmer:

- **Undefined symbols** are those which have not appeared at *name* in a command, DC or DS.
- **Overdefined symbols** have appeared more than once at *name*.
- **Underdefined symbols** have appeared at *name* somewhere but without sufficient information about them.

What $\mathcal{ASLR}$ does about these errors depends on its design. In all cases, it is most desirable to review the source program in its entirety regardless of how early in the program the error is found. It is also desirable to produce an output machine language program even when errors are detected. In this case, $\mathcal{ASLR}$ arbitrarily makes assignments and communicates them to the programmer who can correct them on a later assembly if they are wrong, which they probably are.

Attributes We have already examined the length attribute for a symbol—the length of the area to which it applies. This is written symbolically as L′ *name*. Sometimes it is useful to manipulate the address of a symbol. When the symbol is written as A (*name*), we get the address of *name* rather than the datum itself.

3.4 LITERALS

Purpose **Literals** furnish immediate addressing for commands which would otherwise use only direct addressing. The literal replaces one or more operands in a command, specifying the datum to be operated upon rather than the address to be accessed to obtain the datum. For instance, if the programmer wants to add 123 to GPR4, he may do this with a literal thus:

```
        A       4,=F'123'        (3.4.1)
```

rather than using the DC pseudo to define the constant first thus:

```
C123    DC      F'123'
        A       4,C123           (3.4.2)
```

All literals in BAL are prefixed by =. The rules which apply to a literal are the same as those that apply to the DC pseudo in the *location* field including the alternative that *number* is present since multiple literals are legal (as in STM).

Literals may appear wherever a datum is ordinarily specified by a MEMORY address or a symbol for a MEMORY address. It is not permissible, for instance, to specify a literal in an RR command. A literal may replace a source datum but not a destination datum and, hence, is illegal in an ST command.

Use Use of the literal is best seen with examples. For instance,

```
        L       2,=F'125'        (3.4.3)
```

places a datum in GPR2. If only half of a REGISTER is to be filled, we could use the command

```
        L       3,=H'345'        (3.4.4)
```

A literal can be defined in hexadecimal form too, thus:

```
        L       5,=X'3C4'        (3.4.5)
```

We place EDDY at HERE with

```
        MVC     HERE,=C'EDDY'    (3.4.6)
```

HERE may have more space in it, and we may want to place a hexadecimal constant there. We would do so with a command such as

```
        MVC     HERE+4,=X'0FF0'  (3.4.7)
```

Since immediate addressing is not possible in machine language, $\mathcal{ASLR}$ does the entire job before the program gets into the computer. $\mathcal{ASLR}$ converts the literal to binary and places that quantity in at an address which it allocates from a literal pool as we shall see later. It then replaces the literal in *location* of the command by the address assigned to converted quantity. It is clear that literals cannot be placed in the program as they are encountered.

3.5 EXPRESSIONS

Need A severe limitation would be placed on the programmer if the only thing which he could place in the fields of *location* were symbols. We have already taken the liberty of introducing expressions in this chapter without explaining their use rationale. For instance, if we have a character field which starts at symbolic location HERE, the third byte of the field is addressed as HERE+2. It would be very unwieldy indeed to have to define HERE3 with a DC or DS pseudo instead of being able to use the simple arithmetic expression HERE+2.

At this point, we must carefully distinguish between relocatable and absolute terms. A **relocatable term** is one which changes in value when our program is relocated at load time. For instance, HERE, as described above, applies to a field which will move with the rest of the program and by the same amount. $\mathcal{ASLR}$ and $\mathcal{LOAD}$ handle relocatable quantities in the same way: the relocation quantity is stored in a BASE REGISTER which appears in all commands.

An absolute term is one which must not be altered during relocation. Typical of these are immediate addresses and lengths. For instance, the command

```
CLI     CHAR,K                                   (3.5.1)
```

requests a *compare logical immediate:* the byte at CHAR is compared with K. This command is used to determine if CHAR contains the character K. When this command is relocated, CHAR moves but we still want to compare it to the character K (which is immediately addressed). Hence K is absolute; K is addressed immediately, hence is not preceded by = since it is *not* a literal. Other absolute terms are

- REGISTER designations,
- lengths.

Referents As discussed earlier, the length of a field is obtained by prefixing a symbol with L'. Thus the command

```
MVC     T(L'H),H                                 (3.5.2)
```

moves a datum from H to T. As presented here, T is generally a field larger than H. To indicate the quantity of information transferred, we use L'H and 𝒜𝒮ℒℛ substitutes the length of H there.

Another referent which we may not have explained is the location of the present instruction which is noted symbolically by *. For instance, to jump ahead from this instruction by ten bytes, we use the command

```
B      *+10                                   (3.5.3)
```

Rules The rules for manipulating relative and absolute terms should be clear and are very similar to those which apply to expressions in FORTRAN or PL/1. For instance, an expression may not begin with an operation. These are more or less common sense rules and we shall not review them in detail.

Also the results of manipulating various kinds of terms should be clear to the user after some experience (see problems). For instance, the difference of two relative terms is an absolute term. If we have two addresses in MEMORY and move both of these addresses by the same amount by relocation at load time, the distance between the two addresses remains constant, regardless.

Sometimes it makes sense to do arithmetic with terms; other times it is senseless. For instance, I can see no reason to multiply two relative terms.

Addition and subtraction We have already seen how useful it is to address a location a known distance from our present position as we did in (3.5.3).

We have also seen how to move characters offset from a named field such as in the command below:

```
MVC    A(4),B+3                               (3.5.4)
```

Four bytes starting at B+3 are moved to A. In general, we deal with a relative term which has been offset by addition or subtraction of an absolute term. The absolute term may actually be an expression, such as the difference of two relative terms. For instance, suppose we define BEG and MID thus:

```
BEG    DS      35C
MID    DS      45C                            (3.5.5)
```

Then this command makes sense:

```
MVC    BOT(L'MID-L'BEG),BEG                   (3.5.6)
```

So does this one:

```
MVC    S(L'MID+10-L'BEG),MID                  (3.5.7)
```

Notice that in the parentheses we always have an absolute term since it applies to the number of bytes being moved.

Multiplication and division Occasionally we may come across a command in this form:

```
         MVC     V(5*L'REC),REC                              (3.5.8)
```

Here *length* is a product of two absolute terms. Why would we want to do something like this? Suppose the area REC was defined by

```
         REC     DS     9CL10                                (3.5.9)
```

This conveys that an area of ninety bytes has been set aside. It has been set up in groups of ten bytes each. The first one of these groups is labeled REC. Its length is hence 10. The command at (3.5.8) moves five groups of ten bytes from the area labeled REC to the area labeled V. This is conveyed by indicating the length of the field to be moved as 5*L'REC.

Now let us go about it a different way so as to require division. Let us set aside an area called SPACE, thus:

```
         SPACE     DS     CL120                              (3.5.10)
```

We personally (implicitly) divide this area into ten groups of twelve bytes each. The length of each record is then given as

```
                          L'SPACE/10                         (3.5.11)
```

It now makes sense to perform this operation:

```
         MVC     W(L'SPACE/10),SPACE+5*L'SPACE/10            (3.5.12)
```

This moves the sixth group of twelve bytes to W.

3.6 JOB CONTROL

The programmer must know something about the operating system; it is indeed uncomfortable to work in a vacuum.

Job stream There is one (or more) input to the operating system (OS) which tells it what to do. Actually this stream contains three distinct kinds of entities:

1. statements to OS written in **Job Control Language (JCL)** and distinguished from other entities (each starts with two slashes),
2. programs,
3. data.

There is a subtle difference between data and programs which is extremely important and which we now explicitly define.

The program The program exists in many forms. Actually only when it is in MEMORY and in control is it truly a program. At most other times it is indistinguishable from data and in fact *is* data for some other program.

This is demonstrated in Fig. 3.6.1. I emphasize that this is just one way the job stream is structured. We first encounter the AL program in the job stream as a number of cards. Each contains one AL statement. This AL program is to be translated by *ASLR*. Then, as far as the program, *ASLR*, is concerned, the ALP is merely data to it. At this phase,

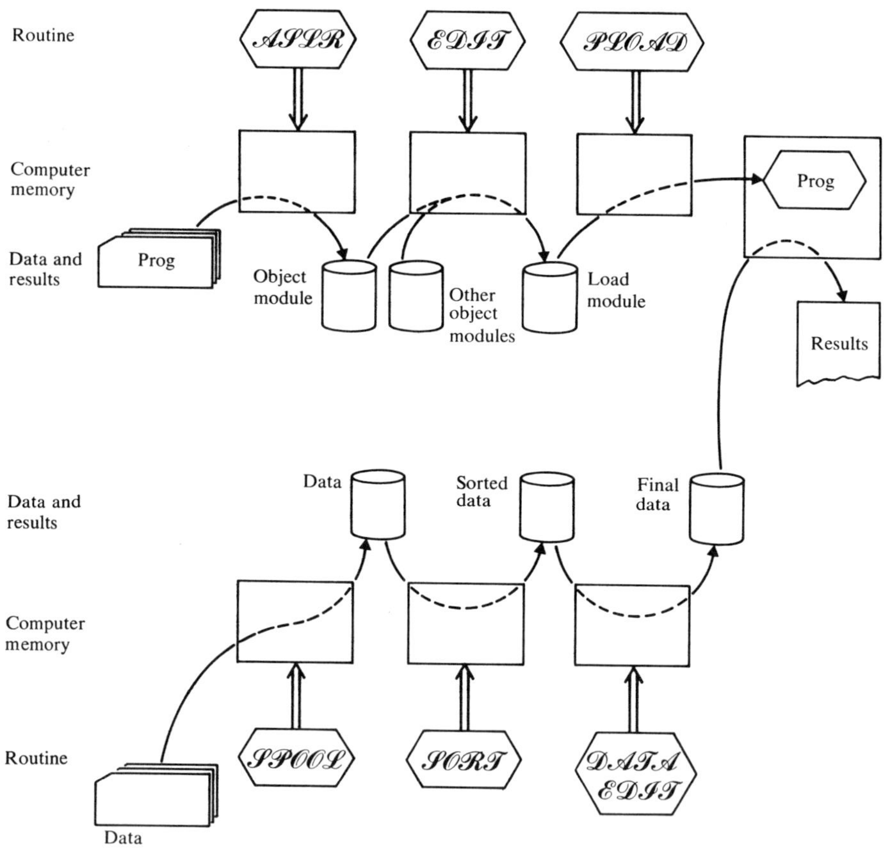

Fig. 3.6.1 The job is composed of several processing steps.

we distinguish three entities:

- ASLR is the program to do the translating (step 1).
- The ALP is the input for ASLR (step 2).
- The output is called an **object module** (step 3).

EDITING

Although some programs are a single unit, many others consist of multiple units. Many object modules and sections of modules are patched together to make a final package, the **load module.** This is done by the linkage editor, EDIT. For this operation we have

- EDIT is the program to do the editing (step 4).
- This object module is one input (step 3).
- Other modules are also used for input (step 5).
- The output is a load module (step 6).

LOADING

When a load module is produced, it is still external to the computer MEMORY. The loader, LOAD, part of OS360, does this task. It gets the program, finds the proper position for it in MEMORY, writes into MEMORY, alters some commands to compensate for their relocation, and links everything together. For this operation we have

- LOAD is the program (step 7).
- The load module is the input (step 6).
- There is no output.
- Control goes to the loaded program (step 8).

RUNNING

We are finally running. During this operation we have

- The translated program in control.
- Data as input, either from the job stream (step 9) or elsewhere.
- Results as output (step 10).

Data preprocessing Data may go through a similar set of steps. This, too, is illustrated in Fig. 3.6.1 but is not as important to us.

Control The transition from one activity—**job step**—to another is not automatic. OS must get instructions on what comes next after each step. JCL describes each

- Separate program with a JOB statement.
- Step to be performed on the program or data with the EXEC statement.
- Input and output for each step with the DD statement.

We need to know about JCL to get our jobs on the computer. We'll only examine what we need. The JCL statement generally has the format

//name function operand comments (3.6.1)

Each JCL statement may be named at *name*. *Function* can be one of JOB, EXEC, DD, or PROC; *operand* depends on *function*.

JOB The entire activity to be worked on is named by JOB; only a name is required and we have

//jobname JOB options (3.6.2)

Actually in some installation something at *options* may be mandatory; for others, the entire field may be blank. Let's see what might be there:

1. information for an accounting routine to change computer time to the proper account,
2. the programmer's name,
3. MSGLEVEL=1 (causing printing of JCL for this job)
   =0 (suppressing JCL printing),
4. statements indicating the conditional performance of sequential steps,
5. restart and multiprogram information.

Step For each JOB there must be one or more steps (EXEC).

For each EXEC there is one or more **data definition** (DD) cards except where procedures are used; this permits all the remaining JCL to be substituted for by a named set of JCL from the procedure library, as we shall see. Without procedures we have

//name EXEC PGM=progname,
options (3.6.3)

Here EXEC may be named by *name* for reference in other JCL. The name of the program such as FORTRAN, EDIT, etc. which operates on our "program" must be supplied at *progname*. Options include

1. conditions for continuing or terminating the step,
2. parameters for *progname*,
3. accounting information associated with the step,
4. multiprogramming specifications.

When a procedure is used, we have

//name EXEC proc,options (3.6.4)

where *proc* can be in the form PROC=*procname* or simply *procname* where *procname* is the procedure name. The same options apply.

Data The DD statement has the format

```
//name          DD       options
```
(3.6.5)

where the data is generally named by *name*.

The options which apply are

1. further data identification,
2. volume where found,
3. unit where volume is or should be mounted,
4. label and DCB description,
5. disposition,
6. space allocation.

We are especially interested in data found in the job stream. They are identified thus:

```
//name          DD       *
```
(3.6.6)

But then how does the Job Manager know when the data end and new JCL begins? A delimiter must be present after the last datum; it has the form

```
/*
```
(3.6.7)

3.7 ASSEMBLING A PROGRAM

JCL IBM has two cataloged procedures which we can use to simplify assembly. The first to *assemble only* for assembler F, (compile) is called ASMFC and is used by placing this in the job stream:

```
//identifier    JOB      name,
//              EXEC     ASMFC
//ASM.SYSIN     DD       *
                program
/*
```
(3.7.1)

where *program* is your deck of AL cards.

To assemble, link, edit, and run (go), use ASMFCLG thus:

```
//identifier     JOB       name,
//               EXEC      ASMFCLG
//ASY.SYSIN      DD        *
                 program                    (3.7.2)
/*
//GO.SYSIN       DD        *
                 data
/*
```

where your AL program cards are at *program*, and *data* is your deck of data cards formatted to suit the program.

Setup To facilitate the writing of programs, we start all programs with the macro SETUP which is defined and examined in Section 17.3. This and the other macros discussed here should be inserted in the system library by the installation manager if student problems are to be run.

For all problems hereafter, we start thus:

```
name             SETUP                      (3.7.3)
```

where the programmer can name his program at *name*. *He should then restrict his choice of* GPRS *to those between 2 and 12, except for linking* (*Chapter 15*). He may *not* place comments with SETUP. To suppress large amounts of unwanted code, he should also say

```
                 PRINT     NOGEN            (3.7.4)
```

The last instruction to be executed should be

```
name             ENDUP                      (3.7.5)
```

Registers To print REGISTER contents, use the macro REG given thus:

```
name             REG       nums             (3.7.6)
```

This causes a printout of one of these bearing the label *name*:

- all GPRS if *nums* is *blank*,
- a single GPR if one number is found at *nums*,
- several GPRS, one for each number in parentheses at *nums*.

Data To get data, use

```
name             GET       RDR,area         (3.7.7)
```

where RDR is established by SETUP as the name of the INPUT DEVICE. The user is responsible for setting up a proper character field of eighty bytes to receive the card reader input, named at *area*, but defined by some DS.

To print, give

name PUT PRTR, area (3.7.8)

where, again, the user is responsible for defining the area of 120 bytes named here at *area*.

Example Figure 3.7.1 shows a small program written in BAL where the register contents are printed out at frequent intervals. Figure 3.7.2 is a program to add three numbers in GPR4 and print out the sum after each addition. The numbers furnished as input cards are 00000012, 00000047, and 00000009.

Program analysis We examine the program of Fig. 3.7.2 referencing the commands by the number at STMT. At (1) is a request to 𝒜𝒮ℒℛ *not* to print command generated by macros. At (2) is the setup macro.

At (147) we set up GPR3 as an index for looping for adding the 3 numbers supplied by the CARD READER. A card is read into AREA defined by DS (177) using GET and addressing RDR (149). Only the first four

LOC	OBJECT CODE	ADDR 1	ADDR 2	STMT		SOURCE STATEMENT	
				1		PRINT	NOGEN
				2	BEGIN	SETUP	
				90	R1	REG	
0000C8	1B33			248		SR	3,3
				249	R2	REG	3
0000DF	5A30	C150	00150	255		A	3,X1
				256	R3	REG	3
0000F6	1A33			262		AR	3,3
				263	R4	REG	3
00010C	5A30	C154	00154	269		A	3,X2
				270	R5	REG	3
000124	5B30	C158	00158	276		S	3,X3
				277	R6	REG	3
				283		ENDUP	
00014F	0000						
000150	0000000A			292	X1	DC	F'10'
000154	00000014			293	X2	DC	F'20'
000158	0000C350			294	X3	DC	F'50000'
00015C				295	EDJ	DS	C
				296		END	
000160	00000000			297			=V(REGISTER)

Fig. 3.7.1(a) AL Program using REG.

CONTENTS OF GENERAL PURPOSE REGISTERS R1

	HEXADECIMAL	DECIMAL
GPR 0	00000048	00000072
GPR I	0001FE10	00130576
GPR 2	00000058	00000088
GPR 3	00000181	00000385
GPR 4	000046C0	00018112
GPR 5	0001EE60	00130912
GPR 6	00002A30	00010800
GPR 7	00000000	00000000
GPR 8	00000040	00000064
GPR 9	6000ED5A	10673498
GPR A	0001EEE0	00130784
GPR B	00002A30	00010800
GPR C	00005020	00020512
GPR D	0001EE10	00130576
GPR E	00005188	00020872
GPR F	00005188	00020872

CONTENTS OF GENERAL PURPOSE REGISTERS R2

	HEXADECIMAL	DECIMAL
GPR 3	00000000	00000000

CONTENTS OF GENERAL PURPOSE REGISTERS R3

	HEXADECIMAL	DECIMAL
GPR 3	0000000A	00000010

CONTENTS OF GENERAL PURPOSE REGISTERS R4

	HEXADECIMAL	DECIMAL
GPR 3	00000014	00000020

CONTENTS OF GENERAL PURPOSE REGISTERS R5

	HEXADECIMAL	DECIMAL
GPR 3	00000028	00000040

CONTENTS OF GENERAL PURPOSE REGISTERS R6

	HEXADECIMAL	DECIMAL
GPR 3	FFFF3CD8	00049960

Fig. 3.7.1(b) Printout.

```
 LOC    OBJECT CODE ADDR1  ADDR2          STMT          SOURCE STATEMENT          Notes
                                            1           PRINT  NOGEN              Suppress macroprinting
                                            2   BEGIN   SETUP                     Macro for setup
000118  5830   C258                000258 147   INITIAL L      3,=F'3'            Enter 3 into INDEX REGISTER 3
00011C  1B44                              148           SR     4,4                Clear GPR4 for addition
                                          149   LOOP    GET    RDR,AREA           Get datum
00012C  F273   C248  C16E   00248  0016E  154           PACK   X,AREA(4)          Put into packed format
000132  4F50   C248                00248  155           CVB    5,X                Convert to binary in GPR5
000136  1A45                              156           AR     4,5                Add to total
000138  4E40   C250                00250  157           CVD    4,T                Convert total to decimal
00013C  F363   C1BF  C254   001BF  00254  158           UNPK   OUT+1(7),T+4(4)    Unpack total
000142  96F0   C1C5         001C5         159           OI     OUT+7,X'F0'        Remove sign from total
                                          160           PUT    PRTR,OUT           Print
000154  4630   C11E                0011E  165           BCT    3,LOOP             Test and loop
                                          166           ENDUP                     Cleanup
00016E                                    177   AREA    DS     CL80               Input area
0001BE  4040404040404040                  178   OUT     DC     CL133' '           Output area
000248                                    179   X       DS     D                  Addend Word
000250                                    180   T       DS     D                  Total Word
                                          181           END                       End of assembly
000258  00000003                          182                  =F'3'              Literal

                                          Relocation dictionary
                                            Cross reference
                                              Edit table

0000012
0000059
0000068
```

Fig. 3.7.2 Assembly of a program to add three input numbers, printing out a sum after each addition. The input cards contain 12, 47, and 9.

characters of AREA are used: they are packed (154) into a doubleWord, X defined by DS(179). A doubleWord is *not* needed by PACK but *is* needed by CVB which we anticipate.

CVB(155) places the binary Word from X into GPR5 from whence it is added to GPR4 (156). Reconversion begins by converting the sum in GPR4 into decimal (157) using the doubleWord T defined with DS (180). Assume at most half of the packed number in T is significant—that half begins at T+4—it consists of four bytes—eight nibbles—seven decimal digits plus sign. It is unpacked into seven characters—the right character will have a sign packed into it. This should explain UNPK (158) except why we start at OUT+1; this is to ensure *blank* at OUT for carriage control.

The right character will be in the form CN or DN where N is a decimal nibble since unpacking will produce a standard sign, C for + and D for —. The PRINTER will not print a numeral for these combos. For instance: C3 for + · · · 3 will print as C; D5 for — · · · 5 will print as U. To get a numeral in the rightmost position, that byte is *or*'ed with hexadecimal F0. Thus C3 V F0 = F3 and DS V F0 = F5; these print respectively as **3** and **5**.

To print use the macro PUT (160) specifying the PRINTER with PRTR and the area by OUT. The index is decremented with BCT (165). The last command in the program (set of commands) must be ENDUP; the last pseudo in the assembly proper must be END; following END is the literal created by $\mathcal{ASLR}$ (182).

Main printout The most important output of $\mathcal{ASLR}$ is an object module which will run and do what the program wants. This is rarely produced on the first submission of the AL program. The AL programmer relies on the main printout to enable him to find errors and correct them. Hence he should know how to read it as well as a novel.

We discuss the fields as they appear from left to right. Generally each page has a heading so that it's easier to find the fields.

LOCATION

At the left is location which is the byte number in hexadecimal at which this command starts in MEMORY before relocation if any. Often the programmer writes his program so that it starts at 0. The location of the first actual ML command would then be 000000. He can alter the origin with ORG (Section 12.2).

OBJECT CODE

A space interferes between the location column and the code. ML commands appear in hexadecimal with a space between each halfWord. Then RR, RX, and SS command present one, two, and three halfWords, respectively.

Constants are written without spaces and vary from one to an unlimited number of bytes. The printout of constants can be limited to eight bytes by the PRINT pseudo (Section 12.2).

Sometimes statements produce no code—pseudos, macrodefinitions—and the location and object code column will naturally be blank. In some cases (USING, START, etc.) a location is given but no code is present since none is generated.

ADDRESSES

We have examined the base/displacement problem and shall consider it again (Section 12.1). MEMORY reference commands address MEMORY in this notation although the programmer does not have to do the accounting for it. To coordinate commands and their referents, the actual five- or six-digit hexadecimal address of the operands is provided in two columns labeled ADDR1 and ADDR2. For a single operand, only ADDR2 is used. This address is the sum of the displacement and the supposed contents of the BASE REGISTER.

STATEMENT

Each statement $\mathcal{ASLR}$ encounters is given a number starting at 1, regardless of whether it is a pseudo, mnemonic, or macro and regardless of whether code is produced but with certain exceptions, SPACE, etc. (Section 12.2). Sometimes, as in the case of a macrocall, $\mathcal{ASLR}$ produces statements not (at this point) furnished by the AL program. It numbers these in sequence, too, but places + (plus) after each to show that *it* ($\mathcal{ASLR}$) has produced them.

COMMAND

The four fields which follow are called *name*, *op*, *operands*, and *comments*. They contain the command as supplied by the programmer or $\mathcal{ASLR}$ accordingly.

SEQUENCE

Punchcards have a characteristic which is both an advantage and disadvantage: as unit documents, we can alter their relative position intentionally; by dropping them, we can alter their relative position unintentionally. It is the latter that we guard against by supplying a sequence number in the last column. $\mathcal{ASLR}$ can check it to see that the cards are in sequence. If they are not, we can use the sequence number to sort the deck.

There is a continuation column just before the sequence number in which we can insert an "X" should a command require more than one card for entry.

Other printouts There is other information furnished; each listing described below is usually placed on a separate page.

JCL

The JCL statements which get the assembler going are printed first.

EXTERNAL

When a program references other programs or vice versa, the external symbol dictionary, ESD, is the means for coordinating the references (see Section 13.3).

RELOCATION

When the obsolete addresses of some locations are required by the program, these locations are set up in a relocation dictionary, RLD.

CROSS-REFERENCE

Additional help is supplied to the programmer by the cross-reference listing. For each symbol at *name*, there is one entry in this listing which contains

1. the symbol itself,
2. its length in bytes,
3. its value or 000000 for DS,
4. the step at which it was defined,
5. all references to it by the step number at which they occur.

To help further, we have

- when undefined, "UNDEFINED" at steps 2, 3, and 4 above.
- when overdefined, "DUPLICATE" at step 5 above for all but the first occurrence of the symbol.

DIAGNOSTICS

When $\mathcal{ASLR}$ detects an error, it flags the printout in two ways:

1. an entry on the line following the error which contains "ERROR" in the object code column,
2. an entry in the diagnostic table consisting of
   (a) the number of the statement where the error was found,
   (b) an error code,
   (c) a message describing the error.

These are examined in detail with examples in Chapter 17.

There is also a summary printed providing

- number of errors detected,
- highest severity code if any error,
- total number of lines printed.

RESULTS

Occasionally, as for some of our problems, the output results appear on the same printout as the assembly itself.

PROBLEMS

3.1 Define the following constants using DCs and then give the contents of the symbolic locations in hex:

(a) F10: fullWord +240;

(b) F11: fullWord −1100;

(c) F12: fullWord +960;

(d) H10: halfWord −999;

(e) P10: three packed bytes 999;

(f) P11: three packed bytes −1234;

(g) Z10: six zoned digits 999;

(h) Z11: six zoned digits −1234;

(i) C10: five characters HARRY;

(j) C11: six characters HARRY;

(k) C12: two fields of seven characters BETTY;

(l) C13: two fields of five characters MILLICENT;

(m) C14: one field of seven characters +987 on a doubleWord boundary.

3.2 Set up storage to hold a record formatted thus:

Record	*Field*	*Subfield*	*Length*
REC			80
	PARTNO		6
	DESCRIP		20
	QUANTITY		8
		ONHAND	4
		ONORDER	4
	REORDER		8
		RPOINT	4
		RQUANT	4

3.3 Reprogram in BAL Probs. 2.17–2.19 using SETUP, ENDUP, GET RDR and PUT PRTR. Assemble and run with sample deck.

3.4 CARD contains a card image with several numbers in adjacent fields each the same size as NUM. Write commands to move the fourth number into NUM; to move NUM into the fifth number; to interchange the sixth and seventh numbers using WORK which you define.

3.5 Restate Probs. 2.12–2.16 so that data is brought in, one datum per card, including the number of items. Write BAL programs to process the cards and print the results. Use SETUP, ENDUP, etc. Provide JCL and run programs on sample decks.

4
SYMBOLIC ASSEMBLY

4.1 BASIC APPROACH

Assumptions We discuss in this chapter a symbolic assembler which does not include any macro facilities. Perhaps this seems a stern requirement but, for assembly in BAL, macros are handled and removed on the first few passes—so what is left for the two or so final passes is much like what is described here.

Further, to introduce assembler operation to the reader, all pseudos are omitted from discussion except for DC, DS, and END (which indicates the end of the assembly). We shall encounter many pseudos associated with programmer macros. Then, starting with Chapter 12, we discuss other pseudos associated with the main program. As pseudos are presented, they are discussed with respect to

- their operation in the program,
- their processing during assembly.

Finally, the whole thing is drawn together in Chapter 16 where full assembly is examined.

Another assumption at this point is the existence of two tables:

- The first is called *SYMTAB* which is made by the assembler and contains all symbols used in the program.
- The second is *OPTAB* which is constructed before symbolic assembly.

We might see *OPTAB* as residing in the assembler. However, this is also a place where macro opcodes exist during earlier passes. This should not confuse the issue since they have been cleaned out during earlier passes and now only mnemonics and pseudos are contained in *OPTAB*. One final assumption is that we have a single assembly language program with no subdivisions or sections. This prospect is reexamined in Chapter 13.

Two passes The symbolic assembler 𝒜𝒮ℒℛ requires two passes. The first is called 𝔖𝔶𝔪 and the second, 𝔒𝔲𝔱.

𝔖𝔶𝔪 analyzes all symbolic references and makes up *SYMTAB*. Here is where errors in symbol definition are detected.

The output pass for assembly, 𝔒𝔲𝔱, examines the entire program, translating it with the help of *SYMTAB*. There is now enough information for producing a machine language output which is the *raison d'être* of 𝒜𝒮ℒℛ. The second product of almost equal stature is a printout which contains both the assembly language input and the machine language output, along with several dictionaries to help the programmer debug his program. Error messages appear in this printout describing errors detected by 𝒜𝒮ℒℛ. The form and content of this printout are postponed to Chapter 16.

Why two passes? First, what is a **pass**? It is a complete review of the entire input—the source language program—to 𝒜𝒮ℒℛ. Each review need not use the same medium as that on which the input is supplied. An assembly language program entered on punchcards may be reproduced by 𝒜𝒮ℒℛ on tape or disk. Succeeding passes review the information as contained on the auxiliary medium.

Any command in the program can reference any other command or datum. This reference can be either forward or backward. It's the forward reference which insists on a second pass. 𝒜𝒮ℒℛ cannot predict where the referenced command or datum will be in the program nor can it preallocate a location for it. This would require a guess or some knowledge of the commands and data which *will* appear.

Is there any way we could make a one-pass assembler? It is possible but the solution is unattractive.†

Referencing ahead to a datum can be eliminated if all the data appear at the beginning of the program: DATUM

1. We could require the programmer to make all data definitions before he writes program commands but he will surely not buy this.

† There is a more complete discussion of the one-pass assembler for the IBM 650 and the Univac SS90 in Ivan Flores, *Computer Software*. Englewood Cliffs, N.J.: Prentice-Hall, Inc., 1965, pp. 110–112.

2. We could have a clerk rewrite the program, placing definitions at the beginning. It would be hard to find a clerk who would settle for such a job.
3. We might pass the program through a PUNCHCARD DEVICE which would separate data cards from others and place them at the beginning. This is workable but still does not grapple with forward references to commands—an absolute necessity.

COMMANDS

Back-referencing to commands is no problem. ASLR similarly could back-reference to a table. Whenever a forward branch appears in the program, it could reference this branch to a table at the front of the program. As assembly proceeded, table entries could be calculated as command labels appear. At the end of the pass, ASLR would have the complete table but the table would not be at the front of the program.

This could be remedied by the loader, LOAD. Thus, ASLR would produce a program followed by the table of forward references. LOAD would place the table at the beginning of the program so that commands would reference backward to the table which, in turn, it would reference forward to the desired command location.

This appears feasible but relies on adequate table sizes which, in turn, would entail restrictions in the number of forward branches appearing in the program. Even so, space would be wasted both during assembly and at run time for the tables.

Objections It was shown that a one-pass assembler is possible but has several objections:

- restrictions on the programmer regarding forward branches,
- provision for tables and lookup facilities for this purpose,
- does not speed up assembly considerably,
- other passes are still required for macrodefinition and expansion.

Limiting the assembler to one pass hence does not afford any saving which would make it practical.

4.2 TABLES

Needs Tables used by the assembler have three requirements which make a special table structure mandatory for speed and accuracy. These are as follows:

- Entries should be found with few "looks.
- It should be easy to add entries.
- No deleting is required.

SYMTAB is constructed by Sym during its pass. Construction and references are both necessary on this pass. The requirements for *SYMTAB* and those for *OPTAB* are very similar as you will find after you have examined the technique for constructing and producing macrodefinitions.

SYMTAB Every occurrence of a symbol requires a search of *SYMTAB*. Whenever a symbol is absent, as it should be if it is being defined, that symbol must be entered into *SYMTAB*. The entry contains a number of fields, one each for at least these needs:

- the symbol name,
- the amount of space allocated to the symbol,
- its type,
- other attributes which may be referenced by the assembler.

Space is of considerable importance to the assembler. Hence table entries should be as compact as possible. Some symbols require much documentation while others can be described tersely. A table structure should therefore provide for variable size entries.

Another need is cross-referencing. The programmer can use different symbols for the same address. A more thorough discussion of this appears in Section 12.3 where the pseudo, EQU, is examined.

Other tables *SYMTAB* is of prime importance because every symbolic reference made by the programmer must be listed and accounted for there. There are many other tables used by ASLR but their importance depends upon the complexity of the particular assembler; some are unnecessary in the lower level assembler. For instance, a table of names of macros isn't needed if no macro facility is provided.

Here are a few tables needed by the higher level assembler.

OPCODES

A list of opcodes, including mnemonics, pseudos and macros is needed by all assemblers. Where no macro facility exists, this table may be fixed and part of ASLR, as reference but not alteration is the full scope of its use. For macros, dynamic fabrication is required.

LOCAL VARIABLES

Where macros can reference variables unique to the definition, a separate variable dictionary is needed for each macro which is reinitialized at each use.

LITERALS

A separate table may be provided for literals. Of course, it is subject to dynamic updating.

Table organization Dynamic construction of tables is a problem for several reasons:

1. The length of the table cannot be anticipated.
2. Lookup during fabrication is usually required.
3. Lookup after fabrication is mandatory.
4. Entries may be variable in size.
5. Cross-references are often needed.

There are many ways to organize these tables. We examine three but pursue in detail only the one used by the OS360ASLR.

REORGANIZATION

A simple approach to construction is to accumulate entries during the first pass and to suppress reference. For *SYMTAB* this means that a separate entry is made for

- each symbol definition,
- *every* reference regardless of duplication.

Only after the first pass is the table reorganized.

- The entries are sorted.
- They are compressed so there is only one entry per symbol.

On later passes only reference is required so the ordered table need not be amended.

IN-PROCESS SORTING

During the first pass with this method, both reference and change are possible. But change is always preceded by reference. When a symbol is encountered by Sym, whether it appears at *name* or *loc*; Sym,

- looks up the symbol in *SYMTAB* and uses it if it is found,
- if it is absent, Sym inserts the symbol in the table, reorganizing it if necessary so that table stays in sequence to facilitate lookup.

There are several techniques for doing this,† including

- sort by insertion,
- loose lists,
- neighborhood locatability with overflow,

but these are omitted here.

LINKED LIST

The combination hash table and link list technique discussed in the next section is particularly effective.

† These are covered in Ivan Flores, *Data Structure and Management*. Englewood Cliffs, N.J.: Prentice-Hall, Inc., 1970.

4.3 THE HASH TABLE

TECHNIQUE

Linked lists A **linked list** resides in a **list area.** Cells in this area may be empty or may contain records. A **record** consists of three parts. We discuss these in terms of *SYMTAB*:

- The **key** is the symbol name.
- The **datum** is the symbol description and the address allocation along with other information.
- The **pointer** is the address of the next record in this list.

Advantages of the linked list structure are as follows:

- It can handle variable size records.
- It is simple to append new records without reorganizing the list.
- If sublists are kept short, it is easy to search them.
- It is not necessary to keep sublists in order.

Instead of a single list structure, consider a number of sublists, each in the linked list format. For 𝒪S360𝒜S𝓛ℛ there are 256 sublists which comprise the symbol table, *SYMTAB*. How do we make up these sublists?

Defining sublists There are many schemes which might be incorporated to determine on which sublist to place a symbol. The very easiest might be to use the first byte of the symbol. This furnishes eight bits to designate 256 sublists. But many USACII-8 and EBCDIC combinations are not letters or characters available in assembly language. Hence these combinations would lead us to sublists which were always empty. The programmer starts a symbol name with one of twenty-six letters. Perhaps using the first two letters to point to sublists might provide a good method. However, the programmer does not select symbols randomly and some sublists might be empty while others become quite long.

We need a method which connects a symbol into 256 categories and where the symbol is equally likely to fall into any one of these categories regardless of how it was made up.

The method chosen is called **hashing**. A symbol can be up to eight bytes long but always contains sixty-four bits since the full amount is set aside, regardless. Hashing designates certain of the sixty-four bits to be used to enter the sublist. The better the choice of bits, the more likely it is that the sublists will be of equal length. The bits designated can best be chosen on an empirical basis. Once chosen, they are fixed *for the life of the assembler*.

To summarize, eight bits are designated as hashing bits for the symbol. These are withdrawn from the symbol code, compacted together, and form an eight-bit address.

HASHTAB With an eight-bit address, the assembler gets to a sublist with the hash table called *HASHTAB*, as shown in Fig. 4.3.1. This table occupies a fixed location, call it H. Suppose that there are four

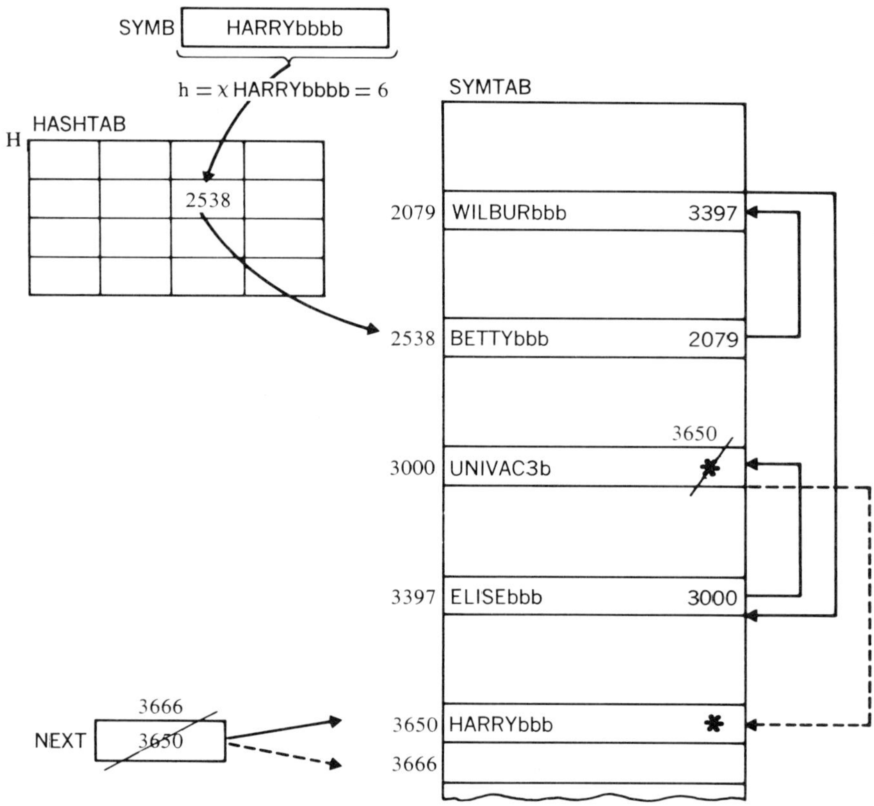

Fig. 4.3.1 *HASHTAB* and *SYMTAB* for the 𝒪𝒮360 𝒜𝒮ℒℛ.

bytes for each entry in the table. The hashing described yields a number which when multiplied by 4 becomes a displacement, h. H is added to h to get a *HASHTAB* entry location, the pointer to a sublist.

When the building of *SYMTAB* starts, most or all sublists are empty. Hence the entries in *HASHTAB* are also empty, which is indicated by setting them to 0's. Hence a symbol which hashes to a *HASHTAB* entry which is 0 indicates an empty sublist.

SYMTAB There is a large area set aside in the assembler which contains the 256 sublists which comprise *SYMTAB*. There is also a pointer called SYMPT which points to the next available space in *SYMTAB*. As entries are made in *SYMTAB*, space is used up and SYMPT is incremented to reflect this. Entries of *SYMTAB* are of variable size and as much space in *SYMTAB* is consumed as is required for the entry.

Search *ASLR* performs the following actions to search for a symbol in *SYMTAB*:

1. The symbol is hashed to an eight-bit number.
2. This number is multiplied by 4 to form a displacement, h.
3. The displacement is added to H to form the address of the *HASHTAB* entry.
4. The *HASHTAB* entry contains a pointer to the first cell in the sublist (or else 0, if this is an empty cell).
5. The key field of the *SYMTAB* entry is examined for a match.
6. When no match is found, the pointer field of the *SYMTAB* entry is examined.
7. This field may indicate the end of the sublist (*) or may contain a pointer to another cell.
8. Search continues using steps 5 through 7 above until the end of the sublist is reached.

Entry To append a new symbol to *SYMTAB*, we go through a search as described above. When the end of the list is reached (provided the symbol has not been previously defined), the assembler performs the following steps:

1. It enters the contents of SYMPT in the pointer field of the last cell of the sublist.
2. It creates an entry in *SYMTAB* beginning at the location indicated by SYMPT.
3. It keeps track of the number of bytes in the entry (including the pointer to be added) and adds this amount to SYMPT, thus updating this pointer.
4. A terminal pointer (*) is placed at the pointer field of the *SYMTAB* entry just added.

Limitations are placed on the programmer as to how many symbols he may use in his program. Generally, this limitation is much greater than the size of *SYMTAB*. Hence overflow is provided on disk or tape for when a large number of symbols are used by the programmer. This is a complication which would add to the explication and hence is omitted.

4.4 SYMBOLS

We examine now the first pass, Sym, of the symbolic assembler using the assumption presented earlier in the chapter.

We divide Sym into four components although further subdivision would be appropriate if this were a macroassembler *and* if all the pseudos introduced later were processed. Here are the names and purposes of the four components:

- SScan (step 1) scans the input text distinguishing the five fields which comprise it by the blanks which separate them.
- Opt (step 2) looks up the opcodes encountered in the *OPTAB*.
- SLook (step 18) looks up the symbols encountered in the *SYMTAB*. and enters new symbols there where necessary.
- Con (step 16) expands constants for Sym.

These are now discussed in order and with respect to the flow chart, Fig. 4.4.1.

Location counter ASLR keeps track of all the locations it assigns in **run time** MEMORY as pictured while the AL program being assembled is running. ASLR has a location counter (LC) within it to do this accounting. This counter (LC) is reset to 0 for the first valid MEMORY location used by the program—the programmer may override this (with ORG, see Section 12.2).

Each command encountered, whether mnemonic or pseudo, reserves bytes in run time MEMORY (except for some pseudos like END, etc., which are considered later). One of Sym's jobs is to find out how much run time MEMORY is consumed by each AL command. Sym then advances the location counter by this much; this is the (run time) address of the next command (before relocation).

SScan The sole purpose of this routine is to separate the fields of the incoming assembly language program. Only three fields are of interest to this pass:

- *name* will be placed in *SYMTAB*;
- *opcode* determines the disposition and space required for *this* command;

- *location* is used by SScan only for DC and DS for allocating space and setting up constants.

SScan separates the three needed fields, placing them in areas where they are available to the other routines.

Opt — The routine called Opt looks up *opcode* in *OPTAB* by the method discussed earlier using the hash table for *OPTAB* (there are separate hash tables for *OPTAB* and *SYMTAB*). Any opcode encountered should be contained in *OPTAB* and recognized there. In Fig. 4.4.1 the Opt (step 2) contains several exits. The first three (steps 4, 5, 6) pertain to bona fide mnemonics. The mnemonic entry indicates whether it is two, four, or six bytes long. This is stored by Opt at D, the amount by which the location counter is incremented. If the opcode should be missing, the error exit, E, is taken. Error exits are indicated simply as E in the rest of the chapter.

The pseudo END is used by the programmer to terminate the assembly.

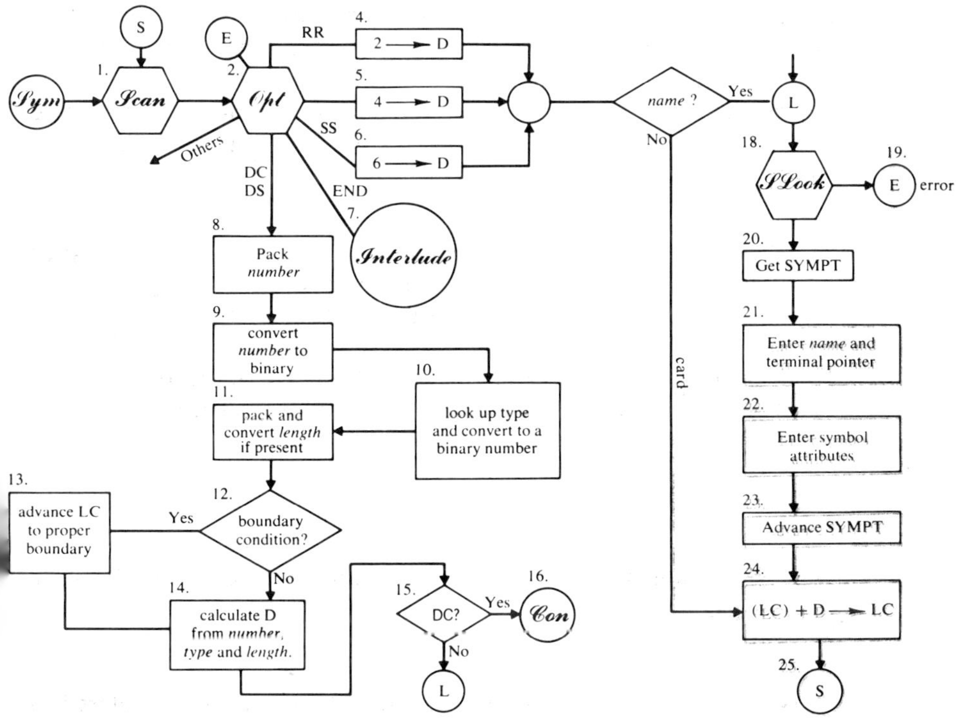

Fig. 4.4.1 Flow chart for Sym.

When encountered by Opt, it recognizes the end of the pass and the exit called Interlude (step 7) is taken.

When the pseudo, DS (or DC), is encountered by Opt, it determines the amount of space in bytes required in the program. It examines *location* to get this information. *Location* contains four subfields you should recall.

NUMBER

The subfield *number* is a number conveying how many fields of *type* are to be set up in this area. When Opt encounters *number*, it is in the form of unpacked decimal digits. Opt packs these digits (step 8) and converts them to binary (step 9).

TYPE

A letter appears at this subfield indicating a type. For each type there is a corresponding length. Opt contains a *type* table where it looks up the type letter to retrieve a binary number (step 10).

LENGTH

When Opt encounters *length*, it removes the prefix L and packs the remaining digits into a decimal number, then converts this to binary (step 11). This is used in conjunction with the numbers obtained from the two previous operations. For a character field, for instance, these three quantities are multiplied to give the storage field length in bytes (step 14).

BOUNDARY

If there is a boundary to be observed such as placing an F type constant on a fullWord boundary (step 12), the LC is advanced to provide for this (step 13).

DATA

The last or data subfield can be ignored for DS except where it must be used to determine the lengths of fields in this area. The reader may examine this requirement. We look at DCs in Section 4.5.

DISPLACEMENT

Opt comes up with the number which is the length of the area to be set aside. This is set into D as a displacement for location encountered.

CONSTANTS

For a DC (step 15) the constant is prepared with Con (step 16)—see the next section.

Sym Now the routine SLook (step 16) is entered to look up *name*, if any (step 17), in the symbol table. SLook goes through the hash table to look up the symbol. Since only *one* symbol combination can appear in any program at *name* (with certain exceptions such as CSECT discussed later), SLook should not find the symbol in its table. If it is present, this is an error (step 19) (handled in different ways for different assemblers).

With the symbol absent, Sym gets SYMPT (step 20) which gives the next available space in *SYMTAB*. The symbol is placed into *SYMTAB* beginning at this point and occupying the full eight bytes (step 21). The attributes which have been obtained by Opt and the processing associated with the DS and DC are compiled and entered as text following the symbol name. In the case of DC, this may require further analysis to determine scaling factors and so forth (step 22).

The entry is now complete except for the pointer. This symbol is the most recent addition to this sublist. It contains a terminal pointer, *, which Sym enters. All the while, Sym is keeping count of the bytes it has used in the *SYMTAB* entry. It needs this for two reasons:

- It uses this prefix field for the entry in *SYMTAB* so that references will know the size of the entry.
- It increments SYMPT by this amount so that the next available space in *SYMTAB* is pointed to (step 23).

The final task is to advance the location counter by the amount contained in D. Notice that, for an unlabeled command, SLook and the steps which follow are omitted but the location counter must be advanced (step 24). It keeps track of the absolute location in the program of each command pseudo. Now control returns to SScan (step 25).

4.5 CONSTANTS

When a DC appears, Sym handles it as shown in Fig. 4.4.1 up to the point where Con is entered.

Con The routine Con for handling constant is type-dependent. Its flow chart appears as Fig. 4.5.1.

CHARACTER

Character (zoned, etc.) strings are simplest. The string is abstracted from its surrounding quotes. It is truncated or padded to make its length equal to *length*. *Number* tells the number of such strings required and Con fabricates them. This compound string is now ready for entry into *SYMTAB*.

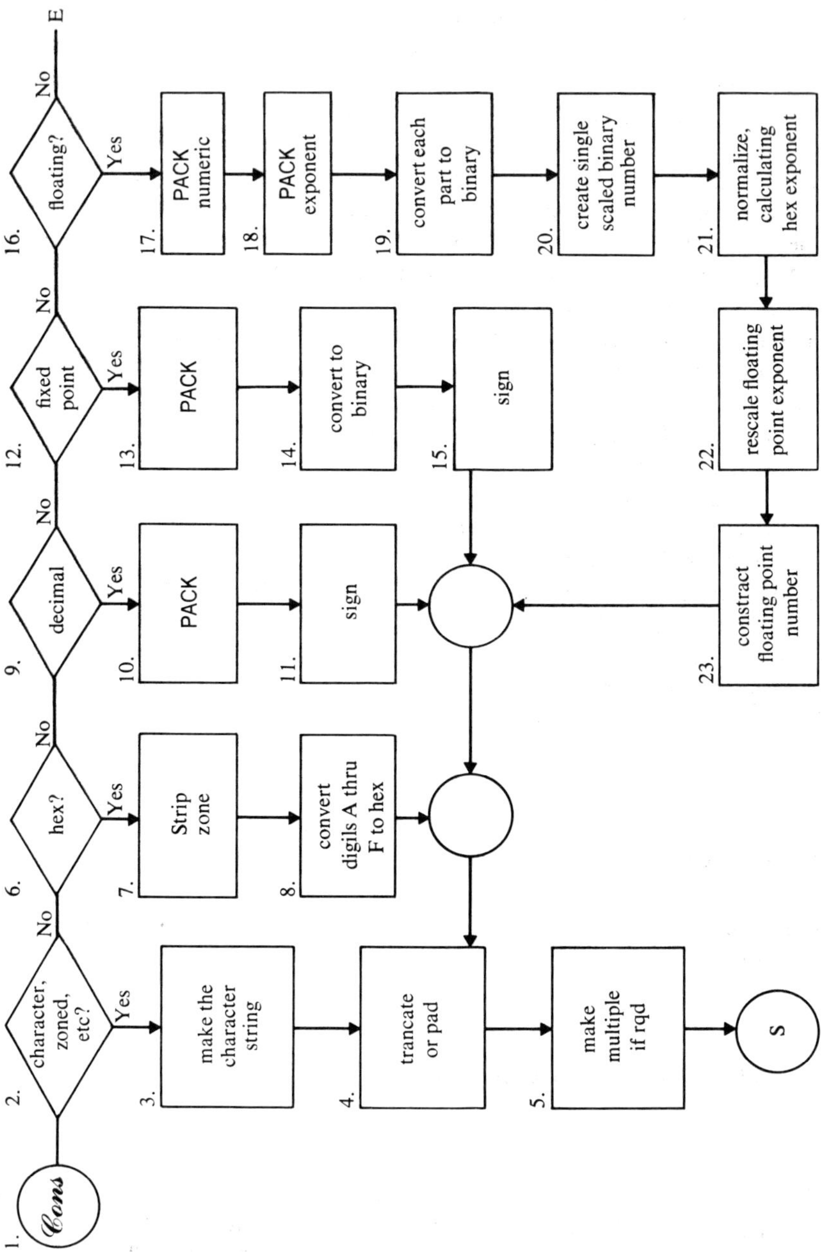

Fig. 4.5.1 How the assembler treats constants with Cons.

To prepare the hex constant, Con in Fig. 4.5.1 HEXADECIMAL

(7) looks up alpha character in a table to convert it to a hex nibble,
(8) strips zone nibble to get hex nibble,
(9) pads or truncates according to length (a zero nibble is required whenever an odd number of hex digits is provided),
(5) creates multiples as needed.

A decimal constant is prepared by Con thus: DECIMAL

(10) Do a PACK on *data*.
(11) Convert the sign byte to a sign nibble and mask in.
(4) Pad or truncate.
(5) Create multiples as required.

A fixed constant is a full- or halfWord: FIXED

(13) *Data* is packed and signed as required.
(14) It is converted to binary.
(15) Sign is entered.
(5) Create multiples as required.

The tasks required to prepare a floating point constant are indeed formidable and they consist of FLOATING

(17) packing the exponent and number separately,
(18–19) converting each to binary,
(20) converting the binary parts to a single fixed point binary number,
(21) normalizing this number constructing a hex exponent,
(22) resetting the exponent by sixty-four,
(23) constructing the floating point number.

4.6 Out

The final assembler pass Out contains a component, ScanO (step 1), which is the output scan. Only two fields are important for the processing routine Out: *opcode* and *location*. ScanO finds these fields and brings them to work areas.

OptO The component OptO (step 2) looks up opcode in the *OPTAB*. Again we limit ourselves to the pseudos DC, DS, and END.

END is simple to take care of, for it means that Out is done. The assembler is not completed though, for printout of the various dictionaries

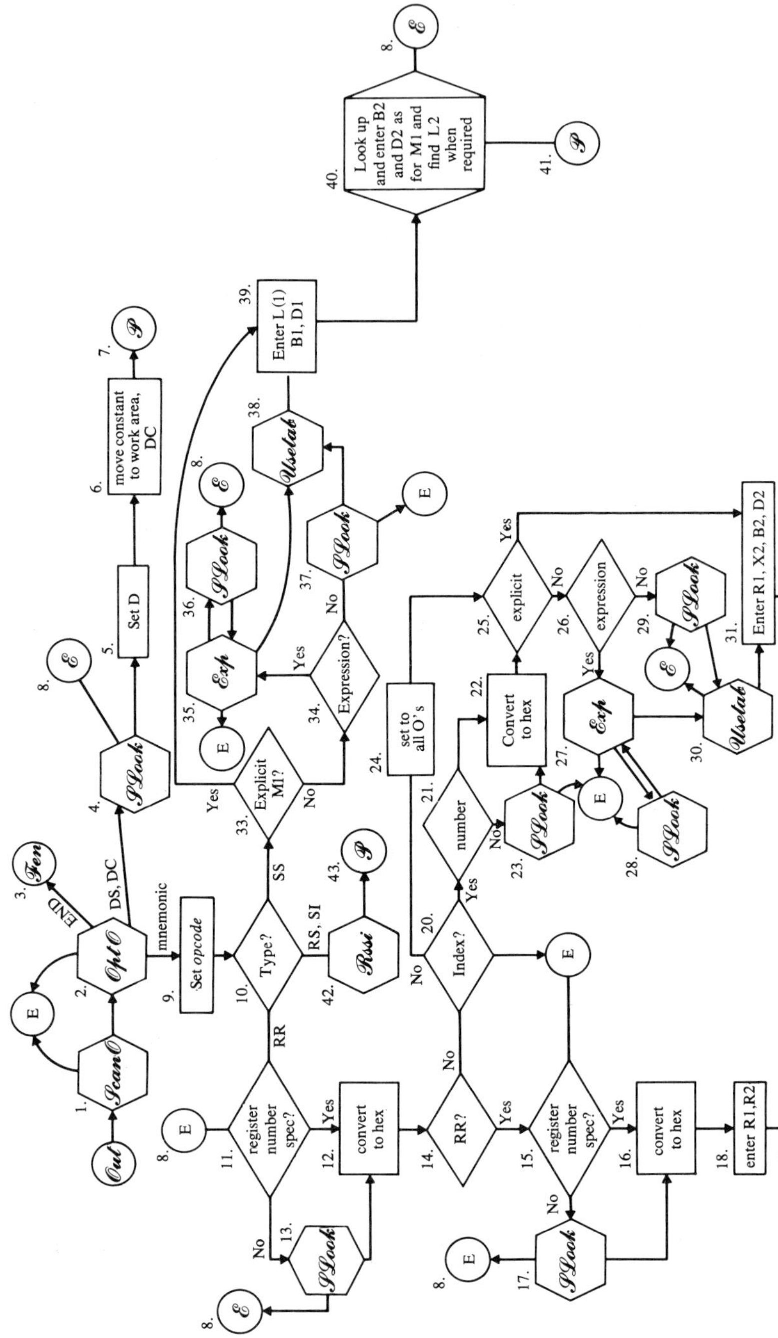
Out
Scan O
Opt O
END
Fen
DS, DC
mnemonic
PLook
Set D
move constant to work area, DC
P
Set opcode
Type?
RR
SS
RS, SI
Rssi
register number spec?
convert to hex
RR?
Yes
No
Index?
number
Convert to hex
set to all O's
explicit
expression
Exp
Uselab
Enter R1, X2, B2, D2
enter R1,R2
Explicit M1?
Expression?
Enter L (1) B1, D1
Look up and enter B2 and D2 as for M1 and find L2 when required
E

Fig. 4.6.1 Out.

is generally required. This is done by 𝓕in (step 3) and we postpone its examination until Chapter 16.

DS, DC

When OptO discovers a DS or DC, it turns over control to the *SYMTAB* search routine SLoof (step 4) which searches the table to find the symbol. There is a length associated with the symbol and this is set into D (step 5) to later be added to the location encountered. That is all that is required for DS. For DC the translated constant is found in the entry and this is moved into the work area (step 6) for printout which we examine later (step 7).

ERRORS

There are many errors that can crop up in this pass. None of them are examined but they will be named E when encountered (step 8). For instance, a missing symbol in *SYMTAB* is always an error.

MNEMONICS

The ML *opcode* is set up and then different things are done according to command type (step 9).

RR All RR, RX, and RS commands require a register designation in the first field of *location* (step 10). If this is a number (step 11), it is simply converted into a single hexadecimal nibble (step 12). It might be a symbol which requires examination of *SYMTAB* by SLoof (step 13).

The beginning of the second field of an RR command is preceded by a comma (step 14). The second register designation is handled in the same fashion as the first (steps 15–17). These two nibbles are now set into the second byte of the command work area (step 18) and we are ready for printout as indicated on Fig. 4.6.1 by the letter P (step 19).

RX The first field of RX command is also a register designation which is handled just as with the RR commands. It is the second field which is different.

If indexing is required, a parenthesized number or symbol follows the address symbol in the second field (step 20). A number is converted into a hex nibble; a symbol is looked up and converted (steps 21–23).

If no index is specified, the index nibble is set to all 0's.

ADDRESS

The second field may contain a symbol address or an explicit designation (step 25). For the latter, no processing is required except conversion into hex/binary form.

The address may also be an expression (step 26). This calls for the component 𝔈𝔵𝔭 to evaluate the expression (steps 27, 28).

Should the second field be a simple symbol (indexed or not), recourse is made to *SYMTAB* by 𝔖𝔏𝔬𝔬𝔨 (step 29). It finds an absolute address there which it turns over to 𝔘𝔰𝔢𝔱𝔞𝔟 (step 30). This component examines the table of base registers set up by the USING statement discussed in Section 12.1. It converts the absolute address supplied by 𝔖𝔏𝔬𝔬𝔨 into base and displacement format. The index nibble determined earlier is added to this and we now have a complete command for output (steps 31, 31).

SS SS commands contain two fields. First a check is made if the first field is explicit—does not have any addressing (step 33). If symbolic addressing is done, an expression appears here (step 34). It must be evaluated by 𝔈𝔵𝔭 (steps 35, 36). This may generate an error (step 8).

When only a symbol is present in the displacement field, this is evaluated by 𝔖𝔏𝔬𝔬𝔨 (step 37). A check is made to see if an explicit length expression appears in parentheses in the field. If so, this is converted to hex and entered as the value for L1 (or L for character commands). If it is the symbol entry, it must be looked up using 𝔖𝔏𝔬𝔬𝔨.

We now have an absolute address which is converted into base displacement notation by 𝔘𝔰𝔢𝔱𝔞𝔟 (step 38).

The same set of operations is performed to find B2 and D2, base and displacement of the second operand (steps 40, 41). In the case of a decimal command, a length is associated with this field. Again, this may be explicit or implied and is determined accordingly.

RS, SI The flow chart of the component ℜ𝔰𝔰𝔦 to process RS and SI commands is left as an exericse (steps 42, 43).

PROBLEMS

4.1 Explain briefly why assemblers use two or more passes.

4.2 Why are variable size entries required in *SYMTAB* of the BAL 𝒜𝔖𝔏ℜ?

4.3 On the first pass a symbol name may appear at *name* or *loc*. How is *SYMTAB* used in each case?

4.4 How does the hashing technique for *SYMTAB* work? Why is a scheme like this required?

4.5 What first pass processing is required for a simple mnemonic?

4.6 Write part of Cons which takes the DC and determine the routine needed to construct the required constant.

4.7 Assume that error checks are made separately. Design BAL routines using the definition in DCWORK to create the constant in CONWORK.

(a) DONEX—create a hex constant;

(b) DOCHAR—create a character constant;

(c) DOWORD—create a Word constant;

(d) DOPACK—create a packed constant.

4.8 Assume that use converts a symbolic address into base/displacement notation, and 𝔊𝔍ℜ converts decimal GPR designation into hex. What activities are required for each mnemonic command type to convert it by 𝔒𝔲𝔱 into ML?

4.9 Write BAL 𝔊𝔍ℜ called GPR to convert decimal designation into hex.

5

MACROS

5.1 THE THEME

The programmer seeks to lighten his burden. Any shortcuts he gets to make his job less tedious he should take advantage of as long as they don't tend to *create* new kinds of errors. One shortcut is to use shorthand for sections of code which may reappear. We let him name the code and then he elicits the production of the code by simply using its name.

The reproduction can be simple and unvarying or can be subject to the alterations the programmer requests. The thread of this chapter is to examine ways to ease the programmer's job by letting him use shorthand for sections of code.

COPY The simplest conceptual entity is a set of code which is copied verbatim. Suppose, as in Fig. 5.1.1, a set of code exists some place external to the program and that it is named SOMCODE. BAL provides a command, COPY, which permits the programmer to call for the code by name and the assembler will enter it into his program. This command has the format

COPY name (5.1.1)

In the figure, the program has the command

COPY SOMCODE (5.1.2)

Commands which precede this one are translated one-for-one (generally). When the assembler reaches COPY, it locates the sequence of assembly language commands, translates it, and inserts it into the machine language program. Commands which follow COPY again are translated one-for-one.

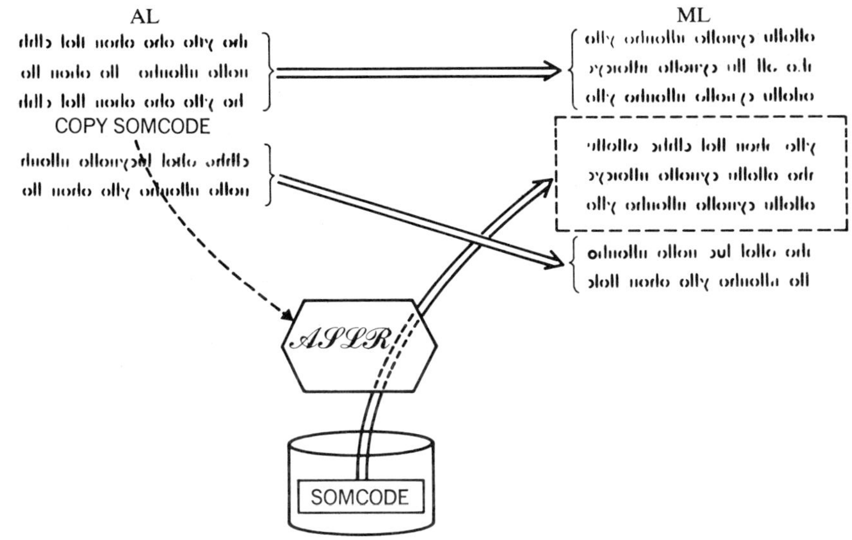

Fig. 5.1.1 COPY causes 𝒜𝒮ℒℛ to obtain named code (SOMCODE) and enter it into the program.

Parameters Generally, copying is not enough. The programmer does not simply want a "copy" of his code to appear at several places. True, he wants the code to recur but with a few changes made so that it does a slightly different job each time.

Hence, we need a way to specify

- that a copy of the desired code is required,
- that certain of its commands are to be modified in ways described to 𝒜𝒮ℒℛ.

This is done as illustrated in Fig. 5.1.2. Again **macrodefinition**—a set of code—appears some place external to the program. This particular definition has the name MORCODE. But places in the code have been set off and given numbers to indicate that they are subject to change from one request of MORCODE to the next. In the case of MORCODE:

- There are nine places in the routine which are subject to alterations.
- Only one of four numbers is associated with any one of these nine places.
- Hence changes which occur in some places will also occur in others.

Insertion To request 𝒜𝒮ℒℛ to copy MORCODE into the program for translation, the programmer places the name assigned to the routine at *opcode* where he wants it in this program. Notice the

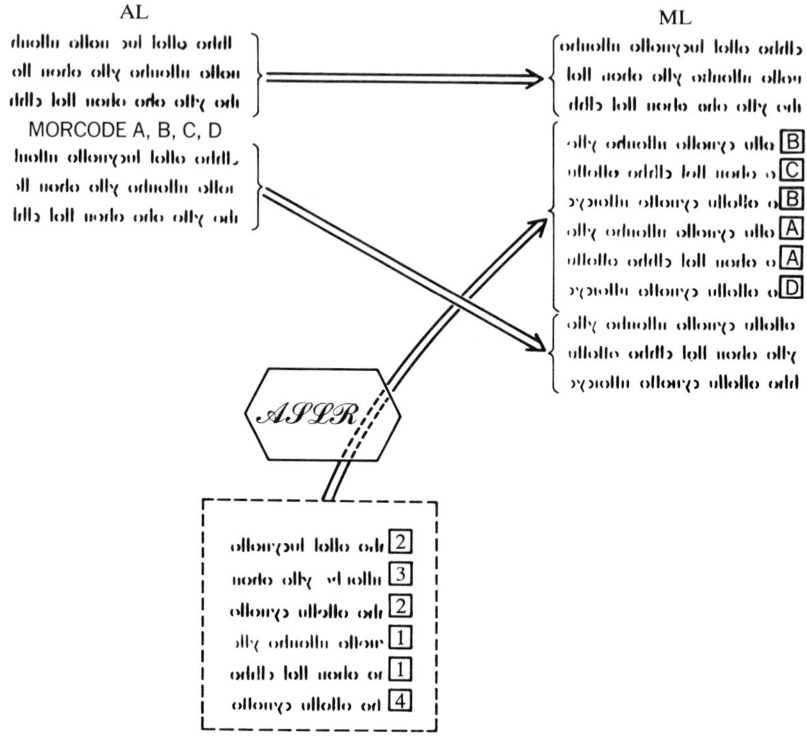

Fig. 5.1.2 The macrocall causes ASLR to find the macrodefinition and plug parameter where arguments used to be and inserts this in the program.

occurrence of MORCODE as an opcode in the assembly language program of Fig. 5.1.2. The assembler will obtain the definition of MORCODE and insert it into the assembly language program. Later it will translate it into machine language output.

Passing parameters Some commands (of MORCODE, for instance) have holes in them to which numbers have been assigned. These are the places where parameters will be inserted. A **parameter** is a value transmitted to ASLR by the macrocall. The **macrocall** is the request for the entry of the named code using its name as an opcode.

When MORCODE appears in the assembly language program, four symbols are supplied, each separated from the other by a comma. These are the parameters. In Fig. 5.1.2, the parameters, in order, are A, B, C and D. They are to be inserted into the numbered holes before the code is put into the program.

Now we see the reason for numbering the holes. The numbers correspond to the order in which the parameters are mentioned in the macrocall:

- The first command in MORCODE contains a hole numbered 2. It is replaced by the second parameter, B, in the macrocall.
- The second command in MORCODE has no hole in it. It's copied intact.
- The third command in MORCODE contains a hole numbered 3 and gets the third parameter from macrocall, C.
- The fourth command in MORCODE contains a hole numbered 2. It, too, will have the second parameter, B, placed there.
- This process of matching up the holes with the parameters continues until all the commands in MORCODE have been copied into the program.

5.2 PROGRAMMERS' MACROS

Method In Section 5.1, I assumed that the code to be entered was available externally. For a programmer's macro, he supplies not only the call but the definition of the macro. Hence we find two distinct phases presented in Fig. 5.2.1:

- **Macrodefinition** sets up the code including the places where there are holes and passes this to the assembler.
- **Macrocall** makes a request for a copy of the code and indicates how the holes should be filled in.

Definition In the figure, the assembly program is shown in the center column. The main portion of the program is subject to direct translation since it consists entirely of assembly language mnemonics. Preceding this, a portion of the program with horizontal lines on it is labeled to tell us that this is a definition of a macro marked MAC. *ASLR* examines the code comprising MAC and incorporates it into tables contained within the assembler at assembly time. However, absolutely no code is produced corresponding to this section of program.

Following the macrodefinition in the figure, notice a crosshatch portion of the program containing only mnemonics and translated directly. Next, we encounter a command which contains MAC at *opcode* and X and Y at *location*. This is a request to the assembler to insert the code previously defined as MAC, replacing the holes, arguments, by the parameters X and Y supplied in the macrocall. *ASLR* obtains this code, plugs in X and Y, translates it, and puts it into the machine language program.

Other code intervenes before a reoccurrence at *opcode* of MAC, this time specifying parameters R and S. The assembler gets the code for MAC, plugs the parameters into the holes, this time R and S, translates it, and puts it into the machine language program.

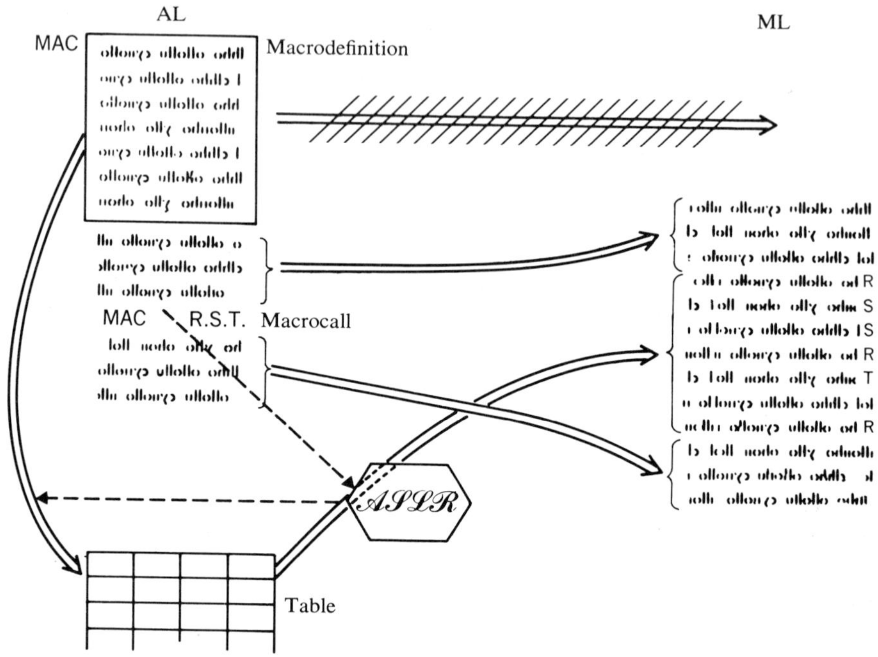

Fig. 5.2.1 The macrodefinition is found by ASLR before the beginning of the program and incorporates it into a table. This table is used to create the code when the macrocall is encountered.

Occurrence Notice that the number of calls of a particular macro is the province of the programmer:

- If he defines a macro and never calls it, he has wasted his own time as well as that of ASLR, for no code will ever be produced for that macrodefinition.
- If he defines a macro and only calls it once, then ASLR has saved him nothing.
- If he makes a macrodefinition for which there are several calls in his program, ASLR really helps him.

5.3 EXTERNAL ROUTINES

Alternatives We have seen good reasons why the programmer wants macro. Such code can be attractive to him if it is

- prewritten,
- easy for him to specify,
- easily accessible to the program.

The code which he may desire may be in three languages:

- Higher language—the routine could be written in a POL, such as FORTRAN or an even higher language such as LISP.
- Assembly language—the macro is the means for obtaining an assembly language code.
- Machine language—the third alternative is to have code already translated into machine language form.

Higher level The programmer can write routines in higher level languages and then call upon these by name. The routines remain in the higher language and have to be compiled into machine language before they can run in the program. The **procedure statement**, for instance, in FORTRAN, enables the programmer to write procedures in his FORTRAN program and then call them later in the program.

An alternative method with which the assembly language programmer is probably familiar is the closed subroutine. He writes a set of code into his program. However, he wants his set of code to be

- reusable,
- reenterable,
- "parametrisable"—he can supply different parameters each time he uses them.

There are several problems associated with the closed subroutine, three of which are

1. getting back and forth to the subroutine,
2. setting up the parameters,
3. passing information between the subroutine and the main program.

These are examined in Chapter 15.

Machine language code The programmer can set up a sequence of machine language code to be executed by his program. He has at least two alternatives for doing this:

- statically,
- dynamically.

In either case, he can do this in his assembly program by naming separate sections using CSECT, explained in Chapter 13. Each of these sections has a distinctive name. Other named sections of assembled program are also available by name.

STATIC

To tie these sections together statically, one or more assembled programs, in machine language, is submitted to the linkage editor which we call EDIT. EDIT gets directions for pasting these sections together so that they form the desired whole:

- The machine language code produced by the assembler is called an **object module**.
- $\mathcal{EDIT}$ can get to object modules furnished as input by $\mathcal{ASLR}$ or from a library.
- The result that $\mathcal{EDIT}$ produces is a **load module** which is ready to be run by the computer.

The directions to $\mathcal{EDIT}$ are in a special control language to tell not only in what order to place the modules but also how control is to pass from one portion of a module to another.

DYNAMIC

Dynamic insertion of machine language code refers to the acquisition and change of control from the main program to a section of code brought in while that program is running. This could not be done by the program alone (normally) and requires the intervention of system software.

Again the assembly language programmer writes his program and other sections which exist on some external accessible library. In his assembly language program, he indicates when these external sections are needed. He does so by giving system macros. These system macros are expanded by $\mathcal{ASLR}$ into code which includes at least one supervisor call. The supervisor call is a command which removes control from the problem program and turns it over to the software. The software determines the code required by the running program, goes out to the library, finds the code, brings it in, properly locates it, and then turns over control to it.

This is done with system macros, such as $\mathcal{LOAD}$, which are discussed in Chapter 15.

PROBLEMS

5.1 (a) What is the difference between a macro and the COPY function? (Explain thoroughly.)

(b) How are parameters transmitted with COPY?

(c) How are parameters transmitted with a macro?

5.2 What is the distinction between:

(a) macrocall and macrodefinition;

(b) parameter and argument;

(c) load module and object module;

(d) static and dynamic insertion?

6

PROGRAMMERS' MACROS

6.1 THE DEFINITION

Introduction We have seen how, when a macro is called, it produces an open subroutine in the main program. When the programmer calls his own macro, it is his responsibility to place its definition preceding the main program (for BAL). The user must be very careful to distinguish the macro*call* from the macro*definition*.

We might *expect* that definition must precede call—after all, how can we request an SR if we have not yet defined it? This is not so! It is sometimes convenient for the programmer to call the subroutine that he has not written yet. Since he has the latitude to define it somewhere else in his program, the call can precede the definition. *For BAL all macrodefinitions must precede the beginning of the program—the first* CSECT *or* START (see later).

Definition The macrodefinition is written by the programmer. It conveys to $\mathcal{ASLR}$ what commands are to appear when the macrocall is given. However, when a macrodefinition is made, it is *not* mistaken for a macrocall. Hence, no code appears in the machine language program corresponding to the point where the definition appears in the assembly language program; code appears only for a macrocall.

The macrodefinition does a number of things:

- names the macro,
- lists the parameters which accompany the call
  - * by giving the order of their appearance,
  - * or by naming them,
- describes the commands which make up the open subroutine.

Notice that commands appear in the macrodefinition:

- These commands do not appear in the program where the definition is made.
- They inform 𝒜𝒮ℒℛ of the makeup of future macrocalls.
- 𝒜𝒮ℒℛ is alerted that these commands are *not for translation* but for later incorporation.

The macrodefinition is parenthesized by a pair of pseudos. The first pseudo, MACRO, alerts 𝒜𝒮ℒℛ that what follows is not to be translated but incorporated. The second pseudo, MEND, signals the end of the definition.

Format The format of the macrodefinition is presented in Fig. 6.1.1. We examine each of the lines which appear in this definition.

Type	*Name*	*Opcode*	*Location*
Header		MACRO	
Prototype	Entry	Macname	Argl 1, arg 2, arg 3, etc.
Model	Name	Opcode	Operand
.			
.			
.			
Model	Name	Opcode	Operand
Trailer		MEND	

Fig. 6.1.1 A macrodefinition.

HEADER

The **header** contains at *opcode* the pseudo MACRO. It must contain blanks at *name* and *location*. This alerts 𝒜𝒮ℒℛ that what follows is a definition and it calls in the macrodefinition generator.

PROTOTYPE

The next line in the definition is a **prototype statement.** It contains the name of the macro Macname at *opcode*. In *name*, we may find an entry point, *entry*, to the macro which we examine in Chapter 8. At *location* are one or more parameters at *arg 1*, *arg 2*, etc. These have a format discussed in the next section.

MODEL

The statements which follow form a **model** which is reproduced when the named macro is called.

The trailer is the pseudo MEND which terminates the macrodefinition. It contains *blanks* at *location* and (generally) *name*. TRAILER

6.2 PARAMETERS

In earlier macroassemblers, it was possible arbitrarily to name the parameters. This may have caused trouble with programmers who could not distinguish definition-time parameters from call-time parameters. In other words, we might use X as a definition-time parameter and Y as a call-time parameter and might even intermix the two. Actually, the definition-time parameter is a hollow structure into which we make a substitution:

- Confusion is reduced when definition-time parameters are called by a different name—IBM calls them **symbolic parameters**—I call them **arguments**.
- Distinguish them and disallow in any other part of the program—for BAL, arguments (symbolic parameters) must be prefixed with &.

Prototype Everything in the prototype must be prefixed with & except *macname*: *entry* is a *label* within the macro and is hence prefixed by &; arguments are always prefixed with &.

In this chapter we only examine positional argument specification. Any argument to be supplied as a parameter at call time must be itemized at *loc* of the prototype. The permissible number of arguments varies from one assembler to another; for BAL, the upper limit of arguments is 200.

Model statements A model statement looks like any command in the main program. At *opcode* is any permissible opcode including a macrocall. The only limitation is a few pseudos including MACRO and MEND. This is because nested macrodefinitions are prohibited in BAL. Although this feature was available in FAP, its usefulness did not make up for the complexity of the assembler which was required.

Any occupant of *location* permissible in the main program may also be present in a model statement. Arguments (prefixed with &) present at *loc* of the prototype may also appear as operands. This is welcome, for we expect that parameters in the macrocall will be used in the code produced.

Model statements may be named by a symbol (dangerous), or by an argument (prefixed by &); other alternatives appear later.

When symbols appear in *location* of a model statement which are not arguments, they may cause trouble. If they name storage defined in the SR, this is dangerous because if the macro is called more than once, the definition will appear more than once and for separate entities leading to multiply-defined symbols. If the symbolic references are not defined in the SR, they must be defined in the main program.

Definition in the main program means setting aside storage with a DS statement or defining constants with a DC statement. Another alternative is to define external symbols with the pseudo EXT, discussed in Chapter 12.

For the sake of simplicity, two other alternatives for the *loc* field are left for Chapter 8. These are

- arguments in *opcode*,
- concatenation.

Example 1 A very simple macro named MOVEW moves a Word from one MEMORY location to another. The macrodefinition for it is shown in Fig. 6.2.1.

```
Header              MACRO
Prototype       &X  MOVEW   &A,&B
Model           &X  L       5,&A
Model               ST      5,&B
Trailer             MEND
```

Fig. 6.2.1 A macrodefinition, MOVEW.

First we find the header, MACRO. It is followed by the prototype statement with *entry*, &X, and *macname*, MOVEW. Arguments are called &A and &B. These are entirely arbitrary. They form a superstructure into which 𝒜𝒮ℒℛ substitutes at call time. The first of the two instructions which make up the macro brings the Word named as the first argument into GPR5. A second instruction stores this Word from GPR5 into the location named as the second argument. After these two instructions, the trailer with opcode MEND appears.

Example 2 Here we find a little bit more complicated macro, the purpose of which is to evaluate the quadratic equation

$$y = ax^2 + bx + c \tag{6.2.1}$$

Ordinarily, we think of this equation as involving three constants, a, b, and c, and two variables, x and y. When asked to *evaluate* the quadratic equation, we are supplied with the three constants and the value of the independent variable, *x*. When these are substituted into the equation, they yield a value for the dependent variable, *y*. Hence, values for everything on the right side of the equals sign (6.2.1) is supplied to subroutine; it produces the value of *y* on the left of the equals sign.

The SR, at call time, is supplied with *addresses* or *symbols* rather than the quantities themselves. Then &Y is a symbol which stands for a location where the result *y* is stored.

Figure 6.2.2 shows the macrodefinition for QUAD, the SR to evaluate

```
            MACRO
&BEG        QUAD        &A,&B,&C,&X,&Y
&BEG        LE              2,&X        }
            ME              2,&A        }   Find ax + b
            AE              2,&B        }
            ME              2,&X            Find ax² + bx
            AE              2,&C            Find y
            STE             2,&Y            Store y
            MEND                            ax² + bx + c = y
```

Fig. 6.2.2 QUAD, the macro to evaluate a quadratic equation.

a quadratic equation. It uses BAL floating point instructions which were explained in Section 2.10 and it should be easy to follow.

Entry A word here about the field called *entry*. It is permissible to write instructions, especially pseudos (and conditional assembly statements, Chapter 10), between the prototype and the first actual instruction produced. In that case, the printout of the macro begins with the statement whose model statement has *entry* for *name*.

6.3 CALLING

When the programmer wants to use a macro he has defined, he simply places its name at *opcode* of the next command. He replaces the arguments with parameters, symbols for addresses of the variables he wishes manipulated by the macro. 𝒜𝒮ℒℛ does the rest. It substitutes the address of the symbol appearing in the *macrocall* for the symbol appearing in that position of the *macrodefinition*. Then, wherever that symbol appears in the model statement, it is replaced by the corresponding symbol in the macrocall. Let's examine some examples.

Example 1 Figure 6.3.1 is a portion of the program. After the command at NOW−1, the programmer needs the macro MOVEW defined in Fig. 6.2.1. He names the macro NOW and calls it

```
              .
              .
              .
              ST          5,HERE
NOW           MOVEW       R,S
NEXT          L           5,THERE
```

Fig. 6.3.1 A call at NOW for MOVEW.

with the *opcode*, MOVEW. He wants to move the word at R to the location named S. Thereafter, he is ready for the next command in the program which appears at NEXT and is *load*, L.

```
              ST          5,THERE
NOW           L           5,R
              ST          5,S
NEXT          L           5,THERE
```

Fig. 6.3.2 𝒜𝒮ℒℛ produces code corresponding to this AL segment when the code of Fig. 6.3.1 is submitted.

In Fig. 6.3.2, we see the results produced by 𝒜𝒮ℒℛ. The macro at NOW is replaced by two statements. The first of these is also given the label NOW. Notice that there are *two* statements between NOW and NEXT.

Actually, I have misrepresented the presentation in Fig. 6.3.2:

- This is not the code produced by the assembler.
- The assembler produces the machine language commands.
- Figure 6.3.2 shows the assembler language form of the machine language produced by the assembler.
- This also appears in the printout.

ONCE MORE

Although it should be clear that a macro is regenerated each time it is called, an example of this is now presented. Figure 6.3.3 shows where our programmer has requested MOVEW a second time in his program at

```
              AR          6,7
AGAIN         MOVEW       FIRST,LAST
MORE          L           6,LAST
```

Fig. 6.3.3 Calling MOVEW again.

AGAIN. He uses different parameters. No matter; the code produced by ASLR corresponds to that of Fig. 6.3.4 where the parameters the programmer desires have been properly substituted.

```
          AR      6,7
AGAIN     L       5,FIRST
          ST      5,LAST
MORE      L       6,LAST
```

Fig. 6.3.4 Producing MOVEW again according to the call of Fig. 6.3.3.

Example 2 Remember the quadratic evaluation macro we defined in Fig. 6.2.2? Let us have our programmer call it in his program as shown in Fig. 6.3.5. He uses A1, A2, and A3 for the three constants and VAR for the independent variable. VAL is the name for the Word which stores the result after QUAD has done its work.

```
          ST      5,THERE
SOLVE     QUAD    A1,A2,A3,VAR,VAL
NEXT      L       5,HERE
```

Fig. 6.3.5 Calling QUAD.

Figure 6.3.6 shows the assembly language equivalent of the code produced by ASLR. Notice that the one macro has produced six commands. There is little limitation of how many commands can be produced when the macro is called; it can range to the hundreds and even thousands.

```
          ST      5,THERE
SOLVE     LE      2,VAR
          ME      2,A1
          AE      2,A2
          ME      2,VAR
          AE      2,A3
          STE     2,VAL
NEXT      L       5,HERE
```

Fig. 6.3.6 Assembly language equivalent of assembler production for the QUAD call of Fig. 6.3.5.

Naming calls The arguments provide the framework for transmitting parameters from the macrocall to 𝒜𝔖𝔏ℜ so that 𝒜𝔖𝔏ℜ can plug the parameters into the code that 𝒜𝔖𝔏ℜ generates. Why do we transmit a *name* to the 𝒜𝔖𝔏ℜ?

𝒜𝔖𝔏ℜ replaces the macrocall by code. The call which appears in the assembly output *does not* appear in the ML equivalent. The name is the means for referencing the beginning of the code from outside *or* within the macro. To branch to the macrocall, it *must* be named; self relative is dangerous, especially if the reference is backward, since the *exact* length of code would have to be known. Naming the macrocall alone will suffice unless the same name applies to the code by which 𝒜𝔖𝔏ℜ replaces the macrocall. This can be done by passing the name down to (usually) the first command in the definition, just as with arguments.

6.4 A FIXED GENERATOR

The generator In a multipass assembler, the macrodefinition is incorporated into tables during one pass and the machine language code is produced on a different pass. The part of the assembler which produces the code corresponding to the macrocall is called the **macrogenerator**. 𝒜𝔖𝔏ℜ contains a single macrogenerator which serves all macrocalls producing code for them from tables constructed at macrodefinition time. This generator is complicated. To prepare ourselves for its examination, we first look at a fixed generator.

If we were to construct a generator for the sole purpose of producing code when QUAD was encountered in the program, how would we construct it? We now address ourselves to this problem, calling the generator associated with QUAD, 𝔔𝔲𝔞𝔡𝔤𝔢𝔫.

Getting to 𝔔𝔲𝔞𝔡𝔤𝔢𝔫 𝒜𝔖𝔏ℜ examines each command in the assembly language program during an earlier pass. It looks up the contents of *opcode* in an opcode table called *OPTAB*. It is assumed that when we enter this pass, the opcode for this macro is now listed in *OPTAB*.

During this pass, we are going to produce code for the macro (and for all other commands perhaps). As each command is encountered in the assembly language program, *opcode* is looked up in *OPTAB*. If it is a mnemonic, it is ignored; if it is a macro, it takes us to the generator. For most assemblers, this would be a variable generator. It would be possible to construct an assembler where there was one generator for *each* macro defined by the program. Of course, we would need a generator generator for this but let us shelve that question.

For the case we examine, ASLR encounters QUAD in the program. This has caused it to locate Quadgen and turn over control to it.

Tables Before we examine the portion of Quadgen, we consider two tables which would be added at definition time:

- *QUADARG* is a blank table with room for the arguments encountered in the call.
- *QUADCOM* is a list of commands corresponding to the commands in the original definition.

These two tables appear in Figs. 6.4.1 and 6.4.2, respectively.

Arguments The first job of Quadgen is to create the argument table shown in Fig. 6.4.1. It knows that six arguments are expected and examines the call to obtain and place these arguments.

Argument number	*Name*	*From call*
1	&BEG	SOLVE
2	&A	A1
3	&B	A2
4	&C	A3
5	&X	VAR
6	&Y	VAL

Fig. 6.4.1 *QUADARG*, the argument table for QUAD *and* its expansion.

The first argument is &BEG and is found at *name*. The remaining five arguments are found at *location*. The table in Fig. 6.4.1 has been filled in for the call which we examined in Fig. 6.3.5.

BLANKS

Some of the argument fields may properly contain blanks. For instance, &BEG is the name of the macrocall. The programmer may leave his call unlabeled for which case Quadgen encounters blanks in his field. It fills in the table to so indicate.

Other argument fields may contain blanks. These must be entered into the argument table. However, the generator must have some way of knowing which fields are *blank* and whether the *blanks* have been properly indicated by the programmer or if he has made a mistake in writing parameters. Parameters in the call are separated by commas:

- To indicate a blank parameter between two commas, the parameter is omitted and two commas appear adjacently in the call.
- A terminal parameter is made blank by omitting its field and the comma which precedes it.

This rule permits the generator to fill in the fields of *QUADARG* correctly.

Addresses In the final machine language output, the addresses assigned to arguments which are found in the call have been substituted in the proper place in the macrodefinition. How do these addresses get there?

- One alternative is to enter them as the argument table is being constructed.
- Another alternative is at the other end of the spectrum and allows us to go from a macrocall into assembly language and, on a separate pass, from assembly language into machine language.

We take the latter alternative and see how the generator might convert on an intermediate pass from a macrocall into assembly language. This would produce a single symbolic program without any macros which would be translated later on a final pass.

Commands Quadgen uses the command table to convert the macro into a set of assembly language commands. The table which we use is shown in Fig. 6.4.2.

Number	*Label*	*Opcode*	*Tag 1*	*Field 1*	*Tag 2*	*Field 2*	*etc.*
1	A1	LE	1	2,A5	—	—	—
2	—	ME	1	2,A2	—	—	—
3	—	AE	1	2,A3	—	—	—
4	—	ME	1	2,A5	—	—	—
5	—	AE	1	2,A4	—	—	—
6	—	STE	1	2,A6	—	—	—

Fig. 6.4.2 *QUADCOM*, the command table for the macro QUAD.

BAL is more complicated than many AL commands since its commands can contain three fields at *loc*. These fields may have commas, parentheses, and so forth in them. As *QUADCOM* is fabricated, each command is checked according to its opcode to determine if it contains the proper fields and if the fields are correctly structured. Therefore, if we have reached this stage, we know that *QUADCOM* is correct in these essentials.

Each command in *QUADCOM* may contain a label but only if that label was present in the prototype. The fields of *loc* may also have the parameter specified or they may be literals or external symbols. There may even be constants; e.g., all the commands in *QUADCOM* refer to GPR2.

When a field in *loc* contains a parameter, it is so tagged. Some fields can be entered directly from the table to the intermediate assembly language stream. Those that are tagged to indicate that they reference arguments must be processed by Quadgen: the arguments from the call replace the original parameter field.

Command entry Figure 6.4.3 is a partial flow chart of command conversion done by Quadgen. It is initialized (step 1) by setting the

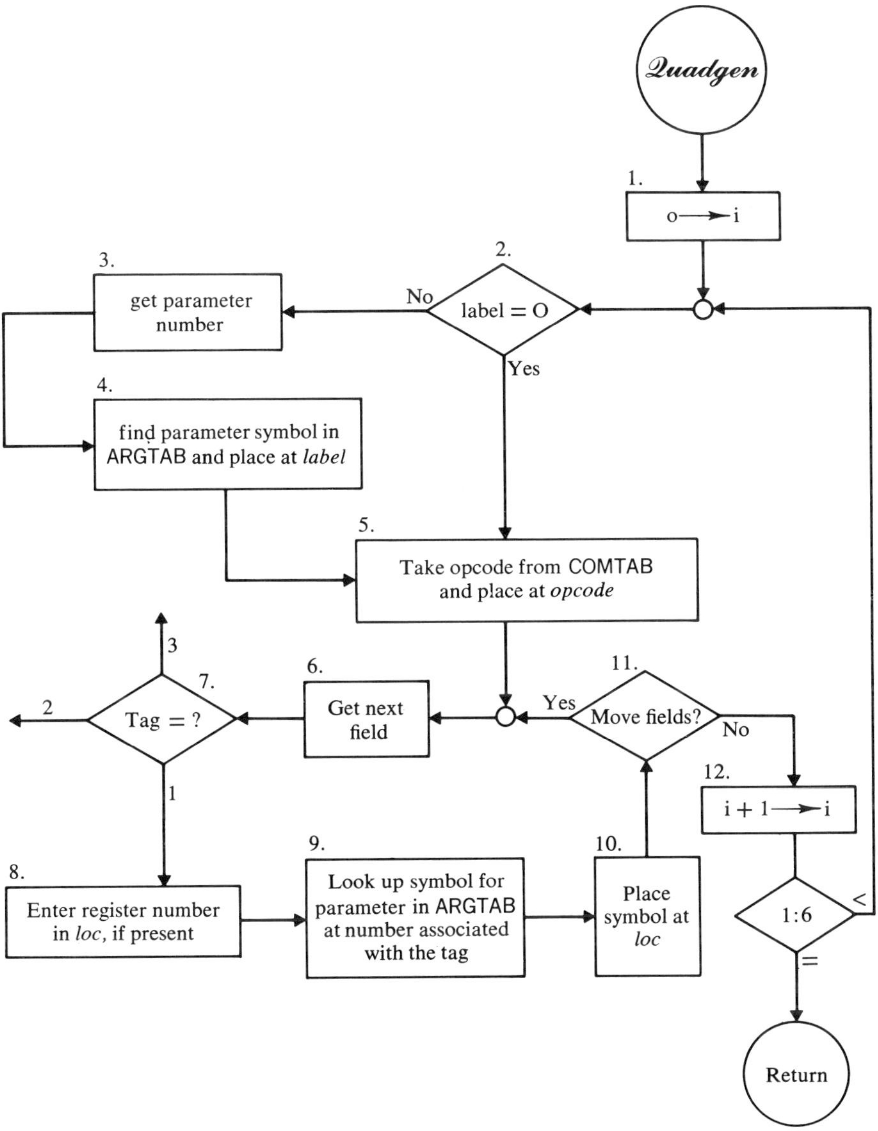

Fig. 6.4.3 Flow chart for Quadgen.

index i to 0. We check for a labeled command (step 2) and if this is one, we get the argument number (step 3), find the argument symbol in the argument table, and place it in *name* (step 4). Next, we obtain the opcode from *QUADCOM* and place it into *opcode* (step 5). We get the next field (step 6) and check its tag.

In the figure, we only examine fields for which a parameter is present. We have tagged such fields with one. After checking the tag (step 7), we enter the REGISTER numbers if any are present (step 8). Since the argument is called for, we look it up in *ARGTAB* (step 9). The symbol that we obtain is placed in *loc* (step 10). We now check to see if there are more fields (step 11) and, if so, we get them and interpret them as described above.

If there are no more fields (step 12), we advance the index (step 13) and check it against the final count, in this case, 6. If the count is less than 6, we have more commands to insert in the intermediate stream. We return to check *label* for the next command (step 2).

Summary In this chapter we have seen how a macro is defined, recorded, and entered into tables at least with respect to a fixed macrogenerator. This technique will be generalized in the next chapter so that $\mathcal{ASLR}$ can accept *any* macro and insert its definition into tables for later interpretation when the macro is called.

PROBLEMS

6.1 Describe the need, format, and restrictions on these macrodefinition components: (a) header; (b) prototype; (c) model; (d) trailer.

6.2 (a) How are arguments distinguished from symbolic variables in BAL?

(b) Do other assemblers make a similar distinction?

(c) Why is it or is it not necessary to make such a distinction?

6.3 Define the macro CUBIC, similar to QUAD, to evaluate in floating point,

$$y = ax^3 + bx^2 + cx + d.$$

6.4 Show the code produced by CUBIC for each of these calls:

(a) CUB1 CUBIC A1,A2,A3,A4,ECKS,WHY;

(b) CUB2 CUBIC A,B,C,X,Y;

(c) CUB3 CUBIC Y,X,S1,S2,S3,S4.

6.5 Write FINDMIN as in Prob. 2.10 called thus:

```
name    FINDMIN    num,listart,min,minloc
```

where *num* is the number of Word in a list starting at *list*. This minimum is put into *min* and its absolute location is supplied at *minloc*.

6.6 Write FINDMAX to find a maximum as above.

6.7 Define QUADW similar to QUAD but use fullWord format.

6.8 Define CUBICW similar to CUBIC but use fullWord format.

6.9 Show CUBICCOM.

7

MACROGENERATION

7.1 OUTLINE

The object of the macrogenerator is to get the code requested by the macrocall and to make the changes required in it to address the call parameters. In this chapter we discuss the multipass assembler where at least two passes are devoted to macrodefinition and macroexpansion. It is possible to create an assembler with macros where only two passes are used for the entire assembly. This alternative is discussed in Section 7.6. We restrict discussion to the technique used by 𝒪S360𝒜S𝓛ℛ where the initial passes define and expand the macro.

Definition We discuss different components of 𝒜S𝓛ℛ using script letters to convey them to the reader. When the definition pass starts, ScanD is in control examining the opcodes of the input stream. When it finds the pseudo MACRO, it calls in the definition component ℳcDef. This component makes all the tables required to incorporate the macrodefinition into the MEMORY to which the assembler has access. ℳcDef absorbs this information as it scans the input stream. When the pseudo MEND turns up, ℳcDef returns control to its scan component, ScanD. This alternation continues until START or CSECT indicates the end of the set of macrodefinitions to be incorporated.

Expansion On the previous pass, we incorporated the definitions into 𝒜S𝓛ℛ. As this pass begins, Scanℳ takes over and examines each opcode. When a macrocall is found as an opcode, ScanM turns over control to McGen. It is now necessary to replace the single call by the code which was defined by an earlier pass. McGen does this replacement and also substitutes the parameters from the call into the hollow arguments presented by the definition. When the replacement is complete, McGen returns control to ScanM which continues to look for macrocalls.

After the expansion pass, the assembly language program looks as though it contains no macrodefinitions and has all the calls expanded; yet it is still untranslated. It is still in assembly language. Other passes are required to do the translation per se.

Nesting We have noted that it is possible for the macrodefinition to include macros as opcodes. This is called **nesting**. Macros which are nested in the macrodefinition are called **inner macros.** A macrodefinition which contains a macrocall is called an **outer macro**. Inner macros may contain further inner macrocalls in *their* definition.

Although nesting is mentioned here, how ASLR accomplishes this is postponed to Chapter 8.

Other features The macro capability can be augmented by other features such as concatenation. It is made even more powerful by conditional assembly. If one goes to the expense of creating a macroassembler, the additional cost of these features more than compensates for their usefulness. As we introduce these features, they are explained and their implementation discussed. This is done in Chapters 9 and 10.

Tables There are at least three sets of tables associated with the macrodefinition and macroexpansion. These are now mentioned and discussed briefly.

ARGTAB

The table called *ARGTAB* holds arguments. It is used for two purposes:

- It holds arguments during definition.
- It holds parameters during expansion.

Only one table is required because the table is temporary and is destroyed and recreated as needed.

COMTAB

COMTAB might be looked at as one large table or several small tables. Actually, there is one subtable for each macro defined. There is one entry in each subtable for each command in the macrodefinition.

OPTAB

This table contains all the opcodes normally used by the assembler. However, because of the unique entry and lookup system incorporated in the OS360ASLR, it is easy to add opcodes to the table as well as easy to look them up. Hence, as macrodefinitions are encountered, their names are added to *OPTAB*.

Variations There are many variations possible in both the conventions in writing a macro and the generation of macros.

The most stringent convention of OS360 conventions is that all macrodefinitions *must* precede the rest of the program. It provides a simplification in assembler design and imposes little hardship on the programmer. I emphasize that *this is not the only way to do things*, and assemblers which permit macrodefinitions almost anywhere in the AL program are rather common.†

Another convention prohibits nested macrodefinitions: it is not permissible to begin one macrodefinition in the middle of another macrodefinition. Truly, this feature is not worth the trouble it engenders.

GENERATION

I describe the in-line generation technique which generates the code for macros in the same order as they appear in the program. It is possible to scan the program, batch macrocalls according to macro type, generate them, and then patch them into the program where they belong. This method has lost favor because it does not *seem* to be as efficient.

Another facility is the ability to do processing during assembly. OS360ASLR does permit this (see Chapter 10) except within the context of conditional assembly. Some AL's broaden this capability tremendously with consequent increase in complexity in their assemblers; the advantage seems dubious and has lost popularity.

7.2 NAMES

As described in the last section, ScanD looks up each opcode as encountered and when it finds MACRO, it turns over control to McDef. What follows next in the assembly language stream is the prototype statement. In the opcode field is the name of the macro which is to be

† The FAP and MAP assembler is discussed with regard to AL's capability in Ivan Flores, *Computer Software*. Englewood Cliffs, N.J.: Prentice-Hall, Inc., 1965, pp. 118–143.

analyzed. The next task is to insert this name into an *OPTAB* and to get the next section of *COMTAB* for building the command table associated with this macro. This is done by the component called *McName*.

Lookup Let us suppose that *McName* is going to look up QUAD, the macro we defined earlier in Chapter 6. The lookup procedure is the same regardless of whether the opcode is a mnemonic, a pseudo, or the name of a macro:

- A logical function is performed on the opcode.
- This takes us to the entry in the hash table, *HASHTAB*.

This operation is shown diagrammatically in Fig. 7.2.1. As described earlier, this entry in *HASHTAB* might be empty, showing that there were no entries in *OPTAB*. The figure shows otherwise.

HASHTAB generally points to an entry in *OPTAB*. This points to another entry in *OPTAB* and so forth.

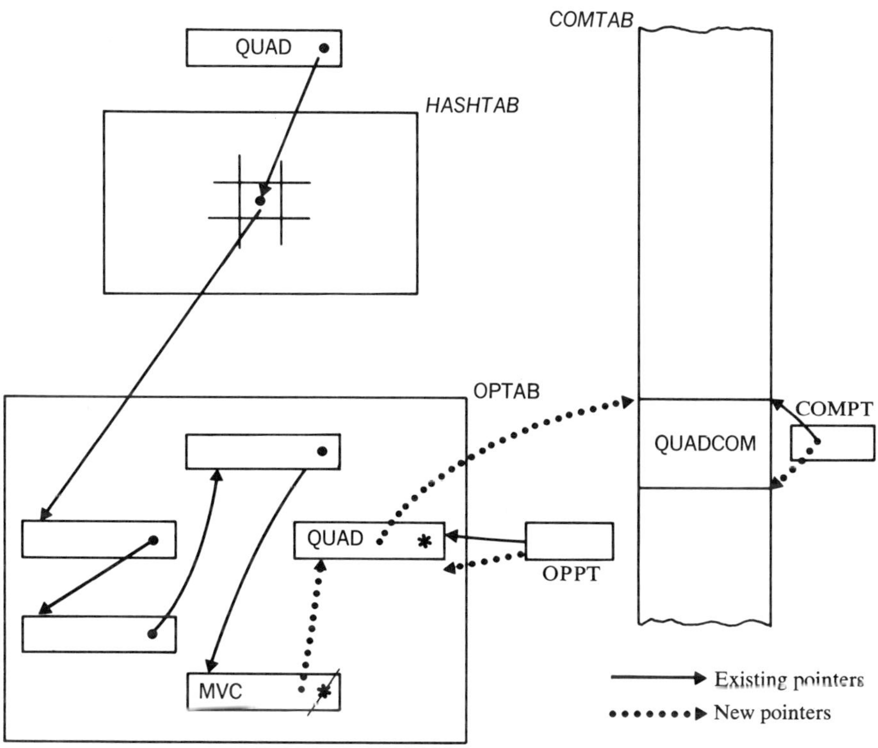

Fig. 7.2.1 The relation of assembly-contained table as *McDef* enters a macrodefinition.

When *McName* takes over, we expect that QUAD has not been previously defined. Hence, as we go through the chain described above, we should not *find* QUAD in *OPTAB*. *McName* will look through *OPTAB* until it comes to the end of the chain. The last entry for this particular hash function will contain * in its pointer thereby indicating that there are no more entries in the *OPTAB*.

Since *OPTAB* is an expanding table, there is a pointer to the next *free* space in *OPTAB*; this pointer is called OPPT. *McName* does three operations now:

- It takes the address which OPPT contains and places it in the last entry of this chain. In the figure, MVC is the last entry since it contains * which is now replaced by the contents of OPPT.
- We go to the cell to which OPPT pointed and we place the name of the macro being defined, viz., QUAD.
- Now QUAD is the last entry in this chain; we place * in its pointer.

Command table The command table, *COMTAB*, is also shown in Fig. 7.2.1. It consists of a number of subtables, one for each macro defined. A subtable is set up as the corresponding macrodefinition is encountered in the assembly language input. Since *COMTAB* is a constantly expanding table, there is a pointer which tells us where the next free space in that table is. This pointer is COMPT. The location to which it points is where we shall now place the commands which make up QUAD. Let us call the subtable of *COMTAB* which is used to store the commands of QUAD, *QUADCOM*. It begins at the location to which COMPT now points.

This information must now be recorded in the QUAD entry of *OPTAB*: the contents of COMPT are copied into this entry.

We have completed this operation and are ready to set up the arguments from the prototype statement. This is done by another component of the assembler which we call *McArg*.

7.3 ARGUMENTS

All arguments must be enumerated in the prototype statement for *OS360AL*. *McArg* will make a list of the arguments, placing it in *ARGTAB*. There is only one *ARGTAB*. The first entry in *ARGTAB* is pointed to by ARGTOP. ARGTOP points to the current entry in *ARGTAB*. Before use, ARGPT is initialized to be identical to ARGTOP.

Entry McArg scans the prototype statement. The first argument may appear at *label*. The first position in *ARGTAB* is preserved for an entry which may occur at *label*. *Opcode* is skipped since we have already used it to enter *OPTAB*. Now the rest of the parameters in the prototype statement are entered into *ARGTAB*.

The first argument in the argument list is placed at the second position in *ARGTAB*. Its name is terminated by a comma or a blank. A comma tells us that further parameters follow. As each comma is encountered, ARGPT is advanced to take us to the next entry in *ARGTAB*. As McArg encounters a new argument, it verifies that the argument is prefixed with &. When McArg encounters *blank*, it assures that no further arguments follow and, hence, terminates the construction of *ARGTAB*.

Now that *ARGTAB* has been constructed, McArg has completed its task and turned over control to McCom.

```
              MACRO                          Header
&NAME         ADDNE    &LIST,&NUM,&SUM       Prototype
              CNOP     0,4                   Boundary maker
&NAME         B        *+12                  Go around save area
              DS       2F                    Save area
              STM      2,3,*-8               Save GPR2, GPR3
              LA       2,&NUM-1              Put number of items in GPR2
              SR       3,3                   Clear GPR3
              LE       4,&LIST,(3)           Load first summand
              AE       4,&LIST+4(3)          Add next number
              LA       3,4(3)                Advance index
              BCT      2,*-8                 Test and branch
              STE      4,&SUM                Store sum
              LM       2,3,*-38              Unsave
              MEND                           Trailer
```

Fig. 7.3.1 Definition of ADDNE to add several floating point numbers.

Example Figure 7.3.1 shows the macrodefinition of ADDNE which adds floating point numbers from a list and returns the sum to MEMORY.

There are four arguments for ADDNE. These are collected and placed in *ARGTAB* as shown in Fig. 7.3.2.

Position	*Name*
1	&NAME
2	&LIST
3	&NUM
4	&SUM

Fig. 7.3.2 How *ARGTAB* might look for ADDNE.

7.4 COMMANDS

Scan *McCom* examines the model statements which follow the prototype statement. It makes one entry in *COMTAB* for each model statement. In this discussion, we only examine nonnested macros. That is, we expect that any opcode we encounter is either a mnemonic or a pseudo.

Entry The entries in *COMTAB* are of variable length. The reason for this is obvious:

- BAL commands are of multiple length—two, four, or six bytes.
- *location* may contain none, one, two, or three fields.

Since information in the command is so variable in nature, it is more appropriate to make the entries also of variable length. Note that the entries are not multiple length but variable length. Hence, each entry has a length associated with it. This should be one of the first fields in the entry so that during expansion we may know where our entry ends. The other alternative would be to terminate the entry with the termination character.

We now examine the variable length entry keeping in mind the following:

- There is one entry for each model statement.
- Each entry has *name*, *opcode*, and *location* just like the model statement.
- These may differ from the model statement, as we now find out.

Label Model statements begin with *name*. This field is often blank, for it is infrequent that we reference the model statement from commands in the macrodefinition.

An argument may be used at *name* in the model statement. This means that the programmer incorporates a label for a model statement in his call.

A symbol may appear at *name* of a model statement. This creates a problem when the macro is expanded more than once.

- A copy of the model statement appears in the program every time the macro is called.
- If the model statement is labeled, the statement which appears in the program will be similarly labeled.
- Therefore, several statements with the same label may appear several places in the program.

In other words, we are faced with a multiply defined symbol since the given symbol stands for several processes in the program. This is the case for BAL.

A way out taken by some assemblers (such as FAP) is to make these labels local rather than global:

- A **local symbol** is defined and meaningful only over a particular segment of the program—in this case, over the macrodefinition or the macrocall.
- A symbol is **global** when it has the same meaning throughout the entire program and all its segments.
- We may also have an **external** symbol whose definition is made neither in the macro nor in any other part of the program. It is defined *externally*. External symbols for BAL are discussed in Chapter 12 using the pseudo EXTRN.

When a symbol is encountered at *name* in the model statement by McCom (for FAP, say), it is converted into a relative address within the macrodefinition and in *COMTAB*. One way to do this uses *ARGTAB*. As a symbol is encountered at *name*, it is entered into *ARGTAB* along with the byte address of this model statement, its relative location with respect to the first model statement.

The description above *does not* apply to BAL. It uses another alternative, &SYSNDX, described in Chapter 9.

Opcodes Several kinds of opcodes can occur at *opcode* in the model statement. Whatever is encountered at *opcode* is checked in *OPTAB* by ASLR to determine its nature. If it is present in *OPTAB*, then its nature is distinguished there as being one of the three types discussed below; if it is missing from the *OPTAB*, it may be because it is a system macro. This is the assumption made by McGen.

MACROS

Macrocalls which appear within macrodefinitions are valid. Encountered at *opcode*, McCom verifies them. If not previously defined, McCom assumes there is a later definition for them and continues. Details on nesting are postponed to Chapter 8.

MNEMONICS

If this opcode is a proper mnemonic, then it has a length associated with it. This length is recorded in *COMTAB* along with the mnemonic and its machine language equivalent.

PSEUDO

When a pseudo occurs at *opcode*, it is checked to determine if it is a permissible pseudo. For instance, MACRO may not appear at *opcode* since nested macrodefinitions are illegal in BAL.

Constants or storage defined in a model statement with DC or DS engender local versus global variables as discussed above with respect to names. If we permit these pseudos within a local definition, the reasonable way to solve the problem of ambiguity is to distinguish them as local variables.

When a DC or DS occurs, it is expanded and incorporated into *COMTAB* so that space is reserved and, if necessary, filled with the defined constant. McSto does this, making all conversions required before entry into *COMTAB*.

Location We may find several different kinds of entities at *loc* in a model statement. We examine these alternatives.

IMMEDIATE

Fields of *loc* may contain the immediate address information. For instance, the command CLI, *compare immediate*, compares the contents of a given byte in MEMORY with a byte found at *loc*. As a second example, RR and RX commands contain nibbles which identify GPRS. This information is viewed as immediately addressed and is stored in *COMTAB* intact.

ARGUMENTS

When an argument occurs in a field of *loc*, it is, of course, prefixed with &. This tells McCom that it is an argument. Hence, McCom goes to *ARGTAB* and looks it up. Since the actual argument name is not important, McCom replaces this name with a number—the relative number of the argument in the argument table.

LITERALS

Literals are permitted in some fields of *loc*. What McCom does with this literal depends on the assembler design. However, at some point in the program, the literal is assigned a location in the literal pool and this location replaces the literal reference in the command. In the BAL ASLR assembler, literal replacement can await a future pass. The literal is recognized by McCom by its prefix, =. It is now entered into the appropriate field of this entry in *COMTAB*.

SYMBOLS

When symbols are encountered at *loc*, they are always global. Hence, they are entered as found in *COMTAB*.

EXPRESSIONS

In some assemblers (and for BAL), expressions are not permitted at *loc* in a model statement. They can be created by concatenation as described in Chapter 9.

Example The macrodefinition of ADDNE was presented in Fig. 7.3.1. The *COMTAB* entries produced for it by McCom are represented in Fig. 7.4.1.

name	*opcode*	*loc*
	CNOP	
#1	B	*+12
	DS	2F
	STM	2,3,*−8
	L	2, #3
	L	3,=F'0'
	CR	2,3
	BE	*+28
	LE	4, #2·(3)
	B	*+8
	AE	4, #2(3)
	A	3,=F'4'
	BCT	2,*−8
	STE	4, #4
	LM	2,3,*−50

N.B.: # is used here to indicate the ordinal number of the parameter to be substituted; e.g., #3—substitute number 3.

Fig. 7.4.1 What BAL *COMTAB* entries for ADDNE *might* look like.

7.5 EXPANSION

A separate pass expands all macrocalls which appear in the user's program. The component called ScanE reviews the assembly language program. It examines *opcode* in each command by the method described in Chapter 4:

- The opcode is hashed to an entry in *HASHTAB*.
- An entry should be found for all opcodes encountered.
- Should the opcode be missing from *OPTAB*, the assumption during ScanD that the entry was a programmer's macrocall is fallacious; if it is not a system macro, an error listing should be produced for this opcode.

ScanG ignores all opcodes except macrocalls. Notice that when a macrodefinition is encountered, it is preceded by MACRO which alerts ScanG to ignore the next opcode encountered since a definition is pending.

When ScanG encounters a bona fide macrocall, it calls in the component McPar.

Parameters McPar scans the macrocall and withdraws the parameters made in the call, placing them in a parameter table, *PARTAB*. This table should correspond exactly to *ARGTAB* when it was established by McDef for this macro:

- The first entry in *PARTAB* is the name of the macrocall. It will be associated with the code produced for the macro if the macro is listed in the output of the assembly run.
- Entries which follow are those at *loc*.
- Each parameter is followed by a comma if further parameters are to come.
- A parameter is omitted where proper by omitting the value for that position but including the comma corresponding to that position.
- A blank indicates that no more parameters follow.

When McPar has finished analyzing the macrocall, it turns over control to McGen, the universal generator which produces the code for the macrocall.

Generation McGen, when it takes over, has a pointer to the position in *COMTAB* where the commands for this macro begin. This was obtained when ScanG found the macroname in *OPTAB*. Associated with the name it found a pointer to *COMTAB*.

McGen reviews the commands in *COMTAB* in order of their occurrence. As each command is examined, substitutions are made where appropriate. We examine the choices which might arise.

PARAMETERS

When an argument occurred in the original macrodefinition, it was replaced by a tagged digit in *COMTAB* indicating the relative position of the argument in *ARGTAB*. McGen goes to the same relative position in *PARTAB* and obtains the corresponding parameter in the macrocall. This parameter is placed in *loc* of a command where the argument was found in the macrodefinition. On a later pass, the symbol for the parameter will be replaced by an address allocated to that symbol.

LITERALS

A literal is copied in its original form into the output for this pass.

LOCAL SYMBOL

A self-relative expression is copied into the program to be replaced later by an address as any other self-relative expression would be.

GLOBAL SYMBOLS

Symbols which were not defined within the macro are copied for later substitution.

EXTERNAL

External symbols are copied too.

Example Figure 7.3.1 showed a macrodefinition of ADDNE which adds several floating point numbers. The three arguments associated with this macro are as follows:

- &LIST is the starting address of the list of fullWords to be added.
- &NUM is the number items to be added.
- &SUM is the address where the result is returned.

The macrodefinition contains a storage reservation. It also contains four labeled commands which refer other commands. The first of these at 581 is a *branch* around the reserve location. The second is STM at 6H to *save* in the reserved space. The third, BCT at 67+, is a loop in the macro. The fourth, LM at 69, is to *unsave*. Figure 7.5.1 shows a call of

LOC	OBJECT	CODE	ADDRI	ADDR2	STMT	SOURCE	STATEMENT
000000					56	USING	*,2
					57	ADDNE	LIST,5,SUM
000000					58+	CNOP	0,4
000000	47F0	2000		00000	59+	B	*+12
000004					60+	DS	2F
000000	9023	2004		00004	61+	STM	2,3,*−8
000010	4120	0004		00004	62+	LA	2,5−1
000014	1B33				63+	SR	3,3
000016	7843	2098		00098	64+	LE	4,LIST(3)
00001A	7A43	209C		0009C	65+	AE	4,LIST+4(3)
00001F	4133	0004		00004	66+	LA	3,4(3)
000022	4620	201A		0001A	67+	BCT	2,*−8
000026	7040	20AC		000AC	68+	STE	4,SUM
00002A	9823	2004		00004	69+	LM	2,3,*−38

Fig. 7.5.1 Call and expansion of ADDNE.

ADDNE. Following this is the expansion of the macrocall as it appears in an 𝒜𝒮ℒℛ printout. It uses the rescanned commands of *COMTAB* shown in Fig. 7.4.1. Commands produced by the macrocall and not actually in the program have numbers followed by + at STMT.

Notice how arguments are now replaced by parameters from the call.

Missing parameters What happens when a parameter is missing from a call? It gets a blank in *PARTAB*. But what does 𝓜𝔠𝔊𝔢𝔫 do? Any command which contained an argument for which there is now a blank in *PARTAB* is omitted entirely. If the macroprogrammer realizes this, he may intentionally omit parameters from the call.

If parameters are omitted accidentally, 𝓜𝔠𝔊𝔢𝔫 *will* create code, omitting the associated commands. These results may occasionally be amusing.

PROBLEMS

7.1 (a) What is nesting?
(b) How does it serve the programmer?
(c) Does nesting simplify programming?
(d) Can an inner macro be: (1) defined by programmer? (2) in the library? (3) a system macro?
(e) What about an outer macro for (d)?

7.2 Describe how the macro name gets in *OPTAB* and its definition into *COMTAB*.

7.3 How can model statements be referenced by other model statements?

7.4 Describe how parameters in the call get into code produced by 𝓐𝔖𝔏𝔑.

7.5 What happens to literals in a macrodefinition?

7.6 How are missing parameters in a call handled by 𝓐𝔖𝔏𝔑?

8
NESTED MACROS

8.1 CONCEPT

Type of macros We have already discussed the two macro types which occur during nesting:

- An **outer macro** is one which contains a macrocall within its definition.
- An **inner macro** is one which is called in a definition of an outer macro.
- An inner macro may contain inner macros within its definition—it may be an outer macro itself for some inner macros.

The usefulness of macros is enhanced through nesting. With simple macros the programmer is able to place a set of code in his program by using a single symbol. When we permit nesting, we allow him to use this symbol which he defines (to mean a set of codes) in defining more and more complex statements.

Nesting without macros appears in nested closed subroutines and nested loops. Once we have implemented this principle, we obtain a power matched only by higher level languages such as FORTRAN and PL1 (which also permit nesting).

Levels of nesting We have distinguished inner and outer macros above and we have stated that multilevel nesting is possible. Let us reiterate the meaning of this for emphasis:

- Imagine a definition for a macro, call it MAC1.
- MAC1 includes in its definition a call to MAC2.
- MAC2 includes in its definition a call to MAC3.

The **level** of a macro is defined by convention going toward the innermost macro. The outer or first level macro may contain in it a second level macro. The second level macro may contain a third level macro and so forth. This concept is subject to ambiguity since MAC3 is a second level macro for MAC2; whereas it is a third level macro for MAC1.

A macrodefinition may contain more than one macrocall. The level of the macro called is always second level with respect to that definition. But

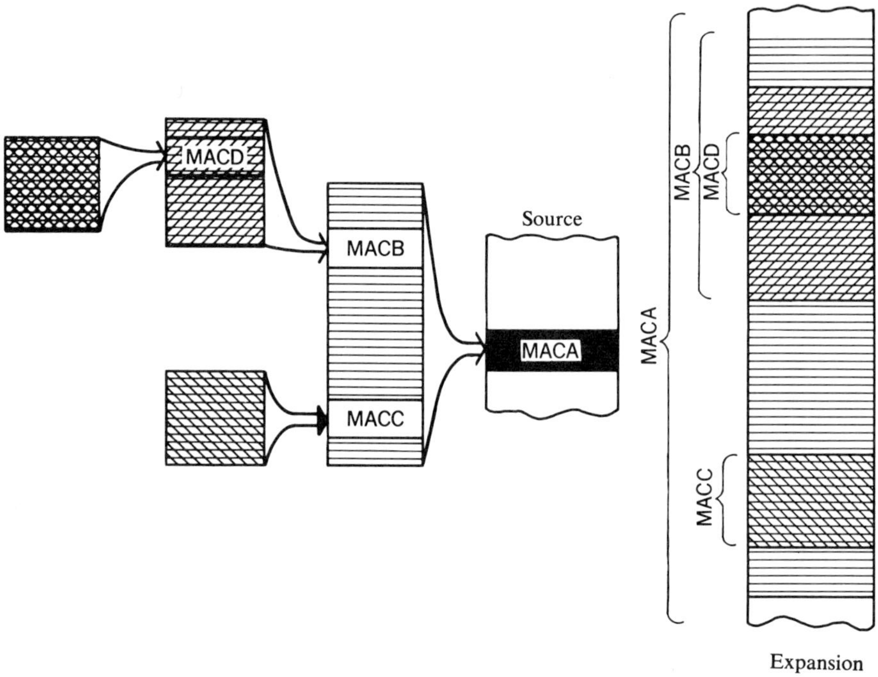

Fig. 8.1.1 MACA is an outer macro—its definition contains microcalls of MACB and MACC. MACB's definition also contains a macrocall to MACD. The expansion of MACA (right) contains the code for all three inner macros as shown.

that outer macro may be an inner macro—a macrocall for another definition. The reader can best see this in Fig. 8.1.1. It should be clear that every time the outer macro is called, its code together with the code for all its inner macros (called within its definition) is reproduced and placed in the machine language output as shown in Fig. 8.1.1.

Definition nesting When a macrodefinition (inner) may appear *within* another (outer) macrodefinition, this is **macrodefinition nesting**;

it is permitted in some assemblers (FAP) but not in BAL. It adds little convenience at a high cost.

Nesting resolution When all nested macros are resolved before other calls are expanded in the program, this is called **static resolution.** Static resolution is simple to perform and the concept is examined in detail in Section 8.3. In brief, the command table for the outer macro is expanded at resolution time by the assembler so as to include the definitions of all the inner macros contained in its definition, no matter what their level.

Dynamic nesting **Dynamic resolution** or **dynamic nesting** is not available in BAL. Even so, it does deserve attention from the reader. Dynamic nesting postpones the resolutions of inner macros until the time that the outer macro is called. The work involved in this may seem superfluous with one important exception. That is when the inner macros required at one call might differ from the inner macro used at another call. How could this be possible if the outer macro is defined and fixed before its call?

Of course, dynamic nesting is required only if an inner macrocall varies from one call to another of the outer macro and it could only vary if the **macroname** were brought in as one of the parameters of the outer macrocall. This is entirely feasible and is realized in the FAP and MAP assembler for IBM 7090 series computers. These assemblers use a "suspension" *scheme* to halt generation of the outer macro and a new generator is called in to generate the inner macro. Parameters, constants, place markers, etc., must be accumulated in tables and kept track of as discussed in detail in *Computer Software*.†

Other methods for nested macrogeneration include a "recursive" generator such as used with the IBM 7070, but here again parameters, constants, etc., must be kept track of.

Nesting depth There is an undeniable advantage to nesting macros. This device expedites the programmer's chores and at a small cost which is usually paid at assembly time. Regardless of the generation technique, greater nesting depth makes more work and uses more assembly space. Time and space are consumed at accelerating rates as depth is increased because bookkeeping and tables proliferate. The programmer should use this nesting facility but keep alert to the penalty involved.

† Ivan Flores, *Computer Software*. Englewood Cliffs, N.J.: Prentice-Hall, Inc., 1965, pp. 143–151.

Self-calling macros The classic example of the self-calling macro is for solving the factorial of *X*, *X*!, call it FACT(X), by this expansion

$$X! = X(X - 1)! \tag{8.1.1}$$

Then FACT(X) will call FACT(X−1) and so forth.

BAL ASLR cannot handle this situation because denesting is done at assembly time and the number of levels is not known until run time. This capability, run time expansion, is hard to implement and one questions whether it is really worth having.

8.2 USE

In this section we examine how nested macros are used by the programmer, but before we do so it is a good idea to examine how we are permitted to get into and out of a macro.

Entries and exits The rectangle in Fig. 8.2.1 represents a macrodefinition within the main assembly language input. There are five arrows pointing into or out of this macro which we now discuss.

JUMP WITHIN

A macro may include a loop without ever including an inner macro. We have seen examples of this in Chapter 7. For a loop to be possible, a *branch* from one point within the macrodefinition to another point within the macrodefinition must be permissible. It can be done with self-relative addressing, as we have seen. Chapter 9 explains how &SYSNDX is used and symbolic labeling is done.

JUMP OUT

If we write a macro which does several alternative tasks, we often wish to leave some of the macro unfinished if a given condition prevails and if one of its given tasks has been completed. Hence, it is permissible to jump out of a macro just as it is permissible to jump out of a closed subroutine. We are no more limited in the places we can jump to from a macro than from any other piece of code:

- We may jump to an argument provided in the macrodefinition and later supplied by the macrocall.
- We may jump to another subroutine.
  - * The name of this subroutine might be an argument in the macrodefinition.

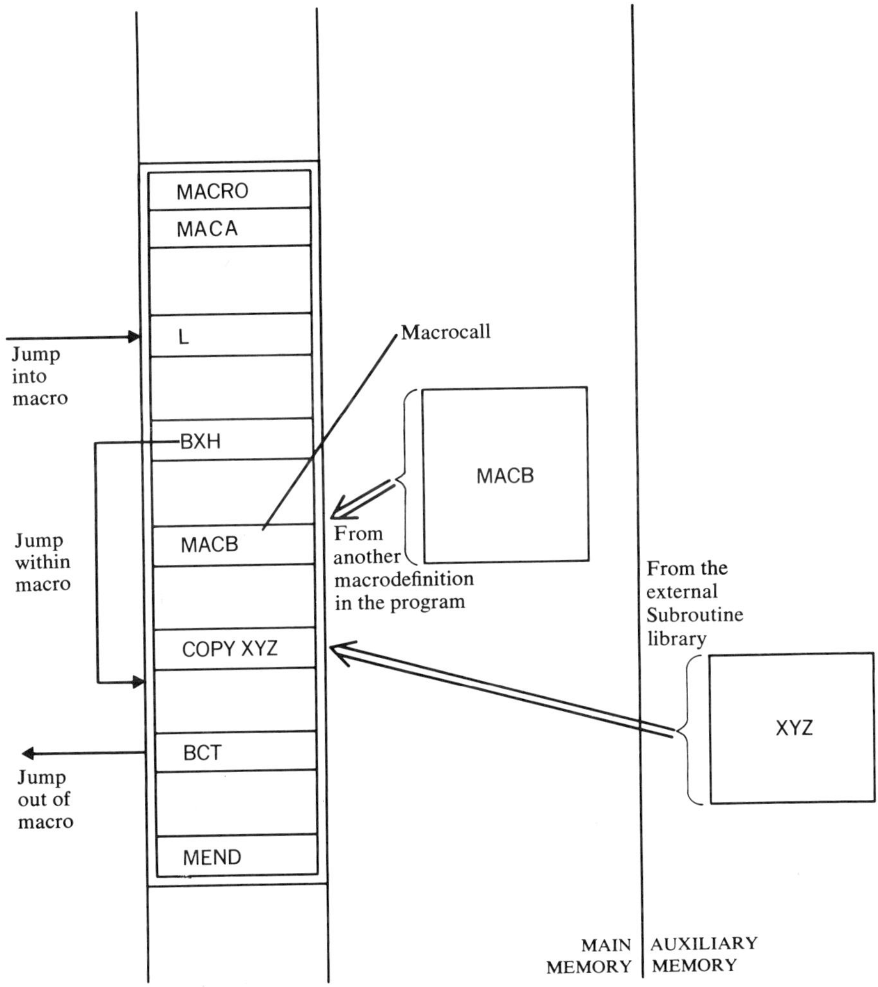

Fig. 8.2.1 Entries, exits, and sources of code for macros.

* It is possible to jump to a point outside the macro in the main program. The programmer has control of this but must take precautions.

JUMP INTO

Although it is possible but difficult for the programmer to jump into a closed subroutine, the technique for him to get into the middle of a macro is to use a global label for one of the model statements. The programmer must be careful, then, that, if this macro is called more than once, a program switch takes us around the entry or an overdefined symbol results.

CODE FROM PROGRAM

The definer of the macro may call another or inner macro that he has defined. This reproduces a set of code in the outer macro as described in Section 8.1.

CODE FROM OUTSIDE

Using the pseudo, COPY, the definer of a macro may request that code from outside his program be copied into the macrodefinition and hence into the macro whenever it is called. Of course, it is actually copied by the assembler into the *COMTAB* during the macrodefinition incorporation. This function is discussed in more detail later.

Outer macro example

Figure 8.2.2 shows a macrodefinition of QDRT which is to solve a quadratic equation.

```
          SOURCE STATEMENT
                MACRO
&N              QDRT      &A,&B,&C,&R1,&R2,&ER
&N              STM       2,5,28(13)     SAVE
                L         3,&B           PUT B IN 3
                M         2,&B           B SQUARE TO 2
                L         5,&A           A TO 5
                SLA       5,2            4A TO 5
                M         4,&C           4AC TO 5
                LTR       2,2            CHECK OVERFLO
                BNZ       &ER
                LTR       4,4            CHECK OVERFLO
                BP        &ER
                SR        3,5            DISC TO 3
                BM        &ER            DISC IS NEGATIVE
                ST        5,&R1          DISC TO R1
                SQRT      &R1,&R1        ROOT OF DISC TO R1
                SR        2,2            CLEAR 2
                L         5,&B           B TO 5
                LNR       3,5            -B TO 3
                S         3,&R1          -B-ROOT TO 3
                L         4,&A           A TO 4
                SLA       4,1            2A TO 4
                DR        2,4            -B-ROOT/2A TO 3
                ST        3,&R2          STORE R2
                SR        2,2            CLEAR 2
                LNR       3,5            -B TO 3
                A         3,&R1          -B+ROOT TO 3
                DR        2,4            -B+ROOT/2A TO 3
                ST        3,&R1          STORE R1
                LM        2,5,28(13)     UNSAVE
                          MEND
```

Fig. 8.2.2 The macrodefinition of QDRT to find the real roots of a quadratic equation.

The equation is given by

$$ax^2 + bx + c = 0 \tag{8.2.1}$$

and the roots of the equation are given as

$$r_1 = \frac{-b + \sqrt{b^2 - 4ac}}{2a} \tag{8.2.2}$$

$$r_2 = \frac{-b - \sqrt{b^2 - 4ac}}{2a} \tag{8.2.3}$$

There are six arguments in the macrodefinition argument list. The first three are the coefficients of the quadratic equation, a, b, and c; the next two are the roots which are to be found by the macro, r_1 and r_2. This leaves the sixth unaccounted for. Actually, QDRT only finds the real roots of the equation. Should the roots be complex, the macro won't function. It rejects the request.

The first commands of the macro (steps 31–43) are used to calculate the discriminant which is given as

$$\text{DISC} = b^2 - 4ac \tag{8.2.4}$$

The command which makes the final calculation of the discriminant is SR (41). This command sets the condition code according to the sign of the discriminant. Should it be negative, the command BM, *branch negative* (42), takes us out of the macro because the roots are complex.

Notice that the discriminant is stored at one of the locations assigned to the root &RI (42). This removes the need for reserving space within the macro.

After ST, we find SQRT (43), a macrocall for the square root subroutine. Two addresses are transmitted to it. These are identical addresses, namely &R1. Thus, the discriminant is supplied to the subroutine at &R1 and the answer is returned to the same cell, &R1. SQRT is an inner macro which we discuss shortly.

The rest of the commands in the macrodefinition determine the valuc of the two roots and put them away where they are supposed to be: &R2, then &R1.

Inner macro Figure 8.2.3 is the macrodefinition for SQRT, the inner macro for QDRT. First let us put x into GPR2 and GPR3, testing it during the latter with LTR (5). If x is zero, *branch* to the end (6). Also, we do not expect a negative x to be supplied—there is no error exit—in such cases the original x is supplied as the root by a *branch* to the end. One more check is done to see if x is equal to 1 (8–10). The use of &SYNDX, explained later, is apparent here.

```
STMT           SOURCE STATEMENT
  2                   MACRO
  3   &N              SQRT      &X,&R
  4   &N              L         2,&X         PUT X INTO 2
  5                   LTR       3,2
  6                   BZ        M&SYSNDX     X IS ZERO
  7                   BM        M&SYSNDX     X IS NEGATIVE
  8                   LA        4,1          PUT ONE IN 4
  9                   CR        4,3
 10                   BE        M&SYSNDX     X IS ONE
 11                   SRA       3,1          Y IS X/2
 12                   LR        5,3          PUT Y INTO 5
 13                   MR        4,3          YSQUARE TO 5
 14                   LTR       4,4
 15                   BNZ       *-20         YSQUARE TOO BIG
 16   R&SYSNDX        SR        4,4          CLEAR 4
 17                   LR        5,2          X TO 5
 18                   DR        4,3          X/Y TO 5
 19                   SR        5,3          TWO DEL TO 5
 20                   SRA       5,1          DEL TO 5
 21                   AR        3,5          NEW Y TO 3
 22                   LPR       4,5          ABS DEL TO 4
 23                   SRA       4,1          TEST ABS DEL
 24                   BNZ       R&SYSNDX     LOOP
 25   M&SYSNDX        ST        3,&R         STORE RESULT
 26                   MEND
```

Fig. 8.2.3 SQRT.

Before trying the Newton-Rapheson method, we halve x (11) and square it (12, 13), testing the result (14). We are "rooting" an integer; the square of the root should not overflow the double register GPR5 and GPR4. If it does, we return (15) to halve x again.

The Newton-Rapheson method is now begun. We calculate a correction factor, DEL, different from DEL for QDRT, given as

$$\text{DEL} = \tfrac{1}{2}\left(\frac{x}{y} - y\right) \tag{8.2.5}$$

with a few basic operations (16–20). This correction factor is added to the old root value, y_i, to get a new value, y_{i+1} (21), thus:

$$y_{i+1} = y_i + \tfrac{1}{2}\left(\frac{x}{y} - y\right) \tag{8.2.6}$$

We determine whether to begin by testing the magnitude of DEL. Its absolute value (22) is shifted right one bit (23) and if the result is zero we're satisfied. Otherwise we *loop* (24).

The value for the root is put away (25), and that's it (26).

Call QDRT is called in Fig. 8.2.4. ASLR contains a complete copy of QDRT with SQRT nested into it, as explained in the next section. The call appears (517) and you note that some of the parameters are expressions, C+4, C+8, etc. These are correctly defined (783) and referenced by 690, 694, etc. Notice the inner call, SQRT, is absent. It is shaded in the figure. The parameters, both C+12, are passed to it and their address substituted (e.g., 532+). The programmer has no way of knowing which code belongs to SQRT from the printout, which, in actuality, is *not shaded*! He must go back to the definitions to find out.

8.3 NESTING PASS

Function The nesting pass, which I call McNest, resolves inner macros by inserting complete definitions of all inner macros in the outer macrodefinition subtable in *COMTAB*. McNest first finds outer macros, those macros which contain macrocalls. Then, it inserts the definition of the inner macro into the definition of the outer macro as we soon see.

McNest is a separate pass. Well, it's not really a full pass since examination of the entire input stream is not required; McNest examines only all macrodefinitions found in *COMTAB*. Only outer macros are processed.

COMTAB

COMTAB is the collection of command subtables. *COMTAB* (for the BAL ASLR) contains not only macrodefinitions but also the meaning of various pseudos and opcodes. However, these are found in the beginning of *COMTAB* and it should be easy to find the place where macrodefinitions begin.

OPTAB contains a list of all legal opcodes. When an opcode is a macrocall, it points to a place in *COMTAB*. Macrodefinitions also point back to the *OPTAB* so that they can be properly expanded.

Then McNest need only examine those opcodes in subtables of *COMTAB* which are macrocalls.

Scan The scan of *COMTAB* to find nested macros, called ScanN, looks at all macrodefinition opcodes. Each opcode might be looked up separately in *OPTAB*. However, if the opcodes are examined by some other component of ASLR, it could tag them to distinguish macrocalls from other opcodes. If *this* macrodefinition does not contain macrocalls as opcodes, it is left intact and no nesting is done.

```
LOC     OBJECT CODE    ADDR1  ADDR2   STMT  SOURCE STATEMENT
                                      517          QDRT  C,C+4,C+8,C+12,C+16,ER
00031E  9025 D01C             0001C   518+         STM   2,5,28(13) SAVE
000322  5830 C690             00690   519+         L     3,C+4 PUT B IN 3
000326  5C20 C690             00690   520+         M     2,C+4 B - SQUARE TO 2
00032A  5850 C68C             0068C   521+         L     5,C A TO 5
00032E  8B50 0002             00002   522+         SLA   5,2 4A TO 5
000332  5C40 C694             00694   523+         M     4,C+8 4AC TO 5
000336  1222                          524+         LTR   2,2 CHECK OVERFLO
000338  4770 C64A             0064A   525+         BP    ER
00033C  1244                          526+         LTR   4,4 CHECK OVERFLO
00033E  47B0 C64A             0064A   527+         BP    ER
000342  1B35                          528+         SR    3,5 DISC TO 3
000344  4740 C64A             0064A   529+         BM    ER DISC IS NEGATIVE
00034E  5050 C698             00698   530+         ST    5,C+12 DISC TO R1
00034C  5820 C698             00698   531+         L     2,C+12 PUT X INTO 2
000350  1232                          532+         LTR   3,2
000352  4780 C38A             0038A   533+         BZ    M0031 X IS ZERO
000356  4740 C38A             0038A   534+         BM    M0031 X IS NEGATIVE
00035A  4140 0001             00001   535+         LA    4,1(0,0) PUT ONE IN 4
00035E  1943                          536+         CR    4,3
000360  4780 C38A             0038A   537+         BE    M0031 X IS ONE
000364  8A30 0001             00001   538+         SRA   3,1 Y IS X/2
000368  1853                          539+         LR    5,3 PUT Y INTO 5
00036A  1C43                          540+         MR    4,3 YSQUARE TO 5
00036C  1244                          541+         LTR   4,4
00036E  4770 C34A             0032E   542+         BNZ   *-20 YSQUARE TOO BIG
```

```
000372   1B44                      543+R0031  SR    4,4 CLEAR 4
000374   1852                      544+       LR    5,2 X TO 5
000376   1D43                      545+       DR    4,3 X/Y TO 5
000378   1B53                      546+       SR    5,3 TWO DEL TO 5
00037A   8A50  0001       00001    547+       SRA   5,1 DEL TO 5
00037E   1A35                      548+       AR    3,5 NEW Y TO 3
000380   1045                      549+       LPR   4,5 ABS DEL TO 4
000382   8A40  0001       00001    550+       SRA   4,1 TEST ABS DEL
000386   4770  C362       00372    551+       BNZ   R0031 LOOP
00038A   5030  C698       00698    552+M0031  ST    3,C+12 STORE RESULT
000396   1B22                      553+       SR    2,2 CLEAR 2
000398   5850  C690       00690    554+       L     5,C+4 B TO 5
00039C   1135                      555+       LNR   3,5 -B TO 3
00039E   5B30  C698       00698    556+       S     3,C+12 -B-ROOT TO 3
0003A2   5840  C68C       0068C    557+       L     4,C A TO 4
0003A6   8B40  0001       00001    558+       SLA   4,1 2A TO 4
0003AA   1D24                      559+       DR    2,4 -B-ROOT/2A TO 3
0003A4   5030  C69C       00696    560+       ST    3,C+16 STORE R2
0003AC   1B22                      562+       SR    2,2 CLEAR 2
0003AE   1135                      563+       LNR   3,5 -B TO 3
0003B0   5A30  C698       00698    564+       A     3,C+12 -B+ROOT TO 3
0003B4   1D24                      565+       DR    2,4 -B+ROOT/2A TO 3
0003B6   5030  C698       00698    566+       ST    3,C+12 STORE R1
0003B6   9825  D01C       0001C    566+       LM    2,5,28(13) UNSAVE
 ...     ...   ...        ...      ...        ...        ...
00068C   0000271000000000          783   C    DC    F'10000,0,2000'
000698                             784        DS    2F
```

Fig. 8.2.4 Call and expansion of QDRT.

As soon as ScanN finds a macrocall in *COMTAB* and has verified it in *OPTAB* as legal, ScanN turns over control to the nesting or incorporation component, McInc. If an opcode encountered in a macrodefinition is absent from *OPTAB*, this indicates that it was used, but not defined, in the program and is either a system macro or an error.

Identification There are four kinds of macrocalls which might be encountered:

1. a macrodefinition which the programmer has made and which appears before the program proper;
2. a macrodefinition constructed by the programmer at some earlier time, and for which the definition has been placed in the so-called macro library, a predefined macro;
3. A definition supplied by the manufacturer and stored in the system or linkage library;
4. An undefined opcode.

These calls can appear in three places:

- the program,
- a program macrodefinition (nesting),
- a library definition.

COMPONENTS

ScanN consists of the three components:

- ScanD which examines the definitions which precede the program;
- ScanP which scans the main program;
- ScanF which looks for, finds, and holds library and/or system macros in MEMORY.

For simplicity, system and predefined macros for which definitions are in a library are lumped together as library macros.

FINDING

Before we examine the components, Table 8.3.1 conveys which component unearths the calls and which identifies and procures the definition.

Review by ScanN The first scan is actually done by ScanD. ScanD only reviews the definitions which precede the program. Let us posit two tables: *DEFTAB*, which lists all the definitions encountered, and *CALLTAB*, which lists all calls which are unaccounted for—which are not named in *DEFTAB*. Then ScanD's job is *just* to list all programmer definitions as encountered in *DEFTAB* and nonopcodes in *CALLTAB*.

Table 8.3.1 FINDING MACRODEFINITIONS

Opcode	*In*	*Found by*	*Identified by*
Macrocall	Macrodefinition	Scan𝔇	Scan𝓕†
	Program	Scan𝔗	Scan𝓕†
	Library definition	Unlikely	—
Library call	Macrodefinition	Scan𝔇	Scan𝓕
	Program	Scan𝔗	Scan𝓕
	Library definition	Scan𝓕	Scan𝓕
Error	Macrodefinition	Scan𝔇	Scan𝓕‡
	Program	Scan𝔇	Scan𝓕‡
	Library definition	None	—

† Before.
‡ After.

Scan𝔗 can be viewed as a continuation of Scan𝔇: the program is reviewed and nonopcodes entered in *CALLTAB*.

The entries in *CALLTAB* and *DEFTAB* are reconciled: calls in *DEFTAB* are removed so that *DEFTAB* contains only calls undefined in the program. This can be done "on the run" or separately after Scan𝔗. The remaining calls in *CALLTAB* *should* be in the library. ℜecon

Library and system macros are looked up by Scan𝓕 in the library, probably using BLDL (see Chapter 14). As each is found, its definition is placed in *COMTAB*. But each command is checked by Scan𝓕 since calls may appear in *these* definitions. They obviously are not likely to be programmer defined. It's possible, though: the programmer may wish to override an inner system or library macro. Scan𝓕

Calls in library macros are put in *CALLTAB* to await lookup. Thus, although *DEFTAB* will grow, *CALLTAB* will always diminish. However, when Scan𝓕 is done, *CALLTAB* *should* be empty. Anything left is an error. Errors may appear in macrodefinition calls, program calls, but are unlikely in library calls.

8.4 INCORPORATION

𝓜c𝔍nc incorporates the definition of macros into the definition of outer macros, making a composite definition for the macro in *COMTAB*.

Example Suppose that MACA is an outer macro which contains MACB and MACC, as shown in Fig. 8.1.1. MACB contains the

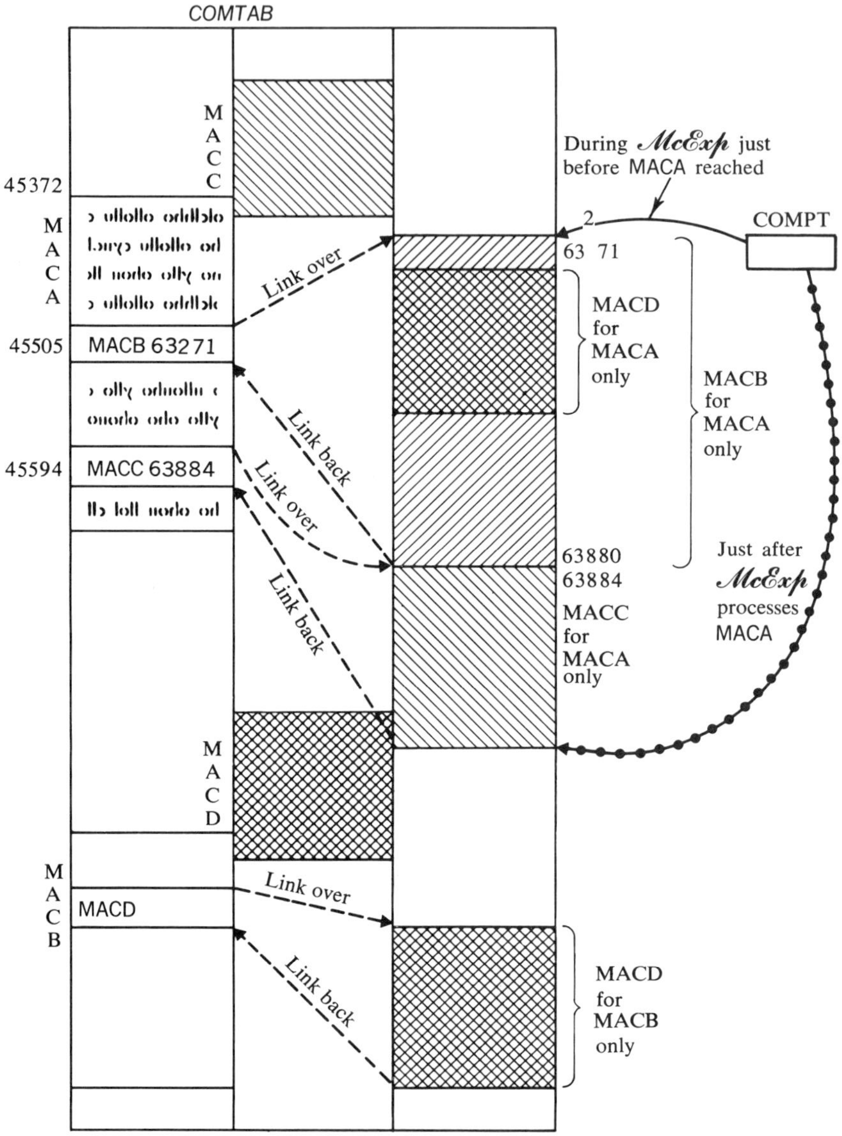

Fig. 8.4.1 The resolution of MACA in *COMTAB*.

second level inner macro MACD. When ScanN' encounters the call MACB in the definition of MACA, it turns over control to McInc. It is up to McInc to *rewrite* the definition of MACA. It can do this in two ways:

- It can rewrite the entire expanded macro in a new section of *COMTAB*.
- It can link to a new section of *COMTAB*, rewrite the MACB portion of MACA there, and link back to the MACA definition.

The latter method does not waste space in *COMTAB* and saves time by not rewriting material already written. The result is shown in Fig. 8.4.1.

McInc does three things to initialize the activity:

- It finds the next empty area in *COMTAB* pointed to be COMPT.
- It links to this area from the macrodefinition of MACA.
- It finds the macrodefinition of MACB.

Now McInc should copy the definition of MACB into the new area of *COMTAB*. However, observe that when MACB is called

- MACB has a parameter list associated with it;
- a parameter for MACB can run the gamut of possibilities including
  * arguments from MACA,
  * normal symbols,
  * literals;
- McInc substitutes the parameters supplied in the MACB call into the arguments of the MACB definition, which is then incorporated into the MACA definition.

Finally, McInc should be alert for other higher level (inner) macrocalls as it expands an inner such as MACB, below.

Higher level macros In Fig. 8.1.1, MACD is called within the definition of MACB. During the MACA resolution of MACB, the MACD call is encountered, checked and validated by McInc as it is writing out MACB in the new portion of *COMTAB*. McInc continues in this area of *COMTAB* by writing out the definition of MACD just as it was doing for MACB. Again, parameters supplied in the call of MACB replace arguments in the definition of MACD as it is being written out. When the definition of MACD is complete (incorporated in MACA), McInc returns to writing out the definition of MACB. When the definition of MACB is complete, a link is inserted to return us to the definition table for MACA in the original area of the *COMTAB*.

McInc continues to scan MACA for other inner macros. When MACC is found, its definition is resolved by a link to the next portion of *COMTAB*, where the definition of MACB (and MACD) was left. Links to and from this MACC table *for MACA only* are constructed. Note that definitions for MACB, MACC and MACD are maintained in *COMTAB*, for calls to them may appear elsewhere in the program and those rewritten copies (which have parameters) *cannot* be used.

Completion McInc continues the scan of the definition of MACA until MEND indicates that the MACA definition is now finished. ScanN then continues to review *COMTAB* looking for macrodefinitions containing macrocalls.

It is important to note that when ScanN encounters MACB independently, before or after MACA, it is resolved separately. MACB is an independent macro which may appear as a call in the program. There parameters from the program call passed from MACB to MACD may be different from those passed to MACD when MACB is a part of MACA.

Hence, when MACB is encountered by ScanN, a new portion of *COMTAB* is appropriated and used to insert MACD as called for when associated with MACB alone.

Generation The reader may wonder why the nesting or resolution is done separately (by McNest) and not included in the generation when the call is expanded (by McGen). McGen is complicated by the many features incorporated to make conditional assembly possible (Chapter 10). These make McGen both large and logically involved. But there are other equally important problems which detract from the desirability of including McNest in McGen (dynamic resolution) such as

- keeping track of the levels of inner macros;
- managing exit and return points of lower level macros;
- handling illegalities at higher levels while maintaining proper generation;
- reinitializing the generator when exiting from high levels;
- passing parameters, arguments, and literals to higher and lower levels;
- *branching* within and between levels.

McGen

Returning to this scheme and Fig. 8.4.1, we investigate how generation is done. When a call appears in the AL program, ScanG detects this from its tag and turns over control to McGen. An *OPTAB* search takes it to *COMTAB* at MACA (45372) where it begins to enter code into the intermediate AL program.

Eventually McGen encounters the link replacing MACB (63271). Code generation for MACB (and MACD) proceeds to completion (63880) where another link appears, this one to the continuation of MACA (45503).

Generation continues until another link appears (45594) to the code for MACC (43884) which McGen inserts, and so forth.

Example In Fig. 8.2.2 we defined the macro QDRT which required the square root defined as the macro SQRT presented in Fig. 8.2.3. An example of a call of QDRT and its resolution was presented in Fig. 8.2.4. It would serve no purpose to duplicate this. McNest creates a definition equivalent to this, except that the shaded section in Fig. 8.2.4 might be written in a separate section of *COMTAB* with a link to it at its beginning and a return to the original definition upon completion.

The definition of SQRT in the QDRT definition refers to arguments. During the call of QDRT, six parameters appear in the *PARTAB* for QDRT. It is these parameters to which the SQRT part of the definition refers. In fact, from Fig. 8.2.2 we find that the parameter for the argument &R1 is the only one referred to in the SQRT part.

Notice that &N is used in both definitions. The name it conveys depends on where it is found. Suppose that SQRT in the definition of QDRT is named CALLRT. Then everytime QDRT is called, the first command produced will have CALLRT for its name. ASLR will reject this STM as a multiply defined symbol.

8.5 RELATION TO OTHER COMPONENTS

Macro components ScanD accepts the macrodefinition and places it into *COMTAB* as we have seen in Chapter 7. This must necessarily precede ScanN. The nesting should be resolved before the calls are expanded. Hence, ScanN precedes ScanE. However, if a rescan were used to replace label references by self-relative addresses, it would occur before calls were expanded, but after nesting is resolved, and, hence, goes between ScanN and ScanE.

ScanD As each opcode is incorporated into *COMTAB*, ScanD can perform an additional function by tagging macrocalls. Now when ScanN comes along and examines the *COMTAB* it can speed right along until it notices an opcode which is tagged as a macrocall—it need not reference *OPTAB* for any other opcode.

Rescan Rescan (not used in the BAL ASLR) would make label reference self-relative. When an inner macro is resolved, it generally goes in the middle of another macro. References to labels past the inner macro to commands which precede the inner macro must be counted so as to include all the commands that appear in the inner macro-definition. Hence, the 𝔑𝔢𝔰𝔠𝔞𝔫 could only be done after resolution of the inner macros.

Assembler In general, one effective way to design 𝒜𝒮ℒℛ is to have all the components concerned with macros operate in the first few passes. The result is assembly language code which would have been produced if the programmer had used open subroutines instead of macros. This can now be assembled as though it were simple symbolic assembly language. Incidentally, conditional assembly commands which we examine later, can be handled during the macroresolution operations.

PROBLEMS

8.1 What is macrodefinition nesting? Describe some provisions in the 𝒜𝒮ℒℛ for providing this feature.

8.2 (a) What is dynamic resolution of macros?
(b) Why might the programmer find it useful? Give some examples.
(c) Describe some provisions required in 𝒜𝒮ℒℛ for dynamic resolution.

8.3 (a) What is a self-calling macro?
(b) Why would one use one?

8.4 Write a cube root macro, CBRT, similar to SQRT except that the correction factor, CDEL, is given by

$$\text{CDEL} = \frac{1}{3}\left(\frac{x^2}{y} - y\right),$$

and the new value for y is given as

$$y_{i+1} = y_i + \text{CDEL}.$$

8.5 We need a macro to solve the cubic

$$y^3 + py^2 + qy + r = 0.$$

It can be solved by converting it into

$$x^3 + ax + b = 0$$

where

$$a = \tfrac{1}{3}(3q - p^2) \text{ and } b = 1/27(2p^3 - 9pq + 27r).$$

For the solution let

$$A = \sqrt[3]{-\frac{b}{2} + \sqrt{\frac{b^2}{4} + \frac{a^3}{27}}}\,;\ B = \sqrt[3]{-\frac{b}{2} - \sqrt{\frac{b^2}{4} + \frac{a^3}{27}}}\,.$$

First write an inner macro to find a and b called thus:

FINDAB p,q,r,a,b.

Next write a macro for A and B called thus:

BIGAB p,q,r,x.

Use doubleWord fixed arithmetic. Use SQRT and CBRT where

$$X = A + B$$

as defined in the text and Prob. 8.4.

8.6 Define TOTHRD to find $y = x^{2/3}$ using CBRT.

8.7 Explain why the BAL ASLR uses a separate nesting pass. Explain how the full macro is expanded with *COMTAB*, discussing the manipulation of pointers such as COMPT, etc.

8.8 Explain how library and system macros are used as inner macro. How does ASLR find the definitions? Where are they? Do the definitions get into *COMTAB*, and, if so, how?

8.9 How does ASLR know which opcodes are:
(a) programmer macrodefinitions;
(b) library macros;
(c) errors;
(d) opcodes;
(e) pseudos;
(f) system macros?

8.10 (a) When are macrocalls *in the program* replaced by code?
(b) Is it AL or ML code?
(c) Where does the code come from?

9

OTHER MACRO FEATURES

9.1 CONCATENATION

Introduction **Concatenation** is placing two or more strings of characters (letters, etc.) together. For macros this means placing characters from different sources together in the same line of a model statement.

The main application of concatenation is to combine information coming in from a macrocall appearing in its parameter list with information arriving by way of the macrodefinition. Concatenation can be applied to any field of a model statement.

Need Concatenation is the only way to make some kinds of improvements on model statements so that they are alterable from one call to the next. We shall discuss the following uses for concatenation:

- forming a single symbol from two arguments,
- forming a *symbol* from an argument and a fixed string in a model statement,
- forming an *expression* from an argument and a fixed string for model statement.

Multiargument symbols One application of multiargument symbols is when the programmer knows that all symbols of a certain kind are prefixed with a fixed string. Suppose all fields which he might move about with the move macrocall, MOVE2, have the same prefix. He need not provide the prefix at macrodefinition time. He might create a simple macro which supplies the prefix thus:

```
        MACRO
&N      MOVE2     &PRE,&TO,&FROM
&N      L         2,&PRE&FROM          (9.1.1)
        ST        2,&PRE&TO
        MEND
```

To apply this to two fields named F1 and F4, he would give the macrocall at M specifying the prefix by F and the suffices as 1 and 4 thus:

```
M       MOVE2     F,1,4                (9.1.2)
```

The code that this call produces is

```
M       L         2,F1
        ST        2,F4                 (9.1.3)
```

Notice that to concatenate two arguments in (9.1.1) the arguments are simply placed next to each other at *location*.

Arguments and fixed symbols If an argument and a string of characters are to be concatenated, a period separates the argument name from the fixed string. For instance, suppose we were going to move a field from one area in MEMORY to another. Suppose also that the source field bears the suffix FROM and the destination bears the suffix TO. The only argument in the macrodefinition is the prefix to the field names. We define the macro MOVE3 thus:

```
        MACRO
&N      MOVE3     &P
&N      L         2,&P.FROM            (9.1.4)
        ST        2,&P.TO
```

Notice that the compound source field name in the model statement appears as &P.FROM When the macro is called,

- the parameter will be substituted for &P,
- the period will be removed,
- FROM will be appended to the parameter.

For instance, we might call the macro thus:

```
P       MOVE3     A                    (9.1.5)
```

producing the following code:

```
P        L        2,AFROM
         ST       2,ATO          (9.1.6)
```

As another example, consider concatenating an argument with a string of symbols to produce an expression. Define a macro ADVNC which moves a Word (on a boundary) ahead four bytes in MEMORY to the next Word boundary. We are furnished with a symbolic location of the Word to be advanced. The position to which it is moved is four greater than this. The macro ADVNC is defined thus:

```
         MACRO
&N       ADVNC    &X
&N       L        2,&X           (9.1.7)
         ST       2,&X.+2
         MEND
```

We might use it in a call thus:

```
Q        ADVNC    HERE           (9.1.8)
```

to produce the code

```
Q        L        2,HERE
         ST       2,HERE+4       (9.1.9)
```

Another example Let us design another macro, this one to advance a number of Words, each a single Word position in MEMORY. The starting position of the set of Words and a location containing the number of Words to be moved are the first and second parameters in the call. The macro is named ADVN and appears in Fig. 9.1.1. It is presented without explanation as a challenge to the reader.

```
         MACRO
&NAME    ADVN     &W,&N
&NAME    L        6,&N
         SLA      6,2
         L        5,&N
         L        4,&W.-4(6)
         ST       4,&W.(6)
         S        6,=H'4'
         BCT      5,*-12
         MEND
```

Fig. 9.1.1 The macro, ADVN.

Implementation Concatenation requires only a properly tagged *COMTAB* entry. The argument has been replaced by the argument number. However, prefixes and suffixes to the argument are indicated and tagged with the *COMTAB* entry. When a call is expanded by McGen, the entire string is worked upon. The parameter is obtained from *PARTAB*, replacing the argument number in the entry. The prefix and suffix are concatenated, removing periods, where appropriate.

9.2 ARGUMENTS AS COMMANDS

Argument fields Any legal argument which appears in *location* of the prototype statement can be used in any position of a model statement. Thus an argument can be used at *label*, *opcode*, or *location*. We now examine the use of an argument at *opcode*.

This is a powerful facility but it has an important limitation as far as BAL ASLR is concerned—if an argument in a model statement is used as an opcode, the parameter we substitute for it may be only a mnemonic or a pseudo *but never a marcocall*. As discussed earlier, this limitation is imposed because the resolution of nested macros is static rather than dynamic. The manufacturer has decided that the added complexity for dynamic nesting does not pay for its advantage to the programmer.

Use We examine the use of command arguments by a simple example which is necessarily synthetic. A more realistic example would be unjustifiably complicated.

Suppose that we wish to post from one field in a transaction record into a field of a master record. We might determine whether we add or subtract from the master record according to the type of transaction record. The type of transaction may in turn be determined by some flag within the record. Assume that this is done before the macro, POSTW, is used. This macro is then defined by

```
        MACRO
&N      POSTW     &C,&FROM,&TO
&N      L         6,&TO
        &C        6,&FROM                (9.2.1)
        ST        6,&TO
        MEND
```

Suppose now that we withdraw items from inventory and wish to subtract. The argument, &C, conveys the command to be performed by the macro. We then give the call

```
R        POSTW    S,OUT,SHELF                (9.2.2)
```

When the macro is expanded, the code produced appears as

```
R        L        6,SHELF
         S        6,OUT                      (9.2.3)
         ST       6,SHELF
```

Here the subtract command, S, appears in *opcode* of the second command produced.

With concatenation Sometimes, instead of specifying an entire opcode, we may wish to specify only a portion thereof. Then concatenation can occur in *opcode* of a model statement.

As a simple example as how this might be done, we examine the macro, ADDT. This adds two numbers from named positions and places the result in a third named position. However, although the numbers must be of the same type, this type may differ from one call to the next. The type is specified as an argument in the macrodefinition at &T. The macrodefinition appears as

```
         MACRO
&N       ADDT     &T,&A,&B,&C
&N       L&T      2,&A
         A&T      2,&B                       (9.2.4)
         ST&T     2,&C
         MEND
```

The argument &T is a suffix for the opcodes which comprise the command. According to its specification in the call, we could request halfWord or fullWord fixed arithmetic or full- or doubleWord floating point arithmetic.

For instance for halfWord arithmetic we might give a macrocall thus:

```
S        ADDT     H,SUM,X,SUM                (9.2.5)
```

This is expanded as

```
S        LH       2,SUM
         AH       2,X                        (9.2.6)
         STH      2,SUM
```

An interesting variation arises when we request fullWord arithmetic. Now the suffix should be eliminated. This can be done by omitting the parameter which would ordinarily appear at &T which is the first argument position of *loc*. We must include the comma which is associated with this parameter, however. A typical macrocall, then, appears as

```
T     ADDT     ,A1,A2,A3
```
(9.2.7)

which is expanded as

```
T     L        2,A1
      A        2,A2
      ST       2,A3
```
(9.2.8)

Look what would happen if the comma were omitted and we gave

```
T1    ADDT     A1,A2,A3
```
(9.2.9)

We would get

```
T1    LA1      2,A2
      AA1      2,A3
      STA1     2,
```
(9.2.10)

Implementation Again, it is the *COMTAB* which implements variable opcodes. If the opcode field of the model statement is an argument or uses concatenation, it is so tagged and the argument is replaced by the argument number by McDef.

When the call is examined by McGen, the argument number is replaced by the parameter from *PARTAB*. If concatenation is specified, this is done as described earlier.

9.3 KEYWORDS

Technique We have examined positional notation for transmitting parameters from the main program to the expanded macro. In this format the call contains the parameters in exactly the same sequence as the macrodefinition contains the arguments.

The keyword method of naming parameters permits the caller to use the name of the argument followed by =, after which appears the symbolic name of the parameter which replaces the named argument.

For the macrodefinition to convey the keyword to McDef, the following format is used:

&keyword=default (9.3.1)

This combination appears in every keyword parameter field in the prototype statement. Here *keyword* is the name of the argument. *Default* is the parameter to be used if an expression comparable to (9.3.1) is missing in the call. If "=*default*" is absent, $\mathcal{ASLR}$ performs no default substitution and omits this argument (or parameter) instead. When the macro is called, the programmer writes for each one of the parameters

keyword=value (9.3.2)

where *value* is the symbolic name of the parameter to substitute for the argument, for *keyword*, and the arguments may be named in *any* order.

Notice in (9.3.1) that *default* may appear at *value* where $\mathcal{ASLR}$ uses *default* as the parameter for the omitted *keyword*. This is the same as if (9.32) is omitted for this argument.

Examples We examine a macro, ADDK3, which adds three numbers together, replacing the last number by the result. The macro permits a register to be named for performing the addition and also permits a type to be associated with each of the opcodes. ADDK3 is defined thus:

```
        MACRO
&N      ADDK3     &R=6,&T=H,&A=,&B=,&C=
&N      L&T       &R,&A
        A&T       &R,&B                       (9.3.3)
        A&T       &R,&C
        ST&T      &R,&C
        MEND
```

Notice that defaults are supplied for &R and &T but not &A, &B, nor &C.

CALL

This macro is called at U with

```
U       ADDK3     A=X1,T=E,B=X2,R=4,C=X3      (9.3.4)
```

Notice that the order in which the parameters are named is immaterial. Obviously, this is one advantage gained by the keyword method. The resulting code produced is given as

```
U       LE        4,X1
        AE        4,X2
        AE        4,X3                        (9.3.5)
        STE       4,X3
```

When the keyword is omitted from the call, McGen replaces the argument by *default* of (9.3.1). In the macrodefinition for ADDK3 of (9.3.3) there were two arguments for which a default was specified. The omission of any other argument will cause a null string to replace that argument and that command will have a missing operand address thereby probably causing an assembly error. DEFAULT

Let us see an example of a call using the default option:

```
V       ADDK3       B=C,T=,A=C,C=A                (9.3.6)
```

Since no register is requested, GPR6 is used by McGen in expanding the macrocall. Another feature in this call is the appearance of T=. This is not a default but indicates that the argument, &T, should be replaced by *no* character. T is the type specifier and is used as a suffix for *opcode*. It is proper to omit this suffix in fullWord commands. Hence, the code produced by (9.3.6) is

```
V       L           6,C
        A           6,C
        A           6,A                           (9.3.7)
        ST          6,A
```

Mixed mode For BAL it's possible to mix keywords and positional arguments. If that is done, the positional arguments must precede the keyword arguments of the prototype statement of the macrodefinition.

Figure 9.3.1 is an example, a macrodefinition for ADDKN which adds a list of numbers together. It includes a loop within its structure. Notice that all keyword arguments contain defaults. EXAMPLE

```
        MACRO
&N      ADDKN       &LIST,&SUM,&R=4,&N=3,&C=5
&N      LH          &C,Y(&N-1)
        LR          &C+1,&C
        MH          &C+1,=H'4'
        LE          &R,&LIST
        AE          &R,&LIST.(&C+1)
        S           &C+1,=F'4'
        BCT         &C,*  4
        STE         &R,&SUM
        MEND
```

Fig. 9.3.1 Definition of ADDKN.

Call A typical call of an ADDKN appears in Fig. 9.3.2. Positional parameters must be in their proper position, whereas the keywords can be in any order *after* the positional parameters. Notice that one of the arguments named in this call happens to correspond to one of the parameters named in the list—no problem.

A call of ADDKN is expanded with two default options in Fig. 9.3.2.

```
                                     80  W     ADDKN   N,S,R=2
0004A   4850   20EA    000EA         81+W      LH      5,=Y(3-1)
0004E   1865                         82+       LR      5+1,5
00050   4C60   20E8    000E8         83+       MH      5+1,=H'4'
00054   7820   20C0    000C0         84+       LE      2,N
00058   7A66   20C0    000C0         85+       AE      2,N(5+1)
0005C   5B60   20E0    000E0         86+       S       5+1=F'4'
00060   4650   2058    00058         87+       BCT     5,*-8
00064   7020   20CC    000CC         88+       STE     2,S

000C0   0000000100000002             107  N    DC      F'1,2,3'
000CC                                108  S    DS      F

000E8   0004                         114               =H'4'
000EA   0002                         115               =Y(3-1)
```

Fig. 9.3.2 An expansion of ADDKN.

Implementation Positional parameters are placed in *PARTAB* as for any other macro. Whereas arguments have been replaced by the argument number in the *COMTAB* entry, a keyword argument is maintained along with its default.

After positional parameters have been entered in *PARTAB*, the remaining keyword parameters are entered in their entirety so that both the keyword and its value appear in *PARTAB*.

Now when McGen comes into play, it handles positional parameters as it always has. When it comes to an entry in the *COMTAB* using a keyword, that keyword is also found in the entry. McGen goes to *PARTAB* and examines all keyword entries to see if the desired one is present:

- If so, it makes the appropriate substitution.
- If the keyword is present and *blank*, *blank* is also substituted into this entry for expansion.
- If the keyword is missing from *PARTAB*, McGen looks for a default option in the *COMTAB* entry.
  - * If one is present, it is used.
  - * If none is present, a null string is substituted.

9.4 LISTS

Definition Any argument which appears in the prototype statement of a macrodefinition may be a list. A list argument is not distinguishable in the prototype statement from any other argument. It can only be distinguished in a model statement where it is followed by a parenthesized number, the ordinal number of the desired member of the list. McDef does not need to distinguish if this operand is a single argument or a member of the list. It need only note the complete argument in *COMTAB* as it is encountered.

Call time At call time, each parameter is entered into *PARTAB*. Entries in *PARTAB* are necessarily of variable length so that parameter lists can be accommodated. If a parameter *is* a list, it is surrounded by parentheses and contains symbols set off by commas.

During expansion, McGen may encounter a command accompanied by a list argument in *COMTAB* which is distinguished by the terminal parenthesized number. It goes to this entry in *PARTAB* and looks for the initial parenthesis. It counts the symbols by the demarcating commas. On reaching the proper ordinally numbered symbol, it replaces the argument with that symbol.

Examples A few examples should make clear how one might use the list technique. We define a macro, ADD3L, to add three items from a list, returning the same to the last list item.

```
        MACRO
&X      ADD3L     &N
&X      L         7,&N(1)
        A         7,&N(2)                 (9.4.1)
        A         7,&N(3)
        ST        7,&N(3)
        MEND
```

Here the argument &N is obviously a list; McDef need not know this however.

Let us now call ADD3L, supplying it with a list of the proper length, namely three items.

```
A       ADD3L     (X,Y,Z)                 (9.4.2)
```

This is expanded as we might expect thus:

```
A    L     7,X
     A     7,Y
     A     7,Z                    (9.4.3)
     ST    7,Z
```

Missing list member It is permissible on occasion to omit one or more members in the parameter list, replacing the member by a comma. McGen will enter a blank in the model statement for which an operand or opcode is missing. Let us now call ADD3L, leaving out one of the parameters.

```
B    ADD3L    (X,,Z)              (9.4.4)
```

This has a parameter omitted but the code produced makes no sense. The line which would normally add the second parameter has a blank in the output and the result is, hence,

```
B    L     7,X
     A     7,
     A     7,Z                    (9.4.5)
     ST    7,Z
```

This will assemble but an error will be noted with a severity coding to show that "it probably will not execute."

No list Suppose, in calling the macro ADD3L which requires a list, we make a mistake and use the symbol instead. McGen uses this parameter for the first member of the required list. All other members of the required list will have blank operands. As an example, observe the call

```
C    ADD3L    X                   (9.4.6)
```

This produces code which really makes no sense in the program; namely,

```
C    L     7,X
     A     7,                     (9.4.7)
     A     7,
     ST    7,
```

which will certainly not execute.

9.5 SYSTEM INDEX AND LIST

Function The system index is merely a counter which is tallied after each macrocall whether for an outer or inner macro. It is the means for making symbolic references local instead of global. This is done by concatenating &SYSNDX with any symbol in the macrodefinition. The result is that at call time, the symbol has appended to it the contents of the system index counter. Since this counter remains constant during any given call, the symbol is also constant during expansion of that call but will be different with its occurrence in another macrocall.

Example The use of the system index is best explained with an example. We define a macro ADDNF to add a list of numbers in Fig. 9.5.1. However, instead of making the command BCT operate self-

```
40                     MACRO
41   &NAME             ADDNF     &L,&N,&S
42   &NAME             STM       2,4,28(13)
43                     LA        2,&N—1
44                     SR        3,3
45                     L         4,&L.(3)
46   ADD&SYSNDX        A         4,&L+4(3)
47                     LA        3,4(3)
48                     BCT       2,ADD&SYSNDX
49                     ST        4,&S
50                     LM        2,4,28(13)
51                     MEND
```

Fig. 9.5.1 The macro ADDNF.

relatively, we have it reference a labeled model statement.

Notice that at *name* for A is ADD&SYSNDX. This concatenates ADD with the present contents of the system index. Notice also on the previous line (45) that we have an indexed symbolic reference given as &L.(3). This means of displaying the operand concatenates (3) with the parameter supplied by the macrocall for ADDNF. Notice that if this operand appeared as &L(3), McGen would look for a list at the position &L, expecting to find the list there and wishing to use the third parameter of that list.

Call Suppose that we called ADDNF at HERE as in Fig. 9.5.2, when the system index was set to 0004. Then we would find the label for 95+ to be formed by concatenating ADD and 0004. This is also the case at *loc* of 97+. Hence, the BCT takes us to the proper line of the expanded code. The suffix to ADD only applies locally.

```
90  HERE        ADDNF     A,5,6
91+             STM       2,4,28(13)
92+             LA        2,5-1
93+             SR        3,3
94+             L         4,A(3)
95+ADD0004      A         4,A+4(3)
96+             LA        3,4(3)
97+             BCT       2,ADD0004
98+             ST        4,C
99+             LM        2,4,28(13)
```

Fig. 9.5.2 An expansion of ADDNF.

Suppose that we gave another call when the system index was set to 0036; namely,

```
        NOW          ADDNF SET,4,TOT    (9.5.1)
```

Then we would have

```
NOW+16    ADD0036    A      SET (3)       (9.5.2)
                     LA     3,4(3)
NOW+24               BCT    2,ADD0036     (9.5.3)
```

Nesting The system index reflects the ordered number of the macrocall as encountered in the total number of calls expanded by McGen. Thus as McGen goes inward in nested calls, the index should increase; conversely, as it returns to outer callers, the index reduces. Figure 9.5.3 illustrates this.

As we examine the figure, let us think of *one* way of implementing this need:

- Each level resolved is so labeled in *COMTAB*.
- Counter SI holds the present value of SYSNDX.
- Counter SM holds the maximum value of SYSNDX recalled so far.
- There is one counter for each level for SYSNDX, namely, SL1, SL2, etc.

At M1, (SI) = (SM) = (SL1) = 94. M2 is called so that (SL2) = (SI) = (SM) = 95. It calls M3 so that (SL3) = (SI) = (SM) = 96. M3 returns to M2, (SI) = (SL2) = 95. M2 returns to M1 so that (SI) = (SL1) = 94.

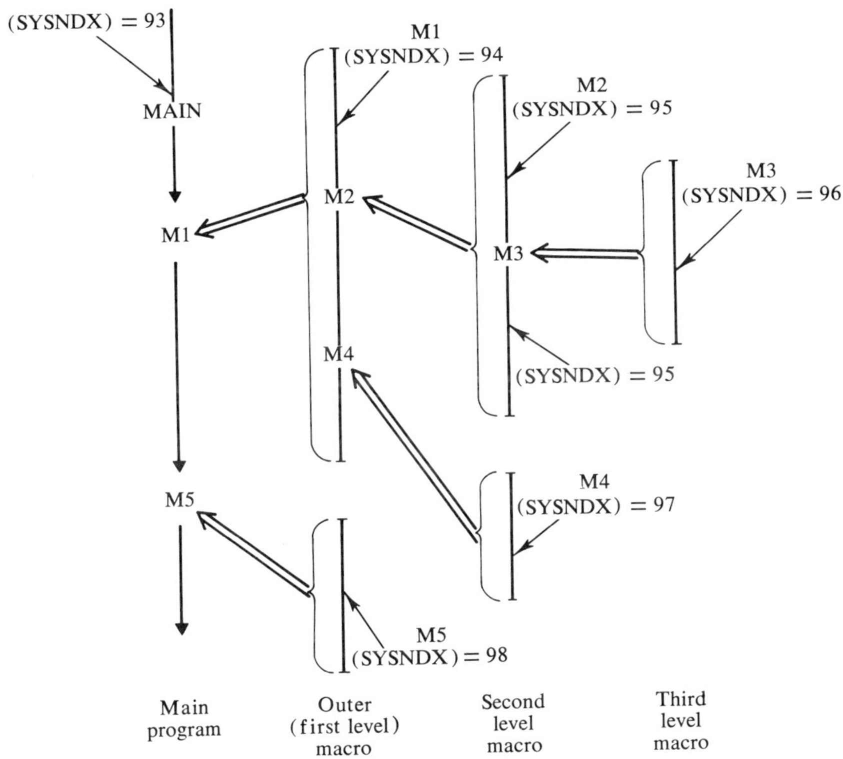

Fig. 9.5.3 Setting and resetting of SYSNDX as McGen passes from one level to another of a nested macro.

Now M1 calls M4. (SI) = (SL2) = (SM) + 1 = 97 = (SM); we add 1 to the old maximum and use that for the current SYSNDX as well as for the level 2 SYSNDX. On return to M1, (SI) = (SL) = 94. On return to the program, the SYSNDX is reset to one more than the maximum resolved.

Entry During McGen when macros are resolved, SYSNDX is set up, used, and labels referencing it are filled in in final form. Trails are left by McNest so that McGen "knows" when it is going to a higher level because of a call or to a lower level because of a return.

System list Sometimes it is desired to address the parameter list—the set of parameters furnished with call and/or definition—by **ordinality**—using the *number* of the parameter. &SYSLIST is a special symbol which enlists the aid of 𝒜𝒮ℒℛ in doing this. It must include a number provided in parentheses directly following &SYSLIST, e.g. &SYSLIST(3).

Examine a sample call:

```
29    HERE    MACX    A,B,(C1,C2,C3),D        (9.5.4)
```

Then we have

```
&SYSLIST(2)=B        (9.5.5)
&SYSLIST(4)=D        (9.5.6)
N'&SYSLIST=4         (9.5.7)
```

To get the last item in the parameter first, we use SET symbols discussed in the next chapter

```
&N    SETA    N'&SYSLIST
&X    SETC    &SYSLIST(&N)        (9.5.8)
      L       4,&X LOADS D
```

Double subscripting procures parameters from parameter sublists—parameters which are themselves lists. This is as far as we go, since subsublists are not permitted. We have for (9.5.4) above

```
N'&SYSLIST(3,1)=C1      (9.5.9)
&SYSLIST(3)=3           (9.5.10)
&SYSLIST(3,3)=C3        (9.5.11)
```

To get at characters in the parameter list, we can use substring notation:

```
&W    SETC    &SYSLIST(3)          (9.5.12)
&C    SETC    '&W'(1,1) &C=(
```

Example Observe the use of &SYSLIST for adding an *open* list of numbers in Fig. 9.5.4. The *add* at .A addresses the *i*th item in the list; the rest is explained in Chapter 10.

```
        MACRO
&NA     ADDOLIST    &L
        LCLA        &I,&N
&N      SETA        N'&SYSLIST
&I      SETA        &N-1
&NA     SR          6,6
.A      A           6,&SYSLIST(&I)
&I      SETA        &I-1
        AIF         ('&I'  GT  '0').A
        ST          6,&SYSLIST(&N)
        MEND
```

Fig. 9.5.4 ADDOLIST adds an open list, placing the result at the last parameter address.

PROBLEMS

9.1 We find &A(4) in some model statement in the macrodefinition of DEFA, and &B.(4) in DEFB.

(a) What does each expand into upon call?

(b) How does ASLR know the difference between them?

(c) How does ASLR handle each?

9.2 If the call MCROW A,B produces the AL statement A S,RADBC, and MCROW I,I produces A S,RIDIC, how might the prototype and the model containing the *add* statement appear in the definition?

9.3 Write a macro to produce storage with the concatenated name NEW, *first*, *second*, and with length equal to the sum of *first* and *second*, and with call MAKENEW first, second.

9.4 Define ADDLK where *list* is a list and the macro is called thus:

```
ADDLK     list,sum R=accno,F=fprno,
```

and the size of *list* is determined with &SYLIST. Use defaults.

9.5 Convert ADDF into a keyword macro, ADDFK. Use defaults.

9.6 Write ADDLISTK in keyword form, specifying also the REGISTER to be used, and *sum* the replace for result.

9.7 Write ADPLISTK for a list of packed numbers with the result to go to *sum*. Assume all locations are defined to be of compatible length.

9.8 Write ADPACK to add *num* packed numbers, each *length* long, into *sum* called thus:

```
ADPACK     NUM=num,LEN=length,SUM=sum.
```

10

CONDITIONAL ASSEMBLY

10.1 OVERVIEW

Principle We have examined the definition and call of macros which are fixed in nature—everytime the macro is called, the same code is produced except for the substitution of parameters for arguments. We have seen elaboration of this principle with concatenation and similar devices. But no way has been presented to logically alter macros from one call to the next.

We now examine **conditional assembly**, the ability to request the inclusion or omission of sections of AL code from the ML program. This ability is especially useful for macros, but it is also available anywhere in the main AL program. We define the macro as previously, except that additional statements may cause $\mathcal{ASLR}$ to skip chosen statements according to conditions prevailing at the time of the macrocall.

We note briefly below and examine in more detail later in this chapter some of the things upon which we can make the assembly of specified statements depend:

- static conditions prevailing in the macrodefinition,
- changing conditions which prevail in the assembly language program,
- the nature of parameters supplied in the call,
- calculations made by $\mathcal{ASLR}$ (these calculations are not made by the program).

Mechanism The pseudo which is central to conditional assembly is AIF, the *assembler conditional branch*. It requests that the assembler go to a designated model statement to continue assembly only if the condition specified in the AIF statement prevails; otherwise the next statement after the AIF is examined and acted upon in a normal fashion.

The form of an AIF statement is

AIF condition.sequence (10.1.1)

Here *condition* is a Boolean expression which is evaluated by the assembler when it is encountered. *Sequence* is a designator of a step in the macrodefinition or program.

In later sections we examine the ways that the conditions are formulated and how the sequence number of the desired step is indicated.

Symbols Of almost equal importance with AIF is the intraassembly, or SET symbol. This symbol is set up and defined by the program and is varied within the assembly but it is not present in the output machine language program. These symbols may be defined in three ways, namely,

- arithmetical expressions,
- Boolean expressions,
- character strings.

Another artifice abstracts the attributes of parameters or symbols and uses them as part of the conditions which determine whether model statements are assembled or ignored.

10.2 ATTRIBUTES

Need One way to tailor our macros is according to the attributes of parameters which are supplied by the macrocall. The means for communicating attributes of parameters to the assembler are attribute operators. An **attribute operator,** when applied to a symbol or an argument, produces a description or value of the symbol with respect to the attribute.

The list of attribute operators presented in Table 10.2.1 is explained in the rest of this section.

Let us get a brief preview. We have already encountered the length operator, L′. If we define or reserve an area in storage of eight bytes and name it FIELD, then the length operator reports that the length of FIELD is 8, thus:

L′FIELD=8 (10.2.1)

Table 10.2.1 ATTRIBUTE OPERATORS

Operator	*Notation*	*Result*	*Outside macro*
Type	T′	Letter	Yes
Length	L′	Number	Yes
Scaling	S′	Number	Yes
Integer	I′	Number	Yes
Count	K′	Number	No
Number	N′	Number	No

Similarly, if we define a short floating point number as E type constant, NUM, then the type operator, when applied to the constant's name, will produce the type designation for the number thus:

T′NUM=E (10.2.2)

The operators as mentioned can be applied equally well to arguments or symbols.

Kinds We examine the operators as they appear in Table 10.2.1.

TYPE

We shall spend a lot more time on the various *type descriptors* which are presented in Table 10.2.2.

LENGTH

The **length operator** is applied to any label field or argument and produces the number of bytes contained in that field.

SCALE, INTEGER

This operator requests the scaling factor applied to fixed and floating point numbers. From it, it can form an integer constant based on scaling and the length of the number defined.

COUNT

The **count operator** counts the number of letters in a symbol. It is superfluous in the main program. However, when parameters of unknown length are supplied in the macrocall, we need some way of determining the number of characters in the symbol for the parameter. Let us examine the rules for counting characters using as an example the sample call below:

```
ADDX     LIST=(A,B,C),N=NUM,T=
```
(10.2.3)

It stems from a macrodefinition, for the prototype statement is

```
&M     ADDX     &LIST=,&N=,&T=
```
(10.2.4)

1. The count of an ordinary parameter is simply the number of characters in the symbol.

$$K'\&N = 3 \tag{10.2.5}$$

2. When a list is supplied, the count includes parentheses, commas, and all the characters which make up the members of a sublist.

$$K'\&LIST = 7 \tag{10.2.6}$$

3. When a parameter is missing, its count is zero:

$$K'\&T = 0 \tag{10.2.7}$$

Table 10.2.2 TYPE ATTRIBUTES AS DETERMINED BY THE TYPE OPERATOR, T′

Type value	*Meaning*	*Length*†	*Alignment*	*For*‡
A	Address constant	4	√	d
B	Binary	—	—	d
C	Character	—	—	d
D	Double floating	8	√	d
E	Short floating	4	√	d
F	Fixed	4	√	d
G	Fixed	X	√	d
H	Half	2	√	d
I	Mnemonic	X	—	s
J	Control section	—	—	s
K	Floating	X	√	d
M	Macro	—	—	s
N	Self-defining	—	—	m
O	Omitted	—	—	m
P	Packed	X	—	d
Q	Address constant	—	√	d
R	Address constant	X	—	d
S	Address constant	—	—	d
U	Undefined	—	—	m
V	V-type constant	4	√	d
W	CCW	8	√	s
X	Hexadecimal	X	—	d
Y	Address constant	—	—	d
Z	Zoned decimal	—	—	d

† Where lengths are fixed and known, they are indicated by numbers; where explicit designation is made, X appears.

‡ Letters indicate what kind of symbols these attributes apply to.
d: *label* in DC or DS,
s: *label* for other statements or EXTRN,
m: parameters of macrocalls.

NUMBER

The number operator applies only when lists are supplied in the macrocall. It counts the number of members in the list. For instance, for the call of ADDX (10.2.4), we have

$$\text{N'\&LIST} = 3 \tag{10.2.8}$$

If some of the numbers are not supplied so that adjacent commas occur in the list, empty members are counted. So, for instance, if we left out B in (10.2.3) so that we had (A,,B), (10.2.8) would still apply—the number of members in the list would still be three.

ALL

All but N′ may be applied to a list member as well as a list. The member is parenthesized after the list name. Thus for (10.2.3) we might have

$$\text{K'\&LIST(1)} = 1 \qquad \text{T'\&LIST(2)} = \text{F} \tag{10.2.9}$$

Type Table 10.2.2 shows the result of applying the type operator, T′, to symbols which have various type attributes. The result is always a letter which appears in the first column which stands for the type of field to which the label applies. The second column contains the meaning or verbal description of the type. We have encountered most of these letters before for the DC and DS pseudos. All those that we have encountered contain *d* in the last column. When an *s* appears in the last column, it indicates that this label is associated with a pseudo. When *m* appears, there the descriptors only apply to parameters of a macrocall.

LENGTH

For some types, field lengths are fixed. For instance, type H is a halfWord fixed point number and always contains two bytes aligned on a halfWord boundary. For other types such as C for *character*, the length of the field is variable. Where an *X* appears in the *length* column, an explicit length qualifier appears parenthesized alongside the symbol (base/displacement notation) where it is used in the program.

10.3 ASSEMBLER VARIABLES

Kinds of SET variables SET variables are used only by the assembler and have no correspondent in machine language. These variables are classified in two ways:

- the area in the program to which they apply:
  - * local,
  - * global,

- the type of variable:
  - ∗ arithmetic,
  - ∗ logical,
  - ∗ character.

Multiplying the three types of variables by the two areas to which they apply yields six different types which must be *declared* within a macro-definition at the beginning before the variables are used.

Symbols A SET symbol is designated by &name where *name* is a legal combination restricted by approximately the same rules which apply to argument symbols. A SET symbol can be subscripted by placing a number or expression in parentheses after the symbol.

Declaration At the beginning of the macro, there should appear a declaration stating the kind of variable at *opcode* and naming the variables to be used at location.

Opcode for declaration can be any one of the following: LCLA, LCLB, LCLC, GBLA, GBLB, GBLC. These declarative opcodes have the following significance:

- LCL for local variables,
- GBL for global variables,
- A for arithmetic variables,
- B for Boolean or logical variables,
- C for character variables.

Here are some examples:

```
LCLA    &A,&B,&C                  (10.3.1)
LCLB    &B1,&B2,&B3               (10.3.2)
GLBC    &REC(50),&F(20)           (10.3.3)
```

In (10.3.3) we find (50) to tell us that &REC can bear subscripts from 1 to 50 noted as &REC(1) through &REC(50).

Initialization All LCLX and GBLX pseudos must appear at the *beginning* of a macrodefinition; none may appear thereafter; all SET variables must be represented in one, and only one, LCLX or GBLX.

LCLX initializes the SET symbol anytime any macrocall containing it is given; GBLX initializes the SET symbol only on the first call in which it appears, or *before the beginning* of program proper. SET variables are initialized thus:

- arithmetic SET variables to 0,
- Boolean SET variables to 0,
- character SET variables to the null character.

Null character *Please note very carefully:* the null character is an absence of characters. It is different from a *blank*.

- When a blank appears between X and Y, we get "X Y."
- When a null character appears between X and Y, we get "XY."

Also,

- The length of a blank is 1.
- The length of a null character is 0.

10.4 SETTING VARIABLE SYMBOLS

Pseudo To set or change an assembler variable symbol, we use one of these three pseudos: SETA, SETB, SETC. To speak generally about these pseudos, let us use SETX to represent any one of them. The format of the SETX pseudo is then

symbol SETX expression (10.4.1)

We find at *symbol* a variable of the form &name which must have been declared by an LCLX or GBLX pseudo. Please note that LCLX or GBLX pseudos initialize the symbol to 0 or the null character, whichever is appropriated to the type of symbol. *Expression* depends upon the type of variable to which we are applying it and the possibilities for this are discussed below.

Arithmetic We can set a symbol to integer by placing that integer at *location*,

```
&A1      SETA   3
```
(10.4.2)

We can change a symbol by adding or subtracting a quantity from that symbol at *location:*

```
&A1      SETA   &A1+2
```
(10.4.3)

We can combine symbols with other symbols or numbers. The only restriction here is that what appears at *location* after evaluation should turn out to be a number. For instance,

```
&A1      SETA   &A1+&A3-3
```
(10.4.4)

When attributes are numerical quantities, they can be used alone or in combination expressions for a SETA. The attribute can apply to a symbol or parameter:

```
&A2      SETA   L'AREA
```
(10.4.5)

or to an argument in the prototype statement:

```
&A3     SETA     L'&LIST                                (10.4.6)
```

It can also be applied to a combination of attributes and numbers such as

```
&A4     SETA     L'&LIST+A*&NUM                         (10.4.7)
&A5     SETA     N'&LIST*L'&LIST(1)                     (10.4.8)
```

```
 1               MACRO
 2  &COUNT       COUNT        &LIST
 3               LCLA         &A
 4  &A           SETA         N'&LIST
 5               B            *+8
 6  &COUNT       DC           F'&A'
 7               MEND
 8  NI           COUNT        (X,Y,Z)
 9+              B            *+8
10+N1            DC           F'3'
11  N2           COUNT        W
12+              B            *+8
13+N2            DC           F'1'
14  N3           COUNT        (V,V+4,V+8,V+12)
15+              B            *+8
16+N3            DC           F'4'
17  NN           COUNT        (N1,N2,N3)
18+              B            *+8
19+NN            DC           F'3'
```

Fig. 10.4.1 Definition and call of COUNT using SETA.

Example To see how SETA is used in a macro, the macrodefinition for COUNT appears in Fig. 10.4.1, along with several calls of COUNT. This is a sample macro with limited purpose and usefulness. A list is supplied at &LIST. The *macro* counts the number of items in the list and establishes a constant containing this number, labeling that constant with the same name given the macrocall.

Here we see that the name of the macro is applied to a constant rather than to the first line of code produced. In the figure an arithmetic SET symbol is defined using LCLA (3). This symbol, &A, is set to the number of items in the list (4). So far no code has been created. We shall create the constant, but first we create a command to *branch* around the constant. Since B contains four bytes, as does the constant, the *branch* must go around eight bytes of information, which accounts for *+8.

COUNT is called at N1 to count a list of three items. It is called at N2 to count a single item and establishes the constant F'1'. The remaining calls should be apparent to the reader.

Characters A character variable can be made equal to the type of a symbol or the type of an attribute using the type operator. For instance, we have

```
&T        SETC      T'&N                    (10.4.9)
```

We can put designated characters into a symbol as long as the string of characters is enclosed in apostrophes. For instance, we have

```
&C1       SETC      'ABCD'                  (10.4.10)
```

A variable symbol can accommodate only eight characters. The characters between the apostrophes can total up to 255. However, unless otherwise indicated, only the first eight characters are used. For instance, we have

```
&C2       SETC      'CONDITIONAL'
          (&C2)=CONDITIO                    (10.4.11)
```

Characters can be alphabetic or numeric or they can be special characters. We could request, for instance,

```
&C3       SETC      '%3,4'                  (10.4.12)
```

To concatenate two strings of characters, these are separated by a period and each string is enclosed in apostrophes thus:

```
&C4       SETC      'ABC'.'DEF'             (10.4.13)
```

We can concatenate a character quantity with a fixed string by separating the two with a period thus:

```
&C5       SETC      '&C3'.'QP'
          (&C5)=%3,4QP                      (10.4.14)
```

To include an apostrophe in the string which the variable will represent, we must use a double apostrophe. For instance, we have

```
&C6       SETC      'L''LIST'
          (&C6)=L'LIST                      (10.4.15)
```

Nulls and blanks We emphasize the roles of nulls and blanks with these set symbols:

```
&BL       SETC      ' '                     (10.4.16)
&NL       SETC      ''                      (10.4.17)
```

Then we get

```
&XB       SETC      'A'.'&BL'.'B'      (&XB)=A B  (10.4.18)
&XN       SETC      'A'.'&NL'.'B'      (&XN)=AB   (10.4.19)
```

and

```
&WOW   SETC'     &XN'.'&BL'.'&XN'.'&NL'.'&XN'.'&BL'.'&XN'
                 (&WOW)=AB ABAB AB                        (10.4.20)
```

Substring notation We can abstract a number of characters starting at a known point in a string of characters with substring notation, the format of which is presented thus:

'expression'(start,number) (10.4.21)

Here *start* is the character at which we begin pulling our characters for the variable symbol; *number* is the number of characters which we are abstracting, starting our count with *start*. For instance, we have

```
&C7     SETC    'CONDITIONAL'(4,3)
                 (&C7)=DIT                                (10.4.22)
```

We can take characters from a character variable using the same substring notation. Thus, using (10.4.15) above, we have

```
&C8     SETC    '&C5'(2,4)
                (&C8)=3,4Q                                (10.4.23)
```

It is interesting to see that an arithmetic variable can be used as either *start* or *number*. For instance, referring to (10.4.14), we could do the following operation:

```
&A7     SETA    4
&C9     SETC    '&C6'(3,&A7)                              (10.4.24)
                (&C9)=LIST
```

It is possible to concatenate two substrings using the substring notation we have described above. For instance, we have

```
&C10    SETC    '&C5'(3,3).'&C6'(3,&A7)
                (&C10)=,4QLIST                            (10.4.25)
```

and further

```
&C11    SETC    '&C7'(4,3).'&BL'.'&NL'.'&C7'(1,1)
                (&C11)=DIT C                              (10.4.26)
```

10.5 LOGICAL

Form The format of a request for a logical variable is

symbol SETB logic (10.5.1)

Here *logic* can be a binary value 1 or 0 or a symbolic variable which has only the truth values 0 or 1 or it can be a parenthesized logical expression.

Within the logical expression we find two kinds of operators not previously defined:

- relations,
- connectives.

There are six logical relations which can be used to compare quantities or character strings. These are defined using verbal phrases which should be otherwise known to the programmer as

EQ—equal to	NE—not equal to	
GT—greater than	GE—greater or equal	(10.5.2)
LT—less than	LE—less or equal	

There are three logical connectives which can be applied to logical or Boolean variables. These have their common meaning and are

AND—and OR—or NOT—not (10.5.3)

Alternatives Instead of listing all the rules for comparing logical operators and variables, a few examples should serve to illustrate how logical expressions are formed. Examine the logical value &B1:

```
&B1        SETB       (L'AREA GT 6)
```
(10.5.4)

&B1 has the value 1 if the length attribute of the symbolic variable AREA is greater than 6; it has the value 0 if this relation is not true—if the length of AREA is less than or equal to 6.

Notice that

- *expression* is within parentheses,
- there is *blank* on each side of the relational operator, GT.

Two attributes are compared with

```
&B2        SETB       (L'&REC LE L'&AREA)
```
(10.5.5)

A more complicated expression is

```
&B3    SETB     (L&F1 LT L'&TOT+3 AND L'&F2 LT L'&TOT+3)
```
(10.5.6)

It uses the connective AND which is surrounded by blanks just as for the relations. It requests that the symbol &B3 is set to one only if both the length attributes L'&F1 and L'&F2 are less than the length attribute L'&TOT after three has been added to it.

To check if a list contains members or is actually empty, we use this variable expression:

```
&B4        SETB       (N'&LIST NE 0)
```
(10.5.7)

Logical expressions can compare character strings. For instance, to determine if the type attribute of &A is F for fullWord, we use

```
&B5      SETB     (T'&A EQ 'F')                (10.5.8)
```

Note the characters or SET symbol must be framed by apostrophes. Here is another example:

```
&B6      SETB     (T'&A NE T'&B)               (10.5.9)
```

We might use a parameter to communicate the setting of a switch to $\mathcal{ASLR}$. Imagine the switch &GO which might have several settings, one of which is STOP. We test against this setting thus:

```
&B7      SETB     (&GO NE 'STOP')              (10.5.10)
```

It is possible to make compound expressions using parenthesized expressions within the total outer parentheses. For instance, we have

```
&B8      SETB     (&B7 AND (K'&A NE 7))        (10.5.11)
```

which sets &B8 to 1 if &B7 is 1 *and* the count of &A is not equal to 7.

10.6 CONDITIONAL BRANCH

AIF As we noted in the beginning of the chapter, the key command for conditional assembly is AIF meaning *branch during assembly if*. It takes the form

```
                  AIF     logic.sequence       (10.6.1)
```

When AIF is encountered by $\mathcal{ASLR}$, it evaluates *logic*. If the value found is 1, the next command examined by $\mathcal{ASLR}$ is that for which the sequence symbol is *sequence*. If the evaluation of *logic* yields 0, $\mathcal{ASLR}$ goes to the next statement in turn for examination and/or assembly. Any *logic* which is permissible in *loc* of SETB is also valid for *logic* in AIF.

Example To illustrate the technique, let us present a simple macrodefinition for MOVEW. This is a fullWord move operation which works with only two fields, &T and &F, usually fullWord attributes. The definition appears in Fig. 10.6.1. Notice that *logic* in the AIF statement (2) reads almost like English. It says that if the type of either variable is not equal to F, we go to the statement with sequence symbol .END. This sequence symbol is found in *name* of the pseudo MEND (6) and causes assembly to be terminated without producing any code.

```
         MACRO
&N       MOVEF     &T,&F
         AIF       (T'&T NE 'F' OR T'&F NE 'F').END
&N       L         2,&T
         ST        2,&F
.END     MEND
```

Fig. 10.6.1 A macro MOVEW for fullWords only.

10.7 OTHER NEEDS

NOOP — We define an assembly NOOP, namely ANOP, which does nothing in the assembly and produces no code. Then why do we need it?

All AIF opcodes have a sequence symbol associated with them. Should *logic* prove to be 1, we go to the command indicated by this sequence symbol. No difficulty arises as long as we place the sequence symbol at *name* of an already unlabeled opcode. However, some model statements may already be labeled with either a symbol or an argument. Neither of these are valid sequence symbols. The solution is to precede such a model statement with ANOP which bears the desired sequence symbol at *label*.

To see an example of the use of ANOP, examine this code:

```
         AIF       (T'&A EQ 'F').START
&AL      SETA      L'SIZE
.START   ANOP
&N       L         4,&A                        (10.7.1)
```

Should *logic* prove *true* for AIF, we should like to go to the *load* command. However, that command bears the label &N. Hence, we precede it with the command ANOP which bears the sequence symbol .START.

Unconditional branch — During assembly, we may wish the next statement assembled to come from someplace else other than the next AL statement in the macrodefinition. We use the *unconditional assembly branch* AGO. It has a sequence symbol at *name*.

When several AIFs occur in the macrodefinition, we often find it necessary to place AGO someplace thereafter to branch around code resulting from some of the conditional branches created by the AIFs.

EXAMPLE

Here we use AGO:

```
         AIF    (T'&A EQ 'F').START
&L       SETA   L'SIZE
         AGO    .END
.START   ANOP
         L      4,&A
.END     MEND
```

(10.7.2)

Notice that should the condition of the AIF be false, $\mathcal{ASLR}$ examines one more command and then *branches* around the commands which would be present for the true condition of the AIF.

Macroexit When a macrodefinition can have several alternative assemblies, the termination of an assembly may also be the termination of the macrocall. We then need to place an AGO statement which takes us to MEND by using the sequence symbol applied to MEND. A simpler way to do this is to use the pseudo, MEXIT. It does the task just mentioned.

Notes It is possible to build tests into the macrodefinition which prevent assembly for improper relations among the parameters. If assembly of the macro is not performed, the programmer should be informed. When a parameter test fails, it is nice to produce a statement telling the programmer why an assembly was not done. This statement can be written directly into the macrodefinition. This is best illustrated with an example.

EXAMPLE

In Fig. 10.7.1, we define a macro MOVEF which is applied to fixed or floating point operands. Statement 2 checks the type of the operands. Should the type be different, we go next to the command MNOTE. It tells the programmer that the reason that assembly did not take place was because the types were different. 8 is the severity code which prevents assembly unless the programmer specifically overrides HMJCL. Following MNOTE, we find MEXIT, which terminates the macro.

Statement 3 checks to see if fixed or floating operands are supplied. If not, we go to another MNOTE. It tells the programmer that the wrong types of operands were supplied.

```
         MACRO
&N       MOVEF     &T,&F
         LCLC      &TY
         AIF       (T'&T NE T'&F).M1
         AIF       (T'&T EQ 'F').L
&TY      SETC      T'&T
         AIF       ('&TY' NE 'H' OR '&TY'
                   NE 'E' OR '&TY' NE 'D').M2
.L       ANOP
&N       L&TY      4,&F
         ST&TY     4,&T
         MEXIT
.M1      MNOTE     8,'TYPE DIFFERENT'
         MEXIT
.M2      MNOTE     8,'WRONG TYPE'
         MEND
```

Fig. 10.7.1 MOVEF moves a fixed or floating operand.

COMMENTS

Sometimes it is desirable to be able to make comments in the macro-definition which are suppressed in the expansion of the call. This may be done with .* as below:

```
*     THIS COMMENT IS FOUND IN THE EXPANSION     (10.7.3)
.*    THIS COMMENT IS ABSENT ON EXPANSION
```

Of course the first (*) comment is also suppressed along with the code when the call is preceded by PRINT NOGEN.

Notice that the purpose of MNOTE would be defeated if it could be suppressed by PRINT NOGEN.

PRINTOUT

MOVEF checks that the type of &T and &F are the same and of proper type. For doubleWords D1 and D2 we have

```
95      MOVEF    D1,D2
96+     LD       4,D2                       (10.7.4)
97+     STD      4,D1
```

But, for halfWord H3 we get

```
98      MOVEF    H3,D1
99+              8 TYPE, DIFFERENT          (10.7.5)
   ***  ERROR  ***
```

The severity code is transmitted, usually, to the Linkage Editor and, if high enough, inhibits its operation. To suppress an error message and suspend the severity code use *. It will print thus:

```
*. THIS MNOTE HAS NO SEVERITY               (10.7.6)
```

10.8 MAIN PROGRAM

All conditional assembly and SET symbol instructions can be used outside macros. Thus the programmer can make this AL program reusable to produce a *different* ML program at another assembly.

Now the AL program acts as a generator: change a few initial conditions with SETX statements and the program produced applies to a weekly instead of a monthly payroll. This is a limited example, and it has limited merit, but it should give food for thought to the AL programmer.

Some rules prevail about how we use which kind of statement. First we know

R1. All macrodefinitions precede the beginning of the program.
R2. GBLXs come right after the prototype.
R3. LCLXs come after GBLXs, if any.

But further we have

R4. GBLXs not in macrodefinitions must come after all macrodefinitions, but before the main program.
R5. LCLXs not in macrodefinitions come after GBLXs, but before the program.

There are a number of command checks that can be used most anywhere:

R6. SETX, AIF, AGO, and ANOP are valid in the macrodefinition or in the main program.
R7. MNOTE, MEXIT, and .* are valid only in the macrodefinition.
R8. &SYSLIST, &SYSNDX, and &SYSECT (Section 13.7) are valid only in macrodefinitions.

Assembler loops Just as the programmer can write "infinite" loops into this program, he can write "infinite" assembly loops with *assembly branches*. These cause ASLR to hang up, not the program. Consider this segment:

```
.FRO    AGO    .TO
.TO     AGO    .FRO
```
(10.8.1)

Obviously it causes the assembler to go "to and fro" indefinitely without producing code. All the worse if code intervenes:

```
&A       SETA  4
.FORTH   AIF   ('&A' LT 8).BACK
.BACK    AR    3,3
         AIF   (&A GT 1).FORTH          (10.8.2)
```

which gets the assembler to spit out AR 3,3's.

The **assembler branch counter** is provided to defeat this. It contains a count of 4095. If any call, inner or outer, or the program individually contains *branches* which exceed this number, assembly is terminated.

The programmer has control of the assembler branch counter, if he chooses, using the pseudo ACTR thus:

```
         ACTR  number                   (10.8.3)
```

which sets in a *different* limit, one he chooses, for this macrodefinition or the whole program specifying it at *number*.

R9. ACTR is valid in the macrodefinition following LCLX or GBLX or before START in the program.

10.9 IMPLEMENTATION

Macro passes All the statements which comprise the macrodefinition, including its conditional assembly statements, are examined and placed in *COMTAB* by McDef. When McNest expands an inner macrodefinition into an outer macrodefinition, conditional assembly statements are brought along with the other model statements. Eventually, on another pass, macrocalls are examined and translated by McGen. This is one time when the conditional assembly statements *could* be evaluated. After evaluation, either one or another section of coding from the macrodefinition is included in the intermediate output coding for later translation. BAL ASLR enters and does the conditional evaluation in one pass but this precedes translation.

Assembler defined symbols Conditional assembly depends on the settings of assembler defined symbols at the time McGen encounters them during call expansion. McGen makes many references to dictionaries which store local or global symbols. The question which arises is how to arrange these dictionaries:

- one universal symbol table containing all program and assembler symbols,
- break out the assembler defined symbols from the normal symbols,
- further separate global and local symbols.

For the BAL 𝒜𝒮ℒℛ, assembly defined symbols are included in *OPTAB*. The reason and needs for this have not been examined. However, to simplify our own explanation, we consider three separate tables:

- *OPTAB* contains opcodes and macro opcodes.
- *GDICT* is the global dictionary.
- *LDICT* is the local dictionary.

When ℳcGen does a scan of a program, it creates *LDICT* and *GDICT* as it goes along from

- SETX which appear in the program,
- SETX in the macrodefinition as they appear in *COMTAB* and are evaluated at the macrocall.

All symbols are established by a declaration such as LCLA or GBLC which precedes any SETX which the programmer might request. Whenever such a declaration is encountered, control goes to ℳcDict, the routine which does the lookup in the appropriate dictionary. If the symbol is absent, it is set to 0's or the null character to initialize it for GBLX; it is initialized regardless for LCLX.

When SETX is encountered, whether in the program or a call, control again goes to ℳcDict to find the named variable in the appropriate dictionary. Then, one of the routines characteristic of the set operation is called in: ℳcValA, ℳcValB, or ℳcValC.

Evaluation The routine ℳcValA evaluates arithmetic expressions. All the information that it needs for this is in one of several places:

- one of the dictionaries,
- the symbol table,
- the parameters associated with the call.

ℳcValA extracts this information and does the arithmetic functions to get a single value. This result can only be an integer since only arithmetic variables are involved. The number is then placed in the dictionary to which the SETA applies.

ℳcValC only manipulates character strings. It uses the dictionaries and the symbol table to get information which it may concatenate. The result is then returned to the eight byte entry in the proper dictionary.

ℳcValB manipulates both arithmetic and character information using relations and logical connectives to come up with a value of 0 or 1. When this value is obtained, it is returned to the eight byte entry in the proper dictionary.

Any one of the routines above may require recourse to the attribute operators. These operators go to the symbol table, argument table, or parameter table to determine attributes of the symbol referenced. The attributes are listed with the symbol to which they are applied. These attributes are then plugged into the expression being evaluated.

Branches Assembly *branches* within a macro as needed for conditional assembly make use of sequence symbols. Each macro should have a local sequence symbol table which we shall call *SEQTAB*. It may be completed only after nesting has been resolved by McNest. Only then do we have an accurate count of a sequence number associated with a sequence symbol. It is placed with macrodefinition in the *COMTAB*.

When AGO is encountered by McGen, it turns over control to McSeq. All that need be done is to look up the sequence symbol in *SEQTAB* and then continue assembly by going to this position in *COMTAB*. If further conditional assembly statements follow, these are evaluated in turn.

MEXIT is equivalent to AGO with the sequence symbol corresponding to MEND. When McGen encounters MEXIT, it terminates the macrocall and searches for the next statement following MEND.

When AIF is encountered by McGen in the program or the expanded call, control is passed to McValB. *Logic* is evaluated in the same manner as for SETB. Recourse may be required to attribute evaluation and placement. The final result of this evaluation is 0 or 1: for 1, control goes to McSeq, which treats this as though it was an AGO statement; otherwise when the value is 0, McGen regains control and examines the next statement in sequence in *COMTAB*.

For MNOTE, no code is produced, only a comment appears printed for the programmer.

10.10 OTHER ASSEMBLERS

Compatibility There is upward compatibility of all the conditional assembly features from BPS (Basic Programming System) through BOS (Basic Operating System) and DOS (Disk Operating System) to OS. Any feature found in DOSAL is available in OSAL. Then what is not available in the lower ALs? Actually everything is! The difference is in the versatility of the SETX commands where specific limitations are found in BPS. What is said hereafter applies also to Spectra 70 POS, TOS, and TDOS assembly languages.

SETX A variable symbol type is determined by its prefix. All have the form

&typerangenumber (10.10.1)

where:

> *type* is A, B, or C for arithmetic;
> *range* is L or G for local or global; (10.10.2)
> *number* is some number between 1 and 127.

The means to set the symbol is the same; here are examples:

```
&AL1    SETA    3                      (10.10.3)
&AL2    SETA    &AL1+&AL2-2            (10.10.4)
&BL3    SETB    (T'&VAR EQ 'F')        (10.10.5)
&CL4    SETC    '&CL1'(3,1).X.'&CL3'   (10.10.6)
        AIF     (L'&X GE 2).SEQ        (10.10.7)
```

One more difference is that *no* LCLA, etc., is required—no declaration is needed. However, symbols are initialized by the assembler before being used, A and B to 0 and C to the null character. Thus &AL2 after (10.10.4) is 1 since it has not appeared previously. Global variables are initialized only once at their first appearance; local variables are reset in each macrocall.

Branch BPS requires separate specification of backward assembly branches. Hence AIF and AGO can be used only as long as *.sequence* is the name of a model statement which follows.

To *assembly branch backward*, AGOB and AIFB *must* be used (compatible with OS).

PROBLEMS

10.1 Use attribute operators to rephrase these statements:

(a) The length C1 is eight;
(b) C1 is a character field;
(c) P2 is a packed field;
(d) "P2" contains two letters;
(e) The list furnished at &START contains four members:
  (1) The first has seven characters;
  (2) The second is a fullWord;
  (3) The third is missing;
  (4) The fourth begins with "X";
(f) The list at &LI is missing;
(g) The list at &S2 has three members:
  (1) The first is FIRST;
  (2) The second is an ADCON;
  (3) The third is a halfWord.

10.2 Declare and set these SET symbols as requested. Intermediate symbols may be required.

(a) &N1 to the length of &X in bytes;
(b) &N2 to the number of characters in &X;
(c) &N3 to the sum of &N1 +&N2;
(d) &N4 to one more than the difference of &N1 and &N2;
(e) &N5 to the product of &N1 and &N2;
(f) &L1 to a blank;
(g) &L2 to a null character;
(h) &L3 to the first five letters in &Y;
(i) &L4 to the letter of &Y with last letter omitted;
(j) &L5 to the first letter of each member in the list at &LIST (less than eight);
(k) &L6 to the last letter in each member in the list at &LIST (less than eight);
(l) &L7 to the first letter of each member of the list at &LIST except the first and last member;
(m) &L8 to the first three letters of &R and the last three letters of &S with a blank between them.

10.3 Construct conditional statements to go to .GO if:

(a) &NP is not *packed:*
(b) &F is floating;
(c) &FX is fixed binary nonfloating;
(d) &C is character;
(e) &MO contains more letters than &S;
(f) &SW (Boolean) is set to 1;
(g) The first member name in &LIST is the largest.

10.4 Explain (1) why these commands are needed; (2) where they are used; and, (3) give new examples of their use:

(a) AGO; (b) ANOP; (c) MEXIT; (d) .*; (e) ACTR.

10.5 (a) What are global SET symbols?
(b) Contrast use and initialization with LCLX and GBLX.
(c) How are global and local symbols used in the main program?
(d) Show code using each.

11

EXAMPLES

Each section of this chapter is devoted to the creation and use of a single macro, the details of logic and construction.

11.1 AN ALL-PURPOSE MOVE, MOVAL

We examine the creation of a universal move macro, MOVAL, which moves a field from one place to another. Its definition is presented in Fig. 11.1.1. The definition, in turn, depends on two macrocalls one of which is also defined later in the section.

```
            MACRO
&N          MOVAL       &T,&F
.*  THIS MACRO MOVES DATUM FROM SECOND FIELD TO FIRST
.*  BUT ONLY IF FIRST FIELD IS LARGER
            AIF         (T'&T EQ 'C' OR T'&T EQ 'D' OR T'&T          X
                          EQ 'Z' OR T'&T EQ 'X').MVC
&N          MOVEF       &T,&F
            MEXIT
.MVC        AIF         (T'&F NE 'C' AND T'&F NE 'P' AND T'&F        X
                          NE 'Z' AND T'&F NE 'X').NV
&N          MOVEC       &T,&F
            MEXIT
.NV         MNOTE       4,'''FROM'' FIELD NOT VARIABLE TYPE'
            MEND
```

Fig. 11.1.1 A universal move macro, MOVAL.

MOVAL uses two macrocalls:

- MOVEF which moves a Word or halfWord to another field;
- MOVEC which moves a character field from one place to another.

These are called within the definition as the reader can see from Fig. 11.1.1. Notice that a call of MOVAL produces no code! Only the inner resulting macrocalls produce code.

Tests The macrodefinition of MOVAL begins with a test to determine if the *to* field is a variable field type. The four alternatives are: character, packed, zoned, or hexadecimal. The test is

```
AIF
(T'&T EQ 'C' OR T'&T EQ 'P' OR T'&T EQ 'Z'
                         OR T'&T EQ 'X').MVC     (11.1.1)
```

Should none of these hold, MOVEF, examined previously, will produce code or MNOTEs accordingly with

```
&N      MOVEF      &T,&F                          (11.1.2)
```

where the name of the outer call and the parameters have been transmitted to the inner macro. Upon completion of the inner macro, the outer macro is also complete and it is left with MEXIT.

Since the *to* field is variable, MOVEC will work, but only if the *from* field is also a variable type. We test with

```
.MVC   AIF     (T'&F NE 'C' AND T'&F NE 'P AND T'&F NE 'Z'
                         AND T'&F NE 'X').NV     (11.1.3)
```

Should this test *pass*, an MNOTE results. Otherwise we give

```
&N      MOVEC      &T,&F                          (11.1.4)
```

Notice that both (11.1.2) and (11.1.4) have the name **&N**. This is no problem, since the two are mutually exclusive: only one call *or* the other may be given, *not* both.

MOVEC1 The first crack at MOVEC, called MOVEC1, is defined in Fig. 11.1.2. It is designed to move fields of any size, even those exceeding 256 bytes. Two local arithmetic variables are declared, thus:

```
        LCLA      &M,&L                           (11.1.5)
```

TESTS

Two tests are made on the length of the fields involved. If the destination field is smaller than the source field, the move is impossible, or at

```
          MACRO
&N        MOVEC1    &T,&F
          LCLA      &M,&L
          AIF       (L'&T LT L'&F).WF
.MORE     AIF       (L'&F LT &M+256).OM
&N        MVC       &T+&M.(256),&F+&M
&M        SETA      &M+256
          AGO       .MORE
.OM       ANOP
&L        SETA      L'&F-&M
          MVC       &T+&M.(&L),&F+&M
          MEXIT
.WF       MNOTE     'WONT FIT'
          MEND
```

Fig. 11.1.2 MOVEC1, the *move character* macro.

least it will endanger other information stored in the computer. We detect this case with

```
          AIF       (L'&T LT L'&F).WF                 (11.1.6)
```

Conditional assembly is terminated, and we tell the programmer that the reason is that "the operands won't fit." Next, we test to see if the source operand is longer than 256 bytes using:

```
.MORE     AIF       (L'&F LT &M+256).0M               (11.1.7)
```

&M has been set to 0 by its declaration.

Should the source field be larger than 256 bytes, we set up a command to move 256 bytes, thus:

```
&M        MVC       &T+&M.(256),&F+&M                 (11.1.8)
```

Upon its completion, advance the variable symbol, &M, which is keeping track of the number of bytes moved, thus:

```
&M        SETA      &M+256                            (11.1.9)
```

Now reach,

```
          AGO       .MORE                             (11.1.10)
```

an *assembly branch* back to the statement labeled .MORE. If we have taken this path in the macro, we know that there are probably more bytes left to be moved. Again (11.1.7) determines if there are more than 256 bytes left to move. If so, we continue (11.1.8), etc.

When there are less than 256 bytes left to be moved, we go to the statement labeled .OM (one more move). It determines the number of bytes left to be moved, thus:

```
.OM       ANOP
&L        SETA      L'&F-&M                          (11.1.12)
```

This is then plugged into an MVC statement which moves the remainder of the field thus:

```
          MVC       &T+&M.(&L),&F+&M                 (11.1.13)
```

MOVEC Examine Fig. 11.1.2. There are two grievous faults:

- For short moves, one unnamed MVC is generated;
- For long moves, several MVCs, most of which are named, are generated.

Neither of these is acceptable. MOVEC in Fig. 11.1.3 cures these problems. Check it through to be sure.

```
             MACRO
&M           MOVEC       &T,&F
             LCLA        &D,&L
.*  &D IS THE DISPLACEMENT WHEN MULTIPLE MOVES
    ARE DONE
.*  &L IS THE LENGTH OF DATUM MOVED
             AIF         (L'&T LT L'&F).WF
&L           SETA        256
             AIF         (L'&F GT 256).FM
&L           SETA        L'&F
.FM          ANOP
&N           MVC         &T.(&L),&F
.MORE        AIF         (L'&F LE &D+256).NM
&D           SETA        256+&D
             AIF         (L'&F GT &D+256).MVC
&L           SETA        L'&F-&D
.MVC         MVC         &T+&D(&L),&F+&D
             AGO         .MORE
.WF          MNOTE       8, 'WON''T FIT'
.NM          MEND
```

Fig. 11.1.3 A proper variable length move, MOVEC.

Calls Figure 11.1.4 shows some calls and their expansion. The first letter of the field named indicates to the reader at least the kind of field for which the move requested is made.

```
        Call                       Expansion
C1   MOVAL   H1,H2         C1   LH      4,H,1
                                STH     4,H2
C2   MOVAL   F1,F2         C2   L       4,F1
                                ST      4,F2
C3   MOVAL   F1,H2                      8,DIFFERENT TYPE
C4   MOVAL   A(F1),F2                   8,WRONG TYPE
C5   MOVAL   C1,P1         C5   MVC     C1(5),P1
C6   MOVAL   C2,Z1         C6   MVC     C2(256),Z1
                                MVC     C2+256(36)Z1+256
C7   MOVAL   C2,C1                      8,WONT''T FIT
C8   MOVAL   C1,F2                      'FROM' FIELD NOT VARIABLE TYPE
```

Fig. 11.1.4 Some calls of MOVAL and their expansion.

11.2 UNIVERSAL ADD MACRO

We shall now design a universal addition macro to add a list of numbers and place it at a given location. We call the macro ADAL. It contains two arguments:

- &L is a *list*—the members of the list name locations which contain numbers to be added.
- &S is a name of the locations where the sum is placed.

ADAL is presented in Fig. 11.2.1.

```
          MACRO
&N        ADAL      &L,&S
          AIF       (T'&L(1) EQ 'P').ADP
          AIF       (T'&L(1) EQ 'F' OR T'&L(1) EQ 'H' OR
                      T'&L(1) EQ 'D' OR T'&L(1) EQ 'E').ADW
          MNOTE     8,'WRONG TYPE'
          MEXIT
.ADP      ANOP
&N        ADP       &L,&S
          MEXIT
.ADW      ANOP
&N        ADW       &L,&S
          MEND
```

Fig. 11.2.1 The macro ADAL adds a list of almost any type of number.

Definition Again, our procedure is to define the outer macro using inner macros. We first perform a number of tests to see what is done. The first test determines if the first number on our list is packed decimal:

AIF (T'&L(1) EQ 'P').ADP (11.2.1)

If so, we assemble the macro following .ADP.

The second test determines if the first number on the list is one of four kinds:

```
AIF    (T'&L(1) EQ 'F' OR T'&L(1) EQ 'H' OR T'&L(1) EQ 'D'
                                 OR T'&L(1) EQ 'E').ADW   (11.2.2)
```

If so, we shall do the word type macro. If the first number on the list is neither of the kinds tested for, MNOTE will write out "WRONG TYPE."

ADW First examine the macro ADW which adds numbers in a word format. It is defined in Fig. 11.2.2. The first few steps declare and define four variables:

- &A is the number of the list member we are working with.
- &M is a number of members in the list supplied at call time.
- &T1 is the type attribute of the *first* member in the list.
- &T2 is the command type suffix.

```
               MACRO
&N             ADW       &L,&S
               LCLA      &M,&A
               LCLC      &T1,&T2
&M             SETA      N'&L
&T1            SETC      T'&L(1)
&T2            SETC      T'&L(1)
               AIF       (&T1 NE 'F').CONT
&T2            SETA      ' '
.CONT          ANOP
&N             ST&T2     2,28(13)
               AIF       (&M EQ 0).Z
               AIF       (&M EQ 1).ONE
               L&T2      2,&L(1)
&A             SETA      2
.LOOP          AIF       (&T1 NE T'&L(&A)).WT
               A&T2      2,&L(&A)
&A             SETA      &A+1
               AIF       (&A LE &M).LOOP
.FIN           ST&T2     2,&S
               L&T2      2,28(13)
               MEXIT
.Z             L&T2      2,=&T1.'0'
               AGO       .FI
.ONE           L&T2      2,&L(1)
               AGO       .FIN
.WT            MNOTE     'FOUND OPERANDS OF ANOTHER TYPE'
               MEND
```

Fig. 11.2.2 The main ADW adds Word type numbers.

Another couple of steps are needed should the type of the first number be F so as to set &T2 equal to *blank*:

```
         AIF      (&T1 NE 'F').CONT           (11.2.3)
&T2      SETA     ''
```

We begin assembly by *saving* GPR2 in an area called SAVE:

```
.CONT    ANOP
&N       ST&T2    2,SAVE                      (11.2.4)
```

Next we see how many operands there are in the list and continue only if there are two or more:

```
         AIF      (&M EQ 0).Z
         AIF      (&M EQ 1).ONE               (11.2.5)
```

We load the first member into GRP2:

```
         L&T2     2,&L(1)                     (11.2.6)
```

We reset the number of the next member to be added, &A, and then check the next one to be sure it is the same type as those that preceded:

```
&A       SETA     2
.LOOP    AIF      (&T1 NE T'&L(&A)).WT        (11.2.7)
```

If they are not the same type, we stop assembling and write the programmer a note.

As long as the operands are the same type, we can produce an add command:

```
         A&T2     2,&L(&A)                    (11.2.8)
```

We now advance &A and check to see if there are more operands left:

```
&A       SETA     &A+1
         AIF      (&A LE &M).LOOP             (11.2.9)
```

The steps above are repeated to generate *add* commands for each member in the list except the first.

When there are no more members left, the test of (11.2.9) fails and we fall through. We put away the sum and restore the contents of GPR2 that were saved:

```
.FIN     ST&T2    2,&S
         L&T2     2,SAVE                      (11.2.10)
```

This is the end of code production. Now we look after the case where there was none or one member in the list.

When the list is empty, we want to set 0 into GPR2 so that &S will have 0 placed there. We use a literal of type &T1 to do this with

```
.Z        L&T2      2,=&T1.'0'
```
(11.2.11)

finishing off the production, thus:

```
          AGO       .FIN
```

When there is only one operand, it can be loaded into GPR2 and the production finished thus:

```
.ONE      L&T2      2,&L(1)
          AGO       .FIN
```

ADP The inner macro, ADP, adds a list of packed numbers furnished at &L, placing the result in the sum field, &S, and is defined in Fig. 11.2.3. We now examine the statements in that macro according to the statement number that appears in the left column.

```
1               MACRO
2     &N        ADP       &L,&S
3               LCLA      &NL,&LS,&I
4     &NL       SETA      N'&L
5     &I        SETA      1
6     &LS       SETA      L'&S
7     &N        MVC       &S.(&LS),=PL&LS.'0'
8               AIF       (&NL EQ 0).Z
9     .AP       AIF       (L'&L(&I) GT &LS).NR
10              AP        &S.(&LS),&L(&I).(L'&L(&I))
11    &I        SETA      &I+1
12              AIF       (&I LE &NL).AP
13              MEXIT
14    .NR       MNOTE     8,'NO ROOM IN SUM FIELD'
15    .Z        MEND
```

Fig. 11.2.3 The main ADP clears the sum field, &S, and adds the numbers from the list of locations supplied.

Statement 3 declares three local arithmetic variables:

- &NL, the number of times in the list, is set in statement 4.
- &I, the item number for which code is being produced, is set to 1 in statement 5.
- &LS, the length of the sum field, is set in statement 6.

Statement 7 is labeled &N, for it is the first command produced when the macro is called. The receiving field, &S, has an implied length. The source field is a literal which places a packed number 0 of the proper length as determined by &LS.

Statement 8 checks if the list provided is empty and, if so, terminates assembly. This is proper since the destination field, &S, now contains 0 as it should.

Statement 9 checks the *next* item to see if its length is greater than the destination field. If so, we know the wrong result would be produced; hence, we write the programmer a note and discontinue assembly. Statement 10 is the *add* command, AP; it's repeatedly produced for each item in the list, provided that item is not too large. Since the lengths of both the list item and the destination field are implied in their symbols, no length is specified in AP.

Statement 11 advances the item pointer. Statement 12 checks to see if there are items left in the list and, if so, moves back to statement 9. Where no items remain, &S contains the proper sum and so we discontinue assembly with MEXIT at statement 13.

Calls Figure 11.2.4 contains examples of the code produced for various calls of ADAL. The first, A1, contains an empty list and a packed result field. The result is a *wrong type* message since an empty parameter does not have the type associated with it.

Call			*Expansion*		
A1	ADAL	,PS1	A1		8,WRONG TYPE
A2	ADAL	P1,PS1	A2	MVC	PS1,=PL3'0'
				AP	PS1,P1
A3	ADAL	(P1,P2,P3),PS2	A3	MVC	PS2,=PL4'0'
				AP	PS2,P1
				AP	PS2,P2
				AP	PS2,P3
A4	ADAL	(P5,P6,P7),PS2	A4		8,NO ROOM IN SUM FIELD
A5	ADAL	F1,FS1	A5	ST	2,SAVE
				L	2,F1
				ST	2,FS1
				L	2,SAVE
A6	ADAL	(F1,H2),FS2	A6	ST	2,SAVE
				L	2,F1
					8,FOUND OPERANDS OF ANOTHER TYPE
A7	ADAL	(E1,E2,E3,E4),ES1	A7	STE	2,SAVE
				LE	2,E1
				AE	2,E2
				AE	2,E3
				AE	2,E4
				STE	2,ES1
				LE	2,SAVE

Fig. 11.2.4 Calls of ADAL and their expansion.

The call, A2, provides a list with only one member and produces code to clear and then add to the destination field. A3 adds a list of three packed items which should present no difficulty.

For A4, the destination PS2 is smaller than the first source word and produces the error message instead of assembly.

A5 is a fullWord *add* of a single item. A6 tries to add a fullWord and a halfWord. It gets to ADW because the first item in the list and the destination are both F type. Statement &N of Fig. 11.2.2 is assembled; tests in the two statements which follow are passed and the next statement is assembled. The test in the statement labeled .LOOP then fails and takes us to an error message accounting for the three lines of code at A7 in Fig. 11.2.4.

A7 adds a list of our fullWord floating point numbers.

11.3 BRING

An interesting use that some programmers have found for a macro is for register management in their own program. We examine the macro, BRING, for it illustrates two features which we have not yet incorporated into the macros:

- the use of global variables,
- the use of subscripted SET symbols.

Purpose BRING manages registers. That is, it keeps track of the symbolic names of Words that we have placed in GPRS. To do this, it contains a sixteen-element character SET array, one element for each GPR. Whenever the program wishes to place a Word into a REGISTER, BRING checks to see if it is already in some REGISTER and makes up the proper command accordingly.

BRING is useful to incorporate in other macros so that it is "invisible" to the user. This is demonstrated shortly.

Definition BRING is defined in Fig. 11.3.1 where the statements are numbered. After the header (1), the prototype statement contains the macro name, BRING, and two parameters:

- &R is the name of the register into which a Word is to be placed.
- &ADRS is the symbolic name for the Word to be placed there.
- Notice that the prototype statement contains no entry at *name* since it is generally an inner macro where its name will not be of consequence.

```
1                        MACRO
2                        BRING     &R,&ADRS
3                        LCLA      &I
4                        GBLC      &GPR(16)
5    &I                  SETA      1
6                        AIF       ('&GPR(&R+1)' EQ '&ADRS').END
7    .EXAM               AIF       ('&GPR(&I)' EQ '&ADRS').SET
8    &I                  SETA      &I+1
9                        AIF       (&I LE 16).EXAM
10                       L         &R,&ADRS
11   .NOTE               ANOP
12   &GPR(&R+1)          SETC      '&ADRS'
13                       MEXIT
14   .SET                LR        &R,&I-1
15                       AGO       .NOTE
16   .END                MEND
```

Fig. 11.3.1 BRING manages the contents of GPRS.

We declare a local arithmetic variable, &I, which will be used to sequence through the list of GPRS. An array of sixteen character variables is declared (4). These are global character variables because we want their settings to remain unchanged from one macro call (of BRING) to the next, except for the one which may be altered within the macro; local variables are always reset to 0 or *blank*.

Now ASLR makes two checks:

- Perhaps the register indicated in the call already contains the Word indicated in the call. If so, (5) takes us to .END and THE MACRO CREATES NO CODE.
- Otherwise, check the contents of the GPRS one at a time starting with register 0 by examining the array &GPR(16) which contains a label for the variable which the corresponding GPR contains:
  - ∗ (5) sets &I to 1,
  - ∗ (7) checks if &GPR(1) notes that &ADRS was set into GPR0.
- If this is the case, we go to .SET.

Generally, this is not the casc and we advance &I, having it act like an index (8) using the SETA pseudo. McGen now performs loop (7–9) as long as &I is less than 15; thus checking &GPR(&I) for all values of &I between 0 and 15, the extent of the global character array.

McGen pops out of the loop because the symbol supplied in the macro-call BRING is not presently in any of the GPRS. Therefore the *load* command enters the Word supplied at &ADRS into GPR&R to do what BRING requires (10). ANOP (11) has no effect. McGen notes that the required symbol has been placed at the required address so that the next BRING will be so informed (12). That is all there is to do so McGen finds MEXIT (13).

A check (7) may reveal that the desired parameter is currently in a GPR and McGen goes to .SET (13) where McGen provides a register transfer, LR, so that the desired Word is placed in the desired GPR. McGen goes back in the macro to .NOTE to note this action for the next occurrence BRING (11–13).

Since there are no more commands in this macrodefinition, it is terminated with MEND (16). Notice that MEND (16) is the object of an AIF statement (6) when the desired item is in the desired register already and hence bears the sequence symbol, .END.

ADSUM We now incorporate BRING into another simple macro, ADSUM, to add a number designated as &NUM to a Word symbolically designated as SUM, doing the addition in GPR1. The definition of ADSUM is in Fig. 11.3.2. The prototype statement (2) contains only one argument &NUM for the number to be added. Note that

1. The word to be added is an argument (&NUM) in the definition.
2. Hence it is supplied as a parameter in the call.
3. SUM is always the location of the accumulated total.

The macro assumes that SUM has been defined or declared elsewhere. This quantity is placed in GPR1 with BRING (3). Addition is done with the fullWord *add*, A (4). That is all there is to the macro (5).

Suppose that for some reason SUM is placed in GPR2 using BRING (6); the only code produced by this macro is the *load* command, L(7+).

At (8) we give the other macro defined above, ADSUM, with the

```
 1     MACRO
 2     ADSUM     &NUM
 3     BRING     1,SUM
 4     A         1,&NUM
 5     MEND
 6     BRING     2,SUM
 7+    L         2,SUM
 8     ADSUM     X1
 9+    LR        1,2
10+    A         1,X1
11     ADSUM     X2
12+    A         1,X2
13     BRING     1,SUM
14     ADSUM     X3
15+    A         1,X3
```

Fig. 11.3.2 Using BRING in a macro, ADSUM, and some code generated for different calls of ADSUM.

parameter X1:

- SUM is now in GPR2.
- ADSUM requires SUM to be in GPR1.
- The inner macro BRING generates the LR to transfer SUM from GPR2 to GPR1.

Now the addition is required and the *add* command, A (10+), is produced.

Let's give ADSUM again (11), this time specifying X2 as the operand. Since SUM is currently in GPR1, the inner macro, BRING, generates no code. Only the *add* (12+) is produced.

Incorporating BRING as an outer command in our program requesting that SUM be placed in GPR1 produces absolutely no code (13). One more request for ADSUM (14) adding X3 produces the single line of code (15+).

11.4 ADLIST

&SYSLST This section presents and examines another feature, the system parameter list quantifier by both description and example. Its purpose is to

- count the total parameters supplied within the call,
- count the number of members in a list in a call,
- select a parameter *or* list member by ordinal number.

The programmer's facility for doing this is &SYSLST and we have

- &SYSLST is the number of parameters in the call,
- &SYSLST(*n*) addresses the *n*th parameter;
- &SYSLST(*n*,*m*) addresses the *m*th member of the *n*th parameter, assuming it is a list.

Use I can't find a good use for the last two features. The first is useful for providing entirely different expansion according to the number of parameters in the call.

ADLIST defined in Fig. 11.4.1 does a task which depends on the number of parameters supplied:

- The last parameter, &B or &C, depending on whether two or three parameters are supplied, is always an accumulating symbolic location.
- &A is
  - * a list of names when only two parameters are supplied;
  - * the starting position of a number of Words.
- &B is used when the first parameter is not a list. Then it is the number of Words starting at &A which are to be added together.

```
1                      MACRO
2    &N                ADLIST         &A,&B,&C
3                      AIF            (&SYSLIST EQ 3).ADWORDS
4                      AIF            (&SYSLIST NE 2).ER
5    &N                ADNAMES        &A,&B
6                      MEXIT
7    .ADWORDS          ANOP
8    &N                ADWORDS        &A,&B,&C
9                      MEXIT
10   .ER               ANOP
11   &N                MNOTE          'OPERAND LIST INCORRECT'
12                     MEND
```

Fig. 11.4.1 Definition of ADLIST demonstrating the incorporation of &SYSLIST.

DEFINITION

In Fig. 11.4.1, check if there are three (3), two (2), or another number (4) of parameters furnished. In the last, .ER causes the assembler to note that the list is incorrect. For the other two cases, one or the other inner macros, ADNAMES or ADWORDS, is called (5, 8).

ADWORDS In Fig. 11.4.2, ADWORDS is defined. The contents of the accumulator, &SUM are put into GPR6 (3). The number of items is loaded into GPR5 (4). GPR7 is cleared to be used as an index (5). *Add* (6), indexing by GPR7. Increment the index by 4(7). *Tally down, test and branch* (8). Put away the result (9).

```
1             MACRO
2    &N       ADWORDS     &START,&NUM,&SUM
3             L           6,&SUM
4             L           5,&NUM
5             SR          7,7
6             A           6,&START(7)
7             LA          7,4(7)
8             BCT         5,*-8
9             ST          6,&SUM
10            MEND
```

Fig. 11.4.2 ADWORDS.

ADNAMES In Fig. 11.4.3, ADNAMES is defined. &I keeps track of the list (3). It may be empty (4); no commands are then produced.

For nonempty lists, &SUM, the accumulator is put into GPR6 (5). &I is counted up (7) and the first (or subsequent) list number added (8).

```
1            MACRO
2   &N       ADNAMES    &NAME,&SUM
3            LCLA       &I
4            AIF        (N'&NAME EQ 0).END
5   &N       L          6,&SUM
6   .BR      ANOP
7   &I       SETA       &I+1
8            A          6,&NAME(&I)
9            AIF        (&I LT N'&NAME).BR
10           ST         6,&SUM
11  .END     MEND
```

Fig. 11.4.3 ADNAMES.

Check to see if the list is exhausted (9). If not, we wish to return to create another *add*. But first the count must be incremented (7). Since a SET symbol is at *name* (7) this command cannot be the object of an *assembly branch* (9). This is the reason for ANOP (6).

When all the *adds* have been assembled, the test (9) fails and the sum is put away (10).

PROBLEMS

11.1 The first card in the input deck appears thus:

Nnnnn,

where *nnnn* is the number of items to follow. Write a program to read the cards which follow and add them together using decimal commands. The data cards take the form:

AAAAAA,

and there are less than 100 of them. Print the answer thus:

ANSWER, nnnn NUMBERS = TTTTTTTT

where TTTTTTTT is the desired sum.

11.2 This is the same as Prob. 11.1, with these three exceptions:

(a) The number AAAAAA is signed. The last (right) digit contains F_H for a positive number and D_H for negative; e.g., $+55 = \cdots$ 0F0F5F5; $-55 = \cdots$ 0F0F5D5.

(b) The answer should now be printed as

ANSWER, nnnn NUMBERS = MTTTTTTTT

where M is minus *only* for a negative total.

(c) The program should handle several sets of data, each of the form of Prob. 11.1, and each producing a separate answer.

11.3 Find the input card with the lowest key. The first card is Nnnnn, where *nnnn* is the number of cards to follow. Other cards are formatted thus:

kkkkkkkkdddd...dddd,

where kkkkkkkk is a key consisting of unpacked characters. The output should read:

THE CARD WITH THE LOWEST KEY IS NUMBER mmmm AND READS: kkkkkkkkdd...ddd.

JCL and the program precedes several sets of cards provided.

11.4 This program finds the root-mean-square of a set of numbers presented—the average of the squares of numbers of which the root is taken. The input is formatted as for Problem 11.2. Use SQRT in the macro library, which has the format:

SQRT number, root,

where *number* is a symbolic location where a number is contained, and *root* is a symbolic location where the root is placed. The convergence quantity is self-contained.
The desired result, y, produced by the full program is described thus:

$$y = \sqrt{\frac{\sum x_i^2}{\mathrm{n}}}\,.$$

Be sure to provide for most errors and results, but use only single precision *binary* calculations—one Word only for intermediate results. Printout might be in this form, but I encourage ingenuity for the messages:

RMS FOR nnnn NUMBERS = rrrrrrr

mmmm CANT BE SQUARED etc.

Again, several sets of data are processed in one run.

11.5 Rewrite the macro, SQRT, which appears in the text, so that a double precision (two Word fixed point binary) number is furnished as the number occupying a double Word in memory. The result, of course, is only a single Word.

11.6 Do Prob. 11.4 as stated, except that now all squares are kept in double precision as is the sum. Now we do not have to check squares, but do have to check for overflow of the sum. Use SQRT from Prob. 11.5.

11.7 Write a macro ADLIST to add a list of numbers. Its call should be as follows:

name ADLIST number,list,sum,

where *list* is the name of a list of fullWords; *sum* is the name of a location for the results; and, *number* is the number (not an address) of items in the list. To show the validity of this macro do the following: Write ODNUMS called by

ODNUMS place,num

to create a list of *num* FullWords starting at *place* where the list contains consecutive odd numbers starting with 1 to 2 * *num* + 1.

To create the first 100 consecutive *odd* numbers as fullWords use ODNUMS. Write a program to test the macro by using three sets of 15, 42, and 100 odd numbers, each from the list made by ODNUM.

(a) Add the lists.
(b) Put the sums in REGISTERS.
(c) Use REG to print the results.
(d) Show that the result is what you calculated beforehand.

11.8 Write a macro QDRT to find the roots of the quadratic equation:

$$ax^2 + bx + c = 0.$$

Restrict yourselves to real roots given by:

$$\text{roots} = \frac{-b \pm \sqrt{b^2 - 4ac}}{2a}.$$

Call $d = b^2 - 4ac$. Write the macro DISC called by:

DISC a,b,c,d,e,

where *a*, *b*, *c*, and *d* are as defined above and *e* is an error exit taken when *d* is negative. Then write QDRT called by:

QDRT a,b,c,r1,r2,e

where *r1* and *r2* are the roots and *e* is the error exit when the roots are complex.

Now write a program which solves six quadratics from coefficients as below, furnished by DCs, puts *a,b,c,r1* and *r2* in consecutive GPRS starting with GPR2, and prints them with REG.

a	*b*	*c*
1,000	2,000	1,000
1,000	0	2,000
1,000	0	−2,000
10,000	−1,000	−3,000
10,000	−1,000	0
−4,000	0	3,000

11.9 Define a macro ADALIST to add the numbers whose symbolic addresses are found in all but the last position in the macrocall; that position contains the address where the sum is to be accumulated. Thus, after ADALIST A,B,C we have (C) = (A) + (B) + (C). When only one parameter is provided, the sum remains unchanged. The amount of code produced is proportional to the parameter list. Test the macro with several lists as

below, using REG to print the values in the list after the call is given.
Start with sum empty and do these calculations:

sum = sum + A + B + C
sum = sum
sum = sum + D + E
sum = sum + F
sum = sum + G + H + I + J + K + L + M + N + O
sum = sum + P

where *A* through *P* are, respectively, 123, 234, 307, 291, 8372, −38708, 2637, 42078, −19, 9091, 7, 17, 39, −999, 368, and −99,000.

12

PSEUDOS

12.1 USING

Need USING, one of the stumbling blocks to the S360 neophyte is peculiar to third generation computers. Those who have used only word type machines may not be familiar with the problem of relativizing.

All *memory reference* commands in the S360 use the contents of one or more GENERAL PURPOSE REGISTERS and the displacement, *D*, added together to form an effective address. The displacement is a three nibble (twelve bit) quantity contained in the command. Twelve bits enable us to obtain a number between 0 and 4095. This would be a hopelessly small span of MEMORY if we were not aided by BASE REGISTERS. By storing different quantities in available BASE REGISTERS, we jump about in all MEMORY without being bound to 4K. Any program of more than minimum size must be able to reference data and other program steps outside its own (present) 4K region.

𝒜𝒮ℒℛ keeps track of BASE REGISTERS and their contents. But it does not have unlimited freedom and no convention is provided for BASE REGISTER management by 𝒜𝒮ℒℛ. Hence, it is up to the programmer to provide for the BASE REGISTERS by informing the assembler which REGISTERS it can use (and, by omission, cannot use) and by having the program fill these REGISTERS with the needed quantities.

USING The format of the USING pseudo is

```
        USING     exp,r1,r2, . . . ,rn                    (12.1.1)
```

Here, *exp* is an expression giving a symbolic or absolute location, the address of which is stored in *r1*. That address, plus 4096, is stored in *r2*. That address (*exp*), plus 8192, is in *r3* and so forth. Up to sixteen GPRS may be mentioned in (12.1.1) but this would leave the programmer with none of his own to work with and would also work against the *save* convention. To reiterate, we have

$$(r1) = \text{exp} \qquad (r2) = \text{exp} + 4096 \qquad (r3) = \text{exp} + 8192 \qquad \text{etc.} \tag{12.1.2}$$

USING only tells the assembler that it *should* find the quantities expected in the GPRS announced. It is the responsibility of the programmer to fill these GPRS before they are needed. Let's see how.

Setting one register

The most effective way to set a GPR just before it is needed is with BALR. Recall the function of BALR

```
BALR        r1, r2: (IAR) ⟶ r1; ⇒ (r2)        (12.1.3)
```

As stated above, BALR is a *branch*; but we don't really want to *branch*! We want to continue the program. If the GPR designated *r2* is 0, GPR0 is not actually used. No GPR is used for *branching*. No *branch* is taken.

Now we have a means for setting a GPR to the present contents of the IAR without taking a branch. For instance, let's set GPR3 to the address of the next instruction and then tell the assembler about it. We have

```
BALR        3,0
USING       *,3                                (12.1.4)
```

Here * tells 𝒜𝒮ℒℛ to use GPR3 for the address of the next *actual* ML command.

Several registers

Setting only one REGISTER would permit us to address only 4K. Suppose our program occupies 12K. To address any byte in the program, three REGISTERS are required. We can set the first REGISTER thus:

```
BALR        3,0                                (12.1.5)
```

We tell the assembler that we are using REGISTERS 3, 4, and 5

```
USING       NEXT,3,4,5                         (12.1.6)
```

We have established GPR3 but not GPR4 and GPR5. Let's suppose that the proper addresses for REGISTERS 4 and 5 are stored at location C. We can load several registers with a *load multiple* command, LM. Thus:

```
NEXT     LM     4,5,C                                   (12.1.7)
```

The existence of LM is a good reason to use consecutively numbered GPRS.

We now want to define the constant, C. Before we do, we provide a *branch* to go around the constant which appears within the program:

```
         B      AFTER                                   (12.1.8)
```

Now the constant appears:

```
C        DC     A(NEXT+4096,NEXT+8192)
                                                        (12.1.9)
```

𝒜𝒮ℒℛ assigns a location for NEXT. The constant defined above contains two words which are each thirty-two bit addresses. 𝒜𝒮ℒℛ forms these addresses by doing the addition indicated and then placing the binary number at these two words in the program.

We are now ready to begin writing the program. If the first command in our program loads GPR7 with the symbolic quantity, NUM, we have

```
AFTER    L      7,NUM                                   (12.1.10)
```

DROP Occasionally the programmer may find that he has assigned too many BASE REGISTERS or that the program no longer requires access to an earlier segment, 4K. He may exercise the slightly dangerous option of freeing BASE REGISTERS using the pseudo, DROP. This tells the assembler that the designated GPRS can no longer be expected to hold the base quantities formerly assigned him and has the format

```
         DROP   regs                                    (12.1.11)
```

where *regs* is a list of REGISTERS; for example,

```
         DROP   3,4                                     (12.1.12)
```

which always drops GPR3 and GPR4.

Of course, it is not necessary to DROP before reassigning a BASE REGISTER. After (12.1.6) we can change the assignment for GPRS thus:

```
         BALR   3,0
         USING  *,3                                     (12.1.13)
```

Assembler 𝒜𝒮ℒℛ takes note of BASE REGISTERS supplied with USING, entering these values in the BASE REGISTER table along with the value of *exp*. That is the only activity associated with USING upon its receipt. Every symbol which appears thereafter is evaluated by ASLR to make a base and displacement assignment. It keeps track of the absolute value of symbols but replaces a symbolic address in a command by a base and displacement. ASLR chooses the proper BASE REGISTER by referring to the BASE REGISTER table, looking for one for which the difference between that REGISTER content and the address of the symbol is greater than 0 but less than 4095. This difference is then the displacement and thus the BASE REGISTER appears at B in the command.

Notice that now FLOAD has practically no work as far as relocation is concerned. For instance, when the two commands of (12.1.4) are encountered, only one appears in the machine language. It places the location contained in the IAR at run time into GPR3. Then, regardless of where FLOAD has placed this segment, references which follow in the program, if they are relative to GPR3, have been properly relocated.

12.2 CONTROL PSEUDOS

This section describes instructions to ASLR about statements that it is going to list, how it is going to accept the program, and other details of operation.

Listing These pseudos affect the printed output of the assembler.

TITLE This pseudo has the format

```
name        TITLE       heading                        (12.2.1)
```

where *name* consists of up to four characters and these characters will appear in columns 73 through 76 on output cards produced by ASLR. Future TITLE cards may not contain *name* since this has now been established. They may only contain a sequence symbol which starts with a period. *Heading* is a set of characters enclosed in apostrophes which becomes the heading on each page of printed output produced by ASLR.

For instance, the following pseudo

```
TS          TITLE       'TOURNAMENT SORT'              (12.2.2)
```

causes each page to be headed TOURNAMENT SORT and causes the characters TS to be punched in card output in columns 73 and 74.

TITLE may appear several places in the program. Its function, then, is to rehead pages which follow in the production. For instance, we may want to title later pages of our sorting program with TOURNAMENT SORT, PART 2. To do this, we issue

TITLE 'TOURNAMENT SORT,PART2' (12.2.3)

EJECT

EJECT causes the ejecting of the remainder of this page of printed output and starts a new page. It takes the form

.sequence EJECT (12.2.4)

Here *sequence* is a sequence symbol or a blank. Following EJECT, there is no operand.

SPACE

The assembler inserts the number of blank lines indicated at *number* for

.sequence SPACE number (12.2.5)

PRINT

PRINT gives instructions to the assembler and is of the format

.sequence PRINT para (12.2.6)

The instructions are actually contained at *para* and can be one or more of the following designations:

- ON/OFF—a listing/no listing is printed.
- GEN/NOGEN—all statements generated by macro instructions are printed/not printed.
- DATA/NODATA—constants which appear in the program are printed out in full/truncated (to eight bytes).

PRINT statements can appear anyplace in the program and reset the assembler switches as stated at *para*. For instance, at one place, we might have

PRINT ON,NODATA,GEN (12.2.7)

This causes a listing of all statements, including expanded macro-commands but data is truncated to eight bytes. If we want the same specifications to prevail, but now wish to see data printed in full, we give

PRINT DATA (12.2.8)

Program control This group of pseudos informs the assembler about the program.

FORMAT

The input control pseudo, ICTL, permits the programmer to depart from normal format which is

- a statement begins in column 1;
- it ends in column 71;
- a continue statement begins at column 16.

To alter this format, the programmer submits

ICTL begin,end,continue (12.2.9)

where rules govern what the programmer can specify for this purpose.

SEQUENCE

The programmer often has punched into his cards a sequence number so that the cards can be kept in sequence or returned to sequence if they get dropped on the floor and get scrambled. ASLR can check if the sequence of the cards is proper if it is told to do so with

ISEQ left,right (12.2.10)

where *left* is the leftmost column and *right* is the rightmost column where the sequence number appears in the programmer's card. ASLR checks the sequence beginning when it receives ISEQ and terminates sequence checking if it receives another ISEQ where *left* and *right* are both blank.

PUNCH

Occasionally a programmer will wish to enter information directly into his program without it being assembled. He can do this with the pseudo

.sequence PUNCH 'message' (12.2.11)

This punches a card with *message* in it wherever the statement appears in the program. An alternative for this is

.sequence REPRO (12.2.12)

This reproduces the data in the next single card which follows this one.

ORIGIN

ASLR can use any origin we desire for a program we submit. If not told otherwise, it would use 0 as an origin. We can set the origin by

.sequence ORG expression (12.2.13)

LITERALS

ASLR sets up a literal pool and places it after the first section of the program. (Sectioning is discussed in the next chapter.) Should the programmer wish to have control over the pool of literals, he may set its origin with this pseudo:

symbol LTORG (12.2.14)

The pool of literals created by ASLR for all literals defined previous to this point are placed in a pool after this pseudo appears.

As we discussed with respect to macros, the program can call for code found in some external library by naming his source in EXTERNAL CODE

COPY symbol (12.2.15)

Before assembly is completed, 𝒜𝒮ℒℛ goes out to the external source, gets the code, and enters it into the program where COPY appears.

To indicate that the assembler has seen the last assembly language statement, that statement is followed by END

END exp (12.2.16)

Here *exp* is an expression naming the statement in the new program to which control should be passed by the loader after the program has been placed in MEMORY.

To tell the programmer where to set the location counter, we use START

symbol START term (12.2.17)

Here *symbol* is the name of the first section of the program and *term* gives an origin for the program so that ORG need not be used.

12.3 DATA AND SPACE

Pseudos We have examined the pseudo to define the constant, DC, and the one to reserve space, DS. The substitution pseudo, EQU, serves a multitude of purposes which we examine immediately below. A fourth pseudo defines channel control word.

EQU This pseudo has the format

symbol EQU exp (12.3.1)

Symbol can be an ordinary symbol or a variable symbol; *exp* is a combination of symbols and numerics. *Symbol* is made equal to *exp* after it is evaluated and takes on the attributes thereof: length, address, value, and relocatability.

One use of EQU is when several programmers work on the same or different segments using different symbols to stand for the same variable. Before the program runs, these symbols are equated using EQU. For instance, one programmer has used GROPAY and another has used GP to stand for the variable, *gross pay*. The assembler should not assign two different addresses to these two symbols and, in fact, must not. After the pseudo below, only one address is assigned to either symbol occurrence in the program:

```
GP        EQU       GROPAY                              (12.3.2)
```

Another use for EQU is when an expression appears frequently in the program. The programmer is saved the trouble of writing out this expression each time by replacing it with a single symbol. Here is an example:

```
NF        EQU       F+L'F1-L'F2                         (12.3.3)
```

Another instance arises when the programmer refers to GPRS symbolically. At the end of the program, he can make an assignment using EQU thus:

```
R1        EQU       3                                   (12.3.4)
```

Now wherever R1 appears in the program as a GPR designation, it is replaced by 3. This is particularly useful when a program must be run on several different models of System 360. To reassemble the program for another model with different software, one EQU card can be replaced with another making a different GPR assignment without going through the whole program and changing it.

Immediate data can be designated symbolically with EQU thus:

```
F         EQU       4X'FF'                              (12.3.5)
```

Now, if we wish to look for a flag of all F's, we can compare with the symbolic entity, F.

CCW When the programmer descends to the level of writing his own channel program, he has to create his own CCWs. Certainly, he can do this with a DC defining the CCW in hexadecimal or binary but this is a lot of trouble. The pseudo, CCW, permits him to make his definition symbolically.

Recall that the CCW contains

- a byte containing a subcommand designation,
- a three-byte address,
- five one-bit flags followed by zeros,
- a two-byte count.

The pseudo, CCW, permits the programmer to specify all these symbolically using the format

```
symbol    CCW       sc,ad,fl,ct                         (12.3.6)
```

Here, *symbol* is a symbolic name; *sc* is a decimal number corresponding to the subcommand; *ad* is an address in symbolic form; *fl* is a flag byte defined in hexadecimal, the first five bits of which are the flags and the last three bits of which are 0's; *ct* is a decimal number specifying *count*, the number of bytes of data to be transmitted.

Action No action is taken for these pseudos until we reach the pass called Symbol. During this pass, the length of the space required for each is calculated and the location counter is advanced by that number of bytes. On the final pass, Output, space is filled with the proper constant for those pseudos which require this.

For these pseudos during Symbol, the following operations are done: DC, DS

1. The multiplier is found and converted into binary.
2. The symbol type is found and interpreted from the SYMTAB.
3. The unit length is determined in bytes and converted to binary.
4. The field length is calculated.
5. The location counter is advanced by this amount.

For Output, only DC is interpreted.

EQU produces a cross-reference so that whenever Symbol is referenced in SYMTAB, the value at *exp* is found and used to replace it during Output. EQU

CCW produces a doubleWord—eight bytes—by which the location counter is advanced during Symbol. For Output, the pseudo is replaced by a doubleWord generated according to the specifications in the pseudo. CCW

PROBLEMS

12.1 Show how to start your program so that GPR8-11 will be used as respective BASE REGISTERS.

12.2 In the last 4K section of the above program, it becomes apparent that the program will occupy 20K. However, the last 4K will never reference the first 4K. How do you reset the last 4K to use GPR8 as a base reference there?

12.3 For Prob. 12.2 I want to use X, defined in the first 4K, in the last 4K. An ADCON is needed. Use GPR2 and get X into GPR2.

12.4 A good idea for documentation is to put a box containing the description of a macro, or of the program, where it will help most. Why are asterisks perfect characters of which to make the box, thus:

```
*************************************************
*                                               *
*               DOCUMENTATION                   *
*                                               *
*************************************************
```

12.5 Explain how symbolic names can be given to GPR's used in the program. How are numbers assigned? What is the advantage of this for documentation? Program revision?

12.6 Each new macrodefinition should begin on a new page. Each page should have a title. One or more blank lines should intervene between important program divisions. What pseudos do this, and how?

12.7 Explain how you would use PRINT to improve documentation.

12.8 SPACE and EJECT are not permitted in macrodefinitions. Explain how to get essentially blank lines in only the macrodefinition; in both the macrodefinition and its expansion.

12.9 Use all the above principles of documentation now. Write, code, document (with comments), and debug three REGISTER management macros and test as described below.

(a) BRING prototype BRING &R,&FROM
(&R is a REGISTER number in which &FROM is placed.)
(1) If &R is 13-1, produce MNOTE.
2,SYSTEM REGISTER REQUESTED
(2) If &R is empty, place &FROM there and note (with global SET array) unless &FROM is *also* in another REGISTER.
(3) If &FROM is in *another* REGISTER, place it in &R and note.
(4) If &R contains a named quantity, return it to MEMORY before placing &FROM there and note.
(5) If &R is a WORK REGISTER, produce MNOTE.
(2,REGISTER &N is a WORK REGISTER.)
Here &GPR(12) is a global character SET array which keeps track of REGISTER assignments. &GPR(i) is
- *blank* if GPRi is unassigned;
- contains *symbol* if GPRi contains *symbol*;
- contains 9 if GPRi is used for *work*.

(b) USE prototype USE &R
(1) sets &GPR(&R) to 9 if it is empty;
(2) puts away *symbol* and sets &GPR(&R) to 9 if a symbol is present.
(3) If &R is in use, produce MNOTE.

(c) RESET RESET &R
(1) releases a WORK REGISTER;
(2) does nothing if &R is not a WORK REGISTER.

Then write ACC, a macro just like ADALIST of Prob. 11.7 with two exceptions:

(1) Use BRING to get the sum from the address furnished by the last parameter into GPR2;
(2) *Do not put the answers back*. It will be returned automatically by the next BRING, if necessary.

Finally, to test your macros, write a program which includes:

```
ACC      A,B,S1
ACC      C,D,S1
ACC      A,B,C,D,S2
ACC      S1
ACC      S1,E,S2
ACC      S2,F,S1
BRING    2,S3
USE      2
ACC      G,S1
RESET    2
ACC      G,S1
BRING    C
ACC      S1,S3
RESET    2
ACC      H,I,J,S3
USE      2
L        2,S4
A        2,A
ST       2,S4
BRING    S4
RESET    2
ACC      S1,S2,S3,S4
```

13

SECTION

13.1 CSECT

Purpose Sectioning permits several different subprograms to be incorporated in the same assembly. These subprograms could be written by the same or a different programmer. Each subprogram is identified by a pseudo, namely CSECT. 𝒜𝒮ℒℛ acts on the subprograms as though they were different programs. Unless otherwise told, each subprogram (or CSECT as it's known familiarly by the BAL programmer) starts at origin 0 in relocatable form.

The CSECT has a further purpose—it enables *pieces* of the subprograms to be scattered throughout the program. The assembler collects them together to form a single subprogram from the pieces which compose it.

The CSECT provides a lot of independence for each subprogram but to the degree where they must be treated almost like separate programs. This has both advantages and disadvantages in modularizing the program.

Program modules have long been a necessity. *Computer Software*† discussed the means provided by FAP. FAP provides the pseudo, HEAD, which accepts all references within the module as local references but also permits global references with a high degree of simplicity. A pseudo like HEAD would be difficult to provide proper assembly for, with BAL, because of the BASE REGISTER problem. Hence, the CSECT method has been adopted.

† Ivan Flores, *Computer Software*. Englewood Cliffs, N.J.: Prentice-Hall, Inc., 1965, Section 8.3.

Format The pseudo, CSECT, has the format

symbol CSECT (13.1.1)

Here *symbol* is a name of the section for which code follows. Since one of the facilities of the CSECT is interspersing pieces of a section throughout the program, we may find several CSECTs which have the same name at *symbol.* This is *not* a multiply-defined symbol as is clear from its use. Notice that *location* is always *blank*.

It is also possible for *symbol* to be *blank*. This is often done when the assembler consists of one CSECT or when it consists of a main CSECT which the programmer wants to be nameless to go with other CSECTs which are named.

START We have already examined the pseudo, START, which has the format

symbol START term (13.1.2)

It may be viewed in a somewhat different light now, for we can see that it serves two purposes:

- It names the CSECT—the main CSECT with the program—as *symbol.*
- It sets the origin to a nonzero quantity when *term* is present.

For instance, we examine the following pseudo:

START 3456 (13.1.3)

It says that the first CSECT in the program is nameless and that its origin is 3456. Similarly, for

SS START 123 (13.1.4)

we find that this is equivalent to

```
        ORG     123
SS      CSECT
```
(13.1.5)

Function Figure 13.1.1 examines how the 𝒜𝒮ℒℛ operates when it encounters several CSECTs in the program. The program on the left of the figure consists of numbered pieces, the first of which begins with START and all the others begin with CSECT.

𝒜𝒮ℒℛ establishes a location counter for each CSECT in the program. A location counter is set to 0 at the first occurrence of a new CSECT. When another CSECT appears in the program, the assembler gets the location counter for that CSECT and continues the count from its present reading.

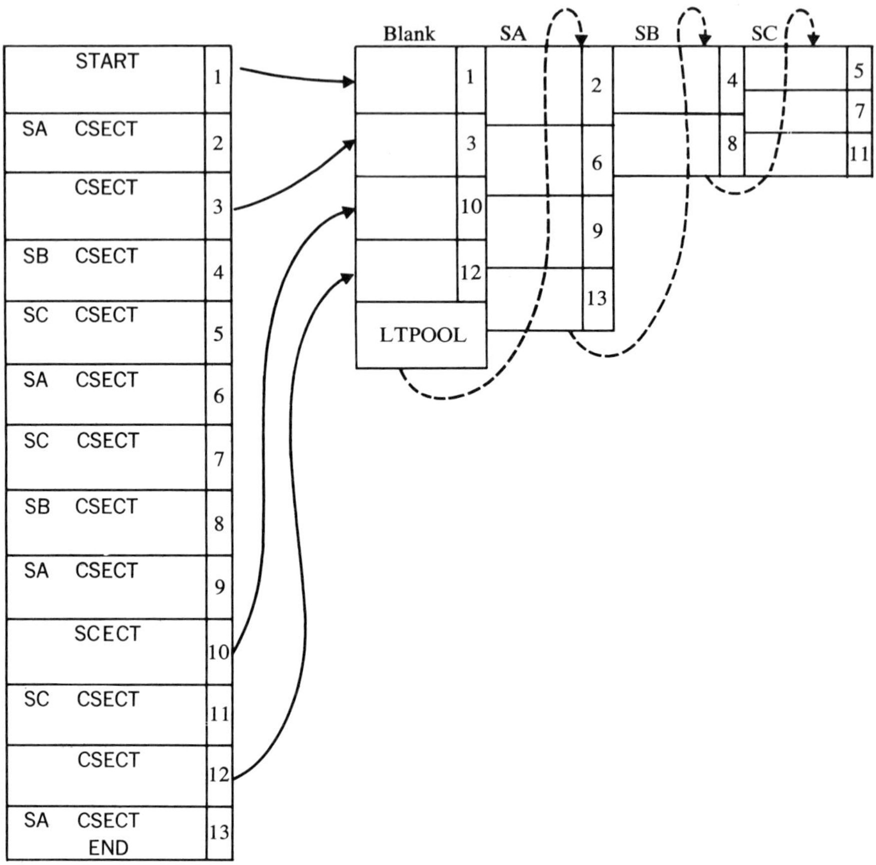

Fig. 13.1.1 Each occurrence of CSECT signals a start of a new program section (first time) or a return to assembly of that (labeled) program section (second time thereafter).

For instance, in the figure, START is unlabeled. This is a blank CSECT; piece 1 of the program uses the blank location counter. When piece 2 of the subprogram prefixed with CSECT labeled SA is encountered, a new location counter is assigned to it and piece 2 of the program is assembled. At the beginning of piece 3, another blank CSECT is encountered. This switches the assembler over to the blank location counter and we continue assembly using it. The reader can follow the remainder of the diagram seeing how the four CSECTs of the program are literally "pieced" together.

After the pieces of the program have been allocated to their proper CSECTs, continuity is restored to the program by the assembler. It now places the CSECTs together in a single program with one CSECT following the other according to the appearance of the first CSECT for that subprogram in the original assembly language program. Thus, the final output contains in order: *blank* CSECT, SA, SB, and then SC.

One more thing is done by the assembler—it inserts the literal pool at the end of the first CSECT, as shown in the figure.

Communication Can two CSECTs talk with each other and exchange data? The answer to this question must be yes—in some way or other. Otherwise, the CSECTs would be totally isolated from each other. Actually there is a high degree of isolation since a symbolic reference to data or commands in another CSECT is prohibited.

In other words, if I name a datum or a command in one CSECT, I can't get that named datum or command from another CSECT *directly*. The reason for this is that same old BASE REGISTER problem.

When I write a CSECT, I establish BASE REGISTERS for that CSECT with USING just as I do for any single program. USING sets up BASE REGISTERS for the assembler so that it can enter addresses into commands in base/displacement format. Since

- each CSECT has different or even overlapping BASE REGISTERS assigned to it and
- ASLR need not be aware of which BASE REGISTERS are available for each CSECT and further
- the same BASE REGISTERS *may* be used for different CSECTs at different times,

intermodular symbolic referencing is possible among CSECTs assembled together but is dangerous and is discouraged (Why?).

Then how can the two CSECTs communicate? They use

- address constants,
- subroutine linkage.

Communication is best explained with an example which appears in Fig. 13.1.2. The blank CSECT is established by START. Later in the program, the CSECT, SA, is established with an appropriate pseudo. Notice that each initial appearance of CSECT (or START) is followed by the usual BALR and USING: EXAMPLE

- The blank CSECT uses GPR2.
- SA uses GPR3.

Somewhere in the blank CSECT, we would like to use part of SA. We link to it using BALR. By convention, the return register is GPR14; the linking register is GPR15. We fill GPR15 with the destination by the *load* command which precedes the BALR. This load command places the address of SA into GPR15.

```
 1              START
 2              BALR      2,0
 3              USING     *,2
                  .
                  .
                  .
 4    X         DS        F
 5              L         15,=V(SA)
 6              BALR      14,15
 7              ST        5,X
-------------------------------------------------------------
 8    SA        CSECT
 9              BALR      3,0
10              USING     *,3
11              L         5,=V(X)        V(X) ——> GPR5
12              L         6,0(5)         X ——> GPR6
                  .
                  .
                  .
13              BR        14
```

Fig. 13.1.2 Branching and getting data to another CSECT.

When we go to SA, we establish immediately the BASE REGISTER appropriate to this CSECT.

Notice that later in SA we need the variable X which has been defined in the blank CSECT. It can't be addressed directly; we refer to it by loading its address in GPR5. But we want the word (labeled X) in GPR6. The command which follows loads GPR6 by using GPR5 as a BASE REGISTER with the displacement of 0. Since S360 does not have indirect addressing, this is a program method for doing indirect addressing.

ADDRESSES

You may ask "How come 𝒜𝒮ℒℛ can get *addresses* of symbols that it needs?" Well, addresses and final code are established only after the entire program has been patched together as it appears in the right of Fig. 13.1.1—the program is then a continuous group of CSECTs. The symbol table contains absolute addresses of all symbols in every CSECT. When 𝒜𝒮ℒℛ is working on a given CSECT, it has a table established by USING so that it can make up a base/displacement address for each command as it occurs. It does this from the absolute address in the assembly table and the BASE REGISTER reference table which lists the available BASE REGISTERS and their contents.

When an address constant is called for, its location is found in absolute terms and placed where requested. For instance, in command 11, Fig. 13.1.2, the address of X is obtained in absolute form from the symbol table. This location is addressed as a literal because 𝒜𝒮ℒℛ has to establish a Word which stores the address of X in the CSECT, SA, just as it would for any other item in statement 4. Next ASLR takes the cell in SA (where it has stored the address of statement 4 in absolute form) and, using the BASE REGISTER table, converts it into base/displacement form. That replaces =A(X) in statement 11. When the *load* command is executed at run time, the contents of literal Word in SA are placed in GPR5 which then contains the address of the symbol, X.

Obviously, the next command can go to the address specified by the contents of GPR5 and, bearing a displacement of zero, place it in GPR6.

13.2 DSECT

Purpose The pseudo, DSECT, divides an externally provided area and names each division so that the program or CSECT can reference each division by a symbolic name. The external area might be provided by another CSECT or by an external program or by software such as an Access Method. (DSECT stands for dummy section; any commands contained in the DSECT are only dummies and supply information to the assembler so that it can make up the symbol reference.)

Need Why would anyone need to reference an external area? This is best made clear with the example presented in Fig. 13.2.1. It concerns the use of an Access Method (discussed elsewhere in detail†) by the assembly language program. To summarize briefly, an Access Method (or simply AMethod) is the means by which the programmer requests IO operations. He does so with a simple macro such as GET. The AMethod completely takes care of the IO need and returns to the program the record requested by it. Of course, it can't return an entire record conveniently and, instead, it places the location of the first byte of that record in a particular REGISTER. For BAL this is GPR1. Hence, after giving GET, the program at some later point finds a location of the desired record in GPR1.

The programmer would like to reference his record symbolically. In the figure, he has called the entire record for a payroll application, MREC. He has also named a number of fields in the record. The first four of these are called

- MKEY for the master record key,
- MNAME for the master record name,
- MGPAY for the gross pay-to-date,
- MYTDW for year-to-date witholding tax.

† Ivan Flores, *Data Structures and the S360*. Englewood Cliffs, N.J.: Prentice-Hall, Inc., 1970.

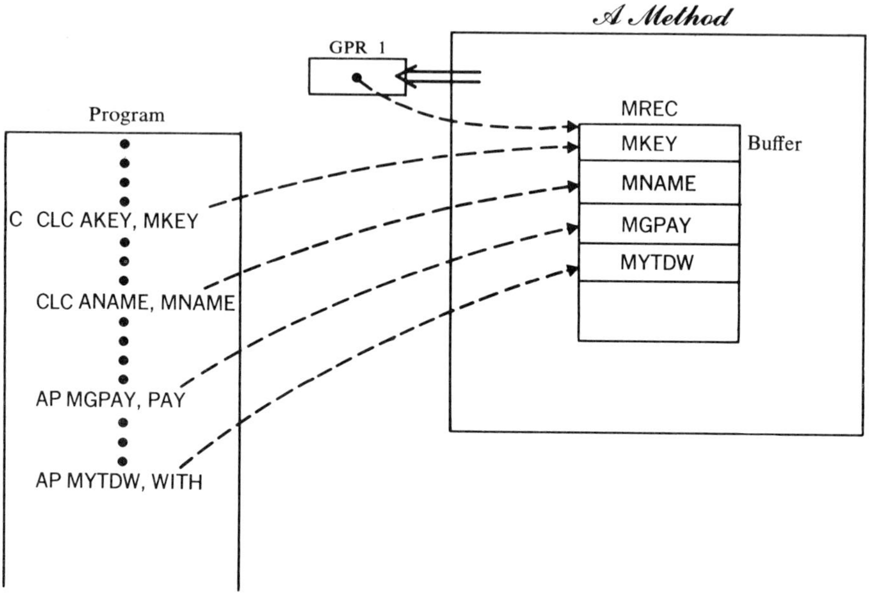

Fig. 13.2.1 The DSECT enables the program to reference a foreign area, such as a buffer provided by the *A Method*, symbolically. The symbols to name the area are provided in the program.

The figure also shows some commands which might appear in the assembly language version of the program. One of these compares the key field of an activity record, AKEY to the key field of a master record, MKEY to verify that the right master was acquired posting. A second check is made with another command to be sure that the name of the employee in both records is identical (MNAME=ANAME?). Commands follow to calculate the gross pay for the previous period. We then come upon an AP which adds the calculated gross pay, PAY to the gross year-to-date pay, MGPAY. A similar command appears later in the program which adds the calculated withholding tax WITH to the year-to-date withholding tax, MYTDW.

You have seen how convenient it is to be able to reference an external area symbolically. But how do we set up this area so that it is addressable?

Method The format of the pseudo, DSECT, is

symbol DSECT (13.2.1)

where symbol names the dummy section. A number of steps of reservations using DSs follow. For instance, in the application of Fig. 13.2.1, we might write this DSECT:

```
MREC     DSECT
MKEY     DS       CL6
MNAME    DS       CL24
MGPAY    DS       PL5
MYTDW    DS       PL4              (13.2.2)
```

This communicates to 𝒜𝒮ℒℛ that the external area is to be broken up as described. To establish labels for the program, we first set up a GPR which contains the location of the first byte in the area to be partitioned. This is an absolute address. 𝒜ℳethod has already provided the location in GPR1. However, it is dangerous to leave this address in GPR1 since the 𝒜ℳethod may make further communications to us via this GPR. Let us shift this address to GPR4:

```
         LR       4,1              (13.2.3)
```

Now all we need do is tell 𝒜𝒮ℒℛ that we are using GPR4 to reference the area we have named MREC and it will permit us to use the symbolic names we have established. We do this with

```
         USING    MREC,4           (13.2.4)
```

Action 𝒜𝒮ℒℛ sets up displacements for each named field, placing these in a table where they are accessible to it. For instance, the displacement associated with the given symbol can be indicated by the displacement operator, D, so that we have

D(MKEY)=0
D(MNAME)=6
D(MGPAY)=30 (13.2.5)
D(MYTDW)=35,etc.

In commands that follow which reference this external area, the assembler converts a symbol into the displacement found in (13.2.5) and attaches the BASE REGISTER furnished by USING.

Example Figure 13.2.2 contains an example of commands of an assembly language program which uses DSECTs. The first three lines of the program establish the main (blank) CSECT and tell 𝒜𝒮ℒℛ that GPRS 8, 9, and 10 are to be used as BASE REGISTERS for this

```
1                START
2                BALR      8,0
3                USING     *,8,9,10
                   .
                   .
                   .
4     MDCB       DCB       DDNAME=MPAY, . . .
5     ADCB       DCB       DDNAME=APAY, . . .
                   .
                   .
                   .
6     AGET       GET       ADCB
7                LR        3,1
8                USING     AREC,3
9     MGET       GET       MDCB
10               LR        4,1
11               USING     MREC,4
12               CLC       AKEY,MKEY
13               BNE       NOPOST
14               CLC       ANAME,MNAME
15               BN        NAMERR
16               GROCAL    ATIME,MRATE, . . . ,PAY
17               AP        MGPAY,PAY
                   .
                   .
                   .
18    AREC       DSECT
18    AKEY       DS        CL6
20    ANAME      DS        CL24
21    ATIME      DS        PL3
                   .
                   .
                   .
22    MREC       DSECT
23    MKEY       DS        CL6
                   .
                   .
                   .
```

Fig. 13.2.2 Using DSECTs in a program.

CSECT. Statements 4 and 5 establish data control blocks for a master file MPAY and an active file, APAY, using the system macro, DCB. These statements are labeled MDCB and ADCB. The first AMethod macro appears at AGET and references the DCB labeled ADCB. The AMethod returns the location of the record it finds in GPR1. The command at statement 7 loads this address from GPR1 into GPR3. We now tell that we are going to be using symbolic names for the record called AREC and that displacements are to be calculated with reference to GPR3.

Down below at statement 18, we find the DSECT for AREC which divides it up and names the sections symbolically for the program.

At MGET, we do the same for the master record called MREC using GPR4 as a BASE REGISTER for referencing this dummy area. Statement 12 compares the keys of the two records. Notice how simple it is to make this symbolic comparison. 𝒜𝔖𝔏ℜ substitutes 0(3) for AKEY and 0(4) for MKEY.

Notice that on line 16 these names are passed as parameters to a macro called GROCAL which does a calculation for us. Should this macro require length or other attributes of the symbols which are passed to it as parameters, these are found by 𝒜𝔖𝔏ℜ by referencing the proper DSECT (or a table made therefrom).

Another use of DSECTs is in getting parameters to a subroutine so that it can refer to them by name. We shall see an example of this in the next chapter.

13.3 EXTERNAL REFERENCES

External symbol dictionary 𝒜𝔖𝔏ℜ produces, as a result of its translation, an object module. This module cannot be loaded without being edited by the linkage editor, 𝔈𝔇𝔍𝔗, which produces a load module. The programmer submits to 𝔈𝔇𝔍𝔗 several programs together with directions for putting these together to form the running package, the **load module.** It's 𝔈𝔇𝔍𝔗, which does the cross-referencing among the programs. Obviously, the programs talk to each other or they would be independent and we would not load them together. For one program to talk to another, the object module of each must reference another. The area in the object module which would have these references is called the **external symbol dictionary.** It precedes the rest of the module and contains two portions as shown in Fig. 13.3.1:

- The *in* portion contains references to *this* program which may be used by other programs.
- The *out* portion lists references to *other* programs made by *this* program.

There are several ways to establish such references; namely,

- incoming references are established by ENTRY and CSECT;
- outgoing references are established by EXTRN and V( ).

References When the programmer realizes that he wishes to reference an external section, he issues the pseudo, EXTRN, which has the format EXTRN

$$\text{sequence} \quad \text{EXTRN} \quad \text{symbol(s)} \qquad (13.3.1)$$

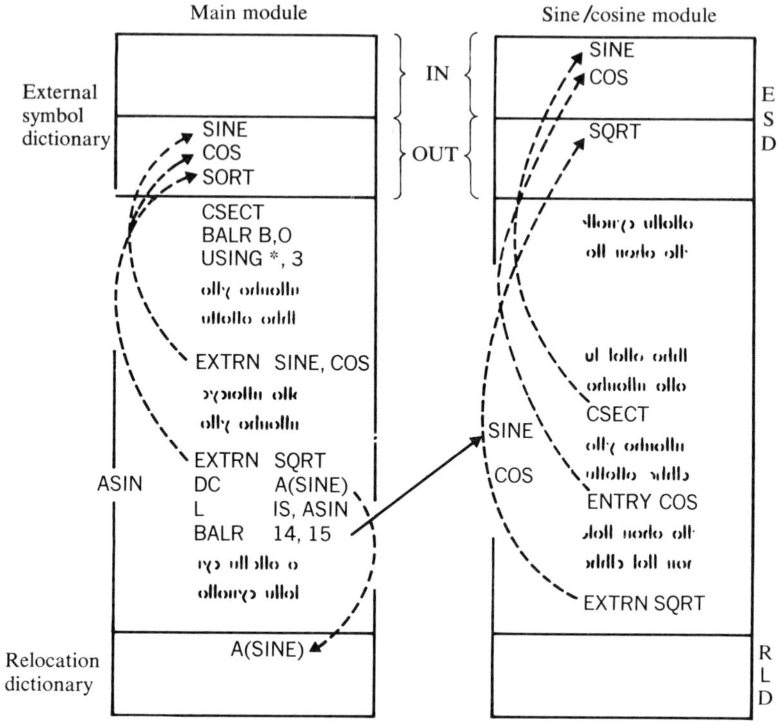

Fig. 13.3.1 EXTRN and V ( ) enters items in ESD (out); CSECT and ENTRY cause entries in ESD (in). A ( ) causes an entry in the RLD.

Sequence is a sequence symbol or blank, *symbol(s)* may not be contained *anywhere* at *name* in this program—it should be either the label of a CSECT or the *symbol* of ENTRY of another (external) program. This pseudo establishes entries in the external symbol dictionary as indicated by the dashed lines in Fig. 13.3.1.

ENTRY

When the programmer realizes that a command in his program will be referenced by another program, he uses ENTRY, thus:

sequence ENTRY symbol(s) (13.3.2)

Again, *sequence* can be a sequence symbol or a *blank* and *symbol* must be the label of some statement in this program. Of course, ENTRY establishes an entry in the external symbol dictionary too, as shown again by dashed lines in Fig. 13.3.1.

LINKAGE

Use To establish linkage with an external CSECT, we first define an address constant. This constant will not be supplied by 𝒜𝒮ℒℛ but will be filled in by ℰ𝒟𝒥𝒯 before run time. For instance, in our program to refer to the sine routine, SINE, we define a constant representing its address thus:

```
ASINE     DC        A(SINE)                (13.3.3)
```

This is loaded into GPR15 if we use the 𝒪𝒮 linkage convention thus:

```
          L         15,ASINE               (13.3.4)
```

We take off with

```
          BALR      14,15                  (13.3.5)
```

Somewhere in our program there should appear

```
          EXTRN     SINE                   (13.3.6)
```

WITHOUT EXTRN

To circumvent EXTRN, we use the variable constant notation. We eliminate (13.3.6) by substituting for (13.3.3).

```
ASINE     DC        V(SINE)                (13.3.7)
```

DATA

To get to data in an external program, we have to make several moves. First, we declare a symbolic location of the data. Call this RESULT:

```
          EXTRN     RESULT                 (13.3.8)
```

Now we need a label for this address. Call it ARES. Then we have

```
ARES      DC        A(RESULT)              (13.3.9)
```

To reference this area, its address is loaded into a register, say GPR4:

```
          L         4,ARES                 (13.3.10)
```

We tell 𝒜𝒮ℒℛ that we are using the contents of GPR4 to represent the label RESULT, thus:

```
          USING     RESULT,4               (13.3.11)
```

Now, to reference the third word in that area and add it to GPR6, we give

```
          A         6,RESULT+8             (13.3.12)
```

VARIABLE CONSTANTS

It is clear how a single variable constant is defined using DC and the label. I note here that it is possible to set up an area in our program to which we transmit several addresses from different programs. For instance, in Fig. 13.3.1, we could establish three variable constants with one pseudo, thus:

```
CONS      DC        V(SINE,COS,SQRT)       (13.3.13)
```

Then we would have

```
          (CONS+8)=V(SQRT)                 (13.3.14)
```

13.4 LITERALS

Literals and sections We run into the BASE REGISTER problem again. All commands and data in a CSECT should be accessible to the CSECT. The pseudo, USING, establishes BASE REGISTERS and permits 𝒜𝒮ℒℛ to convert an absolute address into base/displacement. What about the literal though? When the programmer uses a literal in his command, he wants 𝒜𝒮ℒℛ to be invisible to him so that he need not be worried about that literal's placement. 𝒜𝒮ℒℛ on the other hand, is concerned with all literals which appear in many sections. If it creates a single literal pool and then places that pool in one CSECT, how can other CSECTs reference it? 𝒜𝒮ℒℛ might get around this somehow if it was assured that each CSECT had a different BASE REGISTER but this is not the case. And because the programmer can use DROP and USING, we often find two CSECTs with the same BASE REGISTER where, of course, that BASE REGISTER contains a different base quantity in each CSECT.

So it is not so good to have literals all in one place when the program is sectioned.

Literal placement When the programmer does not tell 𝒜𝒮ℒℛ where he wants the literals, 𝒜𝒮ℒℛ places all literals immediately after the first CSECT. From the discussion of the previous section, it should be clear that a better situation is to have a separate pool of literals for each CSECT. The programmer can tell 𝒜𝒮ℒℛ where he wants the literal pool to begin for this CSECT with the pseudo, LTORG, which has the format

symbol LTORG (13.4.1)

The result of this command is that the assembler places all literals that it has encountered between the *last* LTORG and *this* LTORG in a pool right after *this* LTORG. The pool begins on a doubleWord boundary.

To be effective, 𝒜𝒮ℒℛ refers *this* LTORG to the last one to appear in this CSECT, not to the assembly language input stream in general. Hence, the action of this pseudo can take place only after the CSECTs have been separated.

Action To see the action of LTORG, examine Fig. 13.4.1 which shows the assembly program after CSECTs have been coalesced and separated. During 𝔖𝔶𝔪𝔟, a separate location counter is assigned to each CSECT as it is encountered to assemble them together.

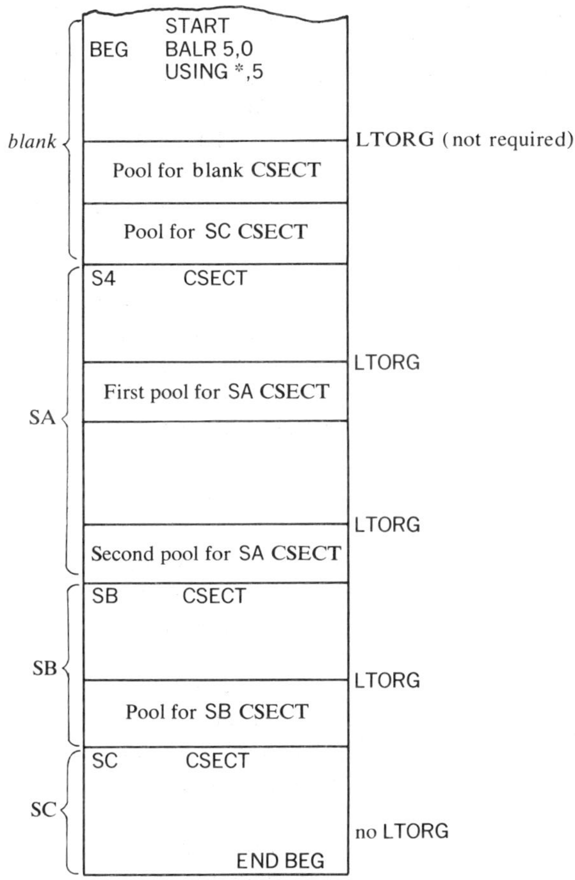

Fig. 13.4.1 Action produced in assembly language equivalent if machine language output for the pseudo LTORG in different CSECTs of a program.

When a new CSECT pseudo is encountered, a new location counter is established. When a CSECT pseudo returns us to an old CSECT, the location counter for that CSECT is obtained and counting continued from its present setting. When a literal is encountered, its name is entered in a symbol table and the literal pool counter for this CSECT is advanced according to the size of the literal. Thus, for each CSECT, we have two counters:

- The location counter marks the present location of commands within a given CSECT.
- The literal pool counter marks the place of literals within the literal pool for this CSECT.

When an LTORG is encountered within a CSECT, the location counter for that CSECT is advanced by an amount equal to the present setting of the literal pool counter. The latter is then reset to 0. This is where a literal pool will go in this CSECT.

It is possible to have more than one LTORG in a CSECT. When this occurs, it is because more commands intervene between LTORG and the CSECT end. Therefore, we continue to step the location counter as new commands are examined; literals encountered advance the literal pool counter after the first LTORG has reset it to 0.

When END is encountered, all literal pool counters are checked in order of the appearance of the CSECTs with which they are associated. If a nonzero literal pool counter is encountered, this indicates that the literal pool for that CSECT has not been totally accounted for. 𝒜𝔖𝔏ℜ moves those literal pools so that they come right after the first CSECT in the program. This is done by advancing that initial location counter by the total amount contained in all the nonzero literal pool counters.

Example Let us examine Fig. 13.4.1, a picture of run time MEMORY after the pass, 𝔖𝔶𝔪𝔟. For the CSECT, SB, the literal pool comes after the CSECT because the programmer used the proper convention here, placing LTORG at the end of the CSECT.

The CSECT, SA, has two LTORGs in it. Thus we find two literal pools, one in the middle and one in the end of the CSECT.

The CSECT, SC, has no literal pool associated with it. When 𝒜𝔖𝔏ℜ found END it made a place for the literals created for SC at the end of the blank CSECT.

Finally, we have the blank CSECT which may or may not have LTORG at the end. The assembler places literals for it at its end without the need for an LTORG. Since CSECT SC has no LTORG, we find its literals also at the end of the blank CSECT.

The programmer may find that he is in trouble with regard to CSECT SC if he has not provided a means for communicating the literals for his section to it from their pool at the end of the blank CSECT.

13.5 ADDRESS CONSTANTS

Addresses Whenever symbols appear in a command to address MEMORY symbolically, recall that the symbol is converted into an absolute address. The base/displacement problem is ever present; this requires 𝒜𝔖𝔏ℜ to convert the absolute address into a BASE REGISTER indication and a displacement by referring to the USING table. It finds a BASE REGISTER with contents less than the desired address by 4K or less. The difference between this BASE REGISTER content and the absolute address is the displacement. It is placed in the command along with the BASE REGISTER indicator.

Often it is necessary to establish an absolute address of a command or datum for use at run time. But 𝒜𝒮ℒℛ does not know this run time address. Yet this runtime address is necessary to establish links to other CSECTs and subroutines within the program. Recall that ENTRY is used to talk to "external" programs.

The means to establish an absolute address in the program is the **address constant,** sometimes referred to by the programmer as **adcon.** It can be set up with a DC or used as a literal. We explore the first occurrence which is declared thus:

AX DC A(X) (13.5.1)

Here AX is a cell which contains the address of the location called X:

- A(X) tells 𝒜𝒮ℒℛ that we want the address of X.
- AX says that this point in the program [where A(X) is placed] will henceforth be called AX.

Quasi Because 𝒜𝒮ℒℛ cannot know the run time address of X, 𝒜𝒮ℒℛ can't fulfill (13.5.1) directly and must provide some information to the loader, ℒ𝒪𝒜𝒟, who will make the proper adjustments and create an actual address as required at runtime. The RLD technique, which I call a **quasi**, is diagrammed in Fig. 13.5.1. The address constant produces an entry in the **relocation dictionary, RLD,** with pointers to two places in the program:

- 𝒜𝒮ℒℛ reserves a cell (here AX) where the desired address is placed—The address of X relative to the beginning of its CSECT.
- 𝒜𝒮ℒℛ creates an RLD entry with a pointer to AX and to the ESD entry for the section containing X.

Examine the example again with some numbers relative to the beginning of the CSECT plugged in. In the figure, the program begins with START, which has blanks in *name* and *location*, meaning that this is a blank CSECT with origin, 0. This sets up a (*blank*) entry in the ESD with ID = 01 ①. The two commands which follow set up and indicate the BASE REGISTERS used in this CSECT. We are examining an object module equivalent as produced by 𝒜𝒮ℒℛ and, at its beginning, find the external symbol dictionary, ESD.

We now note the following addresses from Fig. 13.5.1: X is defined at 6114 as a space occupying one fullWord ②. AX is declared at 7280 and

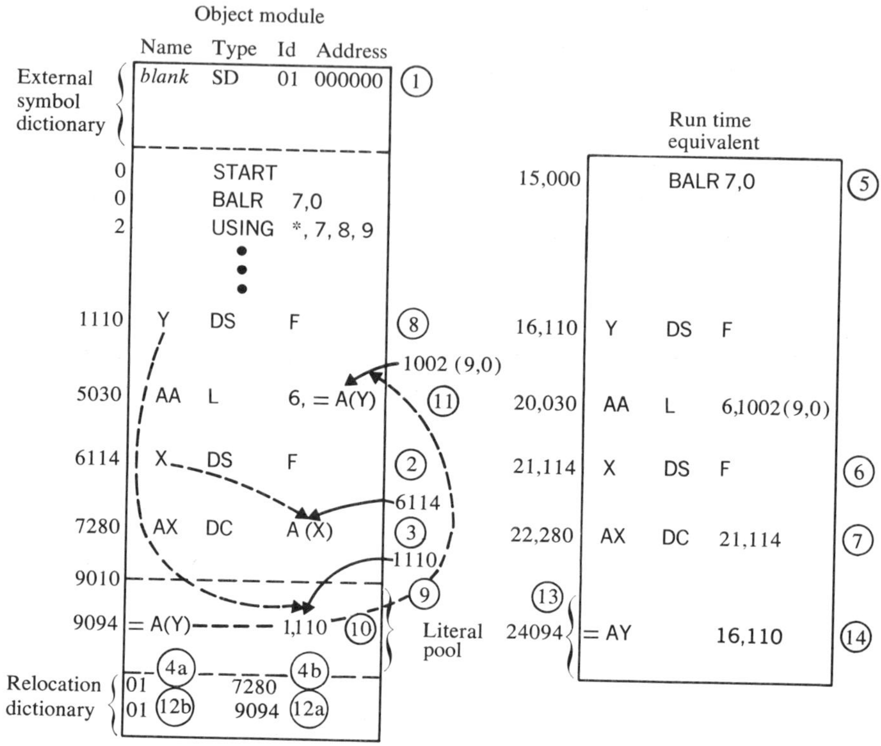

Fig. 13.5.1 The treatment of adcons by ASLR and LOAD.

is the name for the address of X which is placed there relative to 0 (6114) ③. In the relocation dictionary, RLD, which follows the program ④, there is an entry which contains (a) the relative position of AX in the program (7280) and (b) the identification of the CSECT in which X is defined as it appears in the ESD (01).

LOAD

Before the program can run, it is brought in by LOAD. Suppose that LOAD places the program at 15000 as shown at the right side of Fig. 13.5.1. Then, the first command which was

```
BALR     7,0                                        (13.5.2)
```

now appears at 15000 ⑤. There is a blank space of fullWord size at 21114 which bears the name X in the original program ⑥. There is a fullWord cell named AX at 22280.

When LOAD has finished entering the program, it examines the entries in the RLD. The one which concerns us contains 7280 as its first pointer and 01 as the ID. LOAD's task is simple:

- Get the load point (15000) for the CSECT identified in the ESD.
- Add this load point to the contents (6114) of the cell pointed to (22,280) after relativizing that cell (7280) to get the new contents (21114) which are placed there ⑦.

This result appears at the right of the figure. Now notice that because of the cooperation between LOAD and ASLR, the cell labeled AX actually contains the run time address of the cell labeled X.

Literal Now let us see how an adcon can be used in a command. At AA, I can load the address of the symbol, Y, into GPR6 with

```
AA      L      6,=A(Y)
```
(13.5.3)

This example is also incorporated into Fig. 13.5.1. Notice that address assigned to Y at assembly time is 1110 ⑧. ASLR detects = at AA (13.5.3) and realizes that a literal is called for. It therefore creates a literal entry, the name of which is A(Y). An address is not assigned to the literal in the program until after Sym. The literal is placed in the literal table for this CSECT and the literal location counter contents are associated with this literal. In this case, from the figure, you see that A(Y) has been assigned a literal count of 84.

During the final pass, Out, the location of the literal pool ⑨ is known (9010). The location assigned to the literal A(Y) ⑩ is also known (9094). Now, when the program is scanned to enter addresses, ASLR makes one for AA which is assigned the location 5030 ⑪. The assembler replaces =A(Y) by the address assigned to the literal (9094). However, this address must be in base/displacement notation. From USING, note that GPR9 contains 8192. This is the proper base to use to relativize 9094. Hence, =A(Y) is replaced by 902(9,0). The contents of 9094 is the present relative address to which it applies, 1110. Now and at run time, the command at AA references the literal which is at 9094 relative to the beginning of the absolute assembly.

RLD

ASLR is not finished because every adcon requires an RLD entry ⑫. This RLD entry references the literal pool. Therefore, the RLD entry consists of the location of adcon in the literal pool (9094) (12a), the identification of the CSECT to which the symbol name belongs as it appears in the ESD (01) (12b).

LOAD

Before the program can run, LOAD brings it in. This is the same program we discussed earlier and its load point is 15000. After loading,

𝔏𝔒𝔄𝔇 sets up RLD entries. For =A(Y), in this example, it does the following:

- finds the load point of the CSECT referenced in the ESD (15000) which it has set up,
- adds the loadpoint for this CSECT (15000) to the relative location of the literal to find the absolute location (24094) of =A(Y),
- adds the load point (15000) to the contents of 24,094 or (=A(Y)) or 1110 to get 16,110 which is A(Y).

RUN TIME

At run time, the first command, BALR, places 15000 in GPR7. It places 15000 plus 8092 (23092) in GPR9. Let us slide down the program till we come to the *load* command at AA. It is located at 20030 and requests that GPR6 be loaded from the cell whose address is 902 offset by the contents of GPR9. Making this calculation, we came up with the address 24094. Lo and behold, this contains the run time address, 16110, or Y as desired.

13.6 ESD AND RLD PRINTOUT; EXAMPLE

The writer of a multiCSECT program will receive information from 𝔄𝔖𝔏ℜ in a printout about both the RLD and the ESD. If he can give the proper interpretation to this information it will help him in debugging his program. 𝔄𝔖𝔏ℜ prints out both these tables and in the same relative position which they occupy in the object module. We now examine what is contained in this printout and how to interpret it, followed by an actual example together with its interpretation and what the program loader, 𝔓𝔏𝔒𝔄𝔇, will do with them.

RLD The RLD follows the text printout and its error entries. It consists of four columns which are shown in Table 13.6.1.

The first column contains a position identification describing the CSECT which contains the ADCON. It does not reference the ADCON or the CSECT by name; instead it references the CSECT by the position number within the ESD table, which we examine later.

The relocation Id is used for calculating the adjustment quantity to be added to the constant to produce its proper runtime value. The constant to be added is listed in the ESD. It is referred to by a number giving its position in the ESD.

The third column in the RLD entry is a flag which describes the kind of constant with which we are dealing. This flag is one byte, two nibbles. The first nibble is 0 for an address constant and 1 for a VCON. It is 2 for a

Table 13.6.1 THE RLD ENTRY

Byte	*Value*	*Name*	*Use*
1		Position Id	ESD entry for CSECT containing the ADCON
2		Relocation Id	ESD entry for calculating ADCON
3		Flag	
	O_HX		ADCON
	1_HX		VCON
	2_HX *or* 3_HX		pseudo register
	A_HX *or* B_HX		unresolved
	X01xx		two bytes
	X10xx		three bytes
	X11xx		four bytes
	XxxDx		relocate forward
	Xxx1x		relocate backward
	Xxxx0		next RLD entry is different
	Xxxx1		next RLD entry is same
4–6		Address	Hex address of constant to be relocated

pseudo register. This is the special case where the programmer has left room in his own program for code to be brought in by the linkage editor. In this case $\mathcal{ASLR}$ knows the position which the code will occupy even though it is not present in the program. The first nibble is *A* when the symbol is unresolved at assembly time.

The remaining nibble is analyzed bit by bit. The first two bits describe whether the address is two, three, or four bytes long. The next bit describes whether relocation is done in a forward or backward direction. The final bit is used only by $\mathcal{FLOAD}$ so that redundant information can be eliminated. If the position and relocation Id is the same for the next RLD entry, that information can be eliminated and this bit is set to 1.

Table 13.6.2 THE ESD ENTRY

Byte	*Value*	*Name*	*Use*
1–8		Symbol	Identifies ENTRY, CSECT, EXTRN or VCON
9		Type	Incoming or outgoing
	PC	Private Code	
	SD	Selection Definition	Incoming
	LD	Label Definition	
	ER	External Reference	
	PR	Pseudo Register	Outgoing
	CM	Common	Common
10		Id	Ordered number of entry in ESD
11–13		Addr	Address in location counter at beginning of CSECT
14–16		Length	Number of bytes (hex) in CSECT.

Symbol	*Type*	*Id*	*Addr*	*Length*
$BLANK	SD	01	000000	00033C
REGISTER	SD	02	000340	000374
REG010	ER	03	(000654)	
REGISTER	ER	04	(000340)	

```
         Object                        Source
Loc      code        Stmt              statement
..............................................................
000000               28                SETUP
                     29+$BLANK         CSECT
..............................................................
000034   00000000    49+               DC         A($BLANK+0*4096)
..............................................................
00004D   00005C      57+               DC         AL3(RDR)
..............................................................
000051   0000BC      59+               DC         AL3(PRTR)
..............................................................
00005C               66+RDR            DS         OF
..............................................................
00005C   00000000    71+               DC         BL16'0'
..............................................................
00007D   0002F8      85+               DC         AL3(E0J)
..............................................................
0000BC               121+              DS         OF
..............................................................
0000BC   00000000    126+              DC         BL16'0'
..............................................................
000340               191+REGISTER      CSECT
                     192+              USING      REGISTER,15
000340   47F0F00E    293+              B          *+4+10
..............................................................
000374   000340      211+              DC         A(REGISTER+0*4096)
..............................................................
000345   000654      225+              DC         BL16'0'
..............................................................
000654               291+REG010        DS         OF
..............................................................
000654   00000000    296+              DC         BL16'0'
..............................................................
0002F8   4510C308    479+E0J           BAL        1,*+16
0002FC   00          480+              DC         AL1(0)
0002FD   0000BC      481+              DC         AL3(PRTR)
000300   00          482+              DC         AL1(0)
000301   00005C      483+              DC         AL3(RDR)
000304   00          484+              DC         AL1(128)
000305   000000      485+              DC         VL3(REG010)
..............................................................
000338   00000000    491                          =V(REGISTER)
```

Fig. 13.6.1 An example of how RLD and ESD are used.

Pos. Id	*Rel. Id*	*Flags*	*Address*
01	01	0C	000034
01	01	08	00004D
01	01	08	000051
01	01	08	00007D
01	01	08	0002FD
01	01	08	000301
01	03	18	000305
01	04	1C	000338
02	02	0C	000374
02	02	08	0003A5

Fig. 13.6.1 (*Continued*)

The last column in the RLD contains the address of the constant which is to be relocated at load time. The address is in hex and refers to the command location rather than to the command number, as appears in the first column for the particular line of code in the text. Three bytes suffice for this purpose.

ESD The external symbol dictionary appears before any of the code as presented in Table 13.6.2. The first column contains eight bytes which identifies the CSECT, etc., corresponding to this entry.

The next two bytes identify the kind of entry. Most common will be SD for section definition. It may be *blank* for the *blank* CSECT. LD stands for label definition identifying entry points defined by entry. A third source to be identified is private code, PC, embedded in the assembly program.

Outgoing identifiers are usually of type ER for external reference as established by EXTRN or VCON. If space is provided in the program, PR appears for pseudo register.

The last type is CM for common, which is resolved in a slightly different way.

The tenth byte is an identifier of the entry in ESD by ordinal number. This is the number used in the RLD for both the position Id and the relocation Id.

The next column contains the relative address in hex as counted from the beginning of the program at which the CSECT or symbol begins.

The last three bytes indicate the length of the CSECT or symbol. Address and length cannot be filled in for external references which are totally outside of the program. They are filled in by $\mathcal{ASLR}$ for interCSECT references, but this information is not presented in the printout.

Example Figure 13.6.1 provides an example of the ESD and RLD produced for a typical program with two CSECTS. Most of the actual program is not pertinent to the discussion, so that only the pertinent lines of code are provided in the figure. The ESD contains four entries in Id, 01 through 04. The first two represent the two CSECTS named $BLANK and REGISTER. The next two are for VCONs established by the program, and hence are of type ER. No address or length is printed for them. The address in parentheses is that which ASLR has associated with them for relocation.

The RLD is at the bottom of the figure. It is only used by FLOAD when the program is initially brought in. We shall now examine how FLOAD copes with the RLD entries.

After FLOAD has entered the program into MEMORY, it returns to alter some of the constants. It gets these from the RLDs supplied. The first one that FLOAD encounters is at address 34. This is a four-byte ADCON as distinguished by the flag OC. The position and location, or both, are relative to the first CSECT which starts at relative location 0. Let's suppose that FLOAD has placed the program start at location 16,000 of MEMORY. From the printout we can see that a fullWord has been established for this constant in the program. It has been set to all 0's. FLOAD adds 16,000 in hex, and this quantity is resolved.

The next ADCON is at 4D and refers to the address of a DS labeled RDR. The relative position of that address is known and is filled into the ADCON for RDR, namely 00005C. FLOAD fills in the runtime value of the ADCON by adding 16,000. The only difference is that the flag indicates this to be a three-byte ADCON, and ASLR allows for this.

The next four ADCONs are handled in exactly the same fashion: ASLR has filled in a relative address at the ADCON; FLOAD adds the proper ADCON constant. A new activity occurs when we reach the VCON at 305. This is distinguished as a VCON by a flag which also tells us that it is three bytes long. The relative position of this VCON within the program has been resolved by ASLR in the RLD. FLOAD gets this number, adds 16,000 to it, and fills it in at 305, which is presently blank. The same is done for the next VCON which follows in the RLD and is located at 338.

Two more ADCONs follow. Their relative address has been entered into the object code relative to the entire program rather than the CSECT, since the program has control of the CSECTs it assembles. Hence, again all that FLOAD must do is to add the starting position, 16,000, to the contents of these locations, noting whether a three- or four-byte constant is provided.

13.7 COMMON

Purpose The **common area** called **COMMON** provides communication among CSECTs in a given assembly and among programs from different assemblies which are placed in a same load module. Any program or CSECT which wishes to *use* COMMON must include the pseudo, COM. This defines an area which will be common to all programs. 𝒜𝒮ℒℛ communicates the length required by each programmer for COMMON to the linkage editor, ℰ𝒟ℐ𝒯. It's ℰ𝒟ℐ𝒯 which creates the common area and makes the correspondence among references to it by the various programs coinciding. The size of COMMON in each program can be different. Then, ℰ𝒟ℐ𝒯 determines the *maximum* of these and makes COMMON an area of that size. Names for COMMON or parts thereof can be different for the different programs.

Means For a given CSECT we can set up COMMON thus:

COM (13.7.1)

Here *location* must be *blank*; *name* may be present or (generally) absent. In the latter case, we set up areas following the pseudo by using DCs and DSs. Presumably these DS or DC pseudos define the names used in this CSECT or else the CSECT will have no COMMON area to itself. Actually, COM acts much like DSECT in that it creates a labeled subdivision of some remote area of MEMORY. Hence, when COM appears, *no code is produced and no storage is allocated.*

Example Figure 13.7.1 shows a program containing three CSECTs, two of which use COMMON. Statement 8 declares COMMON with COM; statements 9 and 10 make this an area of twenty-eight bytes and label two parts. The entire area is named XCOM since that is the name of the *first* byte in the area.

For the blank CSECT to address COMMON, COM is treated like a DSECT. Thus, at statement 5, we find a *load* command to place the address of XCOM into GPR6. 𝒜𝒮ℒℛ is told about this with USING, statement 6. Statement 7 requests that the three words defined as X in statement 4 are moved to the first twelve bytes of XCOM.

At statement 11, a new CSECT, SECT2, is declared and BASE REGISTERS are set up for it. It, too, contains COM at statement 2. The names for COMMON are different, however, and this area is named SCOM. Another difference is that this COMMON contains thirty-two bytes. Actually, at run time, the maximum—thirty-two bytes—will be allocated to COMMON. For SECT2 to reference COMMON, it loads the address in a register, GPR7, at statement 17 and then it tells 𝒜𝒮ℒℛ about it. Now, information can be moved about between the program and COMMON as shown in statements 19 and 20. SECT2 does calculations with a variable called Y and answers are transmitted to the COMMON region called

```
                START
                BALR    2,0
                USING   *,2
        X       DS      3F
                L       6,=A(XCOM)
                USING   XCOM,6
                MVC     XCOM(12),X
                COM
        XCOM    DS      3F
        MORE    DS      CL16
        SECT2   CSECT
                BALR    3,0
                USING   *,3
                B       SOON
        Y       DS      3F
        Z       DS      CL16
                L       7,=A(SCOM)
                USING   SCOM,7
                MVC     Y(12),ANS
                MVC     ANS(16),Z
                COM
        SCOM    DS      3F
        ANS     DS      CL20
        SECT3   CSECT
                END
```

Fig. 13.7.1 Use of COM.

ANS. If the blank CSECT wishes to get a part of this answer, it will reference part of this area by calling it MORE.

13.8 CSECTS IN MACROS

Large macros Macros can grow very large. This is to be expected. The advantage of having the $\mathcal{ASLR}$ swap code for a call increases with the size of the code substituted.

The second advantage of the macro is having $\mathcal{ASLR}$ tailor the code to suit the needs of the user. Again, this takes much code in the macrodefinition. But, now we see a need to distinguish

1. the AL code generated by the macrocall,
2. the ML code inserted into the ML program by $\mathcal{ASLR}$ resulting from the macrocall.

For conditional assembly, (1) is generally larger than (2). The reader should examine SAVE presented in Section 15.5 and contrast the code produced with definition in Appendix B, noting a factor of about 1 to 50.

Nevertheless, there are occasions where a large amount of ML code is created, and to our advantage. However, this creates a secondary problem associated with base/displacement:

- ML code uses up ML space.
- Space requires BASE REGISTER assignments.
- A single BASE REGISTER accounts for only 4K bytes.

Hence, large macros eat up BASE REGISTER assignments.

Macros in another section A solution to the problem above is to put the code produced by large macros in another section or CSECT. This helps tremendously because the space used in the other CSECT, call it MCSECT, is under the control of another set of BASE REGISTERS. Also the REGISTER for MCSECT can be reset for each new macro placed there.

This poses some new questions which we answer later with respect to the macrodefinition in Fig. 13.8.1:

A. How do we maintain the integrity of BASE REGISTERS used by the caller?
B. How do we get to MCSECT?
C. How do we reset BASE REGISTERS in MCSECT?
D. How do we know what CSECT to return to?
E. How do we return?

Linking To get to the part of a macro which resides in another CSECT requires the establishment of an entry in the external symbol dictionary. This can be done with a VCON or with EXTRN. The former is simpler. We can establish an external reference and at the same time load a register for linkage by using a VCON literal. We then get to the foreign CSECT with BALR, which also loads the return address into a register:

```
        L       15,=V(BEG)
        BALR    14,15                    (13.8.1)
```

If this macro is used several times, then the VCON is loaded several times. The VCON is established as a literal. Once a literal entry is created this same entry can be used for later references. Thus, in future calls the *original* VCON literal created will have its address loaded into GPR15 above.

The CSECT we are entering is foreign and cannot be entered unless an entry point is established. We do this with:

```
MCSECT  CSECT
        ENTRY   BEG                      (13.8.2)
BEG     BALR    3,0
```

External Symbol Dictionary

Symbol	*Type*	*Id*	*Addr*	*Length*	*Ld Id*
$BLANK	SD	01	000000	0001B8	
MCSECT	SD	02	0001B8	00003E	
SQRT	LD		0001B8		02
REGISTER	SD	03	0001F8	000374	
REG010	ER	04			
SQRT	ER	05			
REGISTER	ER	06			

```
Loc.    Object  Addr 1    Addr 2                          Source
        code                       Stmt                   Statement
                                   1               MACRO
                                   2   &N          SQRTC    &X,&R
                                   3               GBLB     &SW           MCSECT
                                                                            SWITCH
                                   4   &N          STM      2,7,28(13)
                                   5               L        2,&X          PUT X INTO
                                                                            GPR2
                                   6               L        7,=V(SQRT)    PUT BRANCH
                                                                            ADDRESS IN
                                                                            GPR7
                                   7               BALR     6,7           GO TO
                                                                            MCSECT
                                   8               AIF      (&SW)         SUPPRESS
                                                              .CONT         MCSECT
                                                                            EXCEPT FIRST
                                                                            TIME
                                   9   MCSECT      CSECT
                                   10  SQRT        BALR     7,0           ESTABLISH BASE
                                   11              ENTRY    SQRT
                                   12              USING    *,7           TELL ASLR
                                   13              LTR      3,2           CALCULATE
                                   14              BZ       M&SYSNDX
                                   15              BM       M&SYSNDX
                                   16              LA       4,1
                                   17              CR       4,3
                                   18              BE       M&SYSNDX
                                   19              SRA      3,1
                                   20              LR       5,3
                                   21              MR       4,3
                                   22              LTR      4,4
                                   23              BNZ      *-20
                                   24  R&SYSNDX    SR       4,4
                                   25              LR       5,2
                                   26              DR       4,3
                                   27              SR       5,3
                                   28              SRA      5,1
                                   29              AR       3,5
                                   30              LPR      4,5
                                   31              SRA      4,1
                                   32              BNZ      R&SYSNDX
                                   33  M&SYSNDX    BR       6
                                   34  .CONT       ANOP
                                   35  &SYSECT     CSECT
                                   36              ST       3,&R
                                   37              LM       2,7,28(13)
                                   38  &SW         SETB     1             SET MCSECT
                                                                            SWITCH
                                   39              MEND
                                   40              SETUP

                                   185             SQRTC    X,R
00011C  9027    D01C      0001C    186+            STM      2,7,28(13)
000120  5820    C194      00194    187+            L        2,X PUT X INTO GPR2
000124  5870    C1B0      001B0    188+            L        7,=V(SQRT) PUT BRANCH
                                                              ADDRESS IN GPR7
```

Fig. 13.8.1 Defining and using the macro SQRTC which uses the CSECT MCSECT for the main routine.

```
         Object                                          Source
Loc.     code    Addr 1   Addr 2    Stmt                 statement
000128   0567                       189+          BALR   6,7 GO TO MCSECT
0001B8                              190+MCSECT    CSECT
0001B8   0570                       191+SQRT      BALR   7,0 ESTABLISH BASE
                                    192+          ENTRY  SQRT
0001BA                              193+          USING  *,7 TELL ASLR
0001BA   1232                       194+          LTR    3,2 CALCULATE
0001BC   4780    703A     001F4     195+          BZ     M0008
0001C0   4740    703A     001F4     196+          BM     M0008
0001C4   4140    0001     00001     197+          LA     4,1
0001C8   1943                       198+          CR     4,3
0001CA   4780    703A     001F4     199+          BE     M0008
0001CE   8A30    0001     00001     200+          SRA    3,1
0001D2   1853                       201+          LR     5,3
0001D4   1C43                       202+          MR     4,3
0001D6   1244                       203+          LTR    4,4
0001D8   4770    700A     001C4     204+          BNZ    *-20
0001DC   1B44                       205+R0008     SR     4,4
0001DE   1852                       206+          LR     5,2
0001E0   1D43                       207+          DR     4,3
0001E2   1B53                       208+          SR     5,3
0001E4   8A50    0001     00001     209+          SRA    5,1
0001E8   1A35                       210+          AR     3,5
0001EA   1045                       211+          LPR    4,5
0001EC   8A40    0001     00001     212+          SRA    4,1
0001F0   4770    7022     001DC     213+          BNZ    R0008
0001F4   07F6                       214+M0008     BR     6
000000                              215+$BLANK    CSECT
00012A   5030    C1A0     001A0     216+          ST     3,R
00012E   9827    D01C     0001C     217+          LM     2,7,28(13)
                                    218           SQRTC  X+4,R+4
000132   9027    D01C     0001C     219+          STM    2,7,28(13)
000136   5820    C198     00198     220+          L      2,X+4 PUT X INTO GPR2
00013A   5870    C1B0     001B0     221+          L      7,=V(SQRT) PUT BRANCH
                                                           ADDRESS IN GPR7
00013E   0567                       222+          BALR   6,7 GO TO MCSECT
000000                              223+$BLANK    CSECT
000140   5030    C1A4     001A4     224+          ST     3,R+4
000144   9827    D01C     0001C     225+          LM     2,7,28(13)
                                    226           SQRTC  X+8,R+8
000148   9027    D01C     0001C     227+          STM    2,7,28(13)
00014C   5820    C19C     0019C     228+          L      2,X+8 PUT X INTO GPR2
000150   5870    C1B0     001B0     229+          L      7,=V(SQRT) PUT BRANCH
                                                           ADDRESS IN GPR7
000154   0567                       230+          BALR   6,7 GO TO MCSECT
000000                              231+$BLANK    CSECT
000156   5030    C1A8     001A8     232+          ST     3,R+8
00015A   9827    D01C     0001C     233+          LM     2,7,28(13)
00015E   9805    C1A0     001A0     234           LM     0,5,R
                                    235           REG
000194   0000001000000271           405  X        DC     F'16,625,1024'
0001A0                              406  R        DS     3F
                                    407           END
0001B0   00000000                   408                  =V(SQRT)
0001B4   00000000                   409                  =V(REGISTER)
```

Relocation Dictionary

Pos. Id	*Rel. Id*	*Flags*	*Address*
01	01	0C	000034
01	01	08	00004D
01	01	08	000051
01	01	08	00007D
01	01	08	000181
01	01	08	000185
01	04	18	000189
01	05	1C	0001B0
01	06	1C	0001B4
03	03	0C	00022C
03	03	08	00025D

Fig. 13.8.1 (*Continued*)

The three commands serve the following purposes:

- To indicate that code is now being produced in another CSECT;
- To establish an entry point called BEG;
- To name the first command of the routine, BEG.

Register integrity It is a good idea with CSECTs (as well as for any routine or subroutine) that system registers and any others used by the routine are saved, as described in the next chapter. This is done thus:

```
MCSECT   CSECT
         STM      14,4,12(13)        (13.8.3)
```

Base reassignment After entering this new section of code it is necessary to establish a BASE REGISTER assignment for this piece of code, which might be done thus:

```
         STM      14,14,12(13)
BEG      BALR     3,0                (13.8.4)
         USING    *,3
```

REGISTERS must be saved to maintain their integrity. Then BALR establishes the runtime address of this command in a designated GPR. USING tells the assembler that the code it fabricates references the designated GPR.

Return We return to the originating CSECT with a *branch*, thus:

```
         BR       14                 (13.8.5)
```

Resetting the section When we reenter the calling CSECT we must notify 𝒜𝒮ℒℛ that code hereafter comes from a different CSECT. How does 𝒜𝒮ℒℛ know which CSECT it is writing unless we tell it? On the other hand, how can we incorporate in the definition the name of the CSECT which is going to be calling this macro? It is impossible.

However, as 𝒜𝒮ℒℛ expands calls, it can note which CSECT is giving the call. In fact, it does this and stores the information internally at assembly time in a cell called &SYSECT. Now when we wish to return to the call &SYSECT we give the call CSECT which bears the label &SYSECT, thus,

```
&SYSECT    CSECT                     (13.8 .6)
```

𝒜𝒮ℒℛ goes to the cell &SYSECT which stores the information about the name of the calling CSECT. It gets that name and applies it to the code written thereafter.

Example Figure 13.8.1 presents an example of a macro, the bulk of which is written in another CSECT. The example begins with the external symbol dictionary, which we examine later.

Definition The definition of the macro SQRTC is found in statements 1–39 of the program. This macro has a code identical to SQRT, which we discussed at length in Chapter 10. The redefinition is only for the purpose of putting the main bulk of the code into another CSECT so that it will occupy less space in the program if multiple calls of SQRTC appear, and so that base allocations in the main program will not be used.

All of the code is created the first time the macro is called. We do not want a large portion of it to be created on subsequent calls. The switch, &SW, is established as a global variable to distinguish if a call has occurred previously. It is set to 0 the first time the macro is called.

At (4) GPRS 2–7 are *saved.* It would be awkward to have the code in the foreign CSECT try to reference parameters, hence &X is passed to the routine in GPR2 (5).

The entry point to the code in the foreign CSECT is loaded into GPR7 (6). A VCON literal is required, specifying the entry point SQRT. We take off to the code in the foreign section with BALR, leaving the return point in GPR6 (7).

Now we test to see if SQRTC has been called before. If so, &SW is set to 1 and $\mathcal{ASLR}$ will jump around the code which is shaded in the figure.

We tell $\mathcal{ASLR}$ that it is producing part of a new CSECT (9). We now name the entry point SQRT (10) and set up the base register. We are using GPR7 for this purpose. This command is really superfluous. (Why?) We establish an entry point to this CSECT using ENTRY and then tell $\mathcal{ASLR}$ that the base register for this portion of the code is GPR7.

The remainder of the code has been explained previously up to (33).

At (34) we provide an entry for $\mathcal{ASLR}$ to resume assembly when multiple calls of SQRTC appear. ANOP is required here. We now return to the caller's CSECT. Its name is identified with the help of $\mathcal{ASLR}$ using &SYSECT (35).

The root obtained by the loop is still in GPR3. It is now stored in &R (36). Registers are unsaved (37). We are done except for the switch, &SW. It must be set to 1 so that a subsequent call of SQRTC will not produce the code in the shaded area of the figure.

Calling Now let us see what happens in a program where SQRTC is called a number of times. The program begins with SETUP (40) which produces much code not shown in Fig. 13.8.1. Finally.

SQRTC is given (185). The code which it produces (186+–217+) is very similar to the original macrodefinition. Most interesting is when the assembler begins to produce code in MCSECT. The actual location of this code is 1B8 in hexadecimal. Notice that the command BALR which directly precedes this is at location 128. MCSECT is the name of another CSECT which 𝒜𝒮ℒℛ will place after *all* the code belonging to the CSECT named $BLANK. Thus we expect that there are other commands which follow 128.

𝒜𝒮ℒℛ finds CSECT in the expansion of SQRT with the code named &SYSECT. It is noted that the calling CSECT is named $BLANK. Therefore this name is applied to that CSECT (215+). The programmer is told that this CSECT has a relative beginning of 0. 𝒜𝒮ℒℛ produces code for $BLANK, where it left off. Hence, the next statement is at location 12A (216+).

Second call A second call of SQRTC follows (218). It produces code belonging to the upper unshaded portion of the macrodefinition. The entry address is filled in by L (221+). This is a VCON belonging to $BLANK. Its location is 1BO (408). This same location is used every time =V(SQRT) appears. BALR (222+) causes a jump to the shaded code in MCSECT. This command also sets up the return address as the command directly following this one and located at 140.

A third call of SQRTC follows and may be analyzed similarly.

The reader should note other details such as the relocation symbol dictionary at the end of the figure, and that code produced in MCSECT uses GPR7 as a base register, as requested in contrast to GPR12, which is used for the main program.

PROBLEMS

13.1 (a) What does the pseudo CSECT do? (b) Are several CSECTs bearing the same name permissible? (c) Why? (d) How about two CSECTs with the same name?

13.2 (a) Why would one write a program containing two CSECTS?
(b) How are base registers assigned in a multiCSECT program?

13.3 The CSECT SD wants C1 and C2 from CSECT SC, and E3 from CSECT SE. Describe *all* the steps required to assure this communication.

13.4 Write the macro PACKIT called thus:

PACKIT dcb,(start,end).

It contains GET and DSECT. GET accesses a 𝒬𝒮𝒜ℳ file defined at *dcb*, which returns an absolute record address in GPR1. DSECT defines the record and a field of interest from byte *start* through byte *end* inclusive in the record. This field is to be packed by the macro and returned there.

13.5 Improve PACKIT so that it is called thus:

PACKIT dcb,field1,field2, . . . fieldn,

where fieldi is given as (*starti*,*endi*).

13.6 (a) What is the need for DSECT?
(b) Can several DSECTs appear in the same CSECT?
(c) How is the DSECT applied to the data?
(d) How does ASLR handle the DSECT?

13.7 Explain the use by the programmer of EXTRN, ENTRY, VCON and, for external references, CSECT. How does ASLR set up the ESD for each?

13.8 In a uniCSECT program where do the literals appear? If that program is large, DROP or USING might alter BASE REGISTER assignment. Why is LTORG needed? How do you use it? What will ASLR do with it?

13.9 Describe how to use LTORG for a sample long double CSECT program. What does ASLR do with LTORG then?

13.10 For each ADCON an RLD entry is created. Describe how ASLR creates it. When is this done? What quantity does this entry contain? What does FLoad do with this entry?

13.11 How are sample literals entries created by ASLR?

13.12 (a) The literal ADCON produces two extra entries; one in the literal pool; the other in the RLD. Why?
(b) How are they related?
(c) Why are they needed?
(d) Suppose =A(X) appears in several commands. How does ASLR treat each? Now how many entries are created?

13.13 (a) For each VCON both an RLD and ESD entry are created. Why?
(b) How are they related by ASLR?
(c) How are they used by FLoad?

13.14 Answer Prob. 13.12 with respect to literal VCONs.

13.15 (a) Why is COM much like DSECT?
(b) How does ASLR use COM in setting up the COMMON area?
(c) How is USING employed with COM?
(d) What do EDIT and FLoad do with COM?

13.16 How is the RLD and ESD used in debugging?

13.17 (a) Why put part of macro in another CSECT?
(b) Then how is linking done?
(c) How do we insure that duplicate names are not produced in call or macro?

(d) How do we produce the macro CSECT code only once?
(e) Give example.

13.18 (a) Describe how a floating BASE REGISTER assignment is achieved in the macro CSECT.
(b) Why is this beneficial?
(c) Show code.

13.19 Write a macro CALLAD which is identical in all respects to the OS system macro CALL, with these exceptions:
(a) An ADCON is created for the name of the called SR instead of a VCON.
(b) No identifier is created.
(c) The action of VL is always performed—hence, VL is not required, and ignored when present.
(d) Provide your own error messages for improper use of CALLAD.
Demonstrate the validity of CALLAD by making requests below in your program and verifying their correctness. Use ASMFC but do not use SETUP; instead use USING and START. Declare SR names, etc.

```
C1      CALLAD    SR1
C2      CALLAD    SR2,ALPH
C3      CALLAD    SR1,(ALPH)
C4      CALLAD    SR2,(3)
C5      CALLAD    SR1,(ALPH,BETA,GAM)
C6      CALLAD    SR2,((5),BETA,(6))
C7      CALLAD    SR2,(ALPH,(A,B,C),GAM)
C8      CALLAD    SR1,(ALPH+4,ALPH-4,ALPH)
C9      CALLAD    SR2,(BETA(3),BETA+2)
C10     CALLAD    SR1,(GAM,,ALPH)
C11     CALLAD    SR2,(GAM,,)
C12     CALLAD    SR1(,,)
C13     CALLAD    SR1((2))
C14     CALLAD    (15),BETA
C15     CALLAD    (15),(ALPH,BETA)
C16     CALLAD    (15),ALPH,BETA
```

14

SYSTEM MACROS

14.1 RUN TIME SOFTWARE

Description **System macros** are assembly language routines which the manufacturer supplies. These routines are stored in the **macro library** on the **system residence volume.** The assembly language programmer can use the macroname as an opcode essentially (with a parameter list, of course) and ASLR will incorporate the proper code into his program—he does not define the macro.

Most (not all) system macros talk to the operating system directly; the rest talk to manufacturer-supplied software brought in dynamically. We should have some idea of how the run time system works. I use OS360 to typify operating systems.

OS360 is usually a multiprogram operating system which permits several programs to reside in MEMORY at the same time. OS360 does the alternation so that parts of each program are performed consecutively under its direction.

For multiprogramming, whether program partitions are fixed (MFT) or dynamically variable (MVT), a MEMORY map might appear like Fig. 14.1.1. There is **fixed** MEMORY, an area which contains the resident part of OS360, including the Task Manager (TM) and the IO Supervisor (IOS).

The remainder of MEMORY is called **variable** MEMORY since its contents vary from one job to another. This area (for multiprogramming only) is cut up into pieces called **partitions**—one for each program which the system can handle.

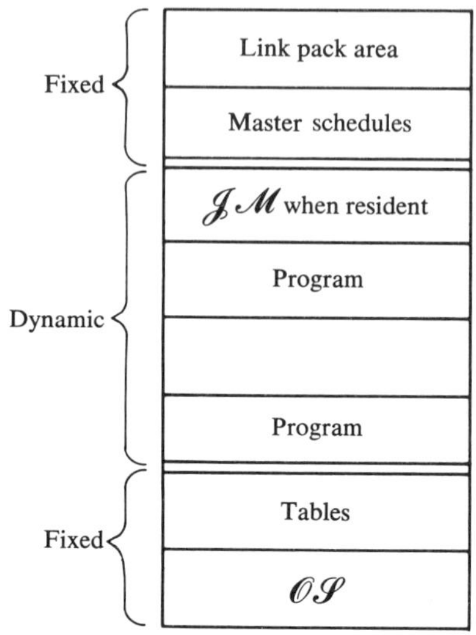

Fig. 14.1.1 MEMORY map OS360.MVT.

Besides the program, this area also contains an Access Method unless the A.Method is stored in another area of MEMORY for semipermanent system software called the **link pack area**. We omit this eventuality to simplify explanation.

Task Manager

In fixed MEMORY we find the Task Manager which handles all interrupts. It sequences between the various tasks which comprise the job which the programmer has submitted. It also provides many of the services which the programmer may request with the SVC, the programmer initiated interrupt.

The SVC tells the Task Manager what service is required. Programs for all possible services could not be kept in MAIN MEMORY—there is simply not enough room. Hence the SVC Transient area is set aside in fixed MEMORY into which the Task Manager brings the requested task. Overlay techniques may be required for large service programs. Upon completion the service program returns control to the Task Manager which normally returns control to the program.

SYSTEM MACRO

The system macro is simply an opcode and a parameter list in the AL program. This is expanded from the macrodefinition in the macro library into a set of AL code. This code does all the setup required to prepare the program to turn over control to the Task Manager. When setup is complete, a SVC appears in this AL code which

- gives control to the Task Manager,
- specifies the service program required,
  transmits parameters via REGISTERS to the service program.

Access Method There is an Access Method associated with every file used by the program. All Access Methods are stored on a system resident volume and are brought in dynamically. They are not brought in until they are needed. The program communicates this with the macro, OPEN. As with other system macros, this gives control to the Task Manager which eventually brings in the proper components of OPEN. The parameters of OPEN indicate which Access Method is required and what portions of it are brought into the portion of variable MEMORY where the problem program resides.

After the AMethod has been established by OPEN, the program talks to the AMethod with system macros, such as GET. We examine these later.

14.2 ACQUIRING SYSTEM MACRODEFINITIONS

Residence As noted, all system macrodefinitions are stored in the system residence volume **(SYSRES)** and are contained in the system macrolibrary, familiarly referred to as SYS1.MACLIB. All the macrodefinitions are supplied by the manufacturer. However, all definitions may not be used at a given installation. To save room on SYS1.MACLIB, only those macrodefinitions used by the installation are placed there. The means for getting the macrodefinitions into the library is the **system generation** process **(SYSGEN)**. All the desired software is placed onto SYSRES by the SYSGEN, which picks and chooses what is required by the installation as specified in the parameters of the SYSGEN request.

Insertion How and when does ASLR get hold of the definitions for the system macros? Recall that McDef gets all programmer macrodefinitions and enters them in *COMTAB*, *their definitions*. To do this, it examines all the AL program. Each opcode is looked up in *OPTAB* regardless of whether it is part of a macrodefinition. In this way, all macrocalls are culled from the program. As McDef enters a macrodefinition into *COMTAB*, it checks off calls to that definition. At the end of McDef, there are a set of calls which are unaccounted for. All these *should* be system macros. Another component, which I shall call McSMc, goes to the library and pulls out these macrodefinitions, placing them in *COMTAB* with appropriate pointers to the code.

In so doing, McSMc will encounter inner macrocalls which are also system macros. Hence, the list of required macrodefinitions may expand and contract as McSMc incorporates definitions into *COMTAB*.

When McSMc gets done, all macrocalls should have a definition in *COMTAB*. Those which do not are illegal calls and are so tagged.

14.3 INTRASYSTEM MACROS

Definition These are system macros provided by the manufacturer but not for use by the program. These macros are used by the system macros. In other words, they are **intrasystem macros,** inner macros for system macros. They are obtained by McSMc from SYS1.MACLIB when they appear as calls within the system macrodefinitions. The intrasystem macro is provided because many system macros need the same kind of service within their definition but these services are not generally required by the programmer. This becomes clear as we examine two of these macros below.

IEBERMAC

The intrasystem macro called IEBERMAC is given this name because

- IEB indicates that this macro belongs to the system,
- ERMAC mnemonically indicates that this is an error macro.

This macro writes out all error messages for all system macros. As you can imagine, this macrodefinition is immense and takes up over five hundred lines of code. It would serve no purpose to examine the whole thing in detail but it is useful to note a few things about it.

PROTOTYPE

The prototype statement takes the form

```
         IHBERMAC    &A,&B,&D,&E,&F
```
(14.3.1)

Here &A is a number which communicates the nature of the error message to be produced; &B, &E, and &F are character strings which are transmitted to the error message for certain difficulties which must be so noted.

VARIABLE SYMBOLS

At the beginning of the macrodefinition, we find the following statement:

```
         LCLC    &G(14)
         LCLC    &C
&C       SETC    '*** IHB'
```
(14.3.2)

&G(14) sets up an array which produces the desired message. Its use is explained later. &C is the prefix for the error message.

Next, in the macrodefinition, are a series of statements which take the form

```
         AIF      (&A EQ 1).E24
         AIF      (&A LE 13).E13
         AIF      (&A EQ 24).E24
.E24     MNOTE    12,'&C.004 REQUIRED OPERANDS
                  NOT SPECIFIED'
         MEXIT                                   (14.3.3)
```

These model statements cause the assembler to go to a portion of the definition appropriate to the error code transmitted by &A. There it will generally find a note as above which will be written in the assembly language printout to tell the programmer the reason for the difficulty in the system macro.

IHBINNRA The entire definition of this intrasystem macro is presented in Fig. 14.3.1. Its purpose is to insert parameters into GPR1 and GPR0. The parameters to be transmitted are given by the arguments &A and &B.

The interesting thing about this macro is that &A or &B is either a

```
           MACRO
&NAME    IHBINNRA &A,&B
         AIF      ('&A' EQ '  ' OR '&A' EQ '(1)').NAMEIT
         AIF      ('&A'(1,1) EQ '(').REGA
&NAME    LA       1,&A                     LOAD PARAMETER REG 1
         AGO      .CHKB
.REGA    ANOP
&NAME    LR       1,&A(1)                  LOAD PARAMETER REG 1
         AGO      .CHKB
.NAMEIT  AIF      ('&NAME' EQ '  ').CHKB
&NAME    DS       OH
.CHKB    AIF      ('&B' EQ '  ' OR '&B' EQ '(0)').END
         AIF      ('&B'(1,1) EQ '(').REGB
         LA       0,&B                     LOAD PARAMETER REG 0
         AGO      .END
.REGB    LR       0,&B(1)                  LOAD PARAMETER REG 0
.END     MEND
```

Fig. 14.3.1 Definition of the intrasystem macro, IHBINNRA.

symbolic location or a REGISTER designation. If it is a REGISTER designation, it is parenthesized. This macro takes care of both cases and treats them properly.

FIRST PARAMETER

The first parameter, &A, may be missing or it may be "(1)." In this case, nothing is loaded into GPR1 and no code is produced for that purpose. A test for this is made (3) and when it proves true we go to .NAMEIT.

If &A contains a REGISTER designation, then the first character in the parameter is a left parenthesis, which we check for (4). For the parenthesis we go to .REGA (7) where we perform an LR (8). Notice that the second field of *loc* is &A (1). This says "take the first number of the list." 𝒜𝒮ℒℛ looks at a parenthesized REGISTER designation as a list since this is the form in which a parameter list is presented. Hence 𝒜𝒮ℒℛ removes the parentheses and places the number enclosed therein as a source REGISTER for the LR command.

If the tests above fail, we fall through (5) and do the LA command which places the address of the parameter designated at &A in GPR1.

NAME

If &NAME is present and no &A, a couple of steps are necessary to get &NAME into the act (10, 11).

SECOND PARAMETER

At the .CHKB an activity similar to that described above is performed to load GPR0. This should now be clear to the reader.

14.4 FILES

Structure There are several file structures available to the 𝒪𝒮 programmer which I now examine.

DIRECT

A **direct file** is one kept on cyclic storage—disk, drum, etc.—and which is addressed randomly—each access is independent of the previous access.

SEQUENTIAL

Sequential files may be kept on most any device. Search and use assumes that the next record in the file will be used next.

PARTITIONED

Programs and irregularly shaped files receive a special structure. The **partitioned file** provides a single directory system† for quicker retrieval. The 𝒜ℳ does automatic search and will help the user update the directory.

INDEXED

The **indexed sequential** structure permits easy accessing *and* sequential processing, thus speeding up both. The cost is a larger, more complex 𝒜ℳ.

Anticipation For sequential files, records required can be anticipated by the 𝒜ℳ which is then said to be **queued.** It gets records before they are needed and then they are immediately available when the program issues GET.

𝒜ℳ NAME

The names for the six kinds of files are presented in Table 14.4.1.

Table 14.4.1 ACCESS METHODS AND THEIR BUFFERS

	Buffering			
𝒜ccess method	*Automatic*	*Pronounced*	*Basic*	*Pronounced*
Direct	—	—	ℬ𝒟𝒜ℳ	beedamn
Sequential	𝒬𝒮𝒜ℳ	cuesam	ℬ𝒮𝒜ℳ	beesam
Partitioned	—	—	ℬ𝒫𝒜ℳ	beepam
Index sequential	𝒬ℐ𝒮𝒜ℳ	kwaisam	ℬℐ𝒮𝒜ℳ	buysam

File description One of the most important aspects of 𝒪S360 is establishing a description of files to be processed for input or output. The **data control block** or **DCB** is a block of information in the problem program at run time which completely describes *each* file used by the program. It is the programmer's responsibility to establish this block:

- In higher level languages he uses **declarative statements.**
- In assembly language he gives the macro, DCB.

DCB is a keyword parameter macro which has the capability of describing the majority of fields in the DCB.

Establishment DCB establishes all fields required for the DCB at load time. However, the programmer need not transmit all

† See Ivan Flores, *Data Structures and Management*. Englewood Cliffs, N.J.: Prentice-Hall, Inc., 1970.

Relative position	Code	Length	Name	Use		Note
0	a	4	DCBRELAD	Relative address of latest reference, TTRN		Device
4		1	DCBKEYCN			Interface
5	2	8	DCBFAD	Absolute address of latest reference MBBCCHHR		
13		3	DCBDVTBL	Address of IO characteristics table entry		
16	md ℓ	1	DCBKEYLE	Key length (KEYLEN)		
17	ℓ	3	DCBREL	Number of relative tracks or blocks in file		
20	md	1	BUFNO	Number of buffers required		Common
21	a	3	DCBBUFCB	Address of pool control block		Interface
24	md	2	BUFL	Length of each buffer		
26	m	2	DSORG	File organization QISAM, BPAM, etc., for BDAM		
				DA—direct organization		
				U—unmovable		
28	a	4	DCBIOBAD	Address of IO Block which keeps track of each IO assignment		
32	ma	1	BFALN	Buffer alignment-full- or doubleWord boundary		
33	—	3	—	Reserved		
36	m	1	RECFM	Record format translated to a binary code	F—fixed	
					V—variable	
					U—undefined	
					T—track overflow	
37	m	3	EXLST	Exit list—a list of address of routines supplied by the user to handle labels, count total block, or fill in the DCB		
40	m		DDNAME	Identifies corresponding name of DD statement		Foundation
48	ma	1	DCBOFLAS	Flags give state of AMethod		Before OPEN
				Input/output OPEN completed		
				Support function taken		
				Support function completed		
				Processing required after support function		
49	ma	1	(DCBIFLA)	Used by IOS to communicate with OPEN		
50	m	2	MACRF	Form of macros to be used by program for this file		
				READ/WRITE		
				blocks added to file		

				CHECK/WAIT	
				KEY/ID search	
				dynamic buffering	
				exclusive use of file during multiprogramming	
40	o	2	(DCBTIOT)	Entry point to Task IO Table	After OPEN
42	o	2	MACRF	(As at 50 before OPEN)	
44	o	1	(DCBIFG)	(As at 49 before OPEN)	
45	o	3	(DCBDEBAD)	Address of associated Data Extent Block which lists extents in volume which apply to this file when multiextent volume	
48	o	1	(DCBOFLGS)	(As in 48 before open but set correctly)	
49	o	3	(DCBREAD)	Absolute MEMORY	
			(DCBWRITE)	Address of entry point to the AMethod	
52	o	1	DCBOPTLD	Option code indicating these options:	
				write relatively dark	
				extended (cylinder) search	
				feedback-return to area of physical read loc	
				actual addressing	
				dynamic buffering	
				exclusive control of reading	
				relative record address	
53	o	3	DCBCHECK	Address of module to do CHECK	
56	o	4	DCBSYNAD	Address of users routine, SYNAD, to handle detected errors	
60	o	2		Reserved	
62	o	2	DCBBLKSI	Maximum block size	
64–104				Other entries	

Notes: 1. Code m = from DCB macro
d = from DD statement
ℓ = from label or JFCB
a = from Access Method
o = from Open
s = from OS360

2. All fields are prefixed by DCB; where this is absent, the name is that which is used in the DCB macro, e.g., BMFL.

Fig. 14.4.1 The DCB for BDAM, disk.

parameters provided in the DCB macrocall. Other parameters may be furnished:

- by default,
- by other means.

It is worthwhile to investigate other ways to fill in the DCB.

LOAD TIME

Information about the file name residence, etc., can be furnished at *load time* by the data definition statement. This is found on a card prefixed DD, the DD statement, brought in with the program at load time by Job Control. DD contains other details of the file not furnished at assembly time. The Job Manager converts the DD statement into the **job file control block, JFCB,** which holds it until OPEN time.

RUN TIME

As the program is running, the expanded macro, OPEN, is encountered. It will cause the AMethod associated with the file to be brought in as discussed in the next section. The AMethod finds the file if one already exists. From the file label, a **data set control block, DSCB,** is produced which may describe fields still lacking in the DCB. Before the file can be processed, information from the DSCB and the JFCB are merged into the DCB to get it into its final form. At that time every necessary field should be filled in.

Description DCBs differ in both total size and the number and kinds of fields they hold according to

- the file organization,
- the device medium.

Various file organizations have been discussed elsewhere.† It is helpful to take one particular structure and examine the DCB created for it. I shall use BDAM—Basic Direct Access Method as it applies to the 2311 DISK DRIVE to exemplify the DCB:

- D in BDAM stands for *direct* indicating that the user directs the AMethod to the particular record of interest whether absolutely or relatively.
- B in BDAM is *basic* meaning that only one record at a time is requested and the system does not do any anticipation.

The fields of the DCB for BDAM are presented in Fig. 14.4.1. The first column gives the byte position of the beginning of the field relative to the beginning of the block. The second column contains a code letter telling the source of information for the field. When several alternative sources exist, several letters appear here. The third column gives the length

† Ivan Flores, *Data Structure and Management*. Englewood Cliffs, N.J.: Prentice-Hall, Inc., 1970.

of the fields in bytes. The fourth column labeled *name*, gives the name of the field as addressed by the programmer in DCB macro using a key parameter. Some fields are not addressable from the parameter list and these are prefixed with DCB. The next column gives the use and contents of each field. The last column may contain a note for clarification.

Since information may be removed and replaced by other information after OPEN is encountered, we find that the final portion of the table is in two parts, *before* and *after*.

The macro The definition of DCB is quite long and contains no real mnemonics. The macro consists entirely of

1. SETs for establishing constants,
2. AIFs for conditional assembly,
3. DCs for establishing space and entering parameters,
4. DSs for establishing space for parameters furnished later,
5. MNOTES for noting errors,
6. inner macro macros for facilitating all the above such as IHB01 and IHBERMAC.

14.5 OPEN

Purpose Opening a file makes that file accessible to the program. The file is described by the Data Control Block examined in Section 14.4. However, further information about the file may be necessary; two other sources exist. The Data Definition statement is supplied at run time, giving information about the particular file as opposed to the general description contained in the DCB. Further, each file begins with a label which contains the properties of the file. This label can provide further information when such is absent from the DCB and the DD statement.

The routine called OPEN is initiated when OPEN appears in the program. It performs a number of tasks summarized as

- setup of initial information required to get the routine going,
- volume request and verification,
- preparation of the DCB in its final form,
- specification of the Access Method required,
- request and establishment of the A.M.

Macro We examine OPEN only in its standard form. The macro may have a list associated with it in its two other forms, *list* and *execute*. The standard format of the macro is

name OPEN dcb,opt1,opt2 (14.5.1)

Here *dcb* is a symbolic address—the name—of the macro, DCB, which establishes the DCB.

We examine OPEN with respect only to $\mathcal{BDAM}$. The two fields *opt1* and *opt2* are options specified in the macrocall. The alternatives and meanings of each of these fields is presented in Table 14.5.1. The first

Table 14.5.1 OPTION MEANINGS

opt1	
INPUT	Input only file
INOUT	File used for input but later as output without another OPEN required (label may override output function)
OUTPUT	Output only
OUTIN	File and for output but later as input without OPEN appearing again (if label contains OUT, input function is overridden)
RDBACK	*Tape only* positions tape to read backward
UPDAT	File may be updated in place and/or records added

opt2	
LEAVE	Do not reposition after volume switching
REREAD	Position to reprocess after switching
DISP	Disposition of volume determined by DD statement

option tells $\mathcal{OPEN}$ how the file will be used; the second option furnishes other information as indicated in the table.

Action OPEN in its standard form produces a parameter list of four bytes:

- The first byte is a coded representation of the two options.
- The other three bytes are an address constant giving the address of the DCB for the file.

This is best seen with the expansion of a typical OPEN in Fig. 14.5.1 where OPEN appears at 251:

- OPEN addresses the DCB called DCBA.
- INOUT indicates that this is an input file which is also used for output.
- DISP indicates that the DD statement notes the disposition of the file.

```
251      OPEN     DCBA,INOUT,DISP
252+     CNOP
253+     BAL      1,*+8
254+     DC       AL1(3)
255+     DC       AL3(DCBA)
256+     SVC      19
```

Fig. 14.5.1 Expansion of OPEN.

At 252+, CNOP aligns the parameter constant on a fullWord boundary. BAL at 253+ inserts the address of the parameter list into GPR1 and then branches around it to 256+. A constant with hexadecimal value 3 at 254+ represents the two options INOUT and DISP. The address of DCBA is established at 255+. At 256+, SVC calls in the Task Manager indicating that OPEN is to be brought in by 19 in *loc*.

OPEN The operation of OPEN is presented in Fig. 14.5.2. OPEN turns over control to the Task Manager by means of the program defined interrupt, SVC. The Task Manager determines that OPEN is required and brings it in to the fixed area of MEMORY from the system residence volume which contains a copy of the routine. When OPEN gets control, it has the address of the parameters in GPR1. From this it gets to the Data Control Block and determines what tasks are required.

The DCB contains a cross-reference to the DD statement in a field called DDNAME. The DD statement has been incorporated by the Job Manager in its own block, the JFCB. OPEN now has enough information to identify either the file or the volume. If it does not have volume identification, it may have to use the system catalog to find which volume contains the file name.

Now it determines whether the desired volume is mounted and, if so, on which DEVICE. If the volume is not mounted, OPEN issues operator directions requesting volume mounting on a designated DEVICE.

OPEN now accesses the volume and through the Volume Table of Contents, it locates the file on the volume. It extracts the volume label to create the Data Set Control Block, DSCB, in MEMORY.

Now all the information about the file is available to OPEN. It performs a merge of the DSCB onto the JFCB and then merges the JFCB into the DCB which is now complete.

OPEN determines the Access Method required and operations needed.

OPEN **execution** As shown in Fig. 14.5.3, OPEN now places the desired AMethod into MEMORY. First from file organization it determines information in the DCB. Each AMethod has an OPEN Executor associated with it which we shall call AMOX. OPEN brings this AMOX

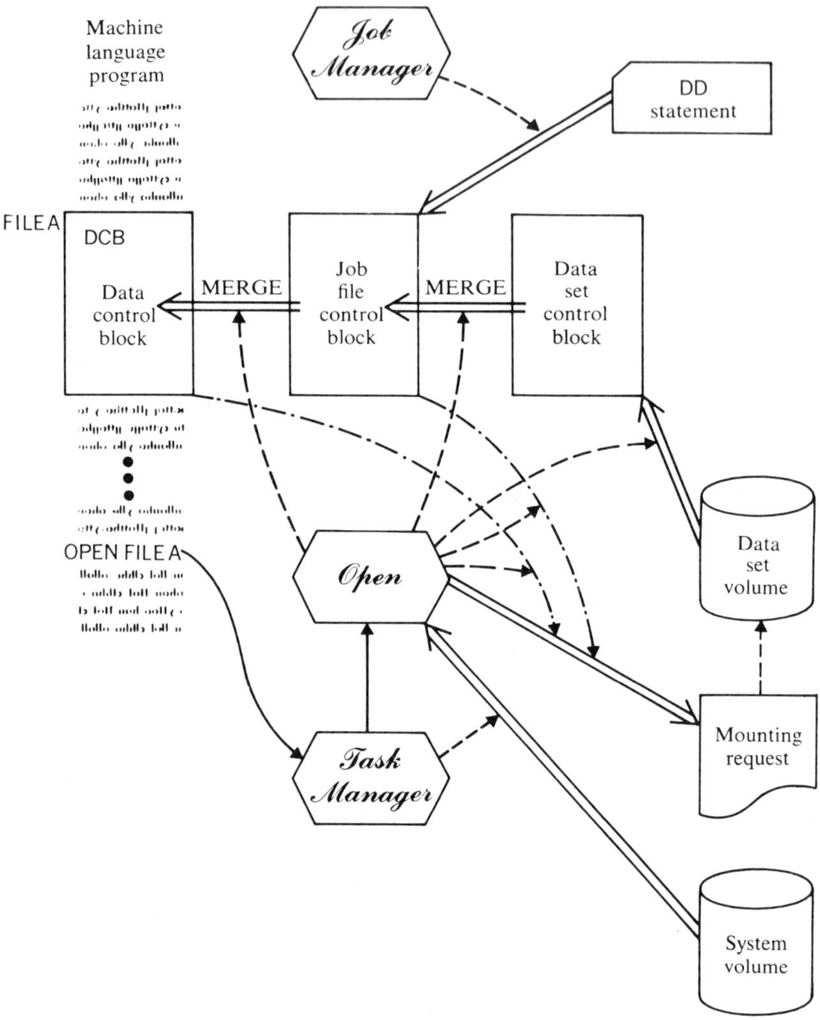

Fig. 14.5.2 Finding OPEN in the program starts a set of operations which fully establishes the DCB.

into the dynamic region of MEMORY and turns control over to it, transmitting the location of the DCB to it.

The $\mathcal{AMOX}$ examines the DCB and from it determines a number of requirements:

- the addressing modules,
- the channel program generating module,
- the option modules,
- the appendage modules.

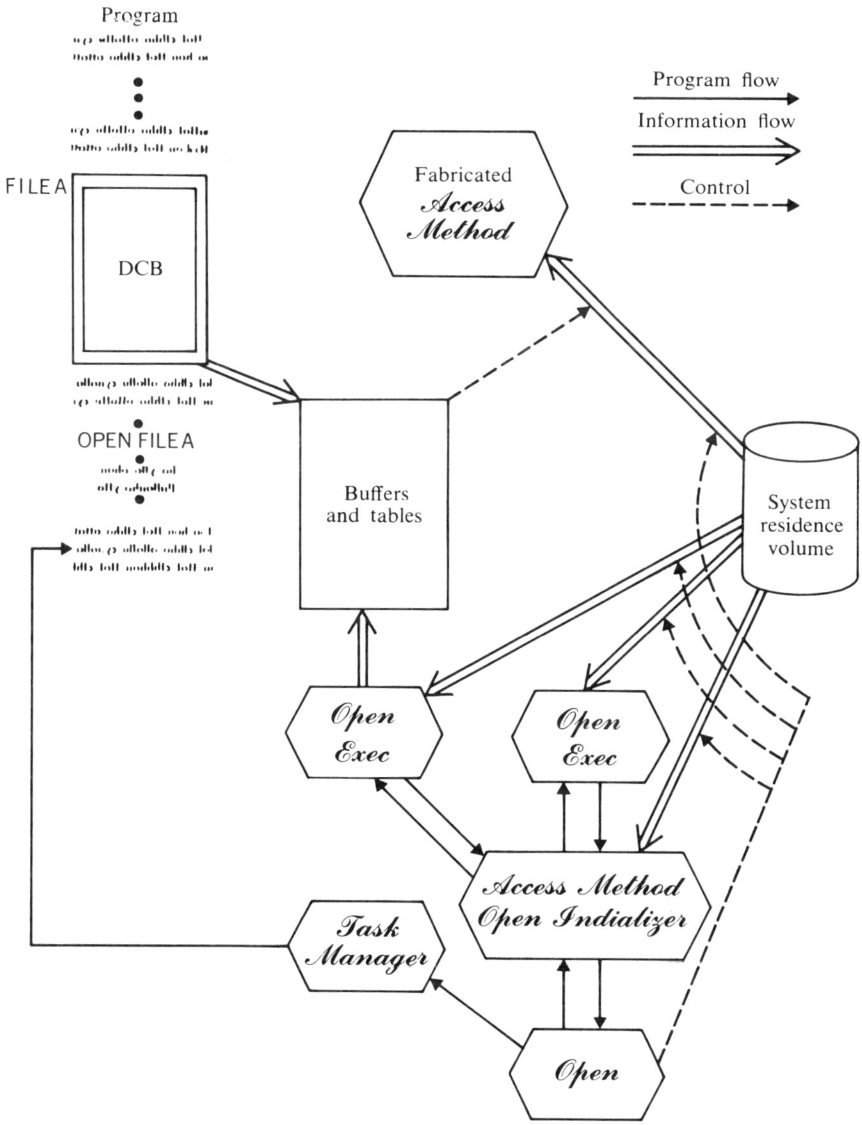

Fig. 14.5.3 OPEN brings in initializers and executors for the requested access method. These build data tables and determine what is the rest of the Access Method which is then brought in by OPEN.

AMOX makes up tables and then brings in these modules from the system residence volume, placing them in a dynamic area of MEMORY *with* the program. It then places the entry point to the AMethod into the forty-eighth byte of the DCB. Finally, the buffers required are created. If this is a queued Access Method, control may go to the AMethod to start reading in information into MEMORY before it is needed by the program.

The program makes use of the AMethod with macros which link directly to the AMethod through the DCB as described in Section 14.6.

14.6 ACCESS MACROS

Meaning These macros talk to the Access Method. Again, we only examine the standard forms.

The program gets to the AMethod with the standard linkage form using BALR where GPR15 contains the entry point to the AMethod and GPR14 contains the return point to the program.

As noted in the last section, OPEN has placed the address of the AMethod at byte 48 of the DCB. We now examine how a macro is expanded so that the proper linkage will be generated.

GET GET is the macro used in QSAM and QISAM to request a record for processing by the programmer. We only examine standard form which is

$$\text{name} \quad \text{GET} \quad \text{dcb,area} \qquad (14.6.1)$$

Here *dcb* is the symbolic address of the macro DCB which defined the DCB. *Area* is the symbolic address of a work area. In some forms *area* may be absent, in which case the Access Method returns the address of the desired buffer in GPR1.

```
          MACRO
NAME      GET        &DCB,&AREA
          AIF        ('&DCB' EQ '').E1
NAME      IHBINNRA   &DCB,&AREA
          L          15,48(0,1)         LOAD GET ROUTINE ADDR.
          BALR       14,15              LINK TO GET ROUTINE
          MEXIT
E1        IHBERMAC   06
          MEND
```

Fig. 14.6.1 GET.

Definition The definition of GET in the system library is presented in Fig. 14.6.1. It includes two intrasystem macros. At (4) IHBINNRA loads *dcb* into GPR1 and *area* into GPR0. At (5) the address of the AMethod (*dcb*+48) is placed in GPR15. At (6) BALR occurs, taking us to the AMethod.

Should the *dcb* be omitted (3), the error printout macro, IHBERMAC, is invoked (8). The pertinent portion of IHBERMAC is presented in Fig. 14.6.2. Notice that the error code associated with the error macro is 06. Examination of the figure will show how the proper error message is printed when *dcb* is omitted.

```
         MACRO
         IHBERMAC  &A,&B,&D,&E,&F
         LCLC      &G(14)
         LCLC      &C
&C       SETC      '***IHB'
           .
           .
           .
         AIF       (&A LE 13).E13
           .
           .
           .
E13      ANOP
           .
           .
           .
&G(5)    SETC      'DCB'
           .
           .
           .
         MNOTE     12,'&C.001 &G(&A—1) OPERAND REQ 'NOT SPECIFIED'
         MEXIT
```

Fig. 14.6.2 Creating an error message for GET (or PUT).

PUT PUT is the macro used in a queued Access Method for outputting information onto a file. The definition of this macro is presented in Fig. 14.6.3.

READ READ is the macro used by the program to obtain input information for a BDAM file (and for all basic access methods for that matter). The format of the READ for BDAM is

name READ decb,type,dcb,area,length,keyadr,blockadr (14.6.2)

```
        MACRO
&NAME   PUT        &DCB,&AREA
        AIF        ('&DCB' EQ '').ERR
&NAME   IHBINNRA   &DCB,&AREA
        L          15,48(0,1)      LOAD PUT ROUTINE ADDR.
        BALR       14,15           LINK TO PUT ROUTINE
        MEXIT
.ERR    IHBERMAC   6
        MEND
```

Fig. 14.6.3 PUT.

As you can see, there are many parameters associated with READ, enough so that Table 14.6.1 is supplied to describe them. Most of the entries are self-explanatory except *decb*. This is the *name*, the symbolic name, by which the program will refer to the data event control block,

Table 14.6.1 PARAMETERS OF READ

Parameter	Description
name	Label for macro
decb	Name for DECB
type	Requirements of AMethod block id versus key return of exact address exclusive use of file
dcb	Symbolic address of DCB
area	Name for area where record is placed
length	Number of bytes to be read
keyadr	Address where key is found
blockadr	Address in MEMORY where address of block is found

DECB. Since buffering cannot be anticipated, each request is a separate event. Each must be mounted for completion. The DECB keeps track of each event. Actually the DECB is created by the READ.

Activity The activity associated with READ is presented in Fig. 14.6.4 where a typical READ is encountered at 204. Notice that it is named RD and that this name is different from the name of the data event control block which is called DECBNAM.

The code produced begins at 205+ which is also named RD, CNOP, which aligns the parameter list on a boundary. At 206+ BAL appears to place the address of the parameter list in GPR1 and *branch* around it. At 210+ *load* places the address of the entry point to the AMethod into

```
204     RD        READ   DECBNAM,DI,DCBADD,etc.
205+    RD        CNOP   0,4
206+              BAL    1*+32
207+    DECBNAM
208+             +------------------------+
                 |                        |  28
209+             |   DECB                 |  bytes
                 +------------------------+
210+              L      15,DCBADD+48
211+              BALR   14,15
```

Fig. 14.6.4 READ and its production.

GPR15. Notice that this address is obtained from the forty-eighth byte of the DCB. Finally at 211+ BALR takes us to the AMethod.

DECB The data event control block consists of twenty-eight bytes as presented in Table 14.6.2. The first column indicates the position of the field with reference to the beginning of the block.

Table 14.6.2 DECB

Location	*Name*	*Description*
0	DECSDECB	Activity posting area
4	DECTYPE	Coded type data
6	DECLNGTH	Length
8	DECDCBAD	Address of DCB
12	DECAREA	Address of destination
16	DECIOBPT	Address of IOB
20	DECKYADR	Address where key is stored
24	DECRECPT	Address of block address

The second column is the name of the block. Finally we have a description of the field.

Most of the fields of the DECB are self-explanatory except for a couple which we now examine:

- DECSDECB is the activity posting area which is used by IOS for indicating the progress of the activity and how it is completed when completion is signaled by IOS.
- DECIOBPT is a pointer to the Input Output Block, IOB. IOS posts the completion status of the activity onto the IOB.

Macro The macrodefinition of READ appears in Fig. 14.6.5. You should note that since READ is used by several AMethods it is *type* which determines the code generated. This, in turn, requests one

```
         MACRO
&NAME    READ       &DECB,&TYPE,&DCB,&AREA,&LENGTH,&KEY,&RCDREF,&MF=I
         GBLB       &IHBWR,&IHBT(2),&IHBS(4)
&IHBS(1) SETB       (K'&TYPE EQ 1)
&IHBS(2) SETB       (K'&TYPE EQ 2)
&IHBS(3) SETB       (K'&TYPE EQ 3)
&IHBS(4) SETB       (K'&TYPE EQ 4)
&IHBWR   SETB       0
&IHBT(1) SETB       (T'&LENGTH EQ ' ')
&IHBT(2) SETB       (T'&RCDREF EQ ' ')
         AIF        ('&DECB' EQ ' ').E1
         AIF        ('&TYPE' EQ ' ').E2
         AIF        ('&TYPE'(1,1) EQ 'S').BSAMR
         AIF        ('&TYPE'(1,1) EQ 'K').BISAMR
         AIF        ('&TYPE'(1,1) EQ 'D').BDAMR
         AIF        ('&TYPE'(1,1) EQ 'T').BTAMR
         IHBERMAC   63,111,&TYPE                              FIRST CHAR OF TYPE INVALID
         MEXIT
.BSAMR   ANOP
&NAME    IHBRDWRS   &DECB,&TYPE,&DCB,&AREA,&LENGTH,&KEY,&RCDREF,MF=&MF
         MEXIT
.BISAMR  ANOP
&NAME    IHBRDWRK   &DECB,&TYPE,&DCB,&AREA,&LENGTH,&KEY,&RCDREF,MF=&MF
         MEXIT
BIAMR    ANOP
&NAME    IHBRDWRT   &DECB,&TYPE,&DCB,&AREA,&LENGTH,&KEY,&RCDREF,MF=&MF
         MEXIT
.BDAMR   ANOP
&NAME    IHBRDWRD   &DECB,&TYPE,&DCB,&AREA,&LENGTH,&KEY,&RCDREF,&MF=&MF
         MEXIT
.E1      IHBERMAC   07,111
         MEXIT
.E2      IHBERMAC   25,111
         MEND
```

Fig. 14.6.5 READ.

of four intrasystem macros which are used by both READ and WRITE. Since we are concerned with 𝔅𝔇𝔄𝔐 where 𝔇 is for Direct, the inner macrocall is IHBRDWRD. Notice the terminal letters RDWRD for ReaD/WRite Direct.

The macrodefinition makes a number of error checks and then defines global symbols which it communicates to the inner macro. This is a saving since this checking can now be done in one place for all four inner macros.

IHBRDWRD is quite long; it does not pay for us to examine it in detail. Its function has been presented in Fig. 14.6.4.

CHECK The purpose of the macro CHECK is to check whether a previously requested activity has been performed. When READ or WRITE is issued, a long train of activity is set up:

- The macro calls the 𝔄𝔐ethod.
- The 𝔄𝔐ethod calls 𝔍𝔒𝔖 and gives it a buffer and CHANNEL program.
- 𝔍𝔒𝔖 places the buffer and program on a queue for later service.
- When this request can be processed, 𝔍𝔒𝔖 issues SIO to the CHANNEL and sets up a pointer to the channel program.
- The CHANNEL connects the DEVICE and puts it to work to satisfy the request.
- Only after the buffer has been filled by the DEVICE can it be made available to the program.

The purpose of CHECK then is to determine if the activity requested has been performed and also to initiate error processing if some kind of error or exception has occurred in the course of the activity.

CHECK has this format:

name CHECK decb (14.6.3)

You will notice that the *symbolic name* of the Data Event Control Block is supplied at *decb*. This is all that is needed to specify the event *and* the file since the DECB points to the DCB.

The macrodefinition for CHECK is presented in Fig. 14.6.6. After an error check (3) the intrasystem macro, IHBINNRA, loads a GPR1 with the address, *decb*, of the DECB (4). The address of the DCB is loaded into GPR14 from the eighth byte of the DECB (5). A different address is used for entry to the 𝔄𝔐ethod for the check routine, namely the fifty-second byte of the DCB. This is loaded into GPR15 (6). Finally link to the 𝔄𝔐ethod (7).

WAIT Another macro, WAIT, serves the same purpose as CHECK in a multiprogramming environment. The difference

```
         MACRO
&NAME    CHECK      &DECB
         AIF        ('&DECB' EQ '')E1
&NAME    IHBINNRA   &DECB
         L          14,8(0,1)       PICK UP DCB ADDRESS
         L          15,52(0,14)     LOAD CHECK ROUT. ADDR
         BALR       14,15           LINK TO CHECK ROUTINE
         MEXIT
.E1      IHBERMAC   07,018
         MEND
```

Fig. 14.6.6 CHECK.

is that WAIT communicates through the Task Manager. Now if the event examined has not been completed, again the program cannot continue. But since this is a multiprogramming environment, the Task Manager does not hold up the computer. Instead, it looks at other programs now in MEMORY and, if there is one which needs servicing, the Task Manager turns control over to it. Later, when IOS is invoked due to the completion of an event mentioned at *loc* of WAIT, IOS will issue the macro, POST, indicating the completion of that event in its DECB. At that time, if all events for all DECBs at *loc* of WAIT are done, the Task Manager will again intervene to determine which program to turn control over to according to the priority of each.

14.7 OTHER AMethod MACROS

Description Table 14.7.1 contains a list of thirty-two AMethod macros. Each macro has a description of its function and some of the parameters which generally accompany the macrocall. In the right-most column are listed the AMethods with which each macro is associated.

Most of the macros are self-explanatory. There is one, however, which may give you trouble, DCBD. This macrocall creates a dummy section called IHADCB. It enables the program to reference any field in a DCB. This macro can be given only once in any program. To make this dummy section apply to a particular DCB, the address of that DCB is entered into a GPR using a *load*, L. Following this, there is a USING statement in the program with the GPR just loaded as one operand and IHADCB as the other. Now whenever a field of the DCB is referenced (such as DCBRAL), it will apply to the named DCB (in this case to byte 17 of that

Table 14.7.1 $\mathcal{AM}$ MACROS

	Macro	*Function*	*Parameters*	$\mathcal{AM}$
1.	BLDL	Place directory obtained from file into a user's list area	dcb, list area	$\mathcal{BPAM}$
2.	BSP	Back space a block (tape only)	dcb	$\mathcal{BSAM}$
3.	BUILD	Create a buffer pool in a named area	area, buf buf length	All
4.	CHECK	Check that data transmission is complete and if errors occur, request an error service routine	decb	Basic
5.	CLOSE	Close file(s)	dcb, option	All
6.	CNTRL	Perform a control function: (a) CARD HOPPER selection (b) PRINTER line skip (c) MTU forward or back space	dcb, code for function required	$\mathcal{BSAM}$
7.	DCB	Construct a DCB	See Table 14.4.2	All
8.	DCBD	Create a dummy section called IHADCB to apply to any DCB giving each portion the names in Fig. 14.4.2. The user gives USING with GPR and DCB address.	Code for organization and device types	All
9.	ESET	End sequential retrieval and release buffers so that retrieval can begin at some other point in file	dcb	$\mathcal{QISAM}$
10.	FEOV	Force *end of volume* condition and cause volume switching when required	dcb	$\mathcal{QSAM}$ $\mathcal{BSAM}$
11.	FIND	Find the beginning of a named member and use as start for next READ	dcb, address of name, code for name versus relative loc	$\mathcal{BPAM}$
12.	FREEBUF	Return a buffer to the pool which was acquired by GETBUF	dcb, register	Basic

Table 14.7.1 *(Continued)*

	Macro	*Function*	*Parameters*	$\mathcal{AM}$
13.	FREEDBUF	Return a buffer obtained dynamically	decb, code for $\mathcal{AM}$, dcb	$\mathcal{BDAM}$ $\mathcal{BISAM}$
14.	FREEPOOL	Release buffer pool area	dcb	All
15.	GET	Get a record	Section 14.6	$\mathcal{QISAM}$,$\mathcal{QSAM}$
16.	GETPOOL	Build a buffer pool in an area supplied by $\mathcal{AM}$	dcb, buffno, bufflength code	
17.	NOTE	Note in GPR1 the relative position of the last block read or written	dcb	$\mathcal{BPAM}$ $\mathcal{BSAM}$
18.	OPEN	Open a file	Section 14.5	All
19.	POINT	Set the DEVICE to the beginning of the indicated block for next operation		
20.	PRTOV	Test for PRINTER carriage overflow	dcb, code, exit	$\mathcal{BSAM}$,$\mathcal{QSAM}$
21.	PUT	Put a record on output	See GET, Section 14.6	$\mathcal{QISAM}$,$\mathcal{QSAM}$
22.	PUTX	Put a record *back* in the file from which it was read (or another file)	dcb, address of original input for two files	$\mathcal{QISAM}$ $\mathcal{QSAM}$
23.	READ	Read a record	Section 14.6	Basic
24.	RELEX	Release exclusive control over file initiated in a foregoing READ	dcb, address containing block adr.	$\mathcal{BDAM}$
25.	RELSE	Release current input buffer immediately so that next GET applies to *next* buffer	dcb	$\mathcal{QISAM}$,$\mathcal{QSAM}$
26.	SETL	Set up to start point of retrieval for sequential file	dcb, code for how address supplied, adr.	$\mathcal{QISAM}$
27.	SETPRT	Load preset message and have printed	dcb, message code	$\mathcal{BSAM}$,$\mathcal{QSAM}$
28.	STOW	Store directory entry into partitioned file	dcb, list adr.	$\mathcal{BPAM}$
29.	SYNADAF	Used by error analysis routine for communication with programmer	Code	All
30.	SYNADRLS	Releases message produced by SYNADAF		All
31.	TRUNC	Release *this* buffer for output after *next* PUT/PUTX	dcb	$\mathcal{QSAM}$
32.	WRITE	Write a record on a file as for READ	See Section 14.6	Basic

DCB). We might load GPR7 with DCBRAL for DCBA, thus:

```
DCBD
L       6,DCBA
USING   IHADCB,6
L       7,DCBRAL
```
(14.7.1)

Definition Macrodefinitions for AMethod macros produce a parameter list where required and a link to the AMethod using BALR. In most cases, the DCB address is one of the parameters of the call. In some few cases, such as CHECK, the DCB is accessed through the DECB.

14.8 CATALOG MANAGEMENT

Catalog The catalog is a list of files or libraries of files. A catalog is necessary so that files specified in DD statements or DCB macros can be both located and retrieved automatically. Finding the volume on which a file resides is done by the Catalog Manager, or Cat. Cat provides a function for both the problem program and the Job Manager who calls in Cat when new jobs are to be started but volumes are unspecified.

The catalog provides for hierarchial structures. It permits libraries to be specified as well as simple files. To specify a file within a library, write the library name and the file name right after it, separated by a period, thus:

library.file (14.8.1)

To indicate the file called MFG, which is part of a sublibrary called PAY, which in turn is part of a library A, we use the same structure, thus:

A.PAY.MFG (14.8.2)

This principle can be extended to any number of levels, provided the total length of the qualified name does not exceed a specified amount, fifty-eight characters.

The catalog is so important to the operating system that it should always be available. This is assured by keeping the catalog on the system residence volume. This does not allow total flexibility; the catalog can grow extremely large. An alternative that can be exercised in OS360 is to have all library names and primary file names on the catalog proper on the system residence volume. Library names can have pointers to the volume on which files for that library exist; then a continuation of that catalog can be found on the volume pointed to.

Table 14.8.1 CATALOG MANAGEMENT MACRO PAIRS

Number	*Function*	*Macro*	*Loc*
1	Read a named block from the catalog	LOCATE	[CAMLST]
		CAMLST	NAME, address where file name is found, address of volume serial number, address where block is to be placed
2	Read a block from the catalog as specified by the block's location	LOCATE	[CAMLST]
		CAMLST	BLOCK, block address, address of volume serial number, address where block is to be placed
3	Build an index	INDEX	[CAMLST]
		CAMLST	BLDX address of index name, address of volume serial number
4	Build a generation index	INDEX	[CAMLST]
		CAMLST	BLDG address of index name, address of volume serial number, DELETE (if space for dropped files is made available) EMPTY (if excess files are to be removed) number of files in group
5	Assign an alias to an index	INDEX	[CAMLST]
		CAMLST	BLDA address of index name, address of volume serial number, address of alias
6	Delete an index	INDEX	[CAMLST]
		CAMLST	DLTX name of index, address of volume
7	Delete an alias	INDEX	[CAMLST]
		CAMLST	DLTA index name, volume address
8	Connect control volumes	INDEX	[CAMLST]
		CAMLST	LINX index name, old volume address, new volume address

Table 14.8.1 (*Continued*)

Number	*Function*	*Macro*	*Loc*
9	Disconnect control volume	INDEX CAMLST	[CAMLST] DRDX index name, volume address
10	Catalog a file	CATALOG CAMLST	[CAMLST] CAT file name, volume address, list indicating volumes where file is stored
11	Remove references to a file from the catalog	CATALOG CAMLST	[CAMLST] UNCAT file names, volume
12	Recatalog a file whose structure has been changed	CATALOG CAMLST	[CAMLST] RECAT file name, volume of catalog, volume description
13	Read the label for the file from its volume table of contents	OBTAIN CAMLST	[CAMLST] SEARCH address of file name, address of VTOC volume number, work area address for label
14	Read the label found at a specified location	OBTAIN CAMLST	[CAMLST] SEEK address of track, cylinder, block location, volume number address, work area address
15	Delete file and reference to it in the catalog	SCRATCH CAMLST	[CAMLST] SCRATCH address of file name, volume description address, OVRD (if expiration date to be overridden)
16	Change the name of a file as it appears in the file label	RENAME CAMLST	[CAMLST] RENAME address of old name, address of new name, volume description

System programmer The system programmer can use the catalog in one of two ways. The normal user really has no need to reference the catalog directly. His access to files is through the Job Manager, which automatically brings in Cat to find the file for the user.

The first way that the system programmer can call in Cat is as one of the steps in his job. An execute card with opcode EXEC calls in the Catalog Manager as any other utility program.

We discuss here the second method to incorporate Cat references with macros. These macros are different from others we have seen because two are always required. The first macro is an imperative indicating the kind of operation desired. The second macro is a declarative and always has the opcode CAMLST. CAMLST is referred to by the symbolic name found next to it at *name* and specifies the subtask, parameters, and lists associated with the imperative. To examine the macros fully, they must be seen in combination. Table 14.8.1 is a list of pairs of macros which are interpreted to convey the kind of thing done by Cat via macros.

Illustration Figure 14.8.1 illustrates how the two macros are associated together. On line 1 we find the imperative with a reference to the name of the name assigned to the macro CAMLST. On line 2 we find the macro CAMLST and its name to the right of it. It has a subtask and one or more lists. The lists are referred to by name and contain constants declared with DC.

Line			
1		Imperative	camad
2	Camad	CAMLST	subtask, list 1, list 2, etc.
	List 1	DC ←	
	List 2	DC ←	

Fig. 14.8.1 How the two catalog macros interact.

Figure 14.8.2 illustrates a catalog entry located by name. The imperative LOCATE references a declarative, CAMLST, named REFER. At REFER we find the macro CAMLST. At *loc* of REFER is NAME, which says that the locating is to be done by name. Next we find TITLE, which is the name of an area where Cat will find the name of the entry. The next entry at REFER would contain the serial number, but it is absent since we expect the Cat to find it. The last entry at REFER is PLACE, the place where the LOCATE routine enters the block from the catalog into the program to be accessible to the system programmer.

```
                LOCATE     REFER

       REFER    CAMLST     NAME,TITLE,PLACE
       TITLE    DC         CL44'PAYFILE'
       PLACE    DS         OD
                DS         265C
```

Fig. 14.8.2 An example of catalog macros.

LOCATE

LOCATE is defined in Fig. 14.8.3 and, after loading GPRS with IHBINNRA, an SVL is created.

```
          MACRO
&NAME     LOCATE     &LIST,&ERCODE=072
          AIF        (T'&LIST EQ '0').E1
&NAME     IHBINNRA   &LIST                 LOAD REG 1
          SVC        26                    LINK TO SERVICE ROUT.
          MEXIT
.EI       IHBERMAC   34,&ERCODE            LIST ADDR MISSING
          MEND
```

Fig. 14.8.3 LOCATE expansion.

14.9 SYSTEM MACROS

This set of macros is called **system macros** because it is not generally used by the BAL programmer. The task of such a macro is to create an SVC and a parameter list. The macros are discussed in categories.

Time Several macros have to do with time. They require the presence of a timer option in the hardware.

The macro TIME has the format

TIME (14.9.1)

It returns the date in GPR1 and the time of day as specified by opt in GPR0; that is its sole function.

STIMER

This macro sets up the timer to monitor an operation and has the format

STIMER type,exit,time (14.9.2)

Here *type* can be one of three alternatives where exit addresses are associated for the first two:

- REAL—the time interval is calculated continuously regardless of what is going on.
- TASK—the time interval is calculated only while the task is active.
- WAIT—the task is held up in a wait condition until the time has elapsed, at which time the task is reactivated.

Exit is the address of an exit routine which takes over after the specified time interval. The third parameter, *time*, consists of two parts separated by an equals sign: the first part indicates the form in which the time is presented; the second part indicates the address where that time interval is to be found. The alternative forms are

- DINTVL—a decimal time interval,
- BINTVL—a binary time interval,
- TUINTVL—a time interval measured in operations relevant to the computer (about 26 microseconds)
- TOD—a time of day specified in hours, minutes, seconds, and hundredths of a second.

TTIMER

This macro permits the programmer to test the interval timer, having it return the time remaining from a previous STIMER macro. It has the format

TTIMER cancel (14.9.3)

If CANCEL appears as *cancel*, then the previous STIMER request is canceled when the remaining time is returned to GPR0.

WAIT

This macro is oriented to an event rather than a time. Frequently events are required to occur sequentially. The next task cannot be done until the preceding one is completed. This is especially necessary in multiprogramming environments to place a job into a wait state until one or more tasks have been completed, such as an IO operation or a subroutine. The task supervisor can then go on to another job until the events associated with this job have been reported as completed. The program gives this macro thus:

WAIT number,event list (14.9.4)

Where there is only one event involved in a uniprogramming environment, *number* is one; *event* then refers to the address of its event control block, ECB.

For multiprogramming, a number of events may be designated by placing that number at *number*. Then, at *event* we find a list of ECBs, all of which must be completed before the job is permitted to continue.

POST

This macro is used by the system or called subroutine when it has determined that an event has been completed. It has the form

POST event,code (14.9.5)

Here *event* is the address of an ECB. This ECB is set so that its first two bits are 01 to indicate a completed event. The *code* is entered in the remainder of the word.

User routines These two macros can specify user routines entered after an interrupt or before abnormal termination.

STAE

The initials of this macro stand for "specify task asynchronous exit." The macro permits the user to specify a routine to be performed before ABEND is entered. In this way he can intercept ABEND and provide processing by this routine before either normal or abnormal termination. This macro has the form

STAE exit,over,para,xctl. (14.9.6)

Here *exit* is the address of the subroutine to which control is passed in the event of ABTERM. At *over* we indicate whether this exit specification overlays a previous one or whether a new block is created. *Para* permits a list of parameters to be transmitted to the exit routine. *Xctl* indicates whether the macro XCTL when given implicitly or explicitly will cancel this STAE.

SPIE

SPIE is used to specify a program interrupt exit and has this format:

SPIE exit,code (14.9.7)

Here *exit* is the address of the exit to be taken when the interruption occurs. *Code* indicates which interruptions produce this exit.

IO The macros described below are used by the programmer to request input or output operations.

EXCP

This request to EXecute a Channel Program is not generally used by the programmer since he has available to him Access Methods and file definitions which do all the work for him. The EXCP macro permits him to create his own channel program elsewhere in his assembly program and then to request the execution of this program. The procedure for doing this requires many considerations which are not discussed here. The macro is simple to request, thus:

EXCP iob (14.9.8)

Here *iob* is the address of the IOB which contains pointers to completely specify the IO action desired.

XDAP

The request to eXecute a Direct Access Program is given with a macro which has the form

XDAP manyfields (14.9.9)

There are many fields to be specified.

WTO

A programmer can request an output message on the output device at any time with the macro

WTO 'message' (14.9.10)

where *message* is any message that the programmer wishes printed.

WTOR

Sometimes a message is insufficient and a reply from the operator is required. To have the system print a message and then wait for a reply, we give a *write to operator with reply* macro:

WTOR 'message'replylen,replyaddr,ecbad (14.9.11)

Again *message* is specified in the macro. *Replyaddr* is an address where the reply is stored; *replylen* is a length in bytes which the maximum reply would be less than; *ecbad* is an address where the event control block is found.

SNAP

Often a program written in assembly language runs into trouble. The programmer can cope with this trouble if he can find out the contents of MEMORY and REGISTERS at various points in his program. He can do this with the macro called SNAP, which takes a snapshot of MEMORY and REGISTERS with respect to *parameters* and which is specified thus:

SNAP param (14.9.12)

The initials are an abbreviation for snapshot, because the programmer is getting a snapshot of the computer at a specific point in this program. He can give parameters which specify the bounds of MEMORY and REGISTERS which are to be presented to him when the snapshot is taken.

SEGWT

This is a request to bring in a segment in a prespecified overlay scheme and to wait until this segment is in before returning control to the program requesting the new segment. Since this is given in a unique programming environment, there is no alternative but to wait for the segment to get in.

System programmer There are a few macros which would really help nobody except the system programmer. These are summarized briefly below:

CVT This macro creates a dummy section to address the communication vector table which permits the system programmer to access that program symbolically.

RDJFCB This is a request to read the JFCB into a given area where it is then available to the programmer for alteration.

PURGE This command is available to the operating system and the system programmer, when trouble arises, to request that waiting requests for IO service be removed from that queue and placed in a safe spot in MEMORY.

RESTORE At some later point in time it may be required to return the request elements to their queues.

14.10 MULTIPROGRAMMING

Priority In a multiprogramming system such as MVT there are a number of programs resident in computer MEMORY. Of course, only one is running at any given time, but switching from one to another is done on a priority basis. This priority is associated with the job step and tasks associated with each. The operator of the program may wish to change this priority and can do so with the macro CHAP.

LOG Under MVT there is a separate log where messages can be written. A program can do this with command WTL.

Tasks During a given job step, new tasks may be started which operate in parallel with old tasks. Thus, within a given program, when one task gets stuck, the other task can be brought in. The macro for doing this is ATTACH.

The entire structure is subject to delegation and subdelegation; thus a task can request a subtask, and so on. Now what happens if the originating task is finished before the subtask? The problem is deleting one without deleting another. The system should monitor the tree of tasks and a special macro is provided to facilitate transition from one completed task to another. Thus, upon completion, the task request is not eliminated until a new macro called DETACH is given.

Segmentation Whereas in a uniprogramming environment we could not expect to load a new segment and operate our program at the same time, with multiprogramming this is possible. We can request loading of the segment to be done simultaneously to the operation of the present program segment. This is done with the macro SEGLD.

Resources Resources are records, programs, areas, and so forth which have names. The resources are called serially reusable when only one program can use them at a time. When such resources exist in the system, it is necessary to lock them out from other programs when they are allocated to another program. When that program is finished with the resources, it releases them to other possibly requesting programs. A resource is designated or allocated using the macro ENQ; it is released with the macro DEQ.

PROBLEMS

14.1 (a) Describe three places where *ASLR* can find macrodefinitions.
(b) Why are all three needed?
(c) When and how does *ASLR* get the definitions from each source?

14.2 (a) Why are intrasystem macros used?
(b) Could *you* call them in your program?

14.3 What generally does IHBINNRA do? IHBERMAC?

14.4 Describe the six *AMethods* IBM furnishes and their use.

14.5 (a) What is the DCB?
(b) How is it defined? Referenced?
(c) Why does it differ in size from one *AMethod* to another?

14.6 (a) How is OPEN used?
(b) What does *ASLR* do with OPEN?
(c) What is SVC 19?
(d) How does *OPEN* get control?
(e) What is *AMOX*?

14.7 (a) Why does READ have so many parameters as compared with GET?
(b) How do GET, PUT get us to the *AMethod*?
(c) What is the result of GET?

14.8 (a) What is the DECB?
(b) How is it established?
(c) How does READ get to the AMethod?
(d) How does CHECK get to the AMethod?

14.9 (a) How did IHBRDWRD get its name?
(b) How does it get control?
(c) What does it do?

14.10 (a) What is the catalog?
(b) How is it arranged?
(c) Who manages it?

14.11 (a) How does Cat get control (two ways)?
(b) For each, state how Cat knows what to do?
(c) Why are double macros provided for Cat?

14.12 (a) What does CAMLST do?
(b) How does ASLR handle it?
(c) How is it related to the imperative?

14.13 (a) What are *system macros*?
(b) How are they expanded?
(c) How used?

14.14 (a) What is the function of POST and WAIT?
(b) How are they used?

15

SUBROUTINES

15.1 KINDS

Reexamination We have examined open and closed subroutines and seen the various ways that they can get into MEMORY:

- brought in with the program during assembly,
- brought in from an external source during assembly,
- at linkage edit time,
- at load time,
- at run time.

We have not found linkage a problem because we have only examined open subroutines so far. Since these routines are duplicated where they occur in the program, no getting back and forth is required.

Linkage is going from the main program to a closed subroutine and at the same time providing a means for the subroutine to return to the main program at the proper place. Linkage also occurs in nested subroutines when we go from an outer subroutine to an inner one.

There are several ways that linkage can be established:

- by the program itself,
- by a macro which does all the work,
- by using the operating system to provide the service.

There are two other considerations when dealing with closed subroutines. The first is the **calling sequence,** a list of parameters or parameter addresses to be used by the subroutine. Since the closed subroutine consists of a fixed sequence of commands, these commands can get to the quantities worked on by the subroutines using the calling sequence.

Another consideration is **saving** REGISTERS. It would be unwieldy for the programmer who constructs the main program and the programmer who constructs the subroutine to have to know what each is doing. We provide the most latitude by establishing conventions which assure the integrity of the registers when going back and forth between the subroutine and its caller.

Macros We have spent a lot of time examining macros. The quick review in Fig. 15.1.1 shows that the management of the macro is left to 𝒜𝒮ℒℛ. The programmer defines the macro before the program proper begins. 𝒜𝒮ℒℛ replaces the name of the macro at *opcode* in the program by the sequence which the programmer has defined.

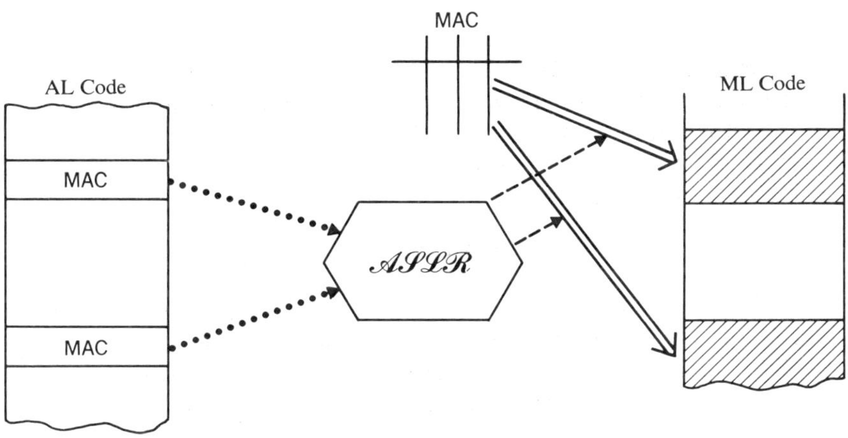

Fig. 15.1.1 For the macro code, MAC, 𝒜𝒮ℒℛ inserts the corresponding defined code into the ML output.

We have seen library macros where the definition does not occur in the program submitted to the assembler, but it was provided at another time. We have also examined COPY which enables the programmer to insert a set of commands any place in his program. The trouble with this is that it lacks provision for transmitting parameters.

Closed subroutines Figure 15.1.2 shows the closed subroutine in diagram form. The code which comprises the closed subroutine appears in the program. Getting to the code is linking. This is generally done with

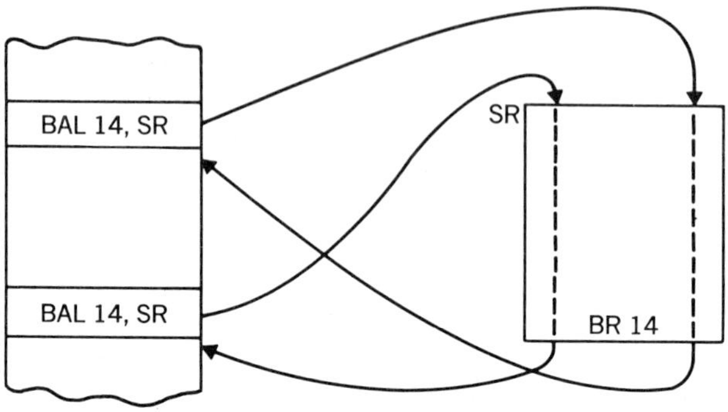

Fig. 15.1.2 𝒜𝒮ℒℛ translates both the calling program and the SR so that the linkage appears as above both for AL and the ML counterpart.

a command such as BAL or BALR which places the departure point from the caller to the exit, in a named REGISTER, by convention, GPR14.

All subroutines know this. They make sure not to destroy the contents of GPR14. When the subroutine has finished its job, it gets back to the main program by **returning**. It simply uses

```
GOBACK    BR    14
```
(15.1.1)

The location of the subroutine is very important to us. If the subroutine is in our program at assembly time and the program has only one CSECT, then things are very easy. However, it is possible to use a subroutine which is further and further distant from the main program. Let's see the alternatives.

The subroutine may be available at assembly time, but it may reside in a different section or CSECT of the total program. The only difference here is the requirement to address the subroutine with a variable address constant (VCON) rather than a simple address constant (ADCON).

Another alternative is for the subroutine to be in another object module. The modules will be brought together by the linkage editor. The only requirement to get to the subroutine is the use of a variable address constant (VCON).

Finally, the subroutine may not be available at load time. It is acquired dynamically during running. Obviously, the program cannot acquire the subroutine without the aid of the operating system. It gets to the operating system with system macros, such as LOAD and LINK, which we examine later in this chapter.

15.2 LINKAGE CONVENTIONS

Conventions Quantities to be transmitted to a subroutine during linkage are left in four REGISTERS thus:

- address of the called subroutine in GPR15,
- return address in GPR14,
- parameters are transmitted by an address in GPR1,
- finally, the *save* convention (described in Section 15.3) requires that the location of the *save* area is transmitted via GPR13.

Local, no parameters First, we examine how to link to a subroutine which is **local**—is contained in this CSECT. We have communicated the BASE REGISTERS which are used for addressing symbolic quantities with the USING statement. This assignment remains applicable to the called subroutine.

For example, to link to the closed routine called CSR, we place its address in GPR15 thus:

```
LA      15,CSR                    (15.2.1)
```

To go to the subroutine, we use BALR to place the exit point in GPR14 since no parameters follow the exit and return is hence to the next subsequent command. We link with

```
BALR    14,15                     (15.2.2)
```

To return from the subroutine, CSR contains as its last command a *branch*, B, using GPR14 thus:

```
BR      14                        (15.2.3)
```

Local, with parameters In this case three GPRS are to be filled. Actually the calling sequence can be any place in the program, or at least in this CSECT. The most convenient place though is right after the exit. Again we would like to link with the command BALR. Since BALR directly precedes the calling sequence, instead of placing the exit address in GPR14, it should place it in GPR1. In so doing, a pointer to the parameter list which follows directly is put in GPR1. Thus the linkage command is

```
BALR    1,15                      (15.2.4)
```

Preceding (15.2.4), we need commands to fill GPR14 and GPR15.

CALLING SEQUENCE

A calling sequence could be structured to contain either the parameters themselves or the addresses of parameters. Approximately the same amount of work is involved. In the first case the main program has to place the parameters to the calling sequence where they are available directly to the subroutine. In the second case the main program does no work; the subroutine gets the addresses and then gets the parameters using the addresses. The latter is more common and most library subroutines are written so that they expect addresses to be transmitted to them. The subroutines know the number of parameters to expect. We examine later a technique for transmitting a variable number of parameters.

Loading of GPR14 and GPR15 is usually done with the *load address* command, LA.

Example Let us now examine the example presented in Fig. 15.2.1.

We call the square root subroutine, the name of which is SQROOT. We present it with two parameter addresses. The first is that of the number, X, for which the square root is desired. The second is that of the root, ROOTX, the location where the subroutine will place its answer.

```
              LA      15,SQROOT      [SQROOT] ──> GPR15
              LA      14,RET            [RET] ──> GPR14
      EXIT    BALR    1,15               [CS] ──> GPR1
                                              ⇒  (GPR15)
      CS      DC      A(X)                [X]
              DC      A(ROOTX)        [ROOTX]
      RET     L       7,ROOTX           ROOTX ──> GPR7
```

Fig. 15.2.1 A call sequence and linkage to SQROOT which use the address of the operand, A(X), and the result, A(ROOTX), for a square root subroutine.

In the figure the first two commands, both LA, place the address of the subroutine, SQROOT, and the address of the return point, RET, into GPR15 and GPR14, respectively. At EXIT we find BALR. Following this, two constants are declared; these are address constants corresponding to the parameters passed to the subroutine. Finally, at RET we find the first command in the main program which follows the calling sequence and is hence the place to which return is made.

Getting parameters The closed subroutine needs parameters, not addresses. The addresses that refer to the desired parameters are at 0(0,1), 4(0,1), etc. In other words, they are at byte numbers 0,4, etc., counting from the beginning of the calling sequence. To get the parameter, its address is loaded into a GPR and then another GPR is loaded by referencing the first register. This complicated method is needed because System 360 does not provide indirect addressing.

An example should make this clear. As part of the square root subroutine, SQROOT, suppose the square of the number for which the root is desired is required. This means placing the number X in a register and then finding its square in another register. To do this, someplace in the subroutine we shall need a total of three registers. Let the address of X be placed in GPR5. The parameter itself, that is, X, will be placed in GPR7. Then we multiply by X. The result is a two-word product spread over two registers. *Multiplication*, M, names the even numbered register of the pair. The product will be stored in GPR6 and GPR7. The sequence for doing this is

```
L     5,0(0,1)
L     7,0(0,5)
M     6,0(0,5)
```
(15.2.5)

First we load GPR5 with A(X), then GPR7 with x, then GPR6 and GPR7 with x^2.

When the square root is found by the subroutine, it should be placed at the answer address XROOT. We cannot store the information directly; this should be done indirectly. Below we load GPR5 with A(ROOTX), the address where the answer is to be placed. The answer is in GPR6. The address where it is to be placed, ROOTX, is now given as 0(0,5); thus we have

```
L     5,4(0,1)
ST    6,0(0,5)
```
(15.2.6)

Using dummy sections Another use for the Dummy Section, the DSECT, discussed in Chapter 13, is in addressing parameters. The writer of the subroutine can enter a DSECT in his routine so that the addresses furnished by the calling sequence can be accessed symbolically, rather than referenced with relation to the beginning of the call sequence. This is best illustrated with the example appearing as Fig. 15.2.2.

At the bottom of the figure is the dummy section. It is named SQPARAD, indicating that these are the addresses of the parameters for the square roots routine. The first word in the section is XADR, the address of X; the second word is ROOTADR, the address where the root is to be returned. Notice the first line named SQROOT begins the subroutine. It is USING, saying that the reference for the dummy section is

```
SQROOT    USING   SQPARAD,1
          L       5,XADR
          L       7,0(0,5)
          M       6,0(0,5)
          L       5,ROOTADR
          ST      6,0(0,5)
          BR      14
SQPARAD   DSECT
XADR      DS      1F
ROOTADR   DS      1F
```

Fig. 15.2.2 Using DSECT for parameter addresses.

GPR1 and that the name of the dummy section is SQPARAD. Multiplication to find x^2 in the first few steps of the subroutine is done as in (15.2.5) with the exception that the first address is provided with XADR instead of 0(0,1).

The usefulness of this technique is limited for the programmer who understands how the subroutine gets addresses from the calling sequence. It does make his subroutine a little bit easier to follow by the casual reader who has not been briefed by the subroutine writer.

Variable number of parameters Some subroutines can be supplied with a variable number of parameters. An example of this is a word addition subroutine, WADD, to add a list of numbers, placing the result at the last parameter address furnished. This assumes a technique to distinguish the last parameter address.

The technique for conveying that an address is the last in a list relies on the fact that the normal address size in System 360 is twenty-four bits, regardless of model. But a fullWord provides thirty-two bits. The leftmost byte is not used when addressing MEMORY from a fullWord stored in a REGISTER, and it is available to convey the nature of the address parameter.

The left byte of the last address in the calling sequence contains 1 in the leftmost position, the flat bit.

Then every address furnished to our subroutine (called WADD) contains a left-hand byte of eight 0's; only the last parameter address in the list is different: The flag bit, the leftmost bit, is set to 1. This can best be seen with an example.

Figure 15.2.3 shows setup and linkage for WADD. The first two commands set up the subroutine address, WADD, and the return point, RETURN. The third command is the actual exit command; following it is the call sequence with the address of three Words, X1, X2, and X3. To tell the subroutine to place the result at a location called SUM (that

SUM is the last address transmitted), the fourth constant declared contains 1 followed by seven 0's. Finally, following this is an address constant of three bytes; $\mathcal{ASLR}$ makes up an address constant, but only provides three bytes for it; this is sufficient, since it only contains twenty-four bits. Then, together, the last two constant declarations in Fig. 15.2.3

```
          LA        15,WADD
          LA        14,RETURN
          BALR      1,15
          DC        A(X1)
          DC        A(X2)
          DC        A(X3)
          DC        X'80'
          DC        AL3(SUM)
RETURN    Continue
```

Fig. 15.2.3 Setup and linkage to WADD.

provide the desired terminal address constant for the subroutine. Naturally it is incumbent upon the subroutine to test each address constant it encounters to see if it is the last address. When it tests X1, X2, etc., the left bit *is* 0, so these are addresses of numbers to be added. When it tests the last address, and finds 1 there, it knows that no more additions are to be done and, after the total is prepared, the result goes into this position.

15.3 SAVING

Need In the transition from the calling program or the called routine, the latter may require the use of REGISTERS, and generally does. It cannot use these REGISTERS as long as they contain quantities proprietary to the calling program. To save the contents of these REGISTERS, two questions arise:

- To whom is the responsibility of *saving* the REGISTERS, the caller or the called?
- In which program are the REGISTERS *saved*?

Either alternative for either question would work as long as a convention is established. In $\mathcal{OS}$360 this is the convention:

- The called program does the *saving*.
- *Saving* is done in the calling program.

This convention provides a number of advantages which accrue when the forward-backward pointer system is also incorporated.

POINTERS

In Fig. 15.3.1 each *save* area has a forward pointer to the *save* area of the called subroutine and a backward pointer to the program which called the program containing that *save* area. In the figure the main program is in the center. It has a backward pointer to the *save* area in OS360. When the program got control from the operating system, operating system REGISTERS were *saved* by the program in the OS *save* area, OSSAVE.

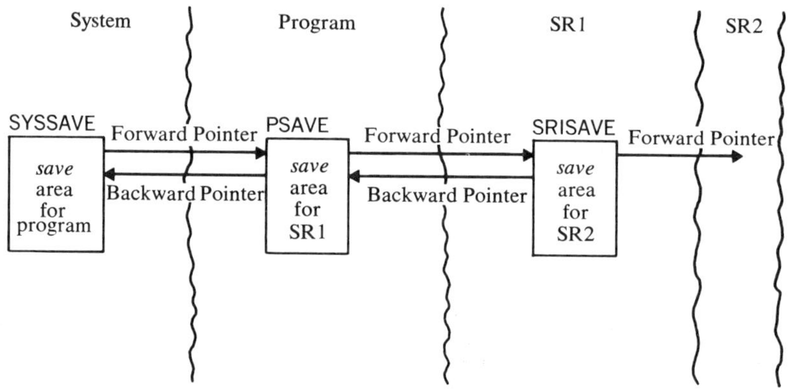

Fig. 15.3.1 *Save* areas for the *called* reside in the caller.

The program, P, calls a first level subroutine SR1. When that subroutine gains control, it *saves* the contents of REGISTERS it will use in the *save* area, PSAVE, in the program which called it. It is the obligation of SR1 to find this area and store the REGISTERS there. When SR1 is done, it must restore these REGISTERS so that, on return to program, P, P finds its REGISTERS intact.

Notice that SR1 calls in another subroutine, SR2. It is the obligation of SR2 to *save* the REGISTERS it uses in the *save* area of SR1, called SR1SAVE. Notice that SR2 contains a *save* area which is not used unless SR2 itself calls another program; it doesn't here so this area doesn't get used. It might, in fact, be eliminated in some cases.

ADVANTAGES

The pointer system yields a debugging advantage: examination of a *save* area can tell the programmer the last subroutine called by a program or subroutine, and also the contents of the REGISTERS *saved* when that subroutine was entered. Further, should trouble arise in the subroutine, the contents of the REGISTERS are safe, since the subroutine will probably harm itself rather than the main program.

The save area As we learned in the last section, the calling program passes the address of the *save* area to the called program in GPR13. Otherwise, how would the called program know where the *save* area is?

The area itself has the format shown in Fig. 15.3.2. The first Word is used by the PL1 compiler and does not concern us. The next two Words are the backward and forward *save* pointers. The fifteen Words which follow are for the contents of GPRS. These are used by the called program only if it so desires.

SAVEA	For PL/1 compiler
SAVEA+4	Backward *save* pointer
+8	Forward *save* pointer
+12	(GPR14)—return address
+16	(GPR15)—entry address
+20	(GPR0)
+24	(GPR1)
...	...
+64	(GPR11)
+68	(GPR12)

Fig. 15.3.2 OS360 *save* area format.

Notice that there seems to be no space in the *save* area for GPR13. Odd? But consider that GPR13 points to the *save* area of the calling program! Hence, it is a backward pointer for the called program. Its contents belong in the backward pointer location of the *save* area for the *called program*. Hence, only the other fifteen GPRS are required to be saved should they all be used. The called program *saves* whatever REGISTERS it will use and also places the backward pointer in *its own save* area, as we soon see.

Saving Before the caller exits, he tells the called program where his *save* area is with a command such as

```
LA     13,PSAVE
```
(15.3.1)

When the called program receives control, it does the saving immediately so that there is no risk of harming the contents of GPRS. Suppose that it expects to use the whole complement of REGISTERS. It *saves* everything with

```
STM    14,12,12(13)
```
(15.3.2)

Notice that this is a *store multiple* requesting the storage of REGISTERS 14 through 12. GPRS are stored in a wraparound fashion: REGISTERS are stored in the sequence, 14, 15, 0, 1, 2, etc. The address at which storing is to be done is 12(13), which says that the area is at a displacement of twelve bytes from the contents of GPR13. Examining Fig. 15.3.2, we note that GPR14 is the fourth Word in the *save* area and its starting byte is numbered 12.

Suppose we only wish to store the REGISTERS 14 through 4. We give

```
STM     14,4,12(13)                    (15.3.3)
```

POINTERS

Now the called program should establish the forward pointer to its own *save* area, SAVE1, in the caller's *save* area at his third Word. It does so thus:

```
MVC     8(4,13)=A(SAVE1)               (15.3.4)
```

This requests that the address of SAVE1 be entered in the caller's *save* area. 8(4,13) addresses the eighth byte, and MVC enters four bytes there referencing relative to GPR13. An alternative to this is

```
LA      6,SAVE1
ST      6,8(13)                        (15.3.5)
```

Now to establish the backward pointer! To store the contents of GPR13 in the backward *save* pointer of SAVE1, give

```
ST      13,SAVE1+4                     (15.3.6)
```

Unsaving Suppose the called program is finished. It is time to restore (***unsave***) the REGISTERS which were *saved.* If GPR13 has been altered at all, it is *unsaved* first. It has been stored in our own *save* area, SAVE1; we *unsave* with

```
L       13,SAVE1+4                     (15.3.7)
```

To restore all the remaining GPRS, we give

```
LM      14,12,12(13)                   (15.3.8)
```

Suppose we only wish to restore a few of the REGISTERS, the ones we stored by (15.3.3). We do

```
LM      14,4,12(13)                    (15.3.9)
```

With all required REGISTERS *unsaved,* return to the main program with

```
BR      14                             (15.3.10)
```

Example Figure 15.3.3 is an example which illustrates the *save* areas discussed in this section and parameter transmission discussed in Section 15.2.

```
1   WADD   STM   14,4,12(13)        Save REGISTERS
2          MVC   8(4,13),A(SAVEW)   Enter forward pointer
3          ST    13,SAVEW+4         Enter backward pointer
4          SR    2,2                Clear GPR2 parameter
                                      pointer
5          SR    4,4                Clear GPR4 sum REGISTER
6          L     3,0(1,2)           Get address of X, [X]
7          LTR   3,3                Test [X], end of para-list?
8          BM    *+16               Yes
9          A     4,0(0,3)           Add next number
10         LA    2,4(0,2)           Alter para-list pointer
11         B     *-18               Continue to next parameter
                                      address
12         ST    4,0(3)             Put away answer
13         LM    14,4,12(13)        Unsave
14         BR    14                 Return
```

Fig. 15.3.3 The closed subroutine WADD. To add a variable number of items, use *save* and *unsave* with a call such as that found in Fig. 15.2.2.

We enter the subroutine WAAD to add a set of numbers at the location called WADD. It stores GPR14 through GPR4 in the caller's *save* area (1). Then the backward pointer in our *save* area is set (2) and the forward pointer in the caller's *save* area is set (3).

We now initialize the routine by clearing GPR2, which is used for addressing the parameter list, and GPR4, which is used for arithmetic (4, 5). Next we begin the routine proper. Get the address of the first parameter (6). Check it to see if it is the last parameter address using the command LTR, *load and test register*, to test the leftmost bit, the sign bit. If this is one, the command views it as a negative number. We know that such an address is tagged to show that it is the last in the series. Hence, following LTR, BM, *branch on minus* (8), causes a jump around the *add* sequence when we have the last parameter address.

We add the next number into GPR4, using the address in GPR3 (9).

The next task will be to add in the following number. But first we must adjust the pointer in GPR2 by adding four to it with the LA command (10), which loads GPR2 with the address formed by the present contents of GPR2 with four added to it. We know that there are more numbers to be added since we have taken this path. Hence, we return to get the next address with the *unconditional branch*, B (11).

Suppose we have acquired the last parameter address. This means that the sum now in GPR4 is to be stored at that address. Since the destination address is in GPR3, we do the *store*, (12).

All that is left is to *unsave* the GPRS which were saved previously (13) and then to return to the calling program (14).

15.4 EXCEPTION EXITS

Need The closed subroutine has a job to do, and usually it can be completed without difficulty. Sometimes the SR is asked to do something wherein it encounters difficulty. For instance, we ask an SR to take the square root of a negative number—this is impossible. Another example is when a group of numbers are supplied to an SR to be added; when one of the numbers is added to the total in the ACCUMULATING REGISTER, it causes an overflow.

It is nice for the SR to be able to tell the main program that it has run into trouble. One way is to provide exits in the calling sequence. When the SR encounters trouble, it exits to the calling sequence where there is a *branch* to the proper exception routine. This is effective, but uses space in the calling sequence. The alternative which is provided is to have the SR place an error code in a GPR. By convention the error code is placed in GPR15; the SR then returns normally to the main program.

In the main program there is a test which determines one of several troubles which may have arisen and then goes to a fix-up routine to take care of the difficulty.

Use The use of the exception exit is demonstrated in Fig. 15.4.1. The main program proceeds to EXIT where the SR, CSR,

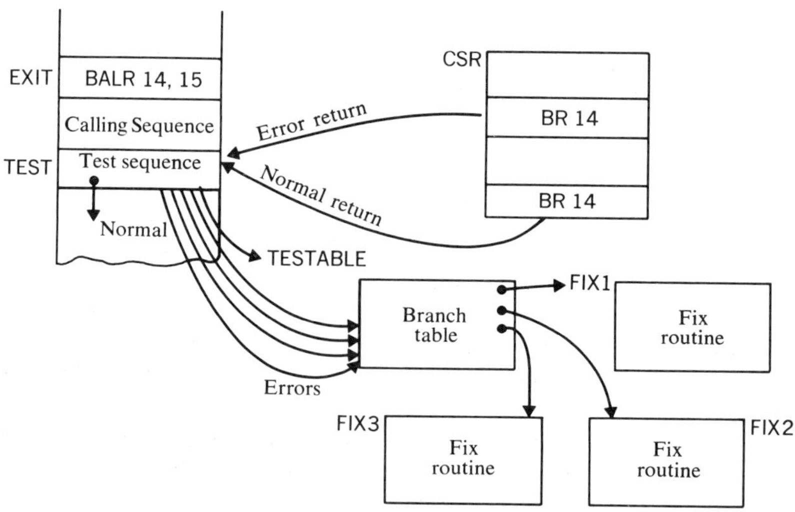

Fig. 15.4.1 The exception exit from CSR permits TEST to involve a fix routine.

is entered by a BALR. CSR uses parameters provided in the call sequence. When CSR is done, it always returns to TEST in the program by using a *branch register*, BR. If CSR has completed its activity satisfactorily, it clears GPR15 (with SR 15,15, say) before returning. If CSR encounters a difficulty, it places a code telling what has been encountered in GPR15.

At TEST the contents of GPR15 are checked. If they are zero, continue the program. If they are nonzero, go off to one of several fix-up subroutines. But which fix-up subroutine should be entered? The SR entry points are in a table and the desired one is chosen according to the code in GPR15.

Test Let's see how we might implement the test operation. We examine the contents of GPR15 with *load and test register* thus:

```
LTR     15,15                    (15.4.1)
```

The result of testing GPR15 is stored in the CONDITION CODE REGISTER, CCR. We test the CCR which tells us now if GPR15 contains zero; if not, we *branch*. The *branch* is to a test table, TESTABLE; it contains *branch* commands spaced one Word apart. The code placed in GPR15 is a multiple of four and hence takes us to one of the Words in TESTABLE. Use *branch nonzero* thus:

```
BNZ     TESTABLE(15)             (15.4.2)
```

We never use TESTABLE per se because that would imply that GPR15 contains zero and that would mean that we never took the *branch*; therefore the test table looks something like this:

```
TESTABLE+4   B     FIX1
TESTABLE+8   B     FIX2
             B     FIX3          (15.4.3)
```

15.5 MACROS

Three macros provided by IBM relieve the programmer of some coding responsibility and implement the conventions discussed. These system macros (not defined by the programmer) reside in the system where they can be called and code for them placed in the program automatically.

CALL The macro CALL creates an exit and a call sequence for a closed subroutine either in the user's main program, in another section of his program, or in a section brought in by the linkage editor or dynamically. It has the format

```
name     CALL     entry,list,tag,id                    (15.5.1)
```

Here, *entry* is the symbolic name of the called subroutine; *entry* may also be (15) when the address of the subroutine at the time of CALL is in GPR15. *List* can be a set of addresses or a single address for the address(es) of the parameter(s), or *list* can be empty. A set of addresses is enclosed in parentheses and separated by commas. Thus, to call WADD and supply addresses for X1, X2, X3, and SUM, we give

```
         CALL     WADD,(X1,X2,X3,SUM)                  (15.5.2)
```

VL at *tag* indicates to CALL that a variable length parameter list is supplied and the last item of the list should be tagged. *Id* is an identifier, a number something less than 64,000,000, which identifies this CALL.

The use of CALL is explained with reference to the subroutine, WADD, which adds a variable number of Words. We supply a number of addresses; it adds up numbers from all but the last address. The last address is tagged by CALL and the sum of the numbers placed at this address by WADD.

```
EXIT     CALL     WADD,(X1,X2,X3,SUM),VL,ID=36         (15.5.3)
```

$\mathcal{ASLR}$ eventually gets the definition of CALL from system library and then CALL at EXIT is expanded as shown in Fig. 15.5.1. Let's make a few observations.

Notice how CNOP is used twice to set up proper boundaries, (2+, 5+). Notice also how the system index was used to provide entry points

```
 1  EXIT            CALL     WADD,(X1,X2,X3,SUM),VL,ID=36
 2+                 CNOP     0,4
 3+EXIT             B        *+8
 4+IHB0036B         DC       V(WADD)
 5+                 CNOP     0,4
 6+                 BAL      0,IHB0037A
 7+                 DC       A(X1)
 8+                 DC       A(X2)
 9+                 DC       A(X3)
10+                 DC       B'10000000'
11+                 DC       AL3(SUM)
12+IHB0037A         L        15,IHB0036B
13+                 BALR     14,15
14+                 DC       X'4700'
15+                 DC       AL2(36)
```

Fig. 15.5.1 An expansion of a CALL.

(4+, 12+) for looping within the open subroutine. At *name* of (4+) is IHB&SYSNDX.B and at (12+) is IHB&SYSNDX.A in the macrodefinition which is found in Appendix C (and should be compared with the CALL in Fig. 15.5.1). Notice the *branch* (3+) around the call sequence and then the call sequence itself (4+ through 11+). The last parameter address is tagged (10+). The address of the closed subroutine, WADD, is created with a DC which declares a V-type address constant (VCON). This is necessary because the CSR may be in a foreign section or a section brought in by the linkage editor and CALL can't know; if WADD is local, no harm is done by using a VCON.

The last two steps of the expansion produce, respectively, a NOP(14+) followed by an identifier corresponding to the ID provided in CALL.

SAVE The macro SAVE does the job of placing a set of GPRS into the *save* area transmitted to SAVE by the address in GPR13. It has the format

name SAVE regs,tag,id (15.5.4)

Here *regs* is a single REGISTER or a pair of REGISTERS (which are *saved* in multiple wraparound, as seen earlier). *Tag*, if it is T, indicates that REGISTERS 14 and 15 are to be saved in Words 4 and 5 of the *save* area, if they do not fall within the range of *regs*; if omitted, this operation is omitted. *Id* is an identification which this time is symbolic; if it is absent, no action is taken. When *id* is a symbol, the number of characters in the symbol is stored at a location indicated by the contents of GPR15 displaced by 4, (GPR15) + 4. The symbol itself is then placed starting at the next byte—it goes to (GPR15) + 5 and the three bytes thereafter. If *id* is an asterisk (*), the name associated with SAVE is stored as described above: length at (GPR15) + 4; *name* at (GPR15) + 5.

```
1     CSR     SAVE     (3,6),T
2+    CSR     DS       OH
3+            STM      14,15,12(13)
4+            STM      3,6,32(13)
5             USING    CSR,15
```

Fig. 15.5.2 An expansion of a SAVE.

An example of an expansion is in Fig. 15.5.2. The commands which follow are set up on a halfWord boundary (2+). Since T is at *tag*, it calls for storing GPR14 and GPR15 (3+). Then *store multiple* saves GPR3 through GPR6. Since *id* is empty, no code identifies SAVE.

RETURN The macro RETURN, which provides steps for an SR to return control to the main program or caller, has the format

name RETURN regs,tag,code (15.5.5)

It creates the command, *branch register*, using GPR14, which has been preserved by the SR. *Regs* is one or two numbers of GPRS which are to be *unsaved* from the *save* area of the caller in a wraparound manner. Again the SR must provide the address of the caller's *save* area in GPR13 where it was preserved. Otherwise the SR should get the backward pointer from its own *save* area and place it in GPR13 before RETURN. *Tag* may be *blank* or may contain a T. When *tag* is T, a pair of hexadecimal F's are put in the first byte, fourth Word of the caller's *save* area. This tells the caller that his *save* area has been used.

When *code* is RC=*number*, *number* is placed in GPR15. If a number was placed there already and it is desired to maintain GPR15, regardless of whether it is present in *regs*, this is indicated by writing RC=(15). If *code* is absent, GPR15 is treated normally.

EXAMPLES Figure 15.5.3 shows two expansions of RETURN. The first has no tag but indicates that a condition code is already stored in GPR15. Hence, two *loads* are created to *unsave*, respectively, GPR14 (2+) and GPR0 through GPR4 (3+). Finally BR is created (4+).

```
1      RETURN   (14,4),RC=(15)
2+     L        14,12(13)
3+     LM       0,4,20(13)
4+     BR       14
5      RETURN   (14,4),T,RC=12
6+     LM       14,4,12(13)
7+     MVI      12(13),X'FF'
8+     LA       15,12
9+     BR       14
```

Fig. 15.5.3 An expansion of RETURN.

In the second example (5), the wraparound REGISTERS specified are *unsaved* first. Then, since *tag* is T, FF is inserted into the *save* area (7+). Next the 12 is placed in GPR15 with LA(8+). Finally, BR command is provided (9+).

15.6 DYNAMIC LINKAGE

Dynamic linkage describes that desired routines or subprograms not present at load time are brought in while the program is running by recourse to OS360. The supervisor call, SVC, is used to get to OS360. Generally, the programmer does not employ SVC directly but, rather, uses a macro which, upon expansion, results in the incorporation of an SVC in the program.

We now examine ways using several macros to provide dynamic linkage.

LOAD The purpose of LOAD is to bring in the subroutine, but not to transfer control to it. When LOAD is given in Fig. 15.6.1, control goes to OS360, which brings in the routine, Load, from the

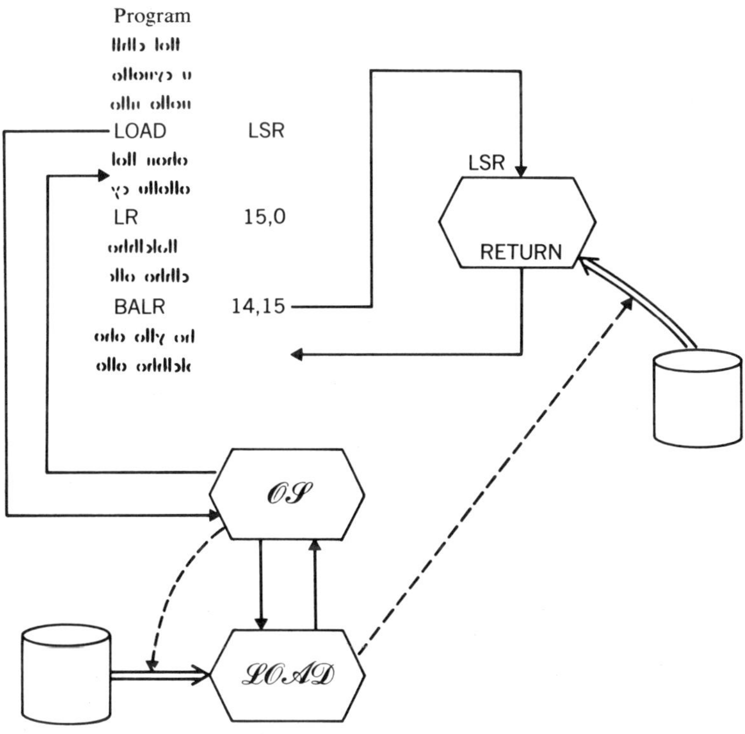

Fig. 15.6.1 LOAD.

system residence volume, placing it in the SVC transient area provided for service routines in MEMORY. Load takes over and provides a number of functions, the final aim of which is to bring in the desired routine. The volume on which the called routine resides is known; its position on the volume is found usually by resorting to the Bldl; space is obtained for the routine in MEMORY by Freemain and the routine is transferred from the volume to the allocated space in MEMORY by Fload, all service routines used by Load and called by SVCs.

MACRO

The macro to do the loading shown in Fig. 15.6.1 has this format:

name LOAD position,dcb (15.6.1)

Here *position* can be one of several things. If it takes the form, EP=*symbol*, then *symbol* is an entry point of the routine name. It must be looked up in the catalog to determine where the desired routine is found. *Position* may have the form EPLOC=*address*, where *address* is the place where the entry point name has been stored in MEMORY. The third alternative is DE=*entry*, where *entry* is a pointer which has been previously obtained by using the macro, BLDL (see p. 308).

Dcb contains the address of the DCB used for addressing the library which contains the desired routine. It may be *blank* or 0 when the linkage library is addressed.

If the desired routine has already been obtained and is presently at MEMORY, Load recognizes this and does not get another copy.

Responsibility count

Space in MEMORY is valuable; one task of OS360 is to monitor MEMORY contents. A called routine is maintained in the user's MEMORY until one of two events occur:

- The task using it is completed.
- OS360 is informed that the routine is not required by the occurrence of the DELETE macro.

A **program request block, PRB,** is established for each dynamically loaded routine. There is a responsibility count contained in this block indicating the number of outstanding requests for it. Each new request increases the count by one. Each task completion decreases the count by one. The latter is requested by DELETE, or when the loaded routine uses XCTL, as explained later. As long as this count is positive, the routine remains in MEMORY; as soon as it becoms zero, the area occupied by the routine becomes available and the routine is no longer accessible.

DELETE

The macro, DELETE, has the format

name DELETE position (15.6.2)

Its sole purpose is to decrease the responsibility count by one. *Position* is satisfied as above with respect to (15.6.1).

Loaded routines A loaded routine can be used in one of two ways:

- linkage by BALR,
- through OS360 with LINK.

The first method is illustrated in Fig. 15.6.1. After issuing LOAD for the routine LSR, the location of LSR is returned in GPR0. The linkage convention requires that the entry point appear in GPR15. Hence, in the figure we notice the command

LR 15,0 (15.6.3)

After setting up the call sequence, control is transferred to the routine using BALR, as shown in the figure.

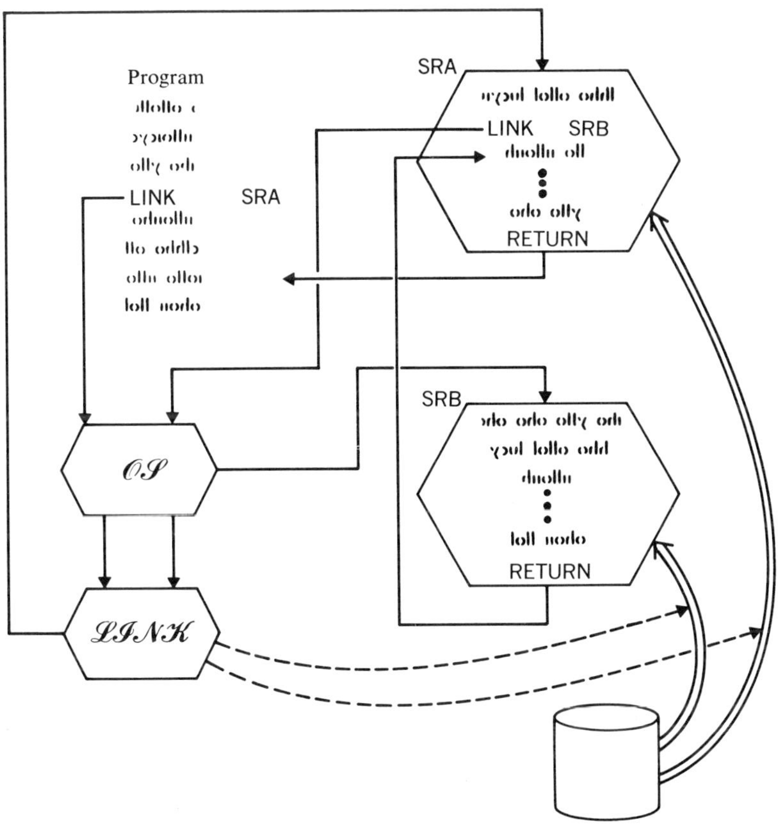

Fig. 15.6.2 LINK.

LINK The macro LINK requests that the OS360 intervene, obtain a routine, and then turn over control to it. This is illustrated in Fig. 15.6.2. Here the program using LINK has requested the subroutine, SRA. The macro, LINK, is expanded to include an SVC. This gives control to OS360, which, in turn, calls in 𝔏𝔦𝔫𝔨. This service routine gets space for SRA, finds the location of SRA, and then enters SRA into MEMORY. Thereafter it gives control to SRA.

The figure illustrates that it is possible to nest LINKs. Thus, SRA includes a dynamic request for SRB using LINK. Here 𝔏𝔦𝔫𝔨 gets SRB, and control is given to it. Notice that SRB contains RETURN as its final command. This returns control to the caller, in this case, SRA. Although not indicated in the diagram, return is made via OS360 so that OS360 can keep its accounting straight.

PRESENT ROUTINE

It is permissible, and, in fact, preferable for the user to anticipate his needs. Thus, he can request the procurement of a routine using LOAD and later request its execution using LINK. When 𝔏𝔦𝔫𝔨 is brought in by OS360, it verifies that a copy of the desired routine is available since a PRB is on file for it. Then it can immediately turn over control to the requested routine.

FORMAT

The format of LINK is

name LINK position, dcb, PARAM=(addresses),tag,id (15.6.4)

The *position* and *dcb* were described above. The next field supplies parameter addresses for the called routine. *Tag* is used when a variable number of parameter addresses may be furnished to the routine; in that case, *tag* contains VL=1. ID=*num* causes the macro expansion to contain a final instruction, NOP, for which *loc* contains *num*, thus providing identification of LINK.

Using BLDL This macro provides a reference for system routines to help them obtain desired programs or routines from the library. Its format is

name BLDL dcb,list (15.6.5)

Here *dcb* is the name of the DCB; *list* is the symbolic name of MEMORY locations where the name and location in AUXILIARY MEMORY of the desired routine are kept. A breakdown of the MEMORY locations referenced by *list* is found in Table 15.6.1.

Notice that BLDL can look up several routines at one time by providing a list of entries.

Table 15.6.1 THE BLDL LIST

Byte	*Field length*	*Use*
0	2	Number of entries in list
2	2	Length of each entry ($58_{\#}$ or $3A_H$ is standard)
		Entry
0	8	Name of desired routine
8	2	Relative track number
10	1	Block number on track
11	1	Concatenation number
12	1	Kind of library in which found
13	1	Notes
14		Subentries

BLDL may be used by the program or by the service routine:

- The program finds the location of the routine SRX with BLDL which, for example, places the location at ENTX; LINK now contains DE=SRX.
- Link finds SRX itself by using BLDL where the name, SRX, is supplied in LINK with EP=SRX.

Example Figure 15.6.3 shows how BLDL is used by the program with LINK.

```
1  BUILD    BLDL   0,ENTRY
2           B      *+64
3  ENTRY    DC     X'0001'        One entry
4           DC     X'003A'        58 bytes in the entry
5  SRNAME   DC     CL8'WADD'      (SRNAME)=WADD
6           DS     50X
7           LINK   DE=SRNAME,DCB=0,PARAM=(X1,X2,X3,SUM),VL=1
```

Fig. 15.6.3 Using BLDL with LINK.

At (1) the macro BLDL is issued indicating that the residence volume contains the library and that a list is supplied at ENTRY. At (2) the program branches around the BLDL entry. ENTRY begins with two bytes, indicating that there is only one entry in the list. Following this, at (4) the hexadecimal constant 3A shows that fifty-eight bytes of MEMORY follow. At SRNAME the name of the routine, WADD, is supplied. Fifty bytes of space are then reserved for the entry made by Bldl. Following this appears LINK which references the BLDL entry by using DE=SRNAME. Link now has the SR name, WADD at SRNAME and its location found by Bldl is at SRNAME+8. The system volume must contain the library with

WADD for this to work. Four parameters are transmitted to WADD, which expects a variable number of addresses. Hence, *tag* is set by VL=1.

XCTL This macro brings in a routine and transfers control to it; when the routine is done, control is returned, not to the caller, but to *his* caller. This is best illustrated by referring to Fig. 15.6.4. Here we link to SRC in the main program with LINK. When OS360 brings

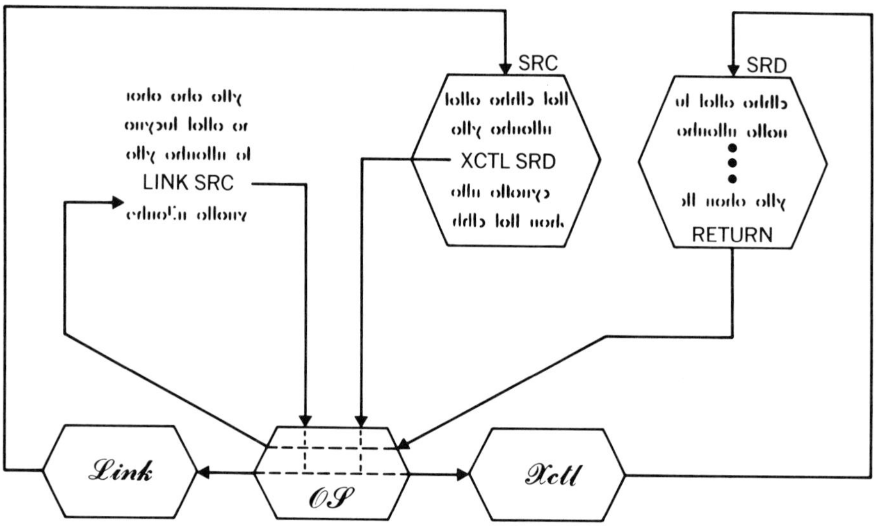

Fig. 15.6.4 XCTL.

in LINK, it, in turn, brings in SRC. During the execution of SRC, we encounter XCTL with a request for SRD. This produces an SVC which requests OS360 to bring in Xctl. This is the service return which will bring in the requested routine.

After Xctl has brought in SRD in the figure, it turns over control to that routine. Notice that at the end of SRD we find RETURN. Normally we would expect that this causes a return to SRC. However, it is mediated by OS360 for Xctl. Control is not returned to the caller, but to the caller's caller. Hence, at RETURN at the end of SRD when OS360 gets control, it passes control to the step after LINK in the main program.

FORMAT

XCTL has this format:

name XCTL regs,position,dcb (15.6.6)

Here *position* and *dcb* serve the same purpose as described for the other macros. *Regs* describes the REGISTERS to be restored from the original caller's *save* area before control is turned over to the called routine. This is a set of REGISTERS specified as for SAVE. This facility permits the original caller to pass REGISTER contents to the routine called with the XCTL, which can *resave* them if required. Thus, for Fig. 15.6.4, REGISTERS specified at *regs* for XCTL are brought from the *save* area pointed to GPR13 with the original information passed from the main program for SRL. This is necessary because RETURN in SRD will function properly only if the integrity of *save* areas is preserved.

ABUSE

XCTL eliminates its caller! This is done by reducing the responsibility count in the caller's PRB by 1; should this count reach 0, Xctl frees this space so that the calling routine is no longer available. The procedure shown in Fig. 15.6.4 assures a proper transition among the routines. This could get messed up if SRC were brought in by the main program and then control transmitted with BALR. Now when XCTL appears in SRC, control goes to SRD, but the caller is eliminated. As far as OS360 is concerned, since SRC was reached through BALR, the caller of SRD is the *program* and not SRC. Hence, there is a good chance that the main program may bomb out and SRD may have no place to return to.

ATTACH

ATTACH differs from the other macros because it turns over parallel control to a called routine. This is possible only in the multiprogramming environment. This provides a far more efficient set of running programs. Now the main program can ATTACH a routine. Either the main program or the called routine can be running. Should the main program get stuck, the routine can take over, and vice versa. The user assigns a priority to the attached task which may be equal to, higher, or lower than the original program. Then when both are available, the task of higher priority will be chosen first.

The format for ATTACH is

```
name    ATTACH    position,dcb,event,exit,para,tag,priority    (15.6.7)
```

where *exit* is an exit routine to be entered upon completion of the routine, and the other parameters are self-explanatory.

PROBLEMS

15.1 Describe when one would choose to use closed SRs as opposed to open SRs (macros). Give the advantages and disadvantages of each.

15.2 Why are linkage conventions needed? Why are as many as five GPRS involved with such conventions?

15.3 Imagine RMS of Prob. 11.4 as a closed SR called CRMS, providing for a calling sequence with a list at DATA of length *n* supplied at LENGTH

15.4 Write CRMS to be called as above. Use RETURN to provide a return code of:
(a) 0 for correct completion;
(b) 4 for square which is not a single word;
(c) 8 for a square which causes an overflow for single word accumulation.
Use the program save area of the caller.

15.5 Write CDRMS for the double precision routine of Prob. 11.6. Supply return code of 8 for double precision accumulation overflow.

15.6 Write CCDRMS for Prob. 15.5 as above, but to call CDSQRT, a closed subroutine for the square root. Provide a save area, RMSAVE, in CCDRMS for CDSQRT, and supply the required pointers.

15.7 Write CDSQRT for Prob. 15.6 using the results of Prob. 11.5.

15.8 (a) Rewrite the RMS and SQRT which you used before, either single or double precision as RMSM and SQRTM. These differ only in that the main code is written in a different CSECT, namely MCSECT. Have RMSM use the system area to save.
(b) Test out your macros on live data as you did before.

15.9 (a) What are the advantages of dynamic linking?
(b) When would you use it?
(c) Call dynamically CDRMS, providing parameters, etc.

15.10 As for Prob. 15.9(c), except use BLDL first.

16

BIG PICTURE

16.1 McDef

The purpose of McDef is multiple:

1. Examine all macrodefinitions which *must* appear before the first CSECT.
2. Perform control functions when necessary.
3. Determine, find and bring in all external macrodefinitions.
4. Determine the attributes of all symbolic references so that conditional assembly can be done later.

Separation of functions Figure 16.1.1 shows McDef separated into several basic functions. The initial scan is called ScanD. The first task done is to examine each statement and look up the opcode in *OPTAB* (1). What is done next depends upon the opcode found in *OPTAB* (2). There may be control statements which bring in the routine called Control, the purpose of which is to incorporate requests made by pseudos into the scan itself (3). Thereafter we return to the scan, ScanD.

When *opcode* is MACRO, a macrodefinition follows and McName is initiated (4). Only after all programmer defined macros are reviewed does the scan of the main program, McDefX, begin. It is so called because it weeds out all external macrocalls (5).

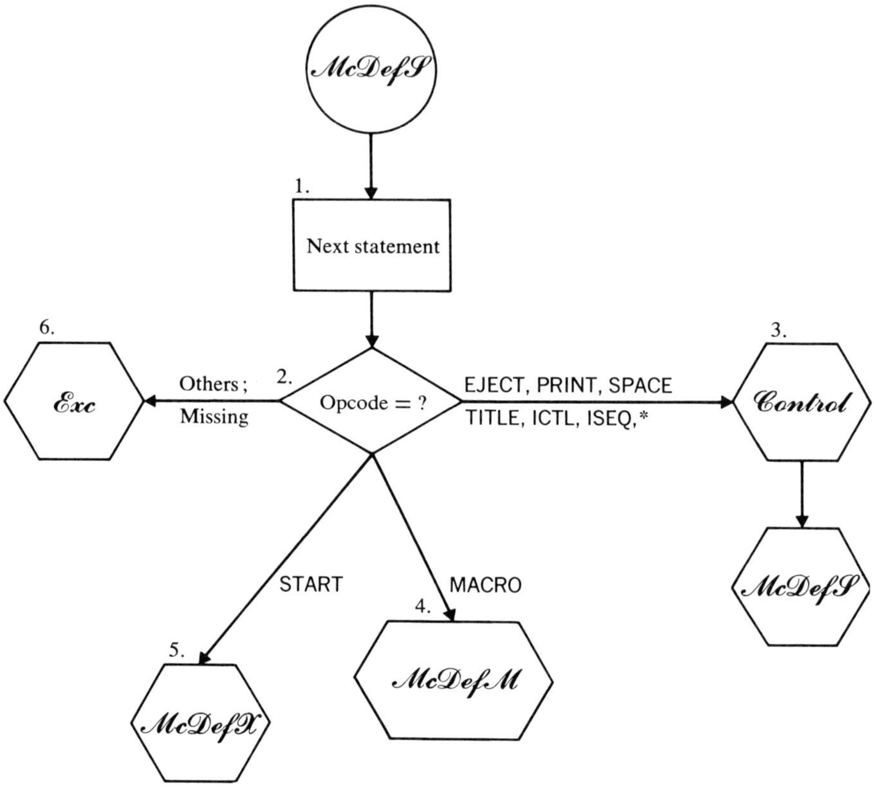

Fig. 16.1.1 Flow chart of McDefS.

It is possible that an opcode is missing from *OPTAB* or is one of the others not mentioned. In this case, the routine Exc is entered (6).

McCom McCom, a routine to incorporate macro-definitions into *COMTAB*, is illustrated in Fig. 16.1.2. Assume that MACRO has been encountered; then a prototype statement is expected next. As such, *opcode* is the name of the macro defined and *opcode* should be inserted in *OPTAB* (1). Next the argument table, *ARGTAB*, is set up by McArg to incorporate the argument at *name*, if any, and the arguments at *location*, if any.

Now begins a scan of the model statements which comprise the macro-definition (3) as shown in Fig. 16.1.2. This scan is generally done several times by ScanM. The first task is to check the opcode from the model

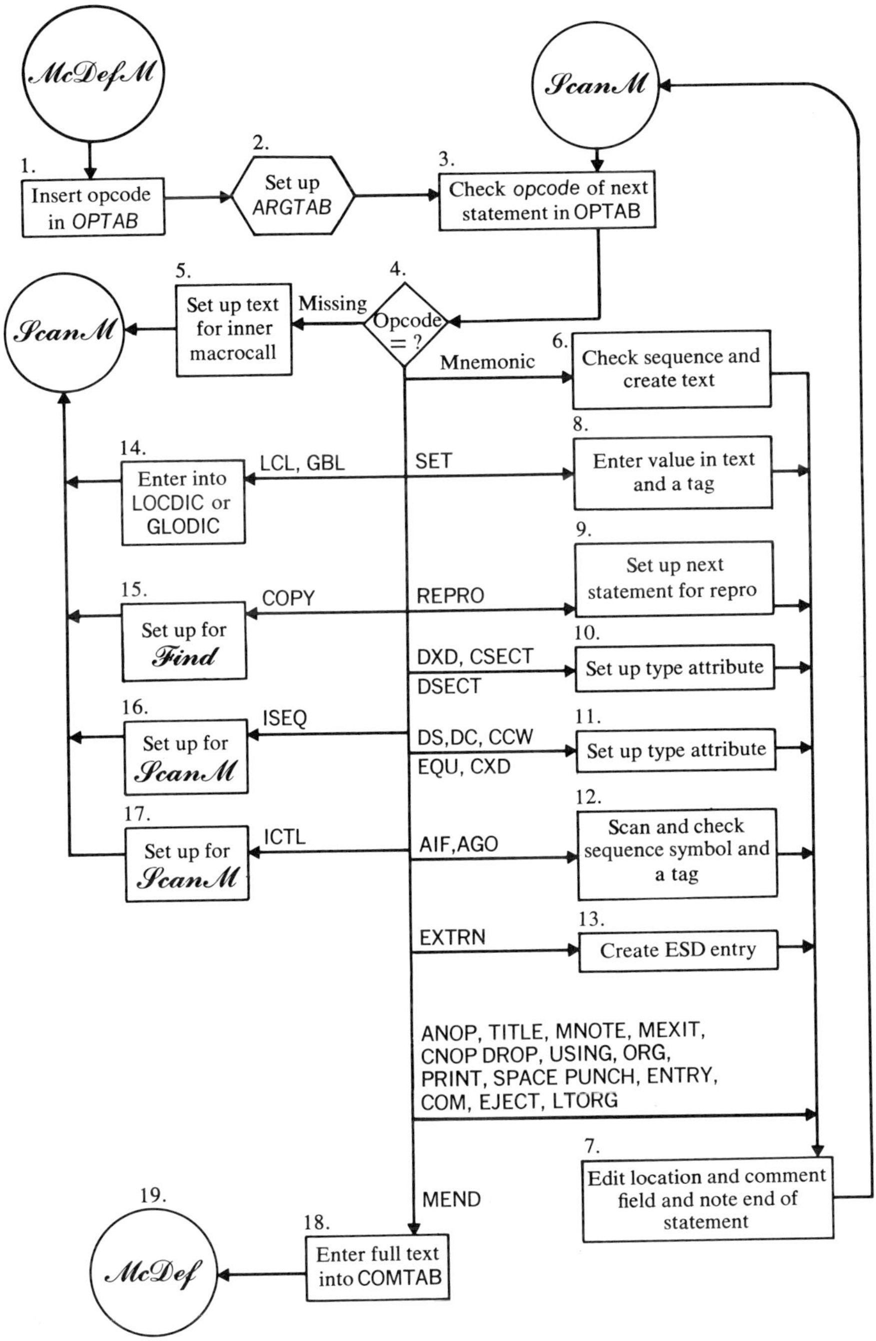

Fig. 16.1.2 Flow chart for McDefM.

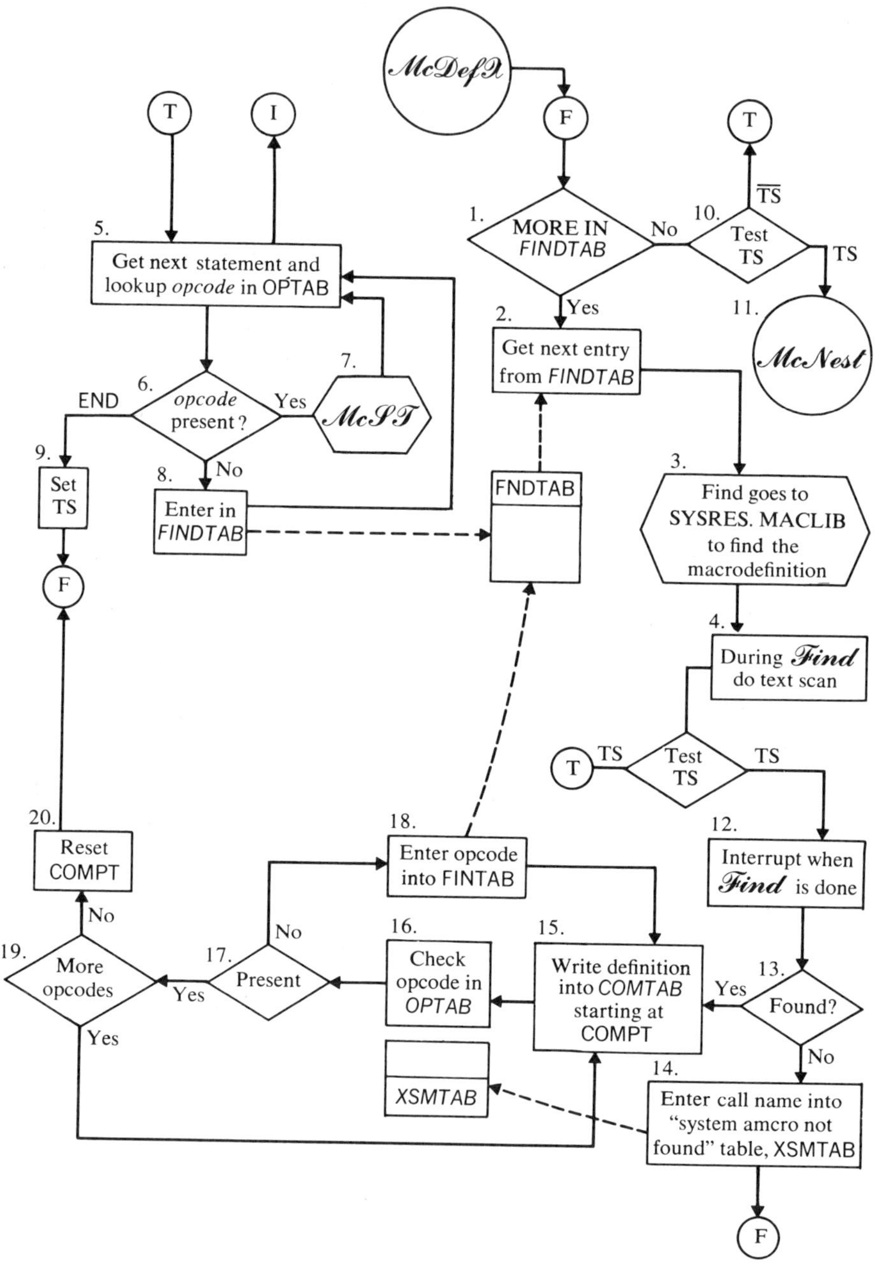

Fig. 16.1.3 Flow chart for McDefX.

statement to determine what kind of model command we have. This is now analyzed (4).

If *opcode* is missing from *OPTAB*, McCom assumes that this is a macrocall and sets up for an inner macro (5). This assumption may be contradicted at a later point.

Most often *opcode* will be a mnemonic. If there is a sequence number associated with it, this is entered into a sequence number table, *SEQTAB*, and text created. Then *location* and *comment* are edited and entered into text for this command (7). This process, by the way, occurs for many of the kinds of commands as you note in the figure.

For SET, the value or expression at *loc* is entered into the text and the text is tagged (8) and edited (7). For REPRO, McCom sets up to reproduce the next statement (9).

The DXD, DSECT, and CSECT do not require processing other than setting up the type attribute in the symbol table (10). Pseudos associated with data and storage definition, such as DC, DS, etc., have their attributes placed in the symbol table (11).

For AIF and AGO, the statement is scanned and checked to see that a sequence symbol is present (12). EXTRN requests a dictionary entry (13).

There are a whole group of pseudos which do not require any processing, merely editing (7).

LCL and GBL declarations cause entry of information into the local or global dictionary, *LOCDIC* or *GLODIC* (4). Notice that no editing is required with this or the pseudos which follow. COPY sets up for the routine Find examined later. ISEQ sets up new information for the scan in progress (16). ICTL does a similar task (17).

When McCom encounters MEND, *this* macrodefinition is complete. The full text produced may require further editing but now comprises a complete entry in *COMTAB* (18). Return is now made to the initial scan, ScanD (19).

McDefX   This routine does three things at one time:

- determines the name of macros externally defined,
- determines the attributes of symbols occurring in the program,
- goes out to the system library and brings in the definitions of the macros, incorporating them into *COMTAB*.

Two of these things go on at once because IO operations are involved. Hence it behooves us to overlap the activities.

McDefX is presented in Fig. 16.1.3. As the routine begins, it looks at the table *FNDTAB* (1) which contains the names of externally defined macros turned up so far. If names are presently in the table, one of them is obtained (2). This is turned over to the routine Find (3). A search request is made to retrieve the definition of the named macro. As search is performed, the remaining program text is scanned (4).

Taking exit T, we now go to the next statement in the program text, get *opcode*, and look it up in *OPTAB* (5). Notice three alternatives for *opcode* (6). If the opcode is present in *OPTAB* and it is not END, then enter the routine 𝓜𝓬𝓢𝓣 which scans this text command as we shall see later (7).

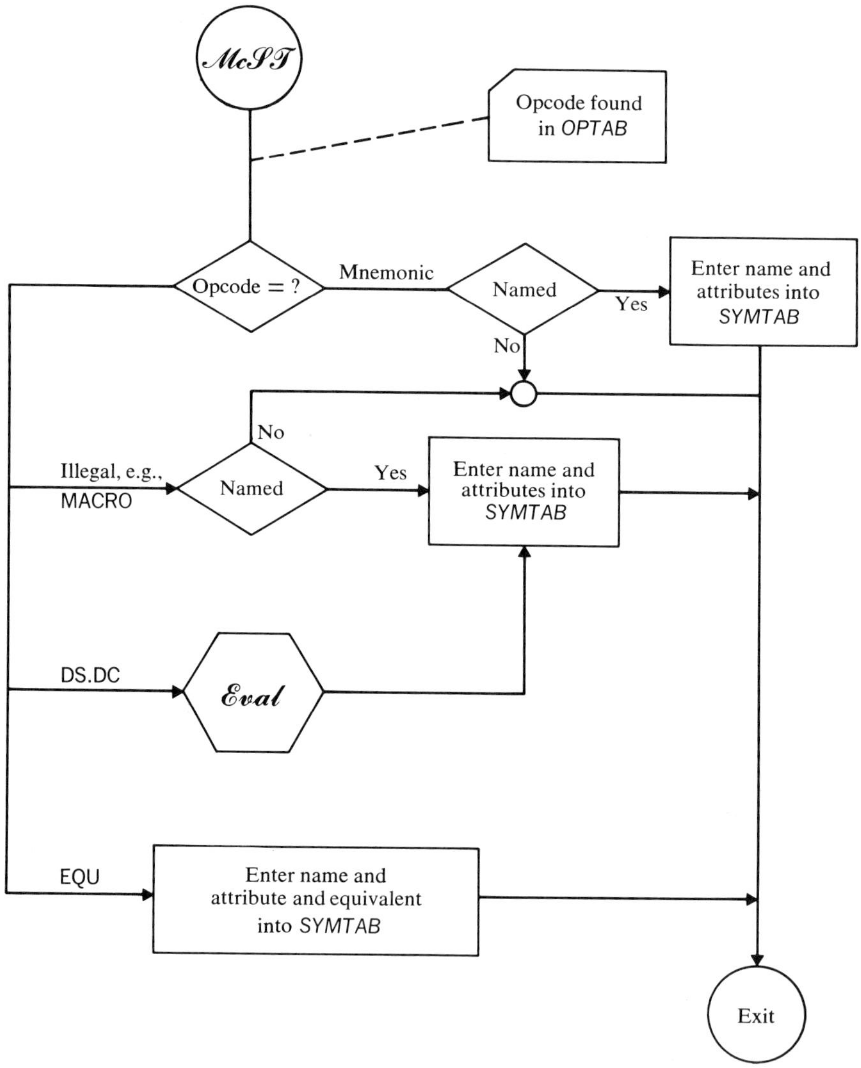

Fig. 16.1.4 Flow chart for 𝓜𝓬𝓢𝓣.

Should *opcode* be absent, it is entered in *FNDTAB* (8); then continue to examine statements.

For END, set a switch called TS (9) to indicate that the entire text has been scanned. Then test the switch, TS, the *Find* switch, to see if all the entries in the *FNDTAB* have been checked. If they have, then McDefX is complete and McNest (11), described in the next section, is entered.

Interrupt During the processing of any statement (5–15), an IO interrupt may occur, indicated by I in the figure. This causes statement processing to stop temporarily to post the macrodefinition (12).

During interrupt processing, the first question asked is, "Is the definition found (13)? If not, the name of the call is placed in the table for unfound system macros, *XSMTAB* (14). Lookup then continues with the next *FNDTAB* entry.

If the macrodefinition is found, it is copied into *COMTAB* and a pointer to the definition is placed in *OPTAB* (15). As each command is placed in *COMTAB*, it is checked in *OPTAB* (16). It is possible that *another* external macro is required (17). If so, its name is entered into *FNDTAB* (18). Further commands are copied (15). If the opcode is present (17) and there are more opcodes (19), these are copied (15).

When the macrodefinition is completely copied, the request is deleted from *FNDTAB* (20).

Now the next thing to be done is to get IO started on finding another macrodefinition if there is any (1).

McST For all commands found in the text, attribute checking is done by McST, flowcharted in Fig. 16.1.4. The kind of opcode has already been determined from *OPTAB*. If it is a mnemonic and it is named, this attribute is entered into *SYMTAB*. DS and DC are evaluated and the attributes placed in *SYMTAB*. For EQU, the name and equivalent and possibly an evaluation are entered into *SYMTAB*. Illegal opcodes must also be dealt with.

16.2 McNest

McNest This routine performs the nesting required as discussed in Section 8.3. It consists first of the major component ScanN which we discussed earlier and review now in relation to Fig. 16.2.1. This is not really a pass but rather an examination in sequence of the entire contents of *COMTAB*. The text of each macrodefinition is scanned in

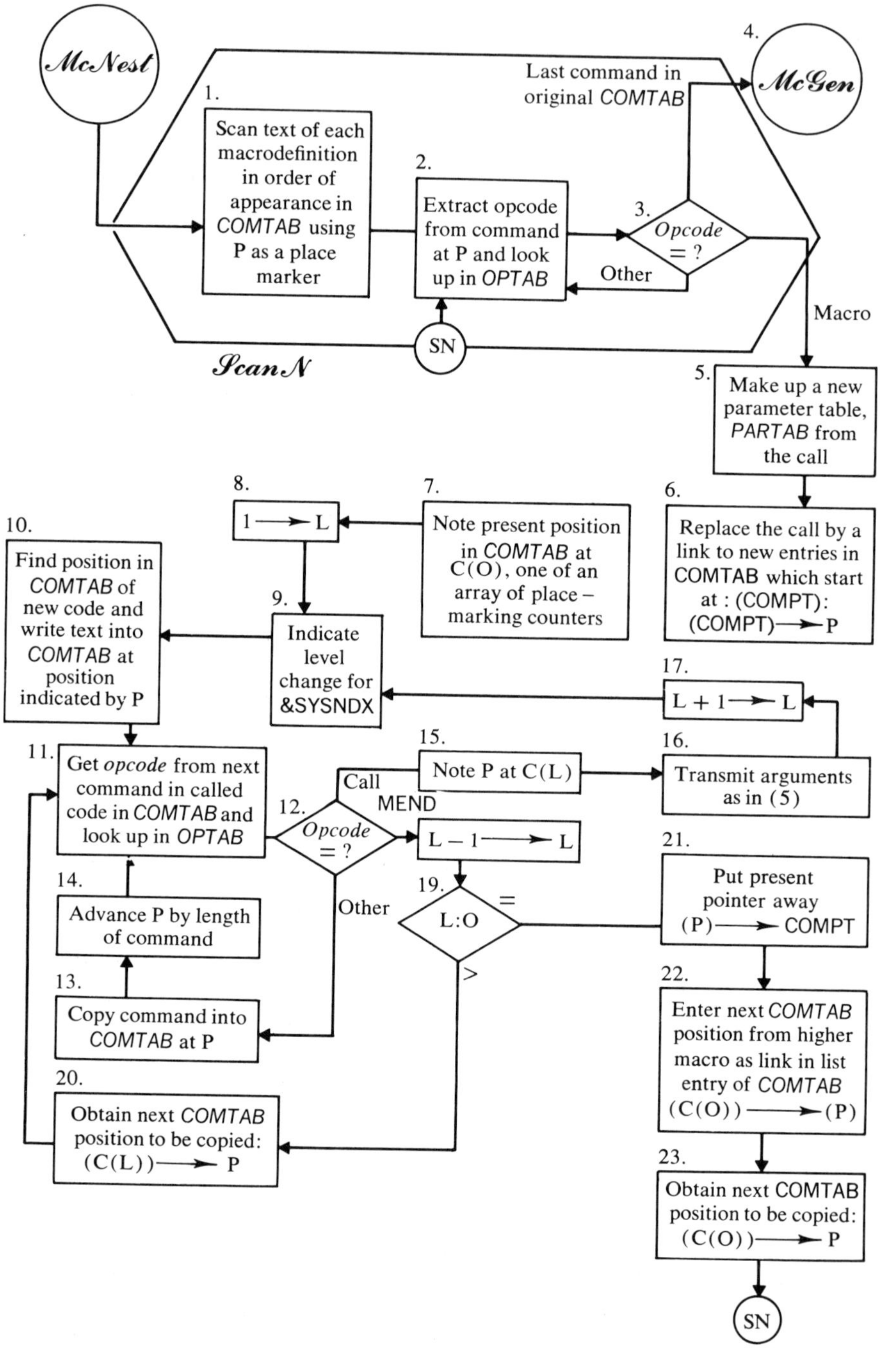

Fig. 16.2.1 Flow chart for *McNest*.

order of its appearance in *COMTAB* (1). It is assumed here that the location counter for ScanN is P and the MEMORY location at the first command in *COMTAB* is placed at P as the scan starts.

Each opcode is examined in turn by lookup in *OPTAB* (2). This pass does nesting and looks only for calls in *COMTAB* (3). Anything else simply causes examination of the next command in sequence. The one exception is END in *COMTAB* as originally constructed. Recall that additions are to be made to *COMTAB* so that after the original commands comprising *COMTAB* are reviewed (3), generation can begin (4).

Call When a call is encountered (5), a new parameter table, *PARTAB*, is built by extracting the parameters from the call so that they can be inserted in the inner macro expansion. The call itself is now replaced by a link to a new set of entries in *COMTAB*. The place to start this set of commands is determined by the present setting of COMPT (6). Since we are leaving one section of *COMTAB* and starting on another, we need to leave a trace of where we have left off. There is an array of counters for this purpose which we call **C( )**. The highest level of counters is called **C(0)**. We note the position from which we are leaving the original call in this counter (7). Now we advance the **level indicator**, L (8). This information should be noted somewhere in the text so that level setting can be done for &SYSNDX (9). We are going to make a copy of the inner macrodefinition starting at a position in *COMTAB* indicated by COMPT. We now have to find the information to be copied. This is obtained from *OPTAB* when the call was looked up there. We now begin to copy the commands from the called section of *COMTAB* into the new section (10). As we do this, each opcode is obtained and examined in the *OPTAB* (11). Again we are looking for two things:

- an inner call,
- MEND, telling us that this inner call is ended (12).

For all other cases the command is copied into the new portion of *COMTAB* indicated by P (13). Then we advance the pointer P by a length of the command inserted (14). We go on to another command to be copied (11).

Another inner call If we find further inner nesting (12), we have to keep track of our present position in *COMTAB*. We do this in the array of counters (15). Before we can proceed, the arguments transmitted from the intermediate macro to the inner macro using the call statement are placed in another *PARTAB* (16). The level setting must also be indicated (17).

Now we go around the loop again, copying commands from the inner macrodefinition into the new area of *COMTAB*.

End Eventually the innermost macro will terminate as indicated by MEND (12). First, we make a level change indication, L (18), and then we check to see if we are still in an intermediate macro (19). If so, we obtain the next higher level pointer, C(L), telling us where we left off in *COMTAB* for the intermediate definition, and we return this to P (20). We go back to the intermediate macrodefinition to continue to copy into the new area of *COMTAB* where we left off for the inner macrodefinition.

Outer When we have reached the outer level as determined when L is 0 (19), we put the present pointer to the new area of *COMTAB* away at COMPT (21). We are through with this new area of *COMTAB*, at least for the moment. We have to enter a pointer, though, from this new section of *COMTAB* back to the outer macro. This link is necessary at expansion time to move back and forth between the old and the new area (22). Now to return to the old area, we get the pointer thereto and insert it into P (23), with the entry point SN (2). We can then continue to examine commands in the *COMTAB* without copying.

If another call arises in the outer definition, we return to the end of the new *COMTAB* area.

16.3 McGen

The purpose of McGen, which is flowcharted in Fig. 16.3.1, is to

1. scan the input text,
2. detect all macrocalls,
3. replace a macrocall by the expanded code,
4. do conditional assembly.

ScanG The generation scan, as most others, examines each statement in the text, looking up *opcode* in *OPTAB* (1). This time we are really making a pass. However, only the text *after* the first CSECT or START is scanned. Only two kinds of opcodes are of interest, END and macrocalls. For all others, statements are ignored and the scan continues (2).

For the case of a macrocall, the *COMTAB* entry is found for the pointer *OPTAB* (3). The local dictionary is obtained (4). This permits setup of the parameters in a table, *PARTAB*, in the local dictionary, *LOCDIC* (5). After parameters are obtained from the macrocall and entered in *PARTAB*, McGenS follows.

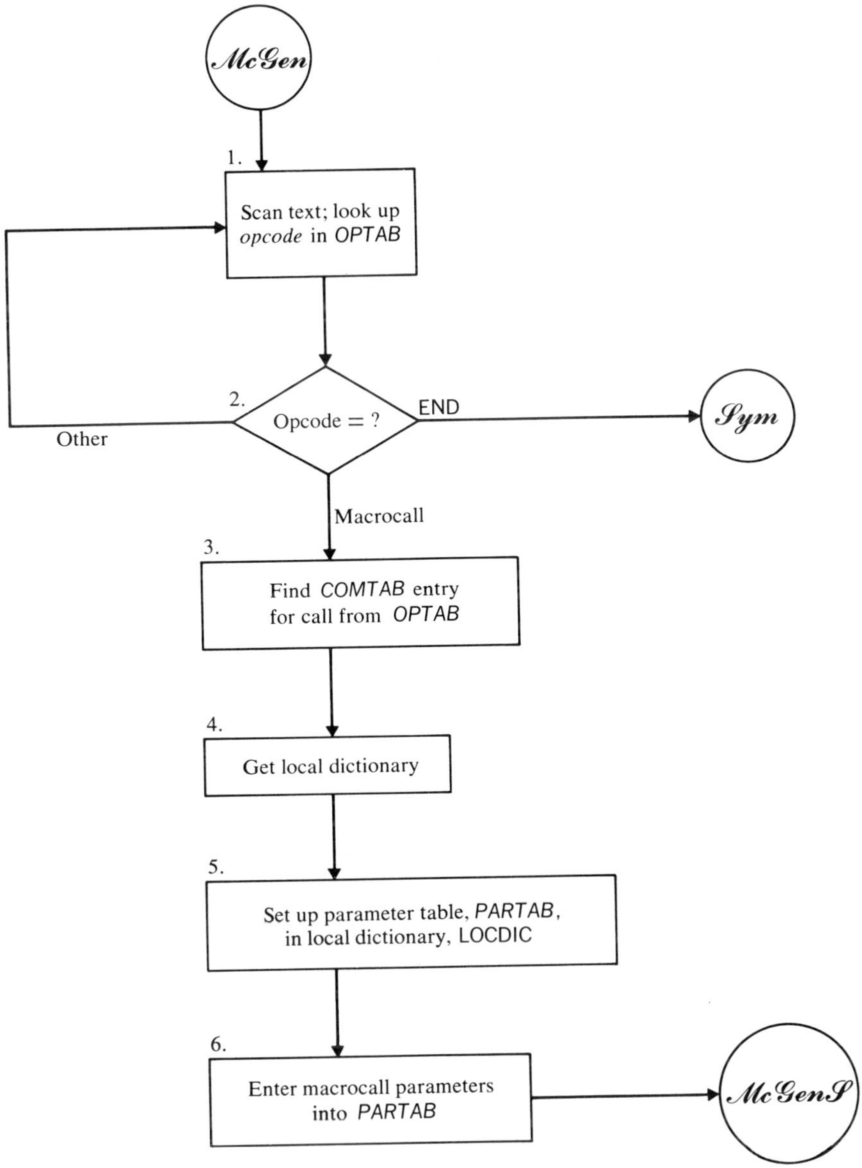

Fig. 16.3.1 Flow chart of the start of McGen.

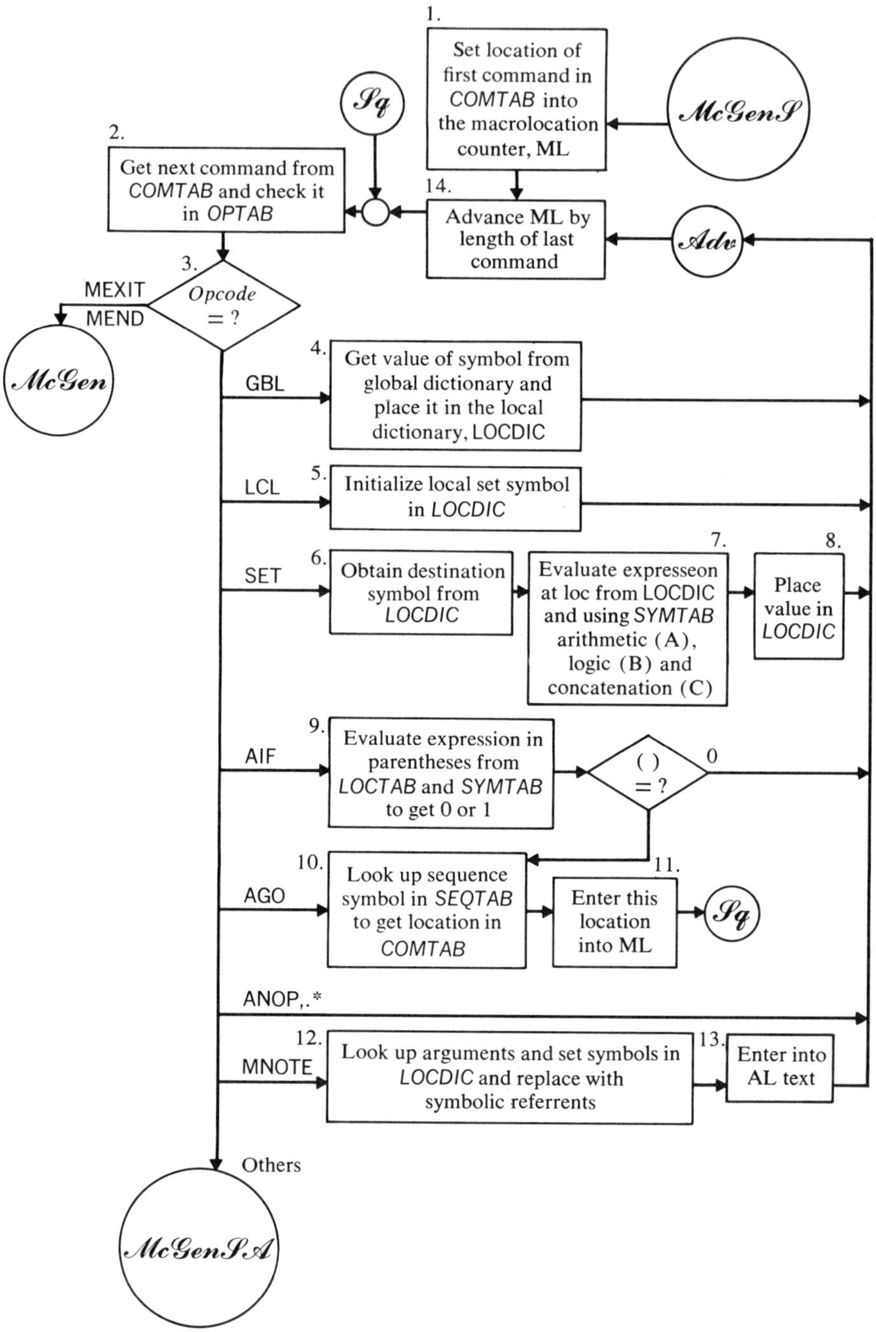

Fig. 16.3.2 Flow chart of McGenS.

McGenS This component enters the code from *COMTAB* in the AL program, *but conditionally*. That is why each command must be checked. As illustrated in Fig. 16.3.2, McGenS begins by setting the location of the first command in *COMTAB* into a macrolocation counter which I shall call ML (1). McGenS scans the text for the macro as it appears in *COMTAB*, the opcode of which command is looked up in *OPTAB* (2).

What we do next depends on the nature of the opcode (3). For GBLX, the value of the symbol is obtained from the global dictionary and placed in the local dictionary (4). For local declaratives the local symbol is initialized by setting it to 0 or the null character (5). Although omitted from the diagram, if GBLX or LCLX occur elsewhere than at the beginning of the macrodefinition, an error should be signaled.

When SETX is encountered, the local dictionary, *LOCDIC*, is entered and the present value of that symbol obtained. Then the expression at *loc* is evaluated by further references to *LOCDIC* and *SYMTAB* (7). The value obtained replaces the old value in *LOCDIC* (8).

For AIF, the evaluation procedure outlined above is performed and a binary number results which is either 0 or 1 (9). If it is 0, McGenS goes on to the next statement. But if it is 1, a branch sequence symbol is required and AIF now looks like AGO, examined next.

For AGO, the sequence symbol is looked up in *SEQTAB*, a listing of the sequence symbols relative to the beginning of the macrodefinition (10). This number is entered into a macrolocation counter ML (11) so that the next statement examined will not be a normal one which follows. ANOP and .* produce no text.

MNOTE produces a message but no code. The message generally contains an argument which requires lookup in *LOCDIC* (12) and entry into the note and the text (13).

All commands except AGO and some AIFs cause advance of ML by the length of command inserted into the text (14). Notice that no inner calls occur because these were resolved by McNest.

Finally if MEXIT or MEND is encountered (3), control is returned to ScanG (15).

Something has been omitted. There are some pseudos which offer storage allocation. These require use of the routine McGenSA which we now examine.

McGenSA As shown in Fig. 16.3.3, again what we do depends on *opcode*. For mnemonics and storage opcodes DS, DC, and EQU, we check to see if there is a name (2). If there is an argument, it is looked up *LOCDIC* and replaced with the corresponding parameter. A symbol is maintained. A sequence number is removed (4).

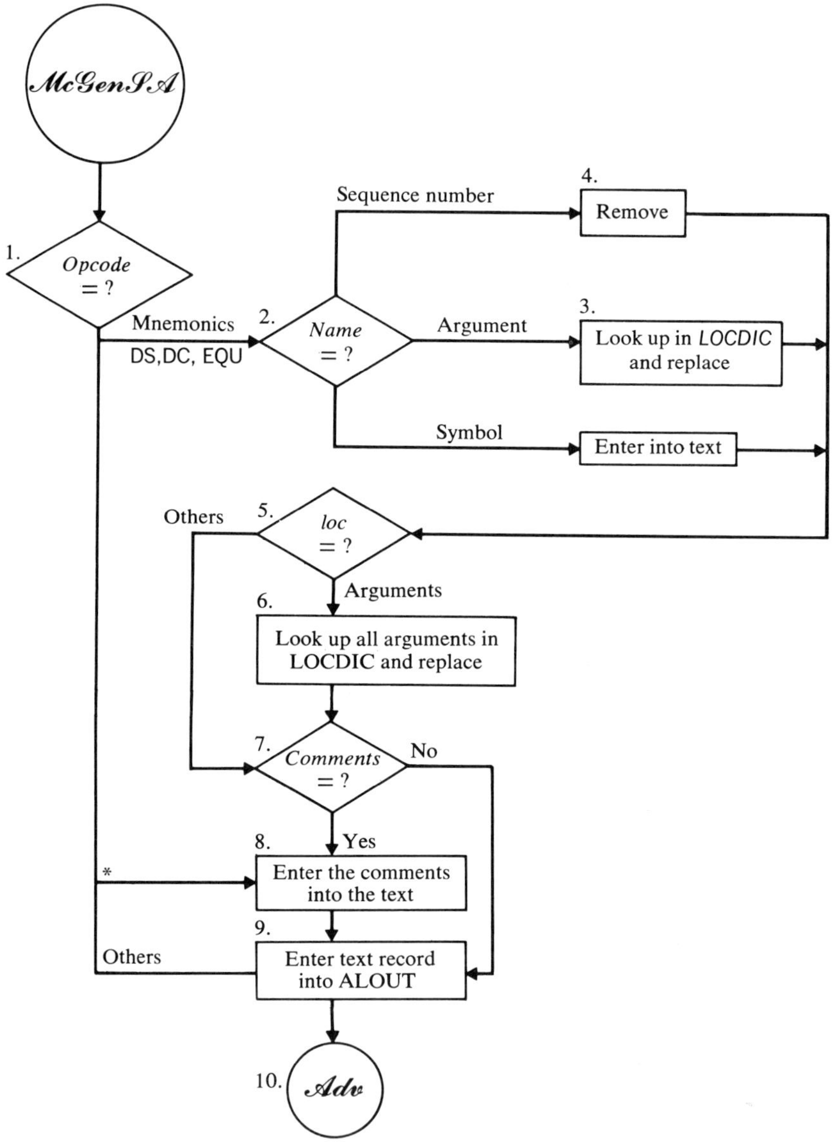

Fig. 16.3.3 Flow chart for McGenSA.

Next we examine *location* (5). If arguments are present, they are picked up from *LOCDIC* (6). If there are comments (7), these are entered directly (8). Notice that a comment without an opcode can be introduced by *. The remainder of the text is now replaced in the assembly language output (9). We then return to A on Fig. 16.3.2 (14).

16.4 Sym

This pass has been discussed to some extent in Section 4.4. We now examine what omissions took place there after a brief review.

Review In Fig. 16.4.1, Scan examines each command checking the opcode. Actually the opcode is examined by Opt. If it is a mnemonic, it is handled by Mnem. If a literal is involved (4), this is handled by Lit, which we examine later (5).

Then again our activity depends on the opcode we have encountered for DS, DC, or DXD. The routine Dcds is required (6). After completion, if a DC has been processed, Scan is returned to (7). Otherwise check to see if an address is specified (8). If so, Lit is called in (5). If not, the routine, Cons, sets up the constant (9).

Others Let us now examine some of the other pseudos which may be encountered by Opt.

For EQU, perhaps an expression must be evaluated and Eval does this.

For CNOP, two numbers appear at *loc*. These are evaluated to determine the number of BALRs to be inserted into the program (11). This is used to advance the displacement counter D (12).

TITLE is easy to handle and simply sets up for printout (13).

LTORG resets the literal counter for this CSECT and notes this for later use (14). Comments can be indicated in three ways. For all of them by this time an argument has been filled in so that the comment is read to printout and can be placed in the text (15). PUNCH and REPRO request the incorporation of the statement coming up which is easy to handle.

ORG simply resets the location counter to the value indicated with the pseudo (17).

START and CSECT both affect the location counter. They either switch over to a different location counter or initiate the use of a new location counter (18).

DSECT and COM set up an external table in the assembler which can be used by the program when a USING statement appears (19).

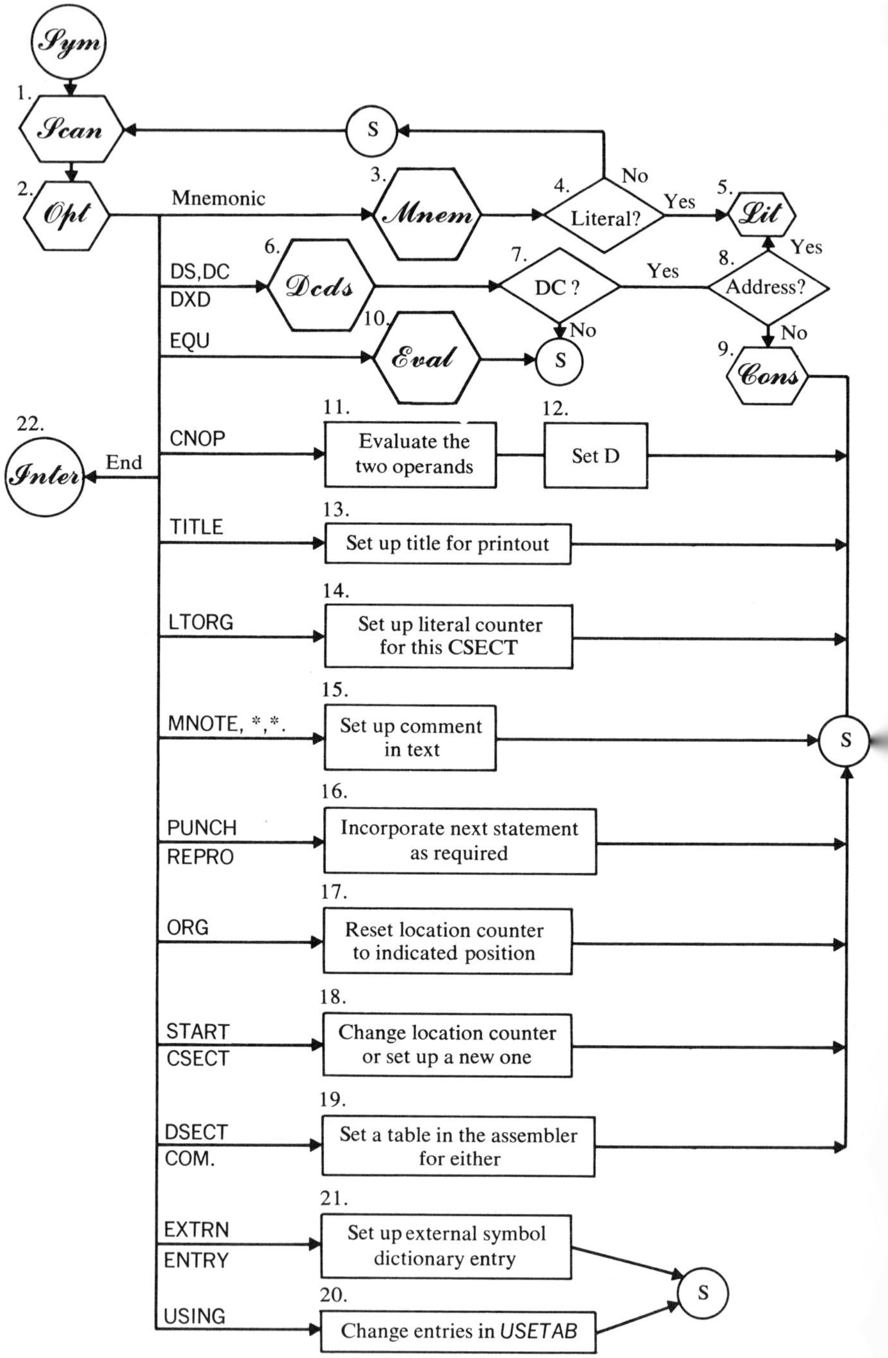

Fig. 16.4.1 Flow chart of $\mathfrak{Sym}$.

USING sets up the *USETAB* for this CSECT as directed in the command (20).

EXTRN and ENTRY set up the external symbol dictionary entry so that other CSECTs can talk with this one.

Finally, END terminates this pass and takes us to a cleanup pass, Inter, an interlude where all symbolic references and tables are straightened out.

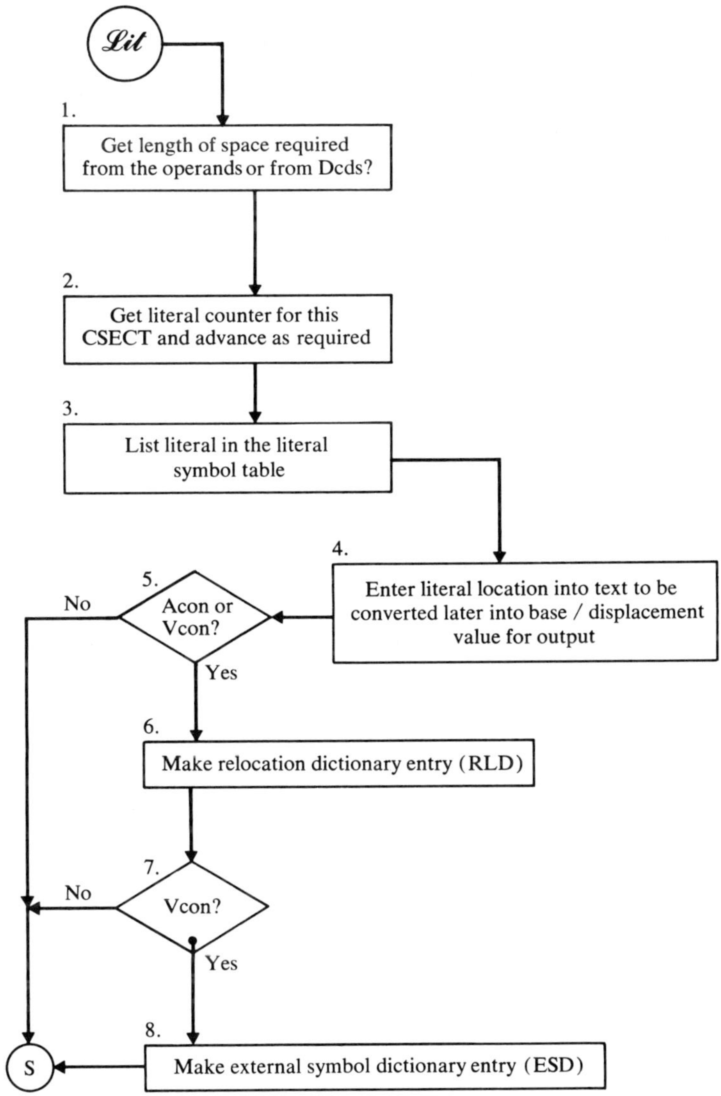

Fig. 16.4.2 Flow chart for Lit.

Literals Literals of three types are examined in Fig. 16.4.2. The first activity is to get space requirement which is transmitted to 𝔏𝔦𝔱 from 𝔇𝔠𝔡𝔰 (1). This quantity is used to advance the literal counter applicable to this particular CSECT (2). The literal is then listed in the literal symbol table for this CSECT (3). Whether this is an actual literal or an address constant, the literal value is entered into the table. Then check for an address constant (4) and, if none, return to 𝔖𝔠𝔞𝔫 (5). For both kinds of address constants, the relocation dictionary entry is fabricated (6). For a variable address constant, one which comes in from an external section, an external symbol dictionary entry is necessary (7). This is fabricated (8). We can now continue to scan.

17

ERROR CODES; ADVANCED MACROS

17.1 ERRORS

Error codes ASLR may find errors when it tries to assemble the program presented to it. These errors may occur on any pass. ASLR must tell the programmer about errors. ASLR detects errors as they occur and keeps track of them so that they will be printed on the final pass. Each error is assigned a severity code according to how it will affect the assembling and running of the program. The codes are as follows:

4 Warning, but the program will probably execute;
8 An error and the execution may fail;
12 A serious error which makes execution improbable;
16 Execution is impossible;
20 The program won't assemble.

There are over a hundred error messages which are described in fair detail in Table 17.1.1. These have been correlated with the example presented in Fig. 17.1.1.

Conveying errors The errors which ASLR has detected and collected from previous passes are stored internally in an error table *ERTAB*. With each error there is associated the (sometimes approximate) statement in the assembly language program where the error occurred. Actually, consider three separate instances:

1. In the macrodefinition—associated with a particular statement in the definition.
2. A command in program may create an error.
3. The error may arise in the code produced when a macro is called.

Table 17.1.1 DIAGNOSTIC MESSAGES

Code	*Message*	*Explanation*	*Severity*	*Example*
IEU001	DUPLICATION FACTOR ERROR	A duplication factor is not an absolute expression, nor is zero in a literal; * in duplication factor expression; invalid syntax in expression.	12	46, 87
IEU002	RELOCATABLE DUPLICATION FACTOR	A relocatable expression has been used to specify the duplication factor.	12	
IEU003	LENGTH ERROR	The length specification is out of permissible range or specified invalidly; * in length expression; invalid syntax in expression; no left-parenthesis delimiter for expression.	12	47, 48, 49
IEU004	RELOCATABLE LENGTH	A relocatable expression has been used to specify length.	12	49
IEU005	S-TYPE CONSTANT IN LITERAL	Self-explanatory.	8	
IEU006	INVALID ORIGIN	The location counter has been reset to a value less than the starting address of the control section; ORG operand is not a simply relocatable expression or specifies an address outside the control section.	12	
IEU007	LOCATION COUNTER ERROR	The location counter has exceeded $2^{24} - 1$, or passed out of control section in negative direction (three-byte arithmetic).	12	
IEU008	INVALID DISPLACEMENT	The displacement in an explicit address is not an absolute value within the range of 0 to 4095.	8	8
IEU009	MISSING OPERAND	Self-explanatory.	12	
IEU010	INCORRECT REGISTER SPECIFICATION	The value specifying the REGISTER is not an absolute value within the range 0–15, an odd register is specified where an even register is required, or a register was used where none can be specified.	8	55, 61
IEU011	SCALE MODIFIER ERROR	The scale modifier is not an absolute expression or is too large, negative scale modifier for floating point, * in scale modifier expression; invalid syntax or illegally specified scale modifier.	8	57
IEU012	RELOCATABLE SCALE MODIFIER	A relocatable expression has been used to specify the scale modifier.	8	91

IEU013	EXPONENT MODIFIER ERROR	The exponent is not specified as an absolute expression or is out of range; * in exponent modifier expression; invalid syntax; illegally specified exponent modifier.	8	110
IEU014	RELOCATABLE EXPONENT MODIFIER	A relocatable expression has been used to specify the exponent modifier.	8	
IEU015	INVALID LITERAL USAGE	A valid literal is used illegally; e.g., it specifies a receiving field or a register, or it is a Q-type constant.	8	61
IEU016	INVALID NAME	A name entry is incorrectly specified; e.g., it contains more than eight characters, it does not begin with a letter, or has a special character imbedded.	8	48, 93
IEU017	DATA ITEM TOO LARGE	The constant is too large for the data type or for the explicit length; operand field for packed DC exceeds thirty-two characters and for zoned DC exceeds sixteen characters (excluding decimal points).	8	113
IEU018	INVALID SYMBOL	The symbol is specified invalidly; e.g., it is longer than eight characters.	8	
IEU019	EXTERNAL NAME ERROR	A CSECT and DSECT have the same name, or a symbol is used more than once in EXTRN or the name field of DXD.	8	122
IEU020	INVALID IMMEDIATE FIELD	The value of the immediate operand exceeds 255, or the operand requires more than one byte of storage, or the operand is not an acceptable type.	8	63
IEU021	SYMBOL NOT PREVIOUSLY DEFINED	Self-explanatory.	8	87, 100
IEU022	*ESDTABLE* OVERFLOW	The combined number of control sections and dummy sections plus the number of unique symbols in EXTRN and V-type constants exceeds 255. (A DSECT which appears as XD makes two entries.)	12	
IEU023	PREVIOUSLY DEFINED NAME	The symbol which appears in the name field has appeared in the name field of a previous statement.	8	103
IEU024	UNDEFINED SYMBOL	A symbol being referenced has not been defined in the program.	8	64

Table 17.1.1 *(Continued)*

Code	*Message*	*Explanation*	*Severity*	*Example*
IEU025	RELOCATABILITY ERROR	A relocatable or complex relocatable expression is specified where an absolute expression is required, an absolute expression or complex relocatable expression is specified where a relocatable expression is required, or a relocatable term is involved in multiplication or division.	8	101, 111
IEU026	TOO MANY LEVELS OF PARENTHESES	An expression specifies more than five levels of parentheses.	12	104
IEU027	TOO MANY TERMS	More than sixteen terms are specified in an expression.	12	105
IEU028	REGISTER NOT USED	A REGISTER specified in a DROP statement is not currently in use.	4	65
IEU029	CCW ERROR	Bits 37–39 of the CCW are set to nonzero.	8	94
IEU030	INVALID CNOP	An invalid combination of operands is specified.	12	66
IEU031	UNKNOWN TYPE	Incorrect type designation is specified in a DC, DS, or literal.	8	
IEU032	OP-CODE NOT ALLOWED TO BE GENERATED	Operation code allowed only in source statement has been obtained through substitution of a value for a variable symbol.	8	
IEU033	ALIGNMENT ERROR	Referenced address is not aligned to the proper boundary for this instruction, e.g., START operand not a multiple of 8.	4	67
IEU034	INVALID OP-CODE	Syntax error, e.g., more than five characters in operation field, not followed by blank on first card, missing.	8	56
IEU035	ADDRESSABILITY ERROR	The referenced address does not fall within the range of a USING.	8	59, 79
IEU037	MNOTE STATEMENT	This indicates that an MNOTE statement has been generated from a macrodefinition. The text and severity code of the MNOTE statement will be found in line in the listing.	Variable	84
IEU038	ENTRY ERROR	A symbol in the operand of ENTRY appears in more than one ENTRY; it is undefined, it is defined in a dummy section or in blank common, or it is equated to a symbol defined by an EXTRN statement.	8	43

IEU039	INVALID DELIMITER	This message can be caused by any syntax error, e.g., missing delimiter, special character used which is not a valid delimiter, delimiter used illegally, operand missing, i.e., nothing between delimiters, unpaired parentheses, imbedded blank in expression.	12	49, 54, 57, 116
IEU040	GENERATED RECORD TOO LONG	There are more than 236 characters in a generated statement.	12	
IEU041	UNDECLARED VARIABLE SYMBOL	Variable symbol is not declared in a defined SET symbol statement or in a macro prototype	8	11, 73, 74, 81
IEU042	SINGLE TERM LOGICAL EXPRESSION IS NOT A SETB SYMBOL	The single term logical expression has not been declared as a SETB symbol.	8	10, 81
IEU043	SET SYMBOL PREVIOUSLY DEFINED	Self-explanatory.	8	8, 81
IEU044	SET SYMBOL USAGE INCONSISTENT WITH DECLARATION	A SET symbol has been declared as undimensioned, but is subscripted, or has been declared dimensioned, but is unsubscripted.	8	13 81
IEU045	ILLEGAL SYMBOLIC PARAMETER	An attribute has been requested for a variable symbol which is not a legal symbolic parameter.	8	14, 22
IEU046	AT LEAST ONE RELOCATABLE Y-TYPE CONSTANT IN ASSEMBLY	One or more relocatable Y-type constants in assembly; relocation may result in address greater than two bytes in length.	4	81, 111
IEU047	SEQUENCE SYMBOL PREVIOUSLY DEFINED	Self-explanatory.	12	15, 81
IEU048	SYMBOLIC PARAMETER PREVIOUSLY DEFINED OR SYSTEM VARIABLE SYMBOL DECLARED AS SYMBOLIC PARAMETER	Self-explanatory.	12	
IEU049	VARIABLE SYMBOL MATCHES A PARAMETER	Self-explanatory.	12	4 81
IEU050	INCONSISTENT GLOBAL DECLARATIONS	A global SET variable symbol, defined in more than one macrodefinition or defined in a macrodefinition and in the source program, is inconsistent in SET type or dimension.	8	

Table 17.1.1 *(Continued)*

Code	*Message*	*Explanation*	*Severity*	*Example*
IEU051	MACRODEFINITION PREVIOUSLY DEFINED	Prototype operation field is the same as a machine or assembler instruction or a previous prototype. This message is not produced when a programmer macro matches a system macro. The programmer macro will be assembled with no indication of the corresponding system macro.	12	
IEU052	NAME FIELD CONTAINS ILLEGAL SET SYMBOL	SET symbol in name field does not correspond to SET statement type.	8	18, 28, 81, 83
IEU053	GLOBAL DICTIONARY FULL	The global dictionary is full, assembly terminated.	12	
IEU054	LOCAL DICTIONARY FULL	The local dictionary is full, current macro aborted. If in open code, assembly terminated.	12	
IEU055	INVALID ASSEMBLER OPTION(S) ON THE EXECUTE CARD	Self-explanatory.	8	0, 111
IEU056	ARITHMETIC OVERFLOW	The intermediate or final result of an expression is not within the range of -2^{31} to $2^{31} - 1$.	8	
IEU057	SUBSCRIPT EXCEEDS MAXIMUM DIMENSION	&SYSLIST or symbolic parameter subscript exceeds 200, or is negative, or zero, or SET symbol subscript exceeds dimension.	8	81
IEU058	REENTRANT CHECK FAILED	An instruction has been detected, which, when executed, might store data into a control section or a common area. This message is generated only when requested via control cards and merely indicates a possible reentrant error.	4	
IEU059	UNDEFINED SEQUENCE SYMBOL	Self-explanatory.	12	
IEU060	ILLEGAL ATTRIBUTE NOTATION	L′, S′, or I′ requested for a parameter whose type attribute does not allow these attributes to be requested.	8	
IEU061	ACTR COUNTER EXCEEDED	Self-explanatory, conditional assembly terminated.	12	84
IEU062	GENERATED STRING GREATER THAN 255 CHARACTERS	Self-explanatory.	8	

IEU063	EXPRESSION 1 OF SUBSTRING IS ZERO OR MINUS	Self-explanatory.	8	81
IEU064	EXPRESSION 2 OF SUBSTRING IS ZERO OR MINUS	Self-explanatory.	8	
IEU065	INVALID OR ILLEGAL TERM IN ARITHMETIC EXPRESSION	The value of a SETC symbol used in the arithmetic expression is not composed of decimal digits, or the parameter is not a self-defining term.	8	81
IEU066	UNDEFINED OR DUPLICATE KEYWORD OPERAND OR EXCESSIVE POSITIONAL OPERANDS	The same keyword operand occurs more than once in the macro instruction; a keyword is not defined in a prototype statement; in a mixed mode macro instruction, more positional operands are specified than are specified in the prototype.	12	
IEU067	EXPRESSION 1 OF SUBSTRING GREATER THAN LENGTH OF CHARACTER EXPRESSION	Self-explanatory.	8	81
IEU068	GENERATION TIME DICTIONARY AREA OVERFLOWED	Self-explanatory.	12	
IEU069	VALUE OF EXPRESSION 2 OF SUBSTRING GREATER THAN 8	Self-explanatory.	8	
IEU070	FLOATING POINT CHARACTERISTIC OUT OF RANGE	Exponent too large for length of defining field, exponent modifier has caused loss of all significant digits.	12	1
IEU071	ILLEGAL OCCURRENCE OF LCL, GBL, OR ACTR STATEMENT	LCLX, GBLX, or ACTR statement is not in proper place in the program.	8	7, 41, 6, 81
IEU072	ILLEGAL RANGE ON ISEQ STATEMENT	Self-explanatory.	4	38, 74
IEU073	ILLEGAL NAME FIELD	Either a statement which requires a name is blank, or a statement has a name which should be blank, or a name entry required to be a sequence symbol is not a sequence symbol.	8	66
IEU074	ILLEGAL STATEMENT IN COPY CODE OR SYSTEM MACRO	Self-explanatory.	8	72

Table 17.1.1 *(Continued)*

Code	*Message*	*Explanation*	*Severity*	*Example*
IEU075	ILLEGAL STATEMENT OUTSIDE OF A MACRODEFINITION	Statement allowed only in a macrodefinition encountered in open code, e.g., period asterisk (.*), mnote statement.	8	80
IEU076	SEQUENCE ERROR	Self-explanatory.	12	
IEU077	ILLEGAL CONTINUATION CARD	Either there are too many continuation cards, or there are nonblanks between the begin and continue columns on the continuation card, or a card not intended as continuation was treated as such because of punch in continue column of preceding card.	8	114
IEU079	ILLEGAL STATEMENT IN MACRODEFINITION	This operation is not allowed within a macrodefinition.	8	25, 81
IEU080	ILLEGAL START CARD	Statements affecting or depending upon the location counter have been encountered before START.	8	46, 62
IEU081	ILLEGAL FORMAT IN GBL OR LCL STATEMENTS	An operand is not a variable symbol.	8	3, 81
IEU082	ILLEGAL DIMENSION SPECIFICATION IN GBL OR LCL STATEMENT	Dimension is other than 1 to 255.	8	3, 81
IEU083	SET STATEMENT NAME FIELD NOT A VARIABLE SYMBOL	Self-explanatory.	8	26, 81
IEU084	ILLEGAL OPERAND FIELD FORMAT	Syntax invalid, e.g., AIF operand does not start with a left parenthesis; operand of AGO is not a sequence symbol; operand of of PUNCH, TITLE, MNOTE not enclosed in quotes.	8	29, 82
IEU085	INVALID SYNTAX IN EXPRESSION	Invalid delimiter, too many terms in expression, too many levels of parentheses, two operators in succession, two terms in succession, or illegal character.	8	
IEU086	ILLEGAL USAGE OF SYSTEM VARIABLE SYMBOL	A system variable symbol appears in the name field of a SET statement, is used in a mixed mode or keyword macrodefinition, is declared in GBLX or LCLX, or is an unsubscripted &SYSLIST in a context other than N'&SYSLIST.	8	

IEU087	NO ENDING APOSTROPHE	There is an unpaired apostrophe or ampersand in the statement.	8	106, 107
IEU088	UNDEFINED OPERATION CODE	Symbol in operation code field does not correspond to a valid machine or assembler operation code or to any operation code in a macro prototype statement.	12	78
IEU089	INVALID ATTRIBUTE NOTATION	Syntax error inside a macrodefinition, e.g., the argument of the attribute reference is not a symbolic parameter.	8	30, 82
IEU090	INVALID SUBSCRIPT	Syntax error, e.g., double subscript where single subscript is required or vice versa; not right parenthesis after subscript.	8	83
IEU091	INVALID SELF-DEFINING TERM	Value is too large or is inconsistent with the data type, e.g., severity code greater than 255.	8	31, 82
IEU092	INVALID FORMAT FOR VARIABLE SYMBOL	The first character after the ampersand is not alphabetic, or the variable symbol contains more than eight characters, or failure to use double ampersand in TITLE or character self-defining term.	8	
IEU093	UNBALANCED PARENTHESIS OR EXCESSIVE LEFT PARENTHESES	End of statement or card encountered before all parenthesis levels are satisfied. May be caused by embedded blank or other unexpected terminator, or failure to have a punch in continuation column.	8	
IEU094	INVALID OR ILLEGAL NAME OR OPERATION IN PROTOTYPE STATEMENT	Name not blank or variable symbol, or variable symbol in name field is subscripted, or violation of rules for forming variable symbol [must begin with ampersand (&) followed by one to seven letters and/or numbers first of which must be a letter], or statement following MACRO is not a valid prototype statement.	12	
IEU095	ENTRY TABLE OVERFLOW	Number of ENTRY symbols, i.e., ENTRY instruction operands, exceeds 100.	8	
IEU096	MACRO INSTRUCTION OR PROTOTYPE OPERAND EXCEEDS 255 CHARACTERS IN LENGTH	Self-explanatory.	12	

Table 17.1.1 (*Continued*)

Code	*Message*	*Explanation*	*Severity*	*Example*
IEU097	INVALID FORMAT IN MACRO INSTRUCTION OPERAND OR PROTOTYPE PARAMETER	This message can be caused by 1. illegal =, 2. a single & appears somewhere in the standard value assigned to a prototype keyword parameter, 3. first character of a prototype argument is not &, 4. prototype argument is a subscripted variable symbol, 5. invalid use of alternate format in prototype statement, e.g., 10 16 72 PROTO &A,&B, or PROTO &A,&B,&C X 6. unintelligible prototype parameter, e.g., &A* or &A&&, 7. illegal (nonassembler) character appears in prototype parameter or macro instruction operand.	12	
IEU098	EXCESSIVE NUMBER OF OPERANDS OR PARAMETERS	Either the prototype has more than 200 parameters, or the macro instruction has more than 200 operands.	12	
IEU099	POSITIONAL MACRO INSTRUCTION OPERAND, PROTOTYPE PARAMETER OR EXTRA COMMA FOLLOWS KEYWORD	Self-explanatory.	12	
IEU100	STATEMENT COMPLEXITY EXCEEDED	More than thirty-two operands in a DC, DS, DXD, or literal DC, or more than fifty terms in a statement.	8	
IEU101	EOD ON SYSIN	EOD before END.	12	
IEU102	INVALID OR ILLEGAL ICTL	The operands of the ICTL are out of range, or the ICTL is not the first statement in the input deck.	16	
IEU103	ILLEGAL NAME IN OPERAND FIELD OF COPY CARD	Syntax error, e.g., symbol has more than eight characters or has an illegal character.	12	76

IEU104	COPY CODE NOT FOUND	The operand of a COPY statement specified COPY text which cannot be found in the library.	12	77
IEU105	EOD ON SYSTEM MACRO LIBRARY	EOD before MEND.	12	
IEU106	NOT NAME OF DSECT OR DXD	Referenced symbol expected to be DSECT name, but it is not.	8	
IEU107	INVALID OPERAND	Invalid syntax in DC operand, e.g., invalid hexadecimal character in hexadecimal DC; operand string too long for X, B, C, DCs; operand unrecognizable, contains invalid value, or incorrectly specified.	4	59, 109, 115
IEU108	PREMATURE EOD	Indicates an internal assembler error; should not occur.	16	
IEU109	PRECISION LOST	Self-explanatory.	8	
IEU110	EXPRESSION VALUE TOO LARGE	Value of expression greater than −16777216 to +16777215. Expressions in EQU and ORG statements are flagged if (1) they include terms previously defined as negative values, or (2) positive terms give a result of more than three bytes in magnitude. The error indication may be erroneous due to (1) the treatment of negative values as three-byte positive values, or (2) the effect of large positive values on the location counter if a control section begins with a START statement having an operand greater than zero, or a control section is divided into subsections.	8	52, 111, 126
IEU111	SYSGO DD CARD MISSING NOLOAD OPTION USED	Self-explanatory.	16	
IEU112	SYSPUNCH DD CARD MISSING NODECK OPTION USED	Self-explanatory.	16	
IEU997	SYSPRINT DD CARD MISSING NOLIST OPTION USED	Self-explanatory. Printed on console typewriter.	0	
IEU998	ASSEMBLY TERMINATED. MISSING DATA SET FOR (ddname)	Self-explanatory. Printed on console typewriter.	20	
IEU999	ASSEMBLY TERMINATED, jobname, stepname, unit address, device type, ddname, operation attempted, error description	Indicates a permanent IO error. This message is produced by a SYNADAF macro instruction and printed on the console typewriter.	20	

```
               SAMP SYMBOL   TYPE   ID   ADDR     LENGTH   LD   ID   EXTERNAL SYMBOL DICT

                  ERROR       SD    01   000000   000000
                              PC    02   000000   FFFC98
                                *** ERROR ***

LOC   OBJECT  CODE          ADDR1 ADDR2  STMT              SOURCE STATEMENT

                                           1                 MACRO
                                           2                 EMAC     &A,&D=,&E=
                                           3                 GBLB     &Q(300),&GLOBALB,TEMP
         *** ERROR ***
                                           4                 LCLA     &P,&LOCALA,&R,&D,&Z(2)
         *** ERROR ***
                                           5                 LCLC     &LOCALC,&T
                                           6                 LCLB     &LOCALB
                                           7                 GBLC     &GLOBALC
         *** ERROR ***
                                           8                 LCLA     &R,&S
         *** ERROR ***
                                           9                 ACTR     25
                                          10                 AIF      (&T).CONT
         *** ERROR ***
                                          11  &UNDEF         SETA     20
         *** ERROR ***
                                          12  .CONT          ANOP
                                          13  &T(5)          SETC     'FIVE'
         *** ERROR ***
                                          14  &P             SETA     L'&T
```

```
*** ERROR ***
                        15  CONT      AIF     (&GLOBALB EQ 1).A
*** ERROR ***
                        16            AIF     ('&A' EQ '  ').A
                        17  &T        SETC    '  '
                        18  &LOCALC   SETB    1
*** ERROR ***
                        19  &Z(&P)    SETA    3
                        20  &T        SETC    '&A'(&R−1,&S)
                        21  &LOCALC   SETC    'LOCALC'
                        22  &P        SETA    L'&LOCALC−2
*** ERROR ***
                        23  &S        SETA    &LOCALC+1
                        24  &LOCALC   SETC    '&A'(&D,&E−3)
                        25            PRINT   DATA
*** ERROR ***
                        26  TEMP      SETB    &P
*** ERROR ***
                        27            PUNCH THIS DATA
                        28  &SYSNDX   SETA    0017
*** ERROR ***
                        29            AIF     ('&A' EQ '  'S')).B
*** ERROR ***
                        30  &Z(1)     SETA    L'TEMP
*** ERROR ***
                        31            AIF     ('&A'(3) EQ 'R').B
```

Fig. 17.1.1 Error problem.

```
LOC     OBJECT   CODE              ADDR1  ADDR2  STMT          SOURCE STATEMENT
             *** ERROR ***
                                                 32            MNOTE   299,'A SERIOUS ERROR'
                                                 33            MNOTE   'THIS IS A VALID MNOTE STATEMENT
                                                 34  .B        ANOP
                                                 35  &P        SETA    &P+1
                                                 36            AIF     (&P NE 30).B
                                                 37            MEND
                                                 38            ISEQ    80,73
             *** ERROR ***
000000                                           40  ERROR     CSECT
                                                 41            GBLB    &GLOBALB(5)
             *** ERROR ***
000000                                           42            START   800
             *** ERROR ***
                                                 43            ENTRY HERE
             *** ERROR ***
000000  0500                                     44            BALR    12,0
000002                                           45            USING   *,12
000002  0000     0000     0000     00000  00000  46  BEGIN     MVC     TEMP,=0CL4
             *** ERROR ***
000008  0000     0000     0000     00000  00000  47            PACK    MOE,MOE
             *** ERROR ***
00000E  0000     0000     0000     00000  00000  48  CLEAR*    XC      JIM(N+TEMP),JIM
             *** ERROR ***
000014  0000     0000     0000     00000  00000  49            CLC     TEMP(2),=S(207(2)
             *** ERROR ***
FFFC96                                           50            ORG     *-900
```

```
FFFC96  1A55                                       51           AR      5,5
00001C                                             52           ORG     *+900
              *** ERROR ***
00001C  0000    0000                     00000     53           LA      2,5000
              *** ERROR ***
000020  0000    0000    0000    00000    00000     54           AP      TIM,
              *** ERROR ***
000026  0000                                       55           SR      5,REG
              *** ERROR ***
                                                   56           BADOPCODE

              *** ERROR ***
000028  0000    0000                     00000     57           AL      2,=FS(SCALE)'100'
              *** ERROR ***
00002C  4C20    C068                     0006A     58           MH      2,MCAND
000030  0000    0000                     00000     59           A       3,=F'10E(N)'
              *** ERROR ***
                                                   60           ACTR    10

              *** ERROR ***
000034  0000    0000                     00000     61  COMP     C       =C'3',=A(47)
              *** ERROR ***
000000                                             62           START   0
              *** ERROR ***
000038  0000    0000            00000              63           MVI     STAT,=X'0'
              *** ERROR ***
000030  0000    0000            00000              64           NI      STAT,MASK
              *** ERROR ***
                                                   65           DROP    7

              *** ERROR ***
                                                   66  ALIGN    CNOP    3,6

              *** ERROR ***
```

Fig. 17.1.1 *(Continued)*

```
LOC      OBJECT  CODE       ADDR1 ADDR2 STMT          SOURCE STATEMENT

000040   47F0    C049             0004B  67                B       AROUND
           *** ERROR ***
000044                                   68  ADR           DS      CL4
000048                                   69                DS      AL3
00004B                                   70  AROUND        EQU     *
                                         71                COPY    BER
                                         72                MACRO
           *** ERROR ***
                                         73  &NAME         BER     &R
           *** ERROR ***
                                         74  &NAME         BCR     8,&R            BR ON EQUAL
           *** ERROR ***
                                         75                MEND
           *** ERROR ***
                                         76                COPY    SYS1.MACLIB
           *** ERROR ***
                                         77                COPY    CODING
           *** ERROR ***
                                         78                ARL     4,5
           *** ERROR ***
00004B   00
00004C   0000    0000             00000  79                EX      0,INSTR
           *** ERROR ***
                                         80                MEXIT
           *** ERROR ***
                                         81                EMAC    VARA,D=10,E=16
```

```
                 *** ERROR ***
                                    82+                     PUNCH THIS DATA
                 *** ERROR ***
                                    83+                     MNOTE 299, 'A SERIOUS ERROR'
                 *** ERROR ***
                                    84                                THIS IS A VALID MNOTE STATEMENT
                 *** ERROR ***
000050                              85   TEMP         DS    CL4
000054   0011                       86   N            DC    H'17'
                                    87   JOE          DC    (N+JIM)C'0'
                 *** ERROR ***
000056   0000000000000000           88   MOE          DC    XL18'1'
                                    89   JIM          DS    ZL17
                 *** ERROR ***
000068   100C                       90   TIM          DC    P'100'
                                    91   MCAND        DC    HS(N)'5E(N)'
                 *** ERROR ***
00006A   2C                         92   BADLNGTH     DC    AL1(300)
00006B   C140D5C1D4C540C7           93   LONGSYMBOL   DC    C'A NAME GREATER THAN 8 CHARACTERS'
                 *** ERROR ***
00008B                              94   STAT         DS    CL1
00008C   D1C1C3D2                   95   JACK         DC    C'JACK'
000090   4200009821000050           96   CHCMDWRD     CCW   X'42',CARD,X'21',80
                 *** ERROR ***
000098                              97   CARD         DS    CL80
000014                              98   REG          EQU   20
000190                              99   SCALE        EQU   400
                                   100   FETCH        EQU   JACK+JILL
```

Fig. 17.1.1 *(Continued)*

```
LOC      OBJECT  CODE    ADDR1 ADDR2  STMT              SOURCE STATEMENT
                *** ERROR ***
                                      101  B            EQU    5*N
                *** ERROR ***
0000EB   D1C9D3D3                     102  JILL         DC     C'JILL'
0000EC   96                           103  COMP         DC     B'10010110'
                *** ERROR ***
                                      104  C            EQU    ((((((*+4)+5)-4*REG)-10)+N)-1)
                *** ERROR ***
                                      105  D            EQU    (((REG+SCALE-15+(L'JACK+L'TIM+L'JIM-2)+
                                                                 MOE-JOE-1)-4*REG+C
                                                               17-2)+L'REG*6+14)/2
                *** ERROR ***
                                      106  SJACK        EQU    S'JACK
                *** ERROR ***
                                      107  UNKNOWN      DS     L'TEMP'
                *** ERROR ***
0000ED   00
0000EE   0054                         108  YCON         DC     Y(N)
                                      109               DC     C'  '
                *** ERROR ***
                                      110  FLOAT        DC     EE80'10'
                *** ERROR ***
                                      111  OFLO         EQU    **X'FFFFFF'
                *** ERROR ***
000350                                112  XX           EQU    50000
0000F0   C350                         113               DC     Y(XX)
                *** ERROR ***
                                      114               DC   C'A',C'B',C'C',C'D',C'E',C'F',C'G',C'H',C'I',C'J',C'K',C'C
```

```
0000F2    C1C2C3C4C5C6C7C8                                  DC      'R',C'S',C'T'
             *** ERROR ***
                                          115               DC      X'ABCDEFG,F4'
             *** ERROR ***
                                          116               DC      B'1010,0001,111'
             *** ERROR ***
000100                                    117               LTORG
000100    F3                              118                       =C'3'
000101    00                              119                       =X'0'
000102                                    120               DS      CL5000
00148A    0A03                            121  INSTR        SVC     3
000000                                    122  ERROR        DSECT
             *** ERROR ***
000000                                    123  X            DS      H
000004                                    124  Y            DS      F
000008    47F0      0000            00002 125  HERE         B       BEGIN
00000B                                    126               ORG     *+X'FFFFFF'
             *** ERROR ***
                                          127               END
```

RELOCATION DICTIONARY

POS.ID	REL.ID	FLAGS	ADDRESS
02	02	08	000091
02	02	04	0000EE

Fig. 17.1.1 *(Continued)*

SYMBOL	LEN	VALUE	DEFN	REFERENCES				
ADR	00004	000044	0068					
AROUND	00001	00004B	0070	0067				
BADLNGTH	00001	00006A	0092					
BEGIN	00006	000002	0046	0125				
CARD	00080	000098	0097	0096				
CHCMDWRD	00008	000090	0096					
COMP	00004	000034	0061					
COMP	00001	0000EC	0103		**** DUPLICATE ****			
ERROR	00001	000000	0040					
ERROR	00001	000000	0122		**** DUPLICATE ****			
FLOAT	00001	0000F0	0110					
HERE	00004	000008	0125	0043				
INSTR	00002	00148A	0121	0079				
JACK	00004	00008C	0095	0100	0105			
JILL	00004	0000E8	0102	0100				
JIM	00001	000068	0089	0048	0048	0087	0105	
JOE	00001	000056	0087	0105				
MASK	**** UNDEFINED ****			0064				
MCAND	00001	00006A	0091	0058				
MOE	00018	000056	0088	0047	0047	0105		
N	00002	000054	0086	0048	0087	0091	0101	0108
REG	00001	000014	0098	0055	0105	0105	0105	
SCALE	00001	000190	0099	0105				
STAT	00001	00008B	0094	0063	0064			
TEMP	00004	000050	0085	0046	0048	0049		
TIM	00002	000068	0090	0054	0105			
X	00002	000000	0123					
XX	00001	000350	0112	0113				
Y	00004	000004	0124					
YCON	00002	0000EE	0108					

STMT	ERROR	CODE	MESSAGE
	IEU046		AT LEAST ONE RELOCATABLE Y-TYPE CONSTANT IN ASSEMBLY
0	IEU055		INVALID EXECUTE CARD PARAMETER(S)
3	IEU082		ILLEGAL DIMENSION SPECIFICATION IN GBL OR LCL STATEMENT
3	IEU081		ILLEGAL FORMAT IN GBL OR LCL STATEMENTS
4	IEU049		VARIABLE SYMBOL MATCHES A PARAMETER
7	IEU071		ILLEGAL OCCURRENCE OF LCL, GBL, OR ACTR STATEMENT
8	IEU043		SET SYMBOL PREVIOUSLY DEFINED
10	IEU042		SINGLE TERM LOGICAL EXPRESSION IS NOT A SETB SYMBOL
11	IEU041		UNDECLARED VARIABLE SYMBOL
13	IEU044		SET SYMBOL USAGE INCONSISTENT WITH DECLARATION
14	IEU045		ILLEGAL SYMBOLIC PARAMETER
15	IEU047		SEQUENCE SYMBOL PREVIOUSLY DEFINED
18	IEU052		NAME FIELD CONTAINS ILLEGAL SET SYMBOL
22	IEU045		ILLEGAL SYMBOLIC PARAMETER
25	IEU079		ILLEGAL STATEMENT IN MACRO DEFINITION
26	IEU083		SET STATEMENT NAME FIELD NOT A VARIABLE SYMBOL
28	IEU052		NAME FIELD CONTAINS ILLEGAL SET SYMBOL
29	IEU084		ILLEGAL OPERAND FIELD FORMAT
30	IEU089		INVALID ATTRIBUTE NOTATION
31	IEU090		INVALID SUBSCRIPT
38	IEU072		ILLEGAL RANGE ON ISEQ STATEMENT
41	IEU071		ILLEGAL OCCURRENCE OF LCL, GBL, OR ACTR STATEMENT
42	IEU080		ILLEGAL START CARD
43	IEU038		NEAR OPERAND COLUMN 1—ENTRY ERROR

Fig. 17.1.1 *(Continued)*

STMT	ERROR CODE	MESSAGE
46	IEU001	NEAR OPERAND COLUMN 7—DUPLICATION FACTOR ERROR
47	IEU003	NEAR OPERAND COLUMN 4—LENGTH ERROR
47	IEU003	NEAR OPERAND COLUMN 8—LENGTH ERROR
48	IEU016	INVALID NAME
48	IEU003	NEAR OPERAND COLUMN 11—LENGTH ERROR
49	IEU005	NEAR OPERAND COLUMN 11—S-TYPE CONSTANT IN LITERAL
49	IEU039	NEAR OPERAND COLUMN 15—INVALID DELIMITER
52	IEU110	NEAR OPERAND COLUMN 1—EXPRESSION VALUE TOO LARGE
53	IEU008	NEAR OPERAND COLUMN 7—INVALID DISPLACEMENT
54	IEU039	NEAR OPERAND COLUMN 5—INVALID DELIMITER
55	IEU010	NEAR OPERAND COLUMN 6—INCORRECT REGISTER SPECIFICATION
56	IEU034	INVALID OP-CODE
57	IEU011	NEAR OPERAND COLUMN 6—SCALE MODIFIER ERROR
57	IEU039	NEAR OPERAND COLUMN 13—INVALID DELIMITER
59	IEU107	NEAR OPERAND COLUMN 9—INVALID OPERAND
59	IEU035	NEAR OPERAND COLUMN 13—ADDRESSABILITY ERROR
60	IEU071	ILLEGAL OCCURRENCE OF LCL, GBL, OR ACTR STATEMENT
61	IEU010	NEAR OPERAND COLUMN 6—INCORRECT REGISTER SPECIFICATION
61	IEU015	NEAR OPERAND COLUMN 7—INVALID LITERAL USAGE
62	IEU080	ILLEGAL START CARD
63	IEU020	NEAR OPERAND COLUMN 11—INVALID IMMEDIATE FIELD
64	IEU024	NEAR OPERAND COLUMN 6—UNDEFINED SYMBOL
65	IEU028	NEAR OPERAND COLUMN 2—REGISTER NOT USED
66	IEU073	ILLEGAL NAME FIELD
66	IEU030	INVALID CNOP
67	IEU033	NEAR OPERAND COLUMN 7—ALIGNMENT ERROR
72	IEU074	ILLEGAL STATEMENT IN COPY CODE OR SYSTEM MACRO
73	IEU041	UNDECLARED VARIABLE SYMBOL
74	IEU041	UNDECLARED VARIABLE SYMBOL

```
75    IEU074    ILLEGAL STATEMENT IN COPY CODE OR SYSTEM MACRO
76    IEU103    ILLEGAL NAME IN OPERAND FIELD OF COPY CARD
77    IEU104    COPY CODE NOT FOUND
78    IEU088    UNDEFINED OPERATION CODE
79    IEU035    NEAR OPERAND COLUMN    8—ADDRESSABILITY ERROR
80    IEU075    ILLEGAL STATEMENT OUTSIDE OF A MACRO DEFINITION
81    IEU082    ILLEGAL DIMENSION SPECIFICATION IN GBL OR LCL STATEMENT
81    IEU081    ILLEGAL FORMAT IN GBL OR LCL STATEMENTS
81    IEU049    VARIABLE SYMBOL MATCHES A PARAMETER
81    IEU071    ILLEGAL OCCURRENCE OF LCL, GBL, OR ACTR STATEMENT
81    IEU043    SET SYMBOL PREVIOUSLY DEFINED
81    IEU042    SINGLE TERM LOGICAL EXPRESSION IS NOT A SETB SYMBOL
81    IEU041    UNDECLARED VARIABLE SYMBOL
81    IEU044    SET SYMBOL USAGE INCONSISTENT WITH DECLARATION
81    IEU045    ILLEGAL SYMBOLIC PARAMETER
81    IEU047    SEQUENCE SYMBOL PREVIOUSLY DEFINED
81    IEU052    NAME FIELD CONTAINS ILLEGAL SET SYMBOL
81    IEU057    SUBSCRIPT EXCEEDS MAXIMUM DIMENSION
81    IEU063    EXPRESSION 1 OF SUBSTRING IS ZERO OR MINUS
81    IEU045    ILLEGAL SYMBOLIC PARAMETER
81    IEU065    INVALID OR ILLEGAL TERM IN ARITHMETIC EXPRESSION
81    IEU067    EXPRESSION 1 OF SUBSTRING GREATER THAN LENGTH OF CHARACTER EXPRESSION
81    IEU079    ILLEGAL STATEMENT IN MACRO DEFINITION
81    IEU083    SET STATEMENT NAME FIELD NOT A VARIABLE SYMBOL
82    IEU084    NEAR OPERAND COLUMN    1—ILLEGAL OPERAND FIELD FORMAT
82    IEU052    NAME FIELD CONTAINS ILLEGAL SET SYMBOL
82    IEU084    ILLEGAL OPERAND FIELD FORMAT
82    IEU089    INVALID ATTRIBUTE NOTATION
```

Fig. 17.1.1 *(Continued)*

```
STMT     ERROR      CODE                       MESSAGE
  82     IEU090          INVALID SUBSCRIPT
  83     IEU091          INVALID SELF-DEFINING TERM
  84     IEU037          MNOTE STATEMENT
  84     IEU061          ACTR COUNTER EXCEEDED
  87     IEU021          NEAR OPERAND COLUMN     4—SYMBOL NOT PREVIOUSLY DEFINED
  87     IEU001          NEAR OPERAND COLUMN     2—DUPLICATION FACTOR ERROR
  89     IEU003          NEAR OPERAND COLUMN     3—LENGTH ERROR
  91     IEU012          NEAR OPERAND COLUMN     7—RELOCATABLE SCALE MODIFIER
  93     IEU016          INVALID NAME
  96     IEU029          NEAR OPERAND COLUMN    17—CCW ERROR
 100     IEU021          NEAR OPERAND COLUMN     6—SYMBOL NOT PREVIOUSLY DEFINED
 101     IEU025          NEAR OPERAND COLUMN     1—RELOCATABILITY ERROR
 103     IEU023          PREVIOUSLY DEFINED NAME
 104     IEU026          NEAR OPERAND COLUMN     6—TOO MANY LEVELS OF PARENTHESES
 105     IEU027          NEAR OPERAND COLUMN    71—TOO MANY TERMS
 106     IEU087          NO ENDING APOSTROPHE
 107     IEU087          NO ENDING APOSTROPHE
 109     IEU107          NEAR OPERAND COLUMN     3—INVALID OPERAND
 110     IEU013          NEAR OPERAND COLUMN     3—EXPONENT MODIFIER ERROR
 111     IEU025          NEAR OPERAND COLUMN     1—RELOCATABILITY ERROR
 111     IEU056          NEAR OPERAND COLUMN     1—ARITHMETIC OVERFLOW
 111     IEU110          NEAR OPERAND COLUMN     1—EXPRESSION VALUE TOO LARGE
 113     IEU017          NEAR OPERAND COLUMN     3—DATA ITEM TOO LARGE
 114     IEU077          ILLEGAL CONTINUATION CARD
 115     IEU107          NEAR OPERAND COLUMN     9—INVALID OPERAND
 116     IEU039          NEAR OPERAND COLUMN     7—INVALID DELIMITER
 122     IEU019          EXTERNAL NAME ERROR
 126     IEU110          NEAR OPERAND COLUMN     1—EXPRESSION VALUE TOO LARGE
  74   STATEMENTS FLAGGED IN THIS ASSEMBLY
  12   WAS HIGHEST SEVERITY CODE
 371   PRINTED LINES
```

Fig. 17.1.1 *(Concluded)*

The assembler enters an indication following a bad statement, as is illustrated in Fig. 17.1.1. After the erroneous statement appears to call

$$*** \quad \text{ERROR} \quad *** \tag{17.1.1}$$

attention to the error. At the end of the printout is a section containing information called the **diagnostic area.** It is correlated to the statements produced by the assembler since each message (17.1.1) names the statement number, the particular line in the printout containing the error.

Diagnostics Figure 17.1.1 contains an example of an assembled program in which errors have been detected by the assembler. At the end of the printout is the diagnostic area. It is titled so as to be distinguished from the rest of the printout by the programmer. Statements in this area have the format

$$\text{stmt} \qquad \text{errorcode} \qquad \text{message} \tag{17.1.2}$$

Here the *stmt* refers to the statement number in which the error occurred; *errorcode* is a number indicating the type of error; *message* is an English sentence describing the type of error which occurred as found in Table 17.1.1.

Thus the programmer can relate an error message in the diagnostic to a statement in his program in which the error was found. The example illustrated in Fig. 17.1.1 will be examined in detail in the next section. A complete list of error codes and their meaning is provided in Table 17.1.1. The description there is more complete than the message printed in the program in the diagnostic area. That message may be a clarification or a pinpointing of the exact error committed.

17.2 ERROR EXAMPLE

The AL code found in Fig. 17.1.1 has been written to produce as many errors as possible so that the reader can be presented with an assortment of error readouts for his examination. It is virtually impossible to cause all possible errors to occur in a single program; those with severity code 20 will prevent assembly anyway. A representative group is provided here.

The job control language for doing the assembly has been omitted. The printout is now discussed in part.

Early errors Two early errors are noted by turning to the error diagnostics at the end of the printout. The first one has no statement number attached to it, and it indicates that a Y-type constant has appeared, which may cause trouble. A Y-type address constant is made up of only two bytes—the left portion of the constant is discarded. If there is useful information to the left of the first sixteen bits, the YCON will be incorrectly recorded.

The second error message indicates that the execute card for the assembly had an error.

Macrodefinition Many errors may arise in macrodefinition, only a few of which we shall now examine. At (3) we find a Boolean variable declared which is too large for $\mathcal{ASLR}$,&Q(300). Also in that statement we find &GLOBALB which contains too many letters. Notice also that a statement can have multiple errors, as this one does.

At (4) we declare an arithmetic symbol, &D, but &D also appears as argument in the prototype statement. At (7) a global declaration follows local declarations, which is illegal. At (8) we declare &R, which has already been declared (4). At (10) AIF is applied to a character variable instead of an expression. Statement (11) tries to set &UNDEF, which was not declared earlier.

There are several other errors pertaining to macrodefinitions appearing in this section of the program which should be scrutinized by the reader.

Other errors There is a total of seventy-four statements in this program that have errors associated with them. These should be examined to get a clear understanding of how the assembler tells the programmer what he has done wrong. Sometimes this is not always clear. For instance, START (42) is not an illegal statement as the message indicates, but it is placed illegally within the program—it is not permitted after CSECT. Often the message and error code interpretation don't give a clear picture of what the programmer has done wrong.

Cross-reference Following the program in Fig. 17.1.1 there is a cross-reference table. The first column, labeled SYMBOL, lists each symbol encountered by $\mathcal{ASLR}$. The next column describes the length of the symbol in bytes. The third column, VALUE, gives the machine language number in hexadecimal where the symbol is defined. The fourth column, DEFN, indicates the statement number which defines the symbol. The last column lists all the statements which refer to or use this symbol. Notice that some symbols, such as ADR, are defined but not used; others, such as AROUND, may be used only once; still others, such as M, may be used many times.

When a symbol is used but not defined, no entries can be placed in the second, third, and fourth columns. Instead, UNDEFINED appears here. This is the case for MASK, for which a reference appears as statement 64. 𝒜𝒮ℒℛ does not produce any code for that statement because of the undefined reference.

When two definitions appear for the same symbol, each is listed in the cross-reference table. However, only the first definition is used by 𝒜𝒮ℒℛ to produce code. The second is flagged under REFERENCES under DUPLICATES, as, for example, COMP.

A symbol may be improper in one way or another. For instance, at (93) we request a constant LONGSYMBOL. Since it is more than eight characters, 𝒜𝒮ℒℛ does not accept it, and it is not listed in the cross-reference table.

Error list Following the cross-reference table is a diagnostic table listing statements, error codes, and error messages as described in Chapter 2. At the end of the table is a summary of the diagnostic table and the code is printed.

17.3 SETUP, ENDUP

We'll now examine some more complicated macros, aimed at aiding the novice programmer.

Objective of SETUP Those who have read the book from the beginning encountered SETUP in Section 3.7, where it facilitates running simple assembly programs on third generation computers by the novice. As such, it provides all the setup required, but the beginning programmer need know nothing of what's being done for him. The experienced programmer can also save himself trouble with SETUP. Here are some of the functions SETUP performs:

- establishes and names the CSECT,
- *saves* GPRS,
- does BASE REGISTER allocation,
- gives DCBs for the PRINTER and the READER so that the programmer can bring in and print data with ease,
- provides references for the completion macro, ENDUP,

- *unsaves* GPRS at the end of the program when ENDUP is invoked,
- provides system return.

Arguments SETUP macrodefinition in Fig. 17.3.1 provides five arguments in the prototype statement, which we now examine. These and the SET symbols are abstracted into Table 17.3.1.

Table 17.3.1 ARGUMENTS AND SET SYMBOLS FOR THE MACRODEFINITION OF SETUP

&FR—First of a consecutive set of registers to be used as base in this CSECT but at least 2.
&LR—Last of the set of consecutive registers to be used as base, but at most 12.
&EXIT—Name of exit for ENDUP.
&LCE—"Last card exit"—exit when READER, RDR, is out of cards.

- - -

&SETUPSW—Switch set to 1 if SETUPS was used before.
&NAME—Name given to this CSECT—either &N or $BLANK if &N is absent.
&REG(1)-&REG(4)—SET symbols for BASE REGISTER specification in USING.
&INDEX—Number used to set up storage for REGISTERS.
&TEST—Number of REGISTERS required by the CSECT.
&CC—Length of CSECT name.
&C1234—Constant to set up &R(i).
&FR—High REGISTER for USING.
&AR—Low REGISTER for USING, also pointer to old *save* area.
&D—Self-relative quantity for branch around name of CSECT.
&COUNT8—Count for the number of characters assigned to &REG(i).

CSECT

A new section of the program is defined by SETUP, and it is given the name which appears at *name* in the macrocall. If the macro is unnamed, we might expect that the section is also unnamed. This would lead to trouble in referencing. Hence, instead, the section is called $BLANK.

BASE REGISTERS

For small programs, SETUP automatically assigns GPR12 as a BASE REGISTER. However, we use SETUP within REG and possibly in other macros where we might employ other GPRS as BASE REGISTERS. A range of BASE REGISTERS is requested by supplying the lower numbered one at &FR and the higher numbered one at &LR, provided that the range of REGISTERS lies between 2 and 12.

EXIT

A windup subroutine is embedded in SETUP at &EXIT and may be named by the user with EXIT. This name is necessary in the call where SETUP appears more than once in the program. (The novice will not do that, hopefully.) Notice that if this exit is not named at &EXIT, a default option is supplied and the exit is named $RESTORE.

It is possible that the programmer may be running his job with no job following. In this case the reader will have no more cards to read after his last data card and the /* card, It requires an exit to the system. The programmer may name his exit; but if none is supplied, SETUP uses as the last card exit, EOJ.

LAST CARD

SET symbols Also in Table 17.3.1 is a list of SET symbols declared at the beginning of SETUP. A globals witch, &SETUPSW, reduces the amount of code produced if the macro should be called a second time. &NAME will have the name of the CSECT after it is determined. As many as eleven BASE REGISTERS can be provided; the subscripted SET symbols &REG(i) store this character information—these should appear in the assembly listing as characters, even though numbers are used in the REGISTER assignment. &TEST and &INDEX are used to set up the REGISTER manipulation within the macro, as is &C1234. &CC contains the length of the CSECT name which is necessary to set up the branch around the constant after it is declared. Other SET symbols are self-explanatory.

CSECT determination Let us now examine the macrodefinition of SETUP in Fig. 17.3.1. The number of characters in the name is counted and entered into &CC (6). Next a number of tests are done to determine which REGISTERS are used as BASE REGISTERS (7–11). The parenthesized numbers are those at the right of each command.

If no name is provided (12), &NAME is set to $BLANK (13), and the character count is set to 6 (14). Otherwise, the actual name is substituted (17); its length has already been counted.

A number of steps is now done to set up the name (51), placing the number of characters in the name in the constant which precedes it (50). Preceding that is, in turn, a *branch* (49). In taking this branch, we must be sure to land on a halfWord boundary (all BAL commands must start on such boundaries). Therefore, &D is calculated and rounded off according to whether the number of characters in the CSECT name is even or odd. This accounts for the tests and setting of SET symbols (23–27).

Registers For no REGISTER specification (7), &AR is set to 12 (8). If the first REGISTER mentioned is less than 2 (10), this is an error and produces an error message (84); otherwise &AR is set to that REGISTER (11).

Later, check if a second REGISTER indication is missing (18): if so, set &ER the same as &AR (19); otherwise, barring specification errors (21, 84), set &ER for that REGISTER (22).

```
         MACRO
&N       SETUP   &FR,&LR,&EXIT=$RESTORE,&LCE=EOJ
         GBLB    &SETUPSW
         LCLC    &REG(4),&NAME
         LCLA    &INDEX,&TEST,&CC,&C1234,&COUNT8,&ER,&D,&AR
&CC      SETA    K'&N
         AIF     ('&FR' NE ' ').W
&AR      SETA    12
         AGO     .S
.W       AIF     (&FR LT 2).IBRA
&AR      SETA    &FR
.S       AIF     ('&N' NE ' ').T
&NAME    SETC    '$BLANK'
&CC      SETA    6
         AGO     .U
.T       ANOP
&NAME    SETC    '&N'
.U       AIF     ('&LR' NE ' ').Q
&ER      SETA    &AR
         AGO     .R
.Q       AIF     (&LR GT 12 OR &LR LT &AR).IBRA
&ER      SETA    &LR
.R       AIF     (&CC/2 EQ (&CC+1)/2).EVEN
&D       SETA    &CC+1
         AGO     .V
.EVEN    ANOP
&D       SETA    &CC+2
.V       ANOP
&INDEX   SETA    &AR
&TEST    SETA    &ER
```

```
&C1234        SETA      1
.LOOP         AIF       (&INDEX LT 10).ADD2
&COUNT8       SETA      &COUNT8+3
              AGO       .CHECK8
.ADD2         ANOP
&COUNT8       SETA      &COUNT8+2
.CHECK8       AIF       (&COUNT8 GT 8).ADD1
&REG(&C1234)  SETC      '&REG(&C1234)'.','.'&INDEX'
&INDEX        SETA      &INDEX+1
              AIF       (&INDEX LE &TEST).LOOP
              AGO       .CSECT
.ADD1         ANOP
&C1234        SETA      &C1234+1
&COUNT8       SETA      0
              AGO       .LOOP
.CSECT        ANOP
&NAME         CSECT
              USING     &NAME,15 TEMPORARY BASE REGISTER
              B         *+4+&D      BRANCH AROUND DCS
              DC        ALI(&CC) NUMBER OF CHARACTERS IN CSECT NAME
              DC        C'&NAME'      CSECT NAME
              STM       14,12,12(13) SAVE REGS IN CSA
              LR        14,15
              GETMAIN   R,LV=72
              LR        15,14
              ST        13,4(1) STORE CSA ADR IN NSA
              LR        &AR,13 STORE CSA ADR IN FIRST REQUESTED BASE REG
              LR        13,1      LOAD R13 W/ADR OF NSA
```

Fig. 17.3.1 Macrodefinition of SETUP.

```
         ST     13,8(&AR) STORE NSA ADR IN PREVIOUS SAVE AREA          000059
         CNOP   0,4                                                    000060
         LM     &AR,&ER,*+8      LOAD REQUESTED BASE REG(S)            000061
         USING  &NAME&REG(1)&REG(2)&REG(3)&REG(4)                      000062
         DROP   15                                                     000063
&INDEX   SETA   0                                                      000064
&TEST    SETA   &ER-&AR                                                000065
         B      *+4+4*(&TEST+1)+14                                     000066
 LOOP1   DC     A(&NAME+&INDEX*4096)                                   000067
&INDEX   SETA   &INDEX+1                                               000068
         AIF    (&INDEX LE &TEST).LOOP1                                000069
&EXIT    L      13,4(13) RESTORE REG13                                 000070
         MVI    12(13),X'FF' RETURN CODE TO R14 IN SAVE AREA           000071
         LM     14,12,12(13) RESTORE R14-R12                           000072
         BR     14                                                     000073
         AIF    (&SETUPSW).END                                         000074
         OPEN   (RDR,(INPUT),PRTR,(OUTPUT))                            000075
         B      $BEGIN                                                 000076
RDR      DCB    DDNAME=SYSIN,DSORG=PS,EODAD=&LCE,                      000077
                EROPT=ABE,LRECL=80,MACRF=(GM),RECFM=FB                 000078
PRTR     DCB    DDNAME=PRINTER2,BLKSIZE=1330,DSORG=PS,EROPT=ACC,      C000079
                LRECL=133,MACRF=PM,OPTCD=U,RECFM=FBA                   000080
$BEGIN   DS     OH                                                     000081
&SETUPSW SETB   1                                                      000082
.END     MEXIT                                                         000083
.IBRA    MNOTE  12,'INVALID BASE REGISTER ASSIGNMENT'                  000084
         MEND                                                          000085
```

Fig. 17.3.1 *(Continued)*

USING

The USING for the CSECT being established is at (62); we want to set up &REG(1) through &REG(4) for it in the loop (29–45). The difficulty is that any character SET symbol can only store a maximum of six characters. Depending upon how many BASE REGISTERS are allocated, we shall need up to four character SET symbols to represent the composite statement to appear at USING. This is best seen as an example.

EXAMPLE

When only one register is to be assigned, the macro SETUP appears as

FIRST SETUP 3 (17.3.1)

creating the USING statement at (62) which appears thus:

USING FIRST,3 (17.3.2)

The original definition statement LCLC (4) establishes four SET symbols named &REG(i). It also initializes these to null characters. The loop which we examine shortly establishes &REG(1) thus:

(&REG(1))=,3 (17.3.3)

Since the other three character symbols are null when concatenated, they provide the proper USING as shown in (17.3.2).

Now let us examine a call of SETUP which will use as BASE REGISTERS the five GPRS numbered 8 through 12. The call is given as

SECOND SETUP 8,12 (17.3.4)

USING should then appear as

USING SECOND,8,9,10,11,12 (17.3.5)

There will not be enough room in one character symbol to represent all the information required. This can be done using two character symbols, thus:

(&REG(1))=,8,9,10 (&REG(2))=,11,12 (17.3.6)

ESTABLISHMENT

An arithmetic SET symbol stores the number of characters allocated so far to the present character SET symbol &REG(i). It is called &COUNT8. When the number of the GPR is less than 10, we are going to add a comma and a numeral to the present SET symbol; when greater than or equal to 10, we add a comma and two numerals.

Now let us examine the loop for setting up &REG(1) which starts at (32). Here we check the contents of &INDEX and if it is greater than or equal to 10, we add 3 to the setting of &COUNT8 (33). Otherwise we add only 2 (36). Then we check and if the addition of the new characters would cause a symbol of greater than eight characters (37), we go to

.ADD1 (42). If not, it is possible to concatenate the comma and the numeral(s) to the present character symbol (38). Thereafter we advance the setting of &INDEX (39) and check to see if all the REGISTERS for USING are accounted for (40). If so, we jump out of this loop (41); otherwise we return (32) to check the next REGISTER assignment.

The arithmetic SET symbol called &C1234 keeps track of what character SET symbol we are operating with. It is set to 1 as we enter the loop (31). It is advanced by 1 after .ADD1 whenever the character SET symbol overflows.

CSECT The CSECT is declared (47) and its name is stored in a fixed location. Thereafter (50, 51), GPR15 is used temporarily, since the address of the start of the program placed there by OS360 is not required (48). The present GPRS are *saved* in the caller's *save* area (52). A new *save* area is obtained with GETMAIN (54). We initialize it thus:

- Use first BASE REGISTER for *save* pointer (57).
- Put pointer to new *save* area in GPR13 (58).
- Provide backward pointer to caller's *save* area (56).
- Provide forward pointer from caller's *save* area (59).

BASE The actual GPRS required as BASE REGISTERS are loaded (61), using an area defined later (67), declared (62), and GPR15 is dropped (63). &INDEX is set to 0 (64) and &TEST to the number of BASE REGISTERS (65) for two reasons:

1. A *branch* around the constant area is created (66):
   (a) measured from the B (*),
   (b) four bytes for each GPR: (4+4*(&TEST+1)),
   (c) fourteen bytes for the exit, &EXIT.
2. The loop creates the proper constants (67–69):
   (a) &NAME is the name of the CSECT (47),
   (b) one multiple of 4096 is added to each GPR area (67),
   (c) &INDEX holds this multiple—it is increased (68) and tested (69).

OPEN OPEN (75) opens the READER and PRINTER and the system input, (INPUT) and (OUTPUT), should they be different. DCBs are needed for RDR (77) and PRTR (79), but not for the others. Note that OPEN is included *only* if SETUP was not used before as noted by &SETUPSW (74)—the *branch* (66) takes us to either the OPEN (75) or the start of the program (85 + 1).

After OPEN, *branch* (76) around the DCBs to $BEGN, which establishes halfWord boundaries (81), sets the SETUP switch (82), and ends (83).

EXIT The exit at &EXIT (70) will be used by ENDUP. It *unsaves* (70–72) and returns to OS360 (73).

```
1                MACRO
2                ENDUP
3                CNOP      0,4
4       EOJ      BAL       1,*+16
5                DC        AL1(0)
6                DC        AL3(PRTR)
7                DC        AL1(0)
8                DC        AL3(RDR)
9                DC        AL1(128)
10               DC        VL3(REG010)
11               SVC       20
12               B         $RESTORE
13               MEND
```

Fig. 17.3.2 Definition of ENDUP.

ENDUP ENDUP is defined in Fig. 17.3.2. It has two purposes:

1. Close files:
   (a) PRTR and RDR as established in SETUP (5–8),
   (b) REG010 as established in REG (9, 10), Section 17.4,
   (c) use CLOSE directly through SVC (11).
2. *Unsave* using $RESTORE in SETUP at &EXIT by default.

17.4 REG

Purpose REG is a macro the purpose of which is to produce a printout in the program of the contents of a list of REGISTERS supplied in the call.

Two parts The macrodefinition in Fig. 17.4.1 consists of two distinct parts. The first is a call interpretation which determines the GPRS to be printed. The second part, below the dashed line, sets up a separate CSECT for the macro, finds the contents of the desired REGISTER, and then prints them out.

The interpretation part of the macrodefinition consists of determining which registers are to be printed and then setting up a halfWord. There is one bit in the halfWord for each one of the GPRS. If a printout is desired, this bit is set to 1; if not, it is set to 0. This halfWord will be transmitted to second part to cause the printout.

```
                MACRO
&NAME           REG         &REG
                GBLB        &REGSW
                LCLA        &X,&Y
                LCLB        &R(16)
                LCLC        &ID
                AIF         ('&NAME' NE '  ').D
&ID             SETC        '$REG&SYSNDX'
                AGO         .E
.D              ANOP
&ID             SETC        '&NAME'
.F              ANOP
&NAME           BAL         1,*+14
                AIF         ('&REG' NE '  ').A
                DC          X'FFFF'
                AGO         .C
.A              ANOP
&X              SETA        1
.B              ANOP
&Y              SETA        &REG(&X)
&Y              SETA        &Y+1
&R(&Y)          SETB        1
&X              SETA        &X+1
                AIF         (&X LE N'&REG).B
                DC          B'&R(1)&R(2)&R(3)&R(4)&R(5)&R(6)&R(7)&R(8)&R(9)
                              &R(10)&R(*11)&R(12)&R(13)&R(14)&R(15)&R(16)'
.C              DC          CL8'&ID'
                L           15,=V(REGISTER)
                BALR        14,15
                AIF         (&REGSW).END
REGISTER        SETUP       2,EXIT=$EXIT
                STM         0,15,REG99S
                L           10,4(13)
                L           8,24(10)
                L           10,28(10)
                ST          10,REG99S+8
                MVC         REGO14+40(8),2(8)
                OPEN        (REG010,OUTPUT)
                PUT         REG010,REG014
                PUT         REG010,REG015
                SR          3,3
                MVI         REG001+3,0
REG009          LA          4,128
REG003          STC         4,REG001+1
REG001          TM          0(8),0
                BO          REG004
REG002          LA          3,1(3)
                SRL         4,1
                LTR         4,4
```

Fig. 17.4.1 Macrodefinition of REG.

```
                BZ        REG008
                B         REG003
REG004          LA        6,4
                LA        7,REG013+9
                LR        5,3
                SLL       5,2
                LA        5,REG99S(5)
                L         9,0(5)
REG005          MVC       REG99H,0(5)
                MVC       REG99L,0(5)
                PACK      REG99H,REG99H
                NI        REG99H,X'OF'
                TR        REG99H,REG99T
                NI        REG99L,X'OF'
                TR        REG99L,REG99T
                MVC       0(2,7),REG99H
                LA        7,2(7)
                LA        5,1(5)
                BCT       6,REG005
                STC       3,REG013+6
                TR        REG013+6(1),REG99T
                CVD       9,REG011
                UNPK      REG012,REG011+3(5)
                OI        REG012+8,X'F0'
                MVC       REG013+25(8),REG012+1
                PUT       REG010,REG013
                B         REG002
REG008          CLI       REG001+3,1
                BE        $EXIT
                MVI       REG001+3,1
                B         REG009
REG99S          DS        16F
REG99T          DC        C'0123456789ABCDEF'
REG99H          DS        CL1
REG99L          DS        CL1
REG014          DC        CL121'1CONTENTS OF GENERAL PURPOSE
                            REGISTERS'
REG015          DC        CL9'0',C'HEXADECIMAL      DECIMAL',CL89'  '
REG013          DC        C'0GPR      *       ',CL112'  '
REG011          DS        D
REG012          DS        CL9
REG010          DCB       DDNAME=SYSPRINT,BLKSIZE=1210,DSORG=PS,
                            EROPT=ACC,LRECL=121,MACRF=PM,
                            OPTCD=U,RECFM=FBA
&REGSW          SETB      1
&SYSECT         CSECT
.END            MEND
```

Fig. 17.4.1 *(Continued)*

SETUP

The setup portion of the macrodefinition creates code which appears only once in the program and acts like a closed subroutine. A new section called REGISTER is created by calling the macro SETUP. This CSECT contains all the commands to find the contents of the desired records and cause them to be printed.

Interpretation Figure 17.4.1 at the beginning contains statements to do the interpretation (99–127). Several set symbols are used:

- &REGSW is a global Boolean variable which indicates whether REG was called before. If so, the setup is omitted.
- &X, &Y are constants for performing an assembly loop, as discussed later.
- &R(16) is an array of sixteen Boolean variables to be used to identify the REGISTERS for printout.
- &ID is a character set symbol which holds the name assigned to the code produced.

NAME

The name assigned to this code is the name of the macrocall provided at &NAME, if such is furnished. If the call is unnamed, then a name is assigned to it, $REG&SYSNDX (106). Of course 𝒜𝔖𝔏ℜ substitutes the present macrocall number for &SYSNDX.

COMMANDS CREATED

The first part of REG creates only a few actual commands:

- BAL (111) causes a jump around constants created to the linkage setup and exit.
- The halfWord either is all 1's (113) or made up from the set symbol array (123);
- Provide the name or identifier of the call (124).

Inner loop The inner loop is to set up the halfWord at 123. First we check to see if any list is furnished (112) and, if not, the halfWord is defined as all 1's (113).

Where a list is furnished, we set up an index to go through the list. We have established an array, &R(i), which consists of sixteen bits. The subscript i ranges from one to sixteen. However, these represent the GPRS which are numbered from 0 to 15.

&X represents the subscript to be used for going through the list of REGISTERS furnished by the user. It is set to 1 (116). This enables us to get the first REGISTER number furnished the first time around, or the *i*th one furnished the *i*th time around. This number is obtained and is used to set &Y. But, we have to add 1 to &Y to get the position in the array which is to be set to 1 (119). This number is used to get into the array and set that bit to 1 (120). Now we advance &X to do this same operation for the next number in the list (121). However, first we check to see if we have taken care of all the numbers in the list (122). If so, we drop through and set up the constants (123).

Setup To establish the second part of the macro-definition, we use the setup macro defined earlier and call SETUP (128). This defines a new CSECT called REGISTER which uses GPR2 as a base and $EXIT as an exit.

Thereafter we store the entire group of GPRS (129). GPR13 has a backward pointer to the previous *save* area, which is now placed in GPR10 (130). We want to get the old GPR1 from the *save* area and put it in GPR8 as a pointer to the parameter list established above at (123, 130). Next we get the contents of old GPR2 and place it in GPR10 (128). These were the contents before SETUP. It is returned to the *save* area that we established above (133).

The parameter pointer is in GPR8. The third byte contains the identifier which is to be placed in the label (134). We now open the printer (135), print the page header (136) and then the column head (137).

Format Let us examine the formatting of the contents of a REGISTER, using different symbols than are in the actual macro for the sake of information. This portion appears in Fig. 17.4.2. The figure is divided into five parts which consist of

- initialization,
- conversion of four bits at a time into hexadecimal,
- entry of the GPR number,
- conversion of the contents into decimal,
- printout.

INITIALIZATION

First put 4 in GPR6 (149) and load the address of the hexadecimal area into GPR7 (150). Load the binary identifier of the REGISTER into GPR5. Shift the number two positions leftward to get the byte number in the *save* area (152). Load the address of the byte number into GPR5 (153). Load GPR9 with the number to be converted.

HEXADECIMAL

Two single character locations are labeled HINIBL and LONIBL. These are filled with eight bits which are to be converted (155–156). The command PACK switches the nibbles within the byte called HINIBL. Its top nibble is zeroed out (158). This byte is used to enter into a table from which is drawn the character equivalent of the hexadecimal nibble used to translate the command (159). Now HINIBL contains the character

```
149   FOUND   LA      6,4
150           LA      7,HEX
151           L       S,BINID
152           SLL     S,2
153           LA      5,SAVE95
154           L       9,0(5)

155   LOOP    MVC     HINIBLE, 0(5)
156           MVC     LONIBL,0(5)
157           PACK    HINIBL,HINIBL
158           NI      HINIBL,X'0F'
159           TR      HINIBL,TABLE
160           NI      LONIBL,X'0F'
161           TR      LONIBL,TABLE
162A          MVC     0(1,7),HINIBLE
162B          MVC     1(1,7)LONIBL
163           LA      7,2(7)
164           LA      5,1(5)
165           BCT     6,LOOP

166           STC     3,NUM
167           TR      NUM,TABLE

168           CVD     9,DW
169           UNPK    CL9,DW+3(5)
170           OI      CL9+8,'X'FO'
171           MVC     DEL(8),CL9+1

172           PUT     REGCONT
173           B
```

Fig. 17.4.2 Formatting for REG.

equivalent of the hexadecimal number in the first nibble of the character withdrawn.

The same thing is done with the lower nibble. Its higher nibble is zeroed out (160) and then translated using the table (160). These two characters are now placed in the proper position for output (162). The output position is then stepped ahead by 2 (163). The address of the next pair of nibbles to be converted is placed in GPR5 (164). If there are more to be converted, we return to LOOP (165).

GPR NUMBER

Assuming that the number of the GPR to be printed is now contained in GPR3, this is placed in a section NUM (166). The same table used in the procedure above is used to replace this number by its character equivalent (167).

DECIMAL

The call for the contents of the GPR to be converted is also placed in GPR 9. To use *convert to decimal* CVD, the source is a GPR and the destination a double Word (168). Thereafter DW contains the packed decimal equivalent of the register contents. It is then unpacked into the nine character area, CR9 (169). The sign byte is then fixed up (170) and the field is moved for output (171).

OUTPUT

Output consists only of PUT.

Identification Let us now examine how REGISTER identification is performed. It is a little tricky and so again its commands are abstracted into Fig. 17.4.3.

```
138          SR      3,3
139          MVI     $TM+3,0
140   MASK   L       4,=X'00000080'
141   MORE   STC     4,$TM+1
142   $TM    TM      0(8),0
143          BO      FOUND
144          LA      3,1(3)
145          $RL     4,1
146          LTR     4,4
147          B2      FIX
148          B       MORE
174   FIX    CLI     $TM+3,1
175          BE      $EXIT
176          MVI     $TM+5,1
177          B       MASK
```

Fig. 17.4.3 Register determination for REG.

MASK

The first thing that we do is set up a mask and GPR3 is cleared to 0, for it will keep count of the number of times that the mask is used (138). Now the test under mask command at $TM is set up so that we are sure it contains a zero in its final byte (139). Now we establish a mask in GPR4 consisting of all 0's except for a 1 in the eighth bit from the right (140). This mask is stored into the second byte of the command at $TM (141). We are now ready to perform the test upon the halfWord provided in the parameter list. The pointer to that list is in GPR8. Therefore 0(8) is the address of the first byte containing 1's or 0's, according to which GPRS were specified in the call of REG. The first time around we check only the leftmost bit (142).

The action of TM is to set the condition code. The condition code is tested with BO to see if the masked bits are all 1's. If so, an identifier bit has been found and a branch occurs to FOUND.

RESET

Now we are going to reset the bit in the mask. Before doing this, we advance the counter by 1 (144). Next we shift the 1 in GPR4 one position rightward (146). After going through the loop eight times, we shall have pushed the 1 in GPR4 out through the right side. GPR4 will be empty, as revealed by (146). We test for this case (147) and, if so, we go to fix the mask. Otherwise we return to check another bit (148).

FIX

We are going to fix up the mask at FIX. We insert a 1 in the fourth byte of $TM so that the command TM will check the next byte of the identifier halfWord (176). This is done only if that byte presently does not contain a 1 (174–175). If that is the case, we are done with all the bits in the identifier and can leave the routine.

APPENDIX **A**

OS360AL COMMANDS

AL	*Code*	*Description*	*Section*
A	b	add fullWord	2.4
ABEND	mos	end job abnormal	14.9
ACTR	c	assy loop limit	10.7
AD	f	add double	2.10
ADR	f	add double register	2.10
AE	f	add short	2.10
AER	f	add short register	2.10
AGO	c	assembly *branch*	10.7
AH	b	add half	2.4
AIF	c	assembly if	10.1
AL	b	add logical	2.4
ALR	b	add logical register	2.4
AND	c	connective *and*	10.5
ANOP	c	assembly NOP	10.7
AP	d	add packed	2.8
AR	b	add register	2.4
ATTACH	ml	get a task	15.1
AU	f	add short unnormalized	2.10
AUR	f	add short unnormalized register	2.10
AW	f	add long unnormalized	2.10
AWR	f	add long unnormalized register	2.10
B	x	branch	2.5
BAL	r	branch and link	2.6
BALR	r	branch and link register	2.6
BC	r	branch, condition	2.5
BCR	r	branch, condition register	2.5
BCT	r	branch on count	2.6

AL	*Code*	*Description*	*Section*
BCTR	r	branch on count register	2.6
BE	x	branch equal	2.5
BH	x	branch high	2.5
BL	x	branch low	2.5
BLDL	ma	build directory	14.7
BM	x	branch minus	2.5
BM	x	branch mixed	2.5
BNE	x	branch not equal	2.5
BNH	x	branch not high	2.5
BNL	x	branch not low	2.5
BNM	x	branch not minus	2.5
BNO	x	branch not zero	2.5
BNP	x	branch not plus	2.5
BNZ	x	branch not zero	2.5
BP	x	branch plus	2.5
BO	x	branch ones	2.5
BO	x	branch overflow	2.5
BR	x	branch	2.5
BSP	ma	backspace a record	14.7
BUILD	ma	pool buffers	14.7
BXH	r	branch index high	2.6
BXLE	r	branch index high equal	2.6
BZ	x	branch zero	2.5
C	b	compare Word	2.4
CALL	ml	⇒ sr	15.0
CAMLST	mc	list for catalog request	14.11
CATALOG	mc	catalog a file	14.11
CCW	p	define CCW	12.3
CD	f	compare double	2.10
CDR	f	compare double register	2.10
CE	f	compare short	2.10
CER	f	compare short register	2.10
CH	b	compare half	2.4
CHAP	mp	change priority	14.10
CHECK	ma	see if IO is done	14.6
CLC	v	compare logical character	2.7
CLI	i	compare logical immediate	2.11
CLOSE	maj	close a file	14.5
CLR	b	compare logical register	2.4
CNOP	x	align on boundary	2.5
CNTRL	ma	control a device	14.7
COM	p	define common	13.6
COPY	p	copy AL code	12.2
CP	d	compare packed	2.8
CR	b	compare register	2.4
CSECT	p	identify section	13.1
CVB	b	convert to binary	2.4
CVD	b	convert to decimal	2.4
CVT	mos	write communication vectors	14.9

AL	Code	Description	Section
CXD	p	external dummy length	
D	b	divide Word	2.4
DC	p	define constant	3.1
DCB	ma	make DCB	14.4
DCBD	ma	make DCECT for DCB	14.7
DD	f	divide double	2.10
DDR	f	divide double register	2.10
DE	f	divide short	2.10
DELETE	mos	reduce use count	14.9
DEQ	mp	release resource	14.10
DER	f	divide short register	2.10
DETACH	mp	delete task	14.10
DEVTYPE	mos	report on device	14.9
DP	d	divide packed	2.8
DR	b	divide register	2.4
DROP	p	drop base register	12.1
DS	p	define storage	3.2
DSECT	p	dummy section	13.2
DXD	p	define external dummy	
ED	v	edit	2.7
EDMK	v	edit and mask	2.7
EJECT	p	start new page	12.2
END	p	end of AL input	12.2
ENTRY	q	entry	13.3
ENQ	mp	request a resource	14.10
EQ	c	relation *equal*	10.5
EQU	p	equate symbols	12.3
ESET	m	end sequential access	14.7
EX	r	execute	2.6
EXCP	mos	do IO program	14.9
EXTRN	q	external reference	13.2
FEOV	ma	force EOV	14.7
FIND	ma	find record	14.7
FREEBUF	ma	return pool buffer	14.7
FREED	ma	free buffer	14.7
FREEMAIN	mos	free part of MEMORY	14.9
GBLA	c	global arithmetic	10.3
GBLB	c	global binary	10.3
GBLC	c	global character	10.3
GE	c	relation *greater equal*	10.5
GET	ma	get	14.6
GETMAIN	mos	get MAIN MEMORY	14.9
GETPOOL	ma	build pool	14.7
GT	c	relation *greater than*	10.5
HDR	f	halve double register	2.10
HER	f	halve short register	2.10
HIO	s	halt IO	2.9
IC	b	insert character	2.4
ICTL	p	new AL input format	12.2

AL	*Code*	*Description*	*Section*
IDENTIFY	mp	set dynamic entry	14.10
INDEX	mc	change index	14.11
ISEQ	p	check AL sequence	12.2
ISK	s	insert system key	2.9
L	b	load Word	2.4
LCDR	f	load complement double register	2.10
LCER	f	load complement short register	2.10
LE	c	relation *less equal*	10.5
LCLA	c	local arithmetic	10.3
LCLB	c	local binary	10.3
LCLC	c	local character	10.3
LCR	b	load complement register	2.4
LD	f	load double	2.10
LDR	f	load double register	2.10
LE	f	load short	2.10
LER	f	load short register	2.10
LINK	ml	get SR and ⇒ SR	15.8
LM	b	load multiple	2.11
LNR	b	load negative register	2.4
LNDR	f	load negative double register	2.10
LNER	f	load negative short register	2.10
LOAD	ml	get SR	15.8
LOCATE	mc	locate subcatalog	14.11
LPDR	f	load positive double register	2.10
LPER	f	load positive short register	2.10
LPR	b	load positive register	2.4
LPSW	s	load PSW	2.9
LR	b	load register	2.4
LT	c	relation *less than*	10.5
LTDR	f	load and test double register	2.10
LTER	f	load and test short register	2.10
LTORG	p	start literal pool	12.2
LTR	b	load and test register	2.4
M	b	multiply	2.4
MACRO	p	start macrodefinition	6.1
MD	f	multiply double	2.10
MDR	f	multiply double register	2.10
ME	f	multiply short	2.10
MEND	p	end of macrodefinition	6.1
MER	f	multiply short register	2.10
MEXIT	c	macro exit	10.7
MH	b	multiply half	2.4
MNOTE	c	note about macro	10.7
MP	d	multiply packed	2.8
MR	b	multiply register	2.4
MVC	v	move	2.7
MVI	i	move immediate	2.11
MVN	v	move numeric	2.7
MVO	d	move with offset	2.8

AL	*Code*	*Description*	*Section*
MVZ	v	move zone	2.7
N	b	*and* Word	2.4
NC	v	*and* character	2.7
NE	c	relation *not equal*	10.5
NI	i	*and* immediate	2.11
NOP	x	no operation	2.5
NOPR	x	no operation register	2.5
NOT	c	connective *not*	10.5
NOTE	ma	note last record	14.7
NR	b	*and* register	2.4
O	b	*or*	2.4
OBTAIN	mc	get DSCB from VTOC	14.11
OC	v	*or* character	2.7
OI	i	*or* immediate	2.11
OPEN	mu	open a file	14.5
OR	b	*or* register	2.4
OR	l	connective *or*	10.5
ORG	p	set location counter	12.2
PACK	d	pack	2.8
POINT	pa	set device per request	14.7
POST	mos	show event done	14.9
PRINT	p	print as specified	12.2
PRTOV	ma	test printer	14.7
PUNCH	p	punch a card only	12.2
PURGE	mos	clear task IOBs	14.9
PUT	ma	write a record	14.6
PUTX	ma	put record from GET	14.7
READ	ma	read a record	14.6
RELSE	ma	release this buffer	14.7
RELEX	ma	release file control	14.7
RENAME	mc	rename a file	14.11
REPRO	p	repro next card only	12.2
RESTORE	mos	put IOB on IOB list	14.9
RDJFCB	mos	read JFCB	14.9
RETURN	ml	SR ⇒ main program	15.8
S	b	subtract Word	2.4
SAVE	ml	(GPRS) → save area	15.8
SCRATCH	mc	uncatalog file	14.11
SD	f	subtract double	2.10
SDR	f	subtract double register	2.10
SE	f	subtract short	2.10
SEGLD	mp	get overlay segment	14.10
SEGWT	mp	get overlay; wait	14.10
SER	f	subtract short register	2.10
SETL	ma	set file start	14.7
SETPRT	ma	print message	14.7
SETA	c	arithmetic set operation	10.4
SETB	c	binary set operation	10.4
SETC	c	character set operation	10.4

AL	*Code*	*Description*	*Section*
SH	b	subtract half	2.4
SIO	s	start IO	2.9
SL	b	subtract, logical	2.4
SLA	b	shift left arithmetic	2.11
SLDA	b	shift left double arithmetic	2.11
SLDL	b	shift left double logical	2.11
SLL	b	shift left logical	2.11
SLR	b	subtract logical register	2.4
SNAP	mos	dump selective	14.9
SP	d	subtract packed	2.8
SPACE	p	skip lines	12.2
SPIE	mos	include interrupt exit	14.9
SPM	s	set program mark	2.9
SR	b	subtract	2.4
SRA	b	shift right arithmetic	2.11
SRDA	b	shift right double arithmetic	2.11
SRDL	b	shift right double logical	2.11
SRL	b	shift right logical	2.11
SSK	s	set system key	2.9
ST	b	store	2.4
STAE	mos	set termination exit	14.9
START	p	start assembly	13.1
STC	b	store character	2.4
STD	f	store double	2.10
STE	f	store short	2.10
STH	b	store half	2.4
STIMER	mos	set timer	14.9
STM	b	store multiple	2.11
STOW	ma	write directory entry	14.7
SU	f	subtract short unnormalized	2.10
SUR	f	subtract short unnormalized register	2.10
SVC	r	supervisor call	2.9
SW	f	subtract long unnormalized	2.10
SWR	f	subtract long unnormalized register	2.10
SYNADAF	ma	analyze error	14.7
SYNADRLS	ma	error message	14.7
TCH	s	test channel	2.9
TIME	mp	enter time, date	14.10
TIO	s	test IO	2.9
TITLE	p	head page with	12.2
TM	i	test under mark	2.11
TR	v	translate	2.7
TRT	v	translate and test	2.7
TRUNC	ma	release output buffer	14.7
TS	i	test and set	2.11
TTIMER	mos	test TIMER	14.9
USING	p	are BASE REGISTERS	12.1
WRITE	ma	write a record	14.6
WTOR	mos	WTO, expect reply	14.9

AL	*Code*	*Description*	*Section*
WTO	mos	write to operator	14.9
WAIT	mos	wait for event(s) end(s)	14.9
WTL	mp	write to log	14.10
X	b	*exclusive or* Word	2.4
XC	v	*exclusive or* character	2.7
XCTL	ml	get, ⇒ w/o return	15.0
XDAP	mos	do disk IO program	14.9
XI	c	*exclusive or* immediate	2.11
XR	b	*exclusive or*	2.4
ZAP	d	zero and add	2.8
&SYSNDX	c	system index	9.4
*	p	comment	10.7
.*	c	macro comment	10.7

Code	*Description*
f	floating point arithmetic
b	binary
r	reflexive
x	extended
v	VFL
d	decimal—packed
s	supervisor mode
i	immediate
p	pseudo
q	quasi
ma	access method macros
mos	operation system macros
mc	catalog macros
mp	multiprogramming macros

APPENDIX **B**

OS360AL COMMANDS BY CLASS

Binary AL	*Description*	*Section*
Fixed point		
A	add Word	2.4
AH	add half	2.4
AL	add logical Word	2.4
ALR	add logical half	2.4
AR	add register	2.4
C	compare Word	2.4
CH	compare half	2.4
CL	compare logical Word	2.4
CLR	compare logical register	2.4
CR	compare register	2.4
CVB	convert to binary	2.4
CVD	convert to decimal	2.4
D	divide Word	2.4
DR	divide register	2.4
IC	insert character	2.4
L	load Word	2.4
LCR	load complement register	2.4
LM	load multiple	2.11
LNR	load negative register	2.4
LPR	load positive register	2.4
LR	load register	2.4
LTR	load and test register	2.4
M	multiply	2.4
MH	multiply half	2.4
MR	multiply register	2.4

AL	Description	Section
N	*and* Word	2.4
NR	*and* register	2.4
O	*or* Word	2.4
OR	*or* register	2.4
S	subtract Word	2.4
SH	subtract half	2.4
SL	subtract logical Word	2.4
SLA	shift left arithmetic	2.11
SLDA	shift left double arithmetic	2.11
SLDL	shift left double logical	2.11
SLL	shift left logical	2.11
SLR	subtract logical register	2.4
SR	subtract register	2.4
SRA	shift right arithmetic	2.11
SRDA	shift right double arithmetic	2.11
SRDL	shift right double logical	2.11
SRL	shift right logical	2.11
ST	store Word	2.4
STC	store character	2.4
STH	store half	2.4
STM	store multiple	2.11
X	*exclusive or* Word	2.4
XR	*exclusive or* register	2.4
Floating		
AD	add double	2.10
ADR	add double register	2.10
AE	add short	2.10
AER	add short register	2.10
AU	add short unnormalized	2.10
AUR	add short unnormalized register	2.10
AW	add long unnormalized	2.10
AWR	add long unnormalized register	2.10
CD	compare double	2.10
CDR	compare double register	2.10
CE	compare short	2.10
CER	compare short register	2.10
DD	divide double	2.10
DDR	divide double register	2.10
DE	divide short	2.10
DER	divide short register	2.10
HDR	halve double register	2.10
HER	halve short register	2.10
LCDR	load complement double register	2.10
LCER	load complement short register	2.10
LD	load double	2.10
LDR	load double register	2.10
LE	load short	2.10

AL	*Description*	*Section*
LER	load short register	2.10
LNDR	load negative double register	2.10
LNER	load negative short register	2.10
LPDR	load positive double register	2.10
LPER	load positive short register	2.10
LTDR	load and test double register	2.10
LTER	load and test short register	2.10
MD	multiply double	2.10
MDR	multiply double register	2.10
ME	multiply short	2.10
MER	multiply short register	2.10
SD	subtract double	2.10
SDR	subtract double register	2.10
SE	subtract short	2.10
SER	subtract short register	2.10
STD	store double	2.10
STE	store short	2.10
SU	subtract short unnormalized	2.10
SUR	subtract short unnormalized reg.	2.10
SW	subtract double unnormalized	2.10
SWR	subtract double unnorm. reg.	2.10
Decimal		
AP	add packed	2.8
CP	compare packed	2.8
DP	divide packed	2.8
MP	multiply packed	2.8
MVO	move with offset	2.8
PACK	pack	2.8
SP	subtract packed	2.8
ZAP	zero and add	2.8
Character		
CLC	compare logical	2.7
ED	edit	2.7
EDMK	edit and mask	2.7
MVC	move	2.7
MVN	move numeric	2.7
MVZ	move zone	2.7
NC	*and*	2.7
OC	*or*	2.7
TR	translate	2.7
TRT	translate and test	2.7
XC	*exclusive or*	2.7
Immediate		
CLI	compare logical immediate	2.11
MVI	move immediate	2.11

AL	*Description*	*Section*
NI	*and* immediate	2.11
OI	*or* immediate	2.11
TM	test under mark	2.11
TS	test and set	2.11
XI	*exclusive or* immediate	2.11
Reflexive		
BAL	branch and link	2.6
BALR	branch and link register	2.6
BC	branch condition	2.5
BCR	branch condition register	2.5
BCT	branch on count	2.6
BCTR	branch on count register	2.6
BXH	branch index high	2.6
BXLE	branch index high equal	2.6
EX	execute	2.6
SVC	supervisor call	2.9
Extended		
B	branch	2.5
BE	branch equal	2.5
BH	branch high	2.5
BL	branch low	2.5
BM	branch minus	2.5
BM	branch mixed	2.5
BNE	branch not equal	2.5
BNH	branch not high	2.5
BNL	branch not low	2.5
BNM	branch not minus	2.5
BNO	branch not zero	2.5
BNP	branch not plus	2.5
BNZ	branch not zero	2.5
BP	branch plus	2.5
BO	branch ones	2.5
BO	branch overflow	2.5
BR	branch register	2.5
BZ	branch zero	2.5
CNOP	align on boundary	2.5
NOP	noop	2.5
NOPR	noop register	2.5
Privileged		
ISK	insert system key	2.9
HIO	halt IO	2.9
LPSW	load PSW	2.9
SIO	start IO	2.9

AL	Description	Section
SPM	set program mark	2.9
SSK	set system key	2.9
TCH	test CHANNEL	2.9
TIO	test IO	2.9
Pseudos		
CCW	define CCW	12.3
COM	define COMMON	13.6
COPY	copy AL code	12.2
CSECT	identify section	13.1
CXD	external dummy length	
DC	define constant	3.1
DROP	drop BASE REGISTER	12.1
DS	define storage	3.2
DSECT	dummy section	13.2
DXD	define external dummy	
EJECT	start new page	12.2
END	end of AL input	12.2
EQU	equate symbols	12.3
ICTL	new AL input format	12.2
ISEQ	check AL sequence	12.2
LTORG	start literal pool	12.2
MACRO	start macrodefinition	6.1
MEND	end macrodefinition	6.1
ORG	set location counter	12.2
PRINT	print as specified	12.2
PUNCH	punch a card only	12.2
REPRO	repro next card only	12.2
SPACE	skip lines	12.2
START	start assembly	13.1
TITLE	head page with	12.2
USING	use BASE REGISTER	12.1
*	comment	10.7
Conditional		
ACTR	assembly loop limit	10.7
AGO	assembly *branch*	10.7
AIF	assemble if	10.1
AND	connective *and*	10.5
ANOP	assembly NOP	10.7
EQ	relation *equal*	10.5
GBLA	global arithmetic	10.3
GBLB	global binary	10.3
GBLC	global character	10.3
GE	relation *greater equal*	10.5
GT	relation *greater than*	10.5
LE	relation *less equal*	10.5
LCLA	local arithmetic	10.3

AL	*Description*	*Section*
LCLB	local binary	10.3
LCLC	local character	10.3
LT	relation *less than*	10.5
MNOTE	note about macro	10.7
MEXIT	macro exit	10.7
NE	relation *net equal*	10.5
NOT	connective *not*	10.5
OR	connective *or*	10.5
SETA	arithmetic set operation	10.4
SETB	binary set operation	10.4
SETC	character set operation	10.4
&SYSNDX	system index	9.4
.*	macro comment	10.7
Quasis		
ENTRY	entry	13.3
EXTRN	external reference	13.2
Macros, access method		
BLDL	build directory	14.7
BSP	backspace a record	14.7
BUILD	pool buffers	14.7
CHECK	see if IO is done	14.6
CLOSE	close a file	14.5
CNTRL	control a DEVICE	14.7
DCB	make DCB	14.4
DCBD	make DCECT for DCB	14.7
ESET	end sequential access	14.7
FEOV	force EOV	14.7
FIND	find record	14.7
FREEBUF	return pool buffer	14.7
FREED	free buffer	14.7
GET	get a record	14.6
GETPOOL	build pool	14.7
NOTE	note last record	14.7
OPEN	open a file	14.5
POINT	set DEVICE per request	14.7
PRTOV	test PRINTER	14.7
PUT	write a record	14.6
PUTX	put record from GET	14.7
READ	read a record	14.6
RELSE	release this buffer	14.7
RELEX	release file control	14.7
SETL	set file start	14.7
SETPRT	print message	14.7
STOW	write directory entry	14.7
SYNADAF	analyze error	14.7

AL	Description	Section
SYNADRLS	error message	14.7
TRUNC	release output buffer	14.7
WRITE	write a record	14.6
Macros, linkage		
ATTACH	get a task in parallel	15.6
CALL	⇒ SR	15.5
LINK	get SR; ⇒ SR	15.6
LOAD	get SR	15.6
RETURN	SR ⇒ main program	15.5
SAVE	(GPRS) ⟶ save area	15.5
XCTL	get SR; ⇒ SR without return	15.6
Macros, operating system		
ABEND	end job abnormal	14.9
CVT	write communication vectors	14.9
DELETE	reduce *use* count	14.9
DEVTYPE	report on DEVICE	14.9
EXCP	do IO program	14.9
FREEMAIN	free part of MEMORY	14.9
GETMAIN	get MAIN MEMORY	14.9
POST	show event done	14.9
PURGE	clear task IOBs	14.9
RESTORE	put IOB on IOB list	14.9
RDJFCB	read JFCB	14.9
SNAP	dump selective	14.9
SPIE	include intrpt exit	14.9
STAE	set termination exit	14.9
STIMER	set timer	14.9
TTIMER	test timer	14.9
WTOR	as WTO, expect reply	14.9
WTO	write to operator	14.9
WAIT	wait for event(s) end(s)	14.9
WAITR	as WAIT	14.9
XDAP	do DISK IO program	14.9
Macros, catalog		
CAMLST	list, catalog rqst	14.11
CATALOG	catalog a file	14.11
LOCATE	locate subcatalog	14.11
INDEX	change index	14.11
OBTAIN	get DSCB from VTOC	14.11
RENAME	rename a file	14.11
SCRATCH	uncatalog file	14.11
Macros, multiprogram		
CHAP	change priority	14.10
DEQ	release resource	14.10

AL	*Description*	*Section*
DETACH	delete task	14.10
ENQ	request a resource	14.10
IDENTIFY	get dynamic entry	14.10
SEGLD	get overlay segment	14.10
SEGWT	get overlay; wait	14.10
TIME	enter time, date	14.10
WTL	write to log	14.10

APPENDIX C

SYSTEM MACROS

```
         MACRO
&NAME    RETURN   &REG,&PARA,&RC=O
         LCLA     &A
         AIF      ('&NAME' EQ '  ').GO
&NAME    DS       OH
.GO      AIF      ('&REC' EQ '  ').CONTA
         AIF      ('&RC' EQ '(15)').SPECRT
.COMBACK ANOP
&A       SETA     &REG(1)*4+20
         AIF      (&A LE 75).CCNTB
&A       SETA     &A-64
.CONTB   AIF      (N'&REG NE 2).CONTG
         LM       &REG(1),&REG(2),&A.(13)                    RESTORE THE REGISTERS
         AGO      .CONTA
.SPECRT  AIF      ('&REG(1)' NE '14' AND '&REG(1)' NE '15').COMBACK
         AIF      ('&REG(1)' EQ '14' AND N'&REG EQ 1).COMBACK
         AIF      ('&REG(1)' EQ '15' AND N'&REG EQ 1).CONTA
         AIF      ('&REG(1)' EQ '14').SKIP
         AIF      ('&REG(2)' EQ '0').ZTWO
.LM      LM       0,&REG(2),20(13)                           RESTORE THE REGISTERS
         AGO      .CONTA
.ZTWO    L        0,20(13,0)                                 RESTORE REGISTER ZERO
         AGO      .CONTA
.SKIP    L        14,12(13,0)                                RESTORE REGISTER 14
         AIF      ('&REG(2)' EQ '15').CONTA
         AIF      ('&REG(2)' EQ '0').ZTWO
         AGO      .LM
.CONTC   AIF      (N'&REG NE 1).ERROR1
         L        &REG(1),&A.(13,0)                          RESTORE REGISTER
```

```
.CONTA    AIF       ('&PARA' EQ '  ').CONTD
          AIF       ('&PARA' NE 'T').ERROR2
          MVI       12(13),X'FF'                                 SET RETURN INDICATION
.CONTD    AIF       ('&RC' EQ 'O').CONTE
          AIF       ('&RC'(1,1) EQ '(').ISAREG
          LA        15,&R0.(0,0)                                 LOAD RETURN CODE
          AGO       .CONTE
.ISAREG   AIF       ('&RC(1)' EQ '15').CONTE
          IHBERMAC  61,,&RC
          MEXIT
.CONTE    BR        14                                           RETURN
          AGO       .END
.ERROR1   IHBERMAC 36,,&REG
          MEXIT
.ERROR2   IHBERMAC 37,,&PARA
.END      MEND
          MACRO
&NAME     LOAD      &EP=,&EPLOC=,&DE=,&DCB=
          AIF       ('&EP' NE '  ').PROCEP                       BRANCH IF EP PRESENT
          AIF       ('&EPLOC' EQ '  ' AND '&DE' EQ '  ').E1
          AIF       ('&EPLOC' NE '  ' AND '&DE' NE '  ').E2
&NAME     IHBINNKA &DCB,&EPLCC&DE                                LOAD REG 0 AND REG 1
          AIF       ('&DE' EQ '  ').DCBCHK
          LNR       0,0                                          COMP RO TO INDICATE DE
.DCBCHK   AIF       ('&DCB' NE '  ').SVC
          SR        1,1                                          SHOW DCB NOT SPECIFIED
```

```
              MACRO
.SVC          SVC        8                                                ISSUE LOAD SVC
              MEXIT
.PROCEP       AIF        ('&EPLOC' NE '   ' OR '&DE' NE '   ').E2
&NAME         LA         0,*+8                                            PUT ADDR OF EP IN REG0
              B          *+12                                             BRANCH AROUND EP
              DC         CL8'&EP'                                         EP SYMBOL
              IHBINNRA   &DCB                                             LOAD REG 1
              AGO        .DCBCHK
.E1           IHBERMAC   31,345                                           EP,DE,EPLOC ALL MISSING
              MEXIT
.E2           IHBERMAC   88,345                                           TOO MANY PARAMETERS PRESENT
.END          MEND
              MACRO
&NAME         LINK       &EP=,&EPLCC=,&DE=,&DCB=,&PARAM=,&VL=,&ID=,&SF=I,&MF=I
              GBLB       &IHBSWA,&IHBSWB
&IHBSWA       SETB       ('&VL' EQ '1')
&IHBSWB       SETB       ('&SF' EQ '(E,(15))')
              AIF        ('&MF' EQ 'L').E1
              AIF        ('&SF' EQ 'L' AND '&MF&PARAM&ID&VL' NE 'T').E2
              AIF        ('&NAME' EQ '   ' OR '&SF' EQ 'L').CONTA
&NAME         DS         OH
```

```
.CONTA      AIF         ('&PARAM' EQ '  ' AND '&MF(1)' NE 'E').CONTB
            IHBOPLST    ,&PARAM,MF=&MF
.CONTB      ANCP
&NAME       IHBINNRB    &EF,&EPLOC,&DE,&DCB,SF=&SF
            AIF         ('&SF' EQ 'L').END
            SVC         6                                          ISSUE LINK SVC
            AIF         ('&ID' EQ '  ').END
            DC          X'470C'                                    NOP INSTRUCTION WITH
            DC          AL2(&ID)                                   'D IN LAST TWO BYTES
            MEXIT
.E1         IHBERMAC 84
            MEXIT
.E2         IHBERMAC 75
.END        MEND


            MACRO
&NAME       CALL        &ENTRY,&OPRNDS,&VLPARA,&ID=,&MF=I
            GBLB        &IHBSWA,&IHBSWB
            GBLC        &IHBNC
            LCLC        &GNAME
&IHBND      SETC        '309'
&GNAME      SETC        'IHB'.'&SYSNDX'
&IHBSWA     SETB        ('&VLPARA' EQ 'VL')
```

```
&IHBSWB    SFTB      ('&ENTRY' EQ '(15)')
           AIF       ('&MF' EQ 'L' AND '&ENTRY' NE '   ').ERROR1
           AIF       ('&MF' EQ 'L' AND '&ID' NE '   ').ERROR2
           AIF       ('&MF' NE 'L' AND '&ENTRY' EQ '   ').ERROR3
           AIF       ('&MF' EQ 'L').CONTC
           AIF       (&IHBSWB).CONTCC
           CNOP      0,4
&NAME      B         *+8                                            BRANCH AROUND VCON
&GNAME.B   DC        V(&ENTRY)                                      ENTRY POINT ADDRESS
.CONTC     AIF       ('&OPRNDS' EQ '   ' AND '&MF(1)' NE 'B').CONTB
.CONTA     IHBOPLST  &ENTRY,&OPRNDS,&NAME,MF=&MF
.CONTB     AIF       ('&MF' EQ 'L').EXIT
           AIF       (&IHBSWB).CONTD
           L         15,&GNAME.B                                    LOAD 15 WITH ENTRY ADR
.CONTD     BALR      14,15                                          BRANCH TO ENTRY POINT
           AIF       ('&ID' EQ '   ').EXIT
           DC        X'4700'                                        NOP INSTRUCTION WITH
           DC        AL2(&ID)                                       ID IN LAST TWO BYTES
.EXIT      MEXIT
.CONTCC    ANCP
&NAME      DS        OH
           AGO       .CONTC
.ERROR1    IHBERMAC  73,&IHBNO,&ENTRY                               ENTRY W/MF=L
           MEXIT
.ERROR2    IHBERMAC  74,&IHBNO,&ID                                  ID W/MF=L
           MEXIT
.ERROR3    IHBERMAC 26,&IHBNO
           MEND
```

```
         MACRO                                          ENTRY SYMBOL MISSING
&NAME    SAVE    &REG,&CODE,&ID
         LCLA    &A,&B,&C
         LCLC    &B,&F,&G,&H
         AIF     ('&REG' EQ '   ').E1
         AIF     ('&ID' EQ '   ').NULLID
         AIF     ('&ID' EQ '*').SPECID
&A       SETA    ((K'&ID+2)/2)*2+4
&NAME    B       &A.(0,15)                              BRANCH AROUND ID
&A       SETA    K'&ID
         DC      AL1(&A)                                LENGTH OF IDENTIFIER
.CONTR   AIF     (&A GT 32).SPLITUP
.CONTAA  AIF     (&A GT 8).BRAKDWN.
&E       SETC    '&ID'(&B+1,&A)
         DC      CL&A'&E'                               IDENTIFIER
         AGO     .CONTA
.BRAKDWN ANOP
&E       SETC    '&ID'(&B+1,8)
         DC      CL8'&E'                                IDENTIFIER
&B       SETA    &B+8
&A       SETA    &A-8
         AGO     .CONTAA
.SPLITUP ANOP
&E       SETC    '&ID'(&B+1,8)
&F       SETC    '&ID'(&B+9,8)
&G       SETC    '&ID'(&B+17,8)
&H       SETC    '&ID'(&B+25,8)
         DC      CL32'&E.&F.&G.&H'                      IDENTIFIER
&B       SETA    &B+32
```

```
&A        SETA      &A-32
          AGO       .CONTB
.NULLID   ANOP
&NAME     DS        OH
          AGO       .CONTA
.SPECID   AIF       ('&NAME' EQ '   ').CSECTN
&E        SETC      '&NAME'
&A        SETA      1
.CONTQ    AIF       ('&E'(1,&A) EQ '&E').LEAVE
&A        SETA      &A+1
          AGO       .CONTQ
.LEAVE    ANOP
&B        SETA      ((&A+2)/2)*2+4
&NAME     B         &B.(0,15)                      BRANCH AROUND ID
          DC        AL1(&A)
          DC        CL&A'&E'                       IDENTIFIER
          AGO       .CONTA
.CSECTN   AIF       ('&SYSECT' EQ '   ').E4
&E        SETC      '&SYSECT'
&A        SETA      1
          AGO       .CONTC
.E4       IHBERMAC  78,360                         CSECT NAME NULL
.CONTA    AIF       (T'&REG(1) NE 'N').E3
          AIF       ('&CODE' EQ 'T').CONTC
          AIF       ('&CODE' NE '   ').E2
&A        SETA      &REG(1)*4+20
          AIF       (&A LE 75).CONTD
```

```
&A       SETA     &A-64
.CONTD   AIF      (N'&REG NE 2).CONTE
         STM      &REG(1),&REG(2),&A.(13)              SAVE REGISTERS
         MEXIT
.CONTE   AIF      (N'&REG NE 1).E3
         ST       &REG(1),&A.(13,0)                    SAVE REGISTER
         MEXIT
.CONTC   AIF      (&REG(1) GE 14 OR &REG(1) LE 2).CONTF
         STM      14,15,12(13)                         SAVE REGISTERS
&A       SETA     &REG(1)*4+20
         AIF      (N'&REG NE 2).CONTG
         STM      &REG(1),&REG(2),&A.(13)              SAVE REGISTERS
         MEXIT
.CONTG   AIF      (N'&REG NE 1).E3
         ST       &REG(1),&A.(13,0)                    SAVE REGISTER
         MEXIT
.CONTF   AIF      (N'&REG NE 2).CONTH
         STM      14,&REG(2),12(13)                    SAVE REGISTERS
         MEXIT
.CONTH   AIF      (N'&REG NE 1).E3
         STM      14,&REG(1),12(13)                    SAVE REGISTERS
         MEXIT
.E1      IHBERMAC 18,360                               REG PARAM MISSING
         MEXIT
.E2      IHBERMAC 37,360,&CODE                         INVALID CODE SPECIFIED
         MEXIT
.E3      IHBERMAC 36,360,&REG                          INVALID REGS. SPECIFIED
         MEND
```

```
         MACRO
         IHBOPLST  &NULL,&OPRNDS,&NAME,&MF=I
         GBLB      &IHBSWA,&IHBSWB
         GBLC      &IHBNC
         LCLC      &GNAME,&AA,&BB
         LCLA      &A,&B,&C,&D,&E,&ATTRN
&ATTRN   SETA      N'&OPRNDS
SGNAME   SETC      'IHB'.'&SYSNDX'
         AIF       ('&MF' EQ 'L').CONTA
         AIF       ('&MF' EQ 'I').IROUT
         AGO       .EROUT
.ERROR1  IHBERMAC  35,&IHBND,&MF                         MF PARAMETER BAD
         MEXIT
.ERROR2  IHBERMAC  69,&IHBNO                             REG. NOT. W/ MF=L
         MEXIT
.CONTA   AIF       ('&NAME' EQ '  ').NONAME
&NAME    DS        OF
.NONAME  ANOP
         AIF       ('&OPRNDS'(1,1) NE '(').CONTXY
         AIF       ('&OPRNDS'(2,1) EQ ',').SKIPC
.CONTXY  AIF       (&ATTRN GT 1).LROUT
&B       SETA      0-1
         AGO       .NEAREND
.LROUT   AIF       ('&OPRNDS(&B+1)' EQ '  ').SKIPC
&AA      SETC      '&OPRNDS(&B+1)'
         AIF       ('&AA'(1,1) EQ '(').ERROR2
         DC        A(&OPRNDS(&B+1))                      PROB. PROG. PARAMETER
         AGO       .AROUND
```

```
.SKIPC     DC     A(0)                                PROB. PROG. PARAMETER
.AROUND    AIF    (&B+2 EQ &ATTRN).NEAREND
&B         SETA   &B+1
           AGO    .LROUT
.NEAREND   AIF    ('&OPRNDS(&B+2)' EQ '  ').SKIPD
&AA        SETC   '&OPRNDS(&B+2)'
           AIF    ('&AA'(1,1) EQ '(').ERROR2
           DC     B'&IHBSWA.0000000'                  SET VL SWITCH BIT
           DC     AL3(&OPRNDS(&E+2))                  PROB. PROG. PARAMETER
           AGO    .END
.SKIPD     DC     B'&IHBSWA.0000000'                  SET VL SWITCH BIT
           DC     AL3(0)                              PROB. PROG. PARAMETER
           AGO    .END
.TROUT     AIF    ('&OPRNDS'(1,1) NE '(').LOOPC
           AIF    ('&OPRNDS'(2,1) EQ ',').SKIPA
.LOOPC     AIF    ('&OPRNDS(&B+1)' EQ '  ').SKIPA
&AA        SETC   '&OPRNDS(&B+1)'
           AIF    ('&AA'(1,1) NE '(').SKIPA
           ST     &OPRNDS(&B+1),&GNAME+&C             STORE INTO PARAM. LIST
.SKIPA     AIF    (&B+1 EQ &ATTRN).THRU
&B         SETA   &B+1
&C         SETA   &C+4
           AGO    .LOOPC
.THRU      AIF    (NOT &IHBSWA).CONTON
           AIF    ('&OPRNDS(&B+1)' EQ '  ').CONTON
           AIF    ('&OPRNDS(&B+1)'(1,1) NE '(').CONTON
           MVI    &GNAME+&C,X'80'                     SET LAST WORD BIT ON
.CONTON    CNOP   0,4
           BAL    1,&GNAME.A                          LOAD LIST ADDR IN REG1
```

```
&GNAME    EQU    *
          AIF    (&ATTRN GT 1).LOOP2
&D        SETA   0-1
          AGO    .NEARCON
.LOOP2    AIF    ('&OPRNDS'(1,2) EQ '(,').SKIPB
.LOOPD    AIF    ('&OPRNDS(&D+1)' EQ '  ').SKIPB
&AA       SETC   '&OPRNDS(&D+1)'
          AIF    ('&AA'(1,1) EQ '(').SKIPB
          DC     A(&OPRNDS(&D+1))                PROB. PROG. PARAMETER
          AGO    .NEXTSTP
.SKIPB    DC     A(0)                            PROB. PROG. PARAMETER
.NEXTSTP  AIF    (&D+2 EQ &ATTRN).NEARDON
&D        SETA   &D+1
          AGO    .LOOPD
.NEARDON  AIF    ('&OPRNDS(&D+2)' EQ '  ').SKIPE
          AIF    ('&OPRNDS(&D+2)'(1,1) EQ '(').SKIPF
          DC     B'&IHBSWA.0000000'              SET VL SWITCH BIT
          DC     AL3(&OPRNDS(&D+2))              PROB. PROG. PARAMETER
          AGO    .ENDOF
.SKIPE    DC     B'&IHBSWA.0000000'              SET VL SWITCH BIT
          DC     AL3(0)                          PROB. PROG. PARAMETER
          AGO    .ENDOF
.SKIPF    DC     A(0)                            PROB. PROG. PARAMETER
.ENDOF    ANOP
&GNAME.A  EQU    *
          AGO    .END
```

```
.EROUT    AIF       (N'&MF NE 2).ERROR1
          AIF       ('&MF(1)' NE 'E').ERROR1
          IHBINNRA  &MF(2)                                LOAD REG 1 WITH LIST ADDR
.CONTB    AIF       ('&OPRNDS' EQ '   ').END
          AIF       (&IHBSWB).CONTC
          AIF       ('&OPRNDS'(1,1) NE '(').LOOPA
          AIF       ('&OPRNDS'(2,1) EQ ',').CONTD
.LOOPA    AIF       ('&OPRNDS(&B+1)' EQ '   ').CONTD
&AA       SETC      '&OPRNDS(&B+1)'
          AIF       ('&AA'(1,1) EQ '(').ISREG
&A        SETA      &C+14
          LA        &A,&OPRNDS(&B+1)                      PICKUP PARAMETER
          AGO       .CONTE
.ISREG    ANOP
          AIF       (&C EQ 0).CONTQQ
.GOBACK   ANOP
&A        SETA      &C+14
          LR        &A,&OPRNDS(&P+1)                      PICK UP PARAMETER
.CONTE    AIF       (&B+1 EQ &ATTRN).ALLDUN
          AIF       (&C EQ 0-14).CONTF
          AIF       (&C EQ 1).CONTG
&C        SETA      &C+1
          AGO       .CONTH
.CONTQQ   AIF       (&B+1 EQ &ATTRN).CONTXX
          AIF       ('&OPRNDS(&B+2)' NE '   ').GOBACK
.CONTXX   ANOP
          ST        &OPRNDS(&B+1),&E.(0,1)                STORE INTO PARAM. LIST
          AGO       .INCRMT
.CONTG    ANOP
&C        SETA      0-14
```

```
.CONTH    ANOP
&B        SETA   &B+1
&D        SETA   &D+4
          AGO    .LOOPA
.CONTD    AIF    (&C EQ 0).INCRMT
          AIF    (&C NE 1).PUTTWO
          ST     14,&E.(0,1)                 STORE INTO PARAM. LIST
          AGO    .INCRMT
.PUTTWO   STM    14,15,&E.(1)                STORE INTO PARAM. LIST
          AGO    .INCRMT
.CONTF    STM    14,0,&E.(1)                 STORE INTO PARAM. LIST
.INCRMT   AIF    (&B+1 EQ &ATTRN).QUIT
&C        SETA   0
&B        SETA   &B+1
&D        SETA   &D+4
&F        SETA   &D
          AGO    .LOOPA
.ALLDUN   AIF    (&C NE 0).CONTJ
          ST     14,&E.(0,1)                 STORE INTO PARAM. LIST
          AGO    .QUIT
.CONTJ    ANOP
```

```
&A        SETA   &C+14
          STM    14,&A,&E.(1)                        STORE INTO PARAM. LIST
          AGO    .QUIT
.CONTC    AIF    ('&OPRNDS'(1,1) NE '(').LOOPB
          AIF    ('&OPRNDS'(2,1) EQ ',').CONTK
.LOOPB    AIF    ('&OPRNDS(&B+1)' EQ '  ').CONTK
&AA       SETC   '&OPRNDS(&B+1)'
          AIF    ('&AA'(1,1) EQ '(').ISAREGA
          LA     0,&OPRNDS(&B+1)                     PICKUP PARAMETER
          ST     0,&D.(0,1)                          STORE INTO PARAM. LIST
          AGO    .CONTK
.ISAREGA  ANOP
          ST     &OPRNDS(&B+1),&D.(0,1)              STORE INTO PARAM. LIST
.CONTK    AIF    (&B+1 EQ &ATTRN).QUIT
&B        SETA   &B+1
&D        SETA   &D+4
          AGO    .LOOPB
.QUIT     AIF    (NOT &IHBSWA).END
&A        SETA   &ATTRN*4-4
          MVI    &A.(1),X'80'                        SET LASTWORD BIT ON
          AGO    .END
.END      ANOP
          MEND
```

APPENDIX **D**

COMPONENTS OF ASLR

Component	*Function*	*Part of*
Cons	Expands constants	Sym
Control	Control statements	McDef
Dcbds	Handle DC and DS	Sym
Eval	Evaluate constant	Sym
Interlude	Before Sym	ASLR
Lit	Handle literals	Sym
McArg	Set up *ARGTAB*	McDef
McCom	Enter macrodefinition into *COMTAB*	McDef
McDef	Macrodefinition handler routine	ASLR
McDefX	Weeds out external macrocalls	McDef
McGen	Generate macrocalls	ASLR
McGenS	Enters commands from *COMTAB* to replace call	McGen
McGenSA	Sets up storage or constants as required during calls	McGen
McInc	Incorporates nested macrodefinition into *COMTAB*	McNest
McName	Look up name of macro in *OPTAB*	McDef
McNest	For nesting	ASLR
McPar	Enters call parameters into *PARTAB*	McGen
McST	Checks or sets type or other attributes	McDef
Mnem	For mnemonics	Sym
Opt	Looks up opcodes in *OPTAB*	Sym
OptO	Final look of *opcode* in *OPTAB*	Out
Out	Creates ASLR output	ASLR
ScanD	Scan for McDef	McDef
ScanF	Looks for and finds library macros	Scan
ScanG	Scan of program for macrocalls to be generated	McGen
ScanM	Model statement scan	McDef
ScanN	Scan for nesting	McNest

Component	*Function*	*Part of*
𝔖𝔠𝔞𝔫𝒪	Scan of code for output	𝒪𝔲𝔱
𝔖𝔠𝔞𝔫𝒯	Scan main program	𝔖𝔠𝔞𝔫𝒩
𝔖ℒ𝔬𝔬𝔨	Loads up symbols in *SYMTAB*	𝔖𝔶𝔪
𝔖𝔖𝔠𝔞𝔫	Separates statement into five fields	𝔖𝔶𝔪
𝔖𝔶𝔪	Examines all symbolic statements	𝒜𝔖ℒℜ
ℜ𝔰𝔰𝔦	Takes care of RS and SI commands	𝒪𝔲𝔱
𝔘𝔰𝔢𝔱𝔞𝔟	Determines base/displacement *loc* from *USETAB* entry	𝒪𝔲𝔱

APPENDIX **E**

TABLES USED BY ASLR

Name	*Function*
ARGTAB	Arguments for macrodefinition
CALLTAB	Opcodes for which macrodefinitions have not been found
COMTAB	Macrodefinition commands
DEFTAB	Opcodes for macrodefinition in *COMTAB*
GLODIC	Global symbols
HASHTAB	Provides entry to main tables
LOCDIC	Local symbols
OPTAB	Opcode
SEQTAB	Sequence symbols
SYMTAB	Symbol, names
USETAB	BASE REGISTERS and their relative assignment for each CSECT
XSMTAB	Unfound macrocalls

APPENDIX **F**

OVEREXTENDED MNEMONICS

Mnemonic	*Description*	*Mnemonic*	*Description*
AI	Add improper	IOR	Illogical or
AME	407 Emulation	IRB	Invert record and branch
ARN	Add and reset to non-zero	LCC	Load and clear core
BB	Branch on bug	LMB	Lose message and branch
BBI	Branch on burned-out indicator	MC	Move continuous
		MLB	Memory left shift and branch
BCF	Branch on chip box full	MLR	Move and lose record
BCR	Backspace card reader	MTI	Make tape invalid
BD	Backspace disk	MWC	Move and wrap core
BPO	Branch on power off	NC	1401 Incompatibility
BSC	Burst selector channel	PAZ	Pack alpha and drop zones
BSO	Branch on sleepy operator	PBC	Print and break chain
CCS	Chinese character set	PI	Punch invalid
CM	Circulate memory	PO	Punch operator
CRN	Convert to roman numerals	PPSW	Pack program status word
DD	Destroy disk	PS	Print and smear
DIA	Develop ineffective address	RBT	Read blank tape
DO	Divide and overflow	RCR	Rewind card reader
DPK	Destroy storage protect key	RCS	Read card and scramble data
ECP	Erase card punch	RD	Remove disk
ED	Eject disk	RDI	Reverse drum immediate
EIO	Execute invalid op-code	RID	Read invalid data
EROS	Erase read-only storage	RIG	Read inter-record gap
FSR	Forms skip and run away	RBT	Rewind and break tape
HCF	Halt and catch fire	RNR	Read noise record
IA	Illogical and	RPB	Read print and blush
II	Inquire and ignore	RPB	Reverse parity and branch

Mnemonic	Description	Mnemonic	Description
RRR	Read record and run away	TPD	Triple-pack decimal
RT	Reduce thruput	TPN	Turn power on
SC	Scramble channels	TPO	Turn power off
SD	Slip disk	UCB	Uncouple CPU and branch
SLP	Sharpen light pencil	UER	Update and erase record
SP	Scatter print	UT	Update transaction
SPSW	Scramble program status word	WLR	Write wrong-length record
		WNR	Write noise record
SRSD	Seek record and scar disk	XOH	Execute NO-OP and hang
SSC	Select reader and chew cards	ROM	Read operator's mind
SSJ	Select stacker and jam	RPM	Read programmer's mind

APPENDIX **G**

MACRODEFINITIONS FOR SETUP, ENDUP, AND REG UNDER DOS

```
         MACRO                                             SETU0001
&N       SETUP    &FR,&LR,&EXIT=$RESTORE,
                    &LCE=EOJ                               SETU0002
         GBLB     &SETUPSW                                 SETU0003
         LCLC     &REG(4),&NAME                            SETU0004
         LCLA     &INDEX,&TEST,&CC,&C1234,&COUNT8,
                    &ER,&D,&AR                             SETU0005
&CC      SETA     K'&N                                     SETU0006
         AIF      ('&FR' NE '').W                          SETU0007
&AR      SETA     12                                       SETU0008
         AGO      .S                                       SETU0009
.W       AIF      (&FR LT 2).IBRA                          SETU0010
&AR      SETA     &FR                                      SETU0011
.S       AIF      ('&N' NE '').T                           SETU0012
&NAME    SETC     '$BLANK'                                 SETU0013
&CC      SETA     6                                        SETU0014
         AGO      .U                                       SETU0015
.T       ANOP                                              SETU0016
&NAME    SETC     '&N'                                     SETU0017
.U       AIF      ('&LR' NE '').Q                          SETU0018
&ER      SETA     &AR                                      SETU0019
         AGO      .R                                       SETU0020
.Q       AIF      (&LR GT 12 OR &LR LT &AR).IBRA           SETU0021
&ER      SETA     &LR                                      SETU0022
.R       AIF      (&CC/2 EQ (&CC+1)/2).EVEN                SETU0023
&D       SETA     &CC+1                                    SETU0024
         AGO      .V                                       SETU0025
```

```
.EVEN         ANOP                                              SETU0026
&D            SETA    &CC+2                                     SETU0027
.V            ANOP                                              SETU0028
&INDEX        SETA    &AR                                       SETU0029
&TEST         SETA    &ER                                       SETU0030
&C1234        SETA    1                                         SETU0031
.LOOP         AIF     (&INDEX LT 10).ADD2                       SETU0032
&COUNT8       SETA    &COUNT8+3                                 SETU0033
              AGO     .CHECK8                                   SETU0034
.ADD2         ANOP                                              SETU0035
&COUNT8       SETA    &COUNT8+2                                 SETU0036
.CHECK8       AIF     (&COUNT.8 GT 8).ADD1                      SETU0037
&REG(&C1234)  SETC    '&REG(&C1234)'.','.'&INDEX'               SETU0038
&INDEX        SETA    &INDEX+1                                  SETU0039
              AIF     (&INDEX LE &TEST).LOOP                    SETU0040
              AGO     .CSECT                                    SETU0041
.ADD1         ANOP                                              SETU0042
&C1234        SETA    &C1234+1                                  SETU0043
&COUNT8       SETA    0                                         SETU0044
              AGO     .LOOP                                     SETU0045
.CSECT        ANOP                                              SETU0046
&NAME         CSECT                                             SETU0047
              BALR    15,0                              DAB     SETU0048
              USING   DAVE&SYSNDX,15 TEMPORARY
                        BASE REGISTER                           SETU0049
DAVE&SYSNDX   B       *+4+&D  BRANCH AROUND DC'S                SETU0050
              DC      AL1(&CC) NUMBER OF CHARACTERS
                        IN CSECT NAME                           SETU0051
              DC      C'&NAME'  CSECT NAME                      SETU0052
              LR      14,15                                     SETU0053
              LR      &AR,13 STORE CSA ADR IN FIRST
                        REQUESTED BASE REG                      SETU0054
              LA      13,$SVE&SYSNDX                            SETU0055
              CNOP    0,4                                       SETU0056
              LM      &AR,&ER,*+8
                        LOAD REQUESTED BASE REG(S)              SETU0057
              USING   &NAME&REG(1)&REG(2)&REG(3)
                        &REG(4)                                 SETU0058
              DROP    15                                        SETU0059
&INDEX        SETA    0                                         SETU0060
&TEST         SETA    &ER-&AR                                   SETU0061
              B       DAB&SYSNDX                                SETU0062
.LOOP1        DC      A(&NAME+&INDEX*4096)                      SETU0063
&INDEX        SFTA    &INDEX+1                                  SETU0064
              AIF     (&INDEX LE &TEST).LOOP1                   SETU0065
&EXIT         EOJ                                       DB/DOS  SETU0066
              AIF     (&SETUPSW).END                            SETU0067
DAB&SYSNDX    DC      OH'O'                                     SETU0068
              OPEN    RDR,PRTR                                  SETU0069
              B       $BEGIN                                    SETU0070
RDR           DTFCD   DEVICE=2540,DEVADDR=SYSRDR,
                        IOAREA1=$READCD,                       CSETU0071
```

```
                       EOFADDR=&LCE,RECFORM=
                         FIXUNB,TYPEFLE=INPUT,
                         WORKA=YES                       SETU0072
              CDMOD    WORKA=YES                         SETU0073
PRTR          DTFPR    DEVICE=1403,BLKSIZE=132,
                         DEVADDR=SYSLST,                CSETU0074
                       WORKA=YES,IOAREA1=$PRINT,
                         CTLCHR=ASA            DAVE B    SETU0075
              PRMOD    WORKA=YES,CTLCHR=ASA      DAB     SETU0076
$READCD       DS       CL80                              SETU0077
$PRINT        DS       CL133                             SETU0078
$SVE&SYSNDX   DS       18F                               SETU0079
$BEGIN        DS       OH                                SETU0080
&SETUPSW      SETB     1                                 SETU0081
.END          MEXIT                                      SETU0082
.IBRA         MNOTE    12,'INVALID BASE REGISTER
                         ASSIGNMENT'                     SETU0083
              MEND                                       SETU0084
              MACRO                                      SETU0177
              ENDUP                                      SETU0178
EOJ           CLOSE RDR,PRTR                   DAVID     SETU0179
              EOJ
              MEND                                       SETU0180
              MACRO                                      SETU0085
&NAME         REG      &REG                              SETU0086
              GBLB     &REGSW                            SETU0087
              LCLA     &X,&Y                             SETU0088
              LCLB     &R(16)                            SETU0089
              LCLC     &ID                               SETU0090
              AIF      ('&NAME' NE '').D                 SETU0091
&ID           SETC     '$REG&SYSNDX'                     SETU0092
              AGO      .E                                SETU0093
.D            ANOP                                       SETU0094
&ID           SETC     '&NAME'                           SETU0095
.F            ANOP                                       SETU0096
&NAME         BAL      1,*+14                            SETU0097
              AIF      ('&REG' NE '').A                  SETU0098
              DC       X'FFFF'                           SETU0099
              AGO      .C                                SETU0100
.A            ANOP                                       SETU0101
&X            SETA     1                                 SETU0102
.B            ANOP                                       SETU0103
&Y            SETA     &REG(&X)                          SETU0104
&Y            SETA     &Y+1                              SETU0105
&R(&Y)        SETR     1                                 SETU0106
&X            SETA     &X+1                              SETU0107
              AIF      (&X LE N'&REG).B                  SETU0108
              DC       B'&R(1)&R(2)&R(3)&R(4)&R(5)&R(6)&
                         R(7)&R(8)&R(9)&R(10)&R(*11)&R(12)&  SETU0109
                         R(13)&R(14)&R(15)&R(16)'        SETU0110
.C            DC       CL8'&ID'                          SETU0111
```

```
         STM   0,15,REG99S                                SETU0112
         AIF   (&REGSW).DAB$                              SETU0113
         LA    11,$EXIT                                   SETU0114
DBREG    LR    8,1 BOY YOU SURE DO THINGS                 SETU0115
                 THE HARD WAY'.'.'.'.
         MVC   REG014+40(8),2(8)                          SETU0116
         PUT   PRTR,REG014                                SETU0117
         PUT   PRTR,REG015                                SETU0118
         SR    3,3                                        SETU0119
         MVI   REG001+3,0                                 SETU0120
REG009   LA    4,128                                      SETU0121
REG003   STC   4,REG001+1                                 SETU0122
REG001   TM    0(8),0                                     SETU0123
         BO    REG004                                     SETU0124
REG002   LA    3,1(3)                                     SETU0125
         SRL   4,1                                        SETU0126
         LTR   4,4                                        SETU0127
         BZ    REG008                                     SETU0128
         B     REG003                                     SETU0129
REG004   LA    6,4                                        SETU0130
         LA    7,REG013+9                                 SETU0131
         LR    5,3                                        SETU0132
         SLL   5,2                                        SETU0133
         LA    5,REG99S(5)                                SETU0134
         L     9,0(5)                                     SETU0135
REG005   MVC   REG99H,0(5)                                SETU0136
         MVC   REG99L,0(5)                                SETU0137
         PACK  REG99H,REG99H                              SETU0138
         NI    REG99H,X'0F'                               SETU0139
         TR    REG99H,REG99T                              SETU0140
         NI    REG99L,X'0F'                               SETU0141
         TR    REG99L,REG99T                              SETU0142
         MVC   0(2,7),REG99H                              SETU0143
         LA    7,2(7)                                     SETU0144
         LA    5,1(5)                                     SETU0145
         BCT   6,REG005                                   SETU0146
         STC   3,REG013+6                                 SETU0147
         TR    REG013+6(1),REG99T                         SETU0148
         CVD   9,REG011                                   SETU0149
         UNPK  REG012,REG011+3(5)                         SETU0150
         OI    REG012+8,X'F0'                             SETU0151
         MVC   REG013+25(8),REG012+1                      SETU0152
         PUT   PRTR,REG013                                SETU0153
         B     REG002                                     SETU0154
REG008   CLI   REG001+3,1                                 SETU0155
         BE    0(11)                                      SETU0156
         MVI   REG001+3,1                                 SETU0157
         B     REG009                                     SETU0158
REG99S   DS    16F                                        SETU0159
REG99T   DC    C'0123456789ABCDEF'                        SETU0160
REG99H   DS    CL1                                        SETU0161
```

```
REG99L    DS     CL1                                        SETU0162
REG014    DC     CL100'-CONTENTS OF GENERAL
                   PURPOSE REGISTERS'                       SETU0163
          DC     CL33'                        '             SETU0164
REG015    DC     CL133'0  HEXIDECIMAL   DECIMAL' DB         SETU0165
REG013    DC     CL133'0GPR   *'                            SETU0166
REG011    DS     D                                          SETU0167
REG012    DS     CL9                                        SETU0168
$PRINT1   DS     CL121                                      SETU0169
&REGSW    SETB   1                                          SETU0170
$EXIT     LM     0,15,REG99S                                SETU0171
          MEXIT                                             SETU0172
.DAB$     ANOP                                              SETU0173
          BAL    11,DBREG                                   SETU0174
          LM     0,15,REG99S                                SETU0175
.END      MEND                                              SETU0176
```

DOS JCL

```
// JOB name
// OPTION LINK, DUMP, NOLOC
// EXEC ASSEMBLY
          AL program
/*
// EXEC LNKEDT
// EXEC
        data
/*
/&
```

Spaces must appear as shown.

INDEX